THE LITERARY CAREER AND LEGACY OF
ELIZABETH CARY, 1613–1680

THE LITERARY CAREER AND LEGACY OF ELIZABETH CARY, 1613–1680

Edited by

Heather Wolfe

THE LITERARY CAREER AND LEGACY OF ELIZABETH CARY, 1613–1680
Copyright © Heather Wolfe, 2007.

All rights reserved. No part of this book may be used or reproduced in any manner whatsoever without written permission except in the case of brief quotations embodied in critical articles or reviews.

First published in 2007 by
PALGRAVE MACMILLAN™
175 Fifth Avenue, New York, N.Y. 10010 and
Houndmills, Basingstoke, Hampshire, England RG21 6XS.
Companies and representatives throughout the world.

PALGRAVE MACMILLAN is the global academic imprint of the Palgrave Macmillan division of St. Martin's Press, LLC and of Palgrave Macmillan Ltd. Macmillan® is a registered trademark in the United States, United Kingdom and other countries. Palgrave is a registered trademark in the European Union and other countries.

ISBN-10: 1-4039-7016-5
ISBN-13: 978-1-4039-7016-9

Library of Congress Cataloging-in-Publication Data

The literary career and legacy of Elizabeth Cary, 1613–1680 / edited by Heather Wolfe.
   p.cm.
   Includes bibliographical references and index.
   ISBN 1-4039-7016-5
   1. Cary, Elizabeth, Lady, 1585 or 6-1639—Criticism and interpretation. 2. Women and literature—Engalnd—History—17th century. I. Wolfe, Heather, 1971-
   PR2499.F3Z75 2006
   822'.3—dc22

                                                                            200604478

A catalogue record for this book is available from the British Library.

Design by Macmillan India Ltd.

First edition: January 2007

10 9 8 7 6 5 4 3 2 1

Printed in the United States of America.

in memoriam
Jeremy Frank Maule
(1952–1998)

CONTENTS

About the Contributors — ix

List of Figures — xiii

Introduction — 1
Heather Wolfe

Part I
The Tragedy of Mariam — 15

1 Private Lyrics in Elizabeth Cary's *Tragedy of Mariam* — 17
   Ilona Bell

2 Mariam and Early Modern Discourses of Martyrdom — 35
   Erin E. Kelly

3 Elizabeth Cary's Historical Conscience: *The Tragedy of Mariam* and Thomas Lodge's Josephus — 53
   Alison Shell

Part II
Edward II — 69

4 "Royal Fever" and "The Giddy Commons": Cary's *History of The Life, Reign, and Death of Edward II* and The Buckingham Phenomenon — 71
   Curtis Perry

5 "Fortune is a Stepmother": Gender and Political Discourse in Elizabeth Cary's *History of Edward II* — 89
   Mihoko Suzuki

6 A Bibliographical Palimpsest: The Post-Publication History
of the 1680 Octavo Pamphlet, *The History of the Most
Unfortunate Prince King Edward II*   107
Jesse G. Swan

7 From Manuscript to Printed Text: Telling and Retelling the
History of Edward II   125
Margaret Reeves

**Part III
Other Writings**   **145**

8 "To informe thee aright": Translating Du Perron for English
Religious Debates   147
Karen L. Nelson

9 Elizabeth Cary and the Great Tew Circle   165
R. W. Serjeantson

10 "Reader, Stand Still and Look, Lo Here I Am": Elizabeth Cary's
Funeral Elegy "On the Duke of Buckingham"   183
Nadine N. W. Akkerman

**Part IV
Literary Patronage and Legacies**   **201**

11 "A More Worthy Patronesse": Elizabeth Cary and Ireland   203
Deana Rankin

12 "To have her children with her": Elizabeth Cary and
Familial Influence   223
Marion Wynne-Davies

Bibliography   243

Index   253

ABOUT THE CONTRIBUTORS

Nadine N. W. Akkerman, a graduate student at the Vrije Universiteit in Amsterdam, has published articles in *The Ben Jonson Journal* and *Early Modern Literary Studies* and is currently preparing her dissertation, "The Letters of Elizabeth Stuart, Electress Palatine of the Rhine, Queen of Bohemia: A Scholarly Edition of the Years 1632–1642." Besides a fully annotated edition of the years 1632–1642, the dissertation will include a census of all the letters, either to or by the Queen of Bohemia, many of which are dispersed in archives across the world and are mostly unpublished.

Ilona Bell is a professor of English literature at Williams College. She is the author of *Elizabethan Women and the Poetry of Courtship* (Cambridge University Press, 1998) as well as numerous articles and book chapters on Donne, Shakespeare, Herbert, Jonson, Elizabeth I, Milton, and Elizabethan women. She is the editor of *John Donne: Selected Poems* (Penguin, 2006). She is currently working on a biographical study of Donne's courtship and a critical interpretation of Donne's love poetry.

Erin E. Kelly is an assistant professor in the Department of English at Nazareth College in Rochester, New York. She is currently working on a book-length study of representations of religious conversion in sixteenth- and seventeenth-century drama.

Karen L. Nelson is the associate director of the Center for Renaissance & Baroque Studies at the University of Maryland. She has coedited the volume *Women, Writing, and the Reproduction of Culture in Tudor and Stuart Britain* with Jane Donawerth, Linda Dove, and Mary Burke. She has published essays on Elizabeth Cary, Henrietta Maria, and Elizabeth of Bohemia. Her research interests include pastoral literature, religious reform and counterreform in England, and women's writing.

ABOUT THE CONTRIBUTORS

Curtis Perry is a professor of English at the University of Illinois at Urbana-Champaign. In addition to essays on various aspects of early modern English literature and culture, he is the author of *The Making of Jacobean Culture: James I and the Renegotiation of Elizabethan Literary Practice* (Cambridge University Press, 1997) and *Literature and Favoritism in Early Modern England* (Cambridge University Press, 2006). He is also the editor of *Material Culture and Cultural Materialisms in the Middle Ages and Renaissance* (Brepols, 2001).

Deana Rankin is fellow and director of studies in English at Girton College, University of Cambridge. She is the author of *Between Spenser and Swift: English Writing in Seventeenth-Century Ireland* (Cambridge University Press, 2005) as well as a number of articles on drama, history-writing, republicanism, and Irish writing in the early modern period. Formerly a theater manager, she maintains close links with the Royal Shakespeare Company's education program.

Margaret Reeves is a sessional assistant professor in the School of Arts and Letters in the Atkinson Faculty of Liberal and Professional Studies at York University in Toronto. She has published articles on Simone de Beauvoir's *The Second Sex,* Elizabeth Gaskell's *Cranford,* Aphra Behn's fiction, and on the writing of literary history in relation to the novel. She is also one of three coeditors of *Shell Games: Scams, Frauds, and Deceits (1300–1650)* (Toronto: Centre for Reformation and Renaissance Studies, 2004), and is currently working on a book-length study of political satiric discourse in seventeenth-century women's prose narratives.

R. W. Serjeantson teaches history at Trinity College, Cambridge. He is the author of a range of studies in early modern intellectual history and the editor of *Generall Learning: A Seventeenth Century Treatise on the Formation of the General Scholar,* by Meric Casaubon (Cambridge: RTM, 1999).

Alison Shell is a reader in English at the University of Durham. She is the author of *Catholicism, Controversy and the English Literary Imagination, 1558–1660* (Cambridge University Press, 1999) and a number of articles on English Catholic literary culture. She is currently working on two books: a survey of Catholicism within the oral culture of early modern England and a study of Shakespeare and religion.

Mihoko Suzuki is a professor of English at the University of Miami and the author of *Metamorphoses of Helen: Authority, Difference, and the Epic* (Cornell University Press, 1989 and 1992) and *Subordinate Subjects: Gender,* the *Political Nation, and Literary Form in England, 1588–1688* (Ashgate, 2003); and the coeditor, with Cristina Malcolmson, of *Debating Gender in Early Modern England, 1500–1700* (Palgrave, 2002). She edited the volumes on Elizabeth Cellier and Mary Carleton for Ashgate's Early Modern Englishwomen facsimile series and is coediting a four-volume collection of women's political writings in seventeenth-century England with Hilda Smith and Susan Wiseman. She is also writing a book on gender, history, and the politics of civil war in early modern England and France.

Jesse G. Swan, an associate professor of English at the University of Northern Iowa, has published on authors ranging from Shakespeare, Cary, and Milton to Conrad Aiken, Flannery O'Connor, and Arundhati Roy and on topics in bibliography and textual studies, critical race studies, silence, and the state of the U.S. academy. He is working on an edition of both the folio and octavo versions of *The History of Edward II* and has recently published, with Richard Utz, *Postmodern Medievalisms* (2005), volume 13 in the series Studies in Medievalism.

Heather Wolfe is the curator of manuscripts at the Folger Shakespeare Library, Washington, D.C. She is the editor of *Elizabeth Cary, Lady Falkland: Life and Letters* (RTM Publications and Arizona Center for Medieval and Renaissance Studies, 2001) and has published several essays on early modern manuscript culture and writing technologies. For the Folger, she has written the exhibition catalogues *The Pen's Excellencie* (2002) and *Letterwritng in Renaissance England* (2005) (with Alan Stewart, and has edited *The Trevelyon Miscellany of 1608* (2006).

Marion Wynne-Davies lectures in the English Department at the University of Dundee, Scotland. She has published two editions of primary material: *Renaissance Drama by Women: Texts and Documents* (with S. P. Cerasano) (Routledge, 1996) and *Women Poets of the Renaissance* (J. M. Dent, 1998), as well as several collections of essays in the same field. She has written two monographs, *Women and Arthurian Literature* (Palgrave Macmillan, 1996) and *Sidney to Milton* (Palgrave Macmillan, 2003), and her most recent work, *Women Writers of the English Renaissance: Familial Discourse,* is forthcoming from Palgrave Macmillan.

LIST OF FIGURES

1 Title page, "Edwarde The Seconde: His Rainge and deathe." Northamptonshire Record Office, Finch-Hatton MS 1.   131
2 Title page, "The Rainge and deathe off Edwarde the Seconde." Fitzwilliam Museum, Cambridge, MS 361.   132
3 "To The Reader," "Edwarde The Seconde: His Rainge and deathe." Northamptonshire Record Office, Finch-Hatton MS 1.   136
4 "To The Reader," "The Rainge and deathe off Edwarde the Seconde." Fitzwilliam Museum, Cambridge, MS 361.   137

INTRODUCTION

Heather Wolfe

Once relegated to the status of a nearly forgotten playwright and eccentric Roman Catholic convert, Elizabeth Cary (1585?–1639) is now increasingly appreciated as a Renaissance woman historian, playwright, translator, and poet. The recent proliferation of editions and facsimiles of Cary's writings has given students and scholars the ability to place the writer in broader and comparative contexts with implications that take her far beyond the domestic sphere.[1] Essays, articles, and chapters devoted to the topical nature of her writings, and a recognition of the ease with which she moved between literary genres, has repositioned her in the milieu of many of her more illustrious male contemporaries. While her small surviving oeuvre prevents her from being considered a major Renaissance writer, she is an intriguing and remarkable writer whose richly complex work actively questions the meaning of political tyranny. As a female author she can be credited with a number of firsts: she is the first English woman to have an original play printed, the first woman to author an English history, and the first woman to publish a translation of a religious polemical work. Cary's resurrection is part of a much larger and rapidly evolving recovery process of women writers in general, spurred on by crosscurrents in literary theory, gender studies, new historicism, textual bibliography, and manuscript studies.

Now that Cary figures so prominently in the inclusive literary landscape of male *and* female writers in early modern England, where do we go from here? Cary criticism, plentiful and robust, has focused almost exclusively on *The Tragedie of Mariam, Faire Queene of Jewry* (London, 1613) and *The History of the Life, Reign, and Death of Edward II* (London, 1680). Building on the Cary scholarship that precedes it, this collection of essays includes new voices, new perspectives, and new discoveries, broadening our understanding of Cary as a writer by incorporating critical and historical analyses of her forays into other genres. Always mindful of the literary, political, and religious backdrop of early Stuart England, the chapters explore the extent of her engagement in both the print *and* manuscript worlds of early modern England. The chapters address crucial questions about authorship, form, and reception and avoid generalizations about gender that would smooth over her consistently ambiguous portrayals of male and female figures and her complicated appropriations of typically "male" genres.

Cognizant of a much wider and more complex culture of literary transmission—often collaborative and anonymous—that operated outside the realm of the printed book, scholars are no longer simply interested in the fact that women wrote, but are now guided by the exciting and frustrating reality that the full extent and nature of women's writing will perhaps never be known. Women writers tended to use the medium of manuscript, rather than print, to construct their public identities, and, as recent studies have shown, manuscripts could be as influential, and often more subversive, than printed texts. But manuscripts have a much lower survival rate than printed books, and women's writing does not always fit neatly into traditional canonical categories. The true scope of women's writing from this period is difficult to estimate.

Cary's autograph remains are limited to fifteen letters, her signature on two depositions, and a youthful translation of Ortelius, which she dedicated to her uncle, Sir Henry Lee.[2] But allusions to her works by others suggest that she was deeply immersed in a variety of networks that transmitted literary and controversial manuscript texts and that her printed corpus represents only the tip of the iceberg. The manuscript of *Mariam* was "stolen out of that sister inlaws (her frinds) chamber, and printed, but by her owne procurement was called in," according to *Lady Falkland: Her Life* (written ca. 1645; hereafter referred to as *Life;* 110). Sir John Davies's dedication to her in 1612 makes mention of "Scenes of Syracuse and Palestine" written by her, which he apparently saw in manuscript.[3] According to Sir James Hayes's preface to the 1680 octavo of Cary's *History of the Most Unfortunate Prince, King Edward II*, he found the source manuscript among the papers of her husband, Henry Cary, Viscount Falkland. While this manuscript no longer appears to be extant, two other contemporary fair copies of Cary's *Edward II* (dated January 7, 1626/27 and February 2, 1627/28), both in the same scribal hand but of differing lengths, do survive. Cary alludes to her use of a copyist to prepare a manuscript of *The Reply of the most illustrious Cardinall of Perron, to the Answeare of the King of Great Britaine* (Douay, 1630) in her "letter to the reader" (sig. [ã2ᵛ]):

> If it gaine noe applause, hee that writt it faire, hath lost more labour then I haue done, for I dare auouch, it hath bene fower times as long in transcribing, as it was in translating.

Cary's epitaph "On the Duke of Buckingham" and its companion elegy were transcribed into dozens of poetical miscellanies and manuscript separates. Oft-repeated statistics culled from *Life* point to many other manuscripts, including an original polemical religious treatise, thought to be "the best thing she ever writ," a letter of advice to her oldest children, and "innumerable slight things in verse."[4] Of her verse, "that which was sayd to be the best" was "the life of Tamberlaine in verse"; she also penned verse lives of many saints, including St. Mary Magdalene, St. Agnes Martyr, St. Elizabeth of Portugal, and "many verses of our Blessed Lady."[5] In addition to her translation of Cardinal du Perron's *Replique* (only the first tome of which was ever published), *Life* cites her translations of Seneca's epistles (found by her son Lucius in her father's study), and the writings of Louis de Blois, a sixteenth-century Benedictine monk.[6] While only a handful of the manuscripts described in this paragraph are known to be extant, the fact that her Catholic children were aware of many of them in the decade after her death suggests that they had seen and read them when they lived with her in England, and that they perhaps took the Catholic writings with them to Cambrai.

The Lady Falkland: Her Life is a valuable tool for understanding Cary's *lived* life and the extent of her literary output. While it is a useful exercise to read it both as a hagiographically motivated conversion narrative of a mother and six of her children produced at a monastery in the Spanish Netherlands, and as a literary work that adheres to the prescribed format for early modern lifewriting, in many cases biographical events can be distilled from providential explanations to corroborate and enhance details about Cary's life and conversion.[7] The utility of this multilayered approach is evident in several chapters included here: Richard Serjeantson begins his chapter with an examination of *Life*'s account of the triangular relationship between Cary, her son Lucius, and his friend William Chillingworth; Deana Rankin reads *Life*'s account of Cary's time in Ireland against the grain to highlight her emergence in the Irish public sphere; and Marion Wynne-Davies uses *Life* as a springboard for understanding Cary's influence on the surviving written remains of four of her children (Lucy, Anne, Patrick, and Lucius). As Alison Shell elegantly argues in her chapter, it is entirely plausible that Cary followed the Renaissance practice of interrogating her own life through an active rewriting of relevant historical exemplars. Thus, it has been, and will continue to be, a useful exercise to use what we know about her life—her extensive learning, the ways in which she defended her conversion, her financial and familial hardships, her active participation in a range of influential literary and religious circles—through *Life*, her letters, and other contemporary print and manuscript sources, to better understand the relationship between form and content in her writings.[8]

★★★★★

Part I of the collection is devoted to *The Tragedy of Mariam*. Printed in 1613 by Richard Hawkins, this Senecan closet drama was written roughly ten years earlier, when the newly married Cary was living with her mother-in-law while her husband honed his soldier-skills in the wars in the Spanish Netherlands.[9] Ilona Bell examines the ways in which the play's meaning is shaped by Cary's deployment of Renaissance lyric— nearly forty sonnets and countless sestets are embedded throughout the play. The use of Petrarchan sonnets and dialogic love poetry allows the female characters to respond to and transform a typically male genre, and in turn, allows the playwright herself to critique the contradictory rhetoric of the Petrarchan sonneteers of the Elizabethan period. The constant undermining and overturning of declaration and judgment by each character is central to the play's meaning and purpose, and Bell suggests that Cary unsettled her audience by providing both an ironic commentary on Renaissance literary conventions and on attitudes toward love, marriage, and women.

Previous scholars have identified Mariam as a proto-Christian martyr. Erin Kelly problematizes this tag by comparing Cary's Mariam to other Mariams and to other descriptions of post-Reformation Protestant and Catholic martyrs by Cary's contemporaries. Cary wrote her play at a critical period in the history of martyrological discourse in England, when stories about Protestant martyrs were deployed by writers *not* to encourage spiritual zealotry and religious dissent, but rather, to encourage conformity. Thus, female martyrs were often depicted as meek and innocent victims, stripped of the rebellious facets of their personalities. Cary, instead, highlights the defiant actions of her Mariam, challenging contemporary readers to accept the heroine-martyr as a chaste, but not silent or obedient, female. The judgments that the chorus pass on Mariam therefore serve as Cary's implicit interrogation of her contemporaries' tendency to strip female martyrs of their rebelliousness, since to condemn this quality is to condemn the very quality that made them martyrs.

While critics have previously compared *Mariam* to Cary's source, Thomas Lodge's translation of Josephus's *Antiquities of the Jews* (1st ed., London, 1602), Alison Shell focuses on the influence of Lodge's approach to history as spelled out in his preface, rather than on the source material itself. Historical exemplars were widely used in early modern England as a means for self-interrogation of the past and as a model for future behavior, and it could be argued that *Mariam* was in part a moral exercise in internalizing an exemplar that bore some relation to Cary's own condition. Autodidactic texts such as Cary's play and Lodge's translation did not require a point-by-point correspondence between writer/reader and character, but instead required the reader to be able to infer the moral utility from only one character trait or incident. Cary's voracious devouring of history and moral treatises, as recounted in *Life*, strongly suggests her belief in the power of a historical text or play to provide matter for the correcting of one's faults. Moving beyond both the readings of *Mariam* as an exploration of female subjectivity and as a confessional work, and the subsequent downplaying of biographical criticism by later scholars, Shell argues that the play be read in light of what we know about Cary's own conscience, and that we fully appreciate the clash of exemplarities that she presents.

★★★★★

Part II turns to Cary's *History of Edward II*, extant in four different versions of varying lengths—two print publications of 1680 and two scribal copies made in the late 1620s. While the story of Edward II, his wife, Isabel, and his favorites Gaveston and Spenser, was taken up by many of Cary's contemporaries, including Marlowe, Hubert, and Drayton, what were Cary's motives in reviving and retelling the story of a king who had died 400 years earlier? Curtis Perry's chapter on the folio version of *The History of the Life, Death, and Reign of Edward II* focuses on the ways in which Cary's concern with domestic tyranny is intertwined with larger questions about the meaning of political tyranny and subjection. In the 1620s, comparisons of Edward II's favorite, Spencer, to James I's and Charles I's favorite, the Duke of Buckingham, were rife, interpreted as a warning against the dangers of favorites and, simultaneously, as a warning about the dangers of unchecked popularity and speech. Cary's adaptation of this deeply contested political fable evinces an interest in its moral ambiguity: the fact that, once the political balance has tipped, nobody in the story is completely innocent, and all actions and motives are suspect. Suggesting that the politics of passion and the lack of self-restraint are Cary's central concerns, Perry invites readers to subordinate character to theme as early modern readers were prone to do; that is, to think of the fundamental narrative structure of the *History* not in terms of the experiences of individual characters but in terms of an outward movement of intemperate passion beginning with Edward himself and then moving in sequence to his court and to the realm as a whole.

Mihoko Suzuki argues that *The History of Edward II* represents a significant intervention in the history of English and continental political thought and historiography. She examines Cary's use of and divergence from Machiavelli's *The Prince* and *Discourses,* and compares Cary's gendered critique of the hierarchical metaphor of the body politic to that in Christine de Pizan's *The Book of the Body Politic*. Suzuki then situates Cary in the tradition of English political thought that advances limited monarchy—whose chief exemplars are John of Salisbury and John Fortescue—and examines her relation to late sixteenth- and early seventeenth-century Catholic proponents of monarchical resistance. Not only does Cary use these political thinkers to shape her historical narrative, her analysis of the fall of Edward II serves as an exemplary narrative through which she tests political theories concerning monarchical prerogative and the claims of the subject, thus challenging the theory of absolute monarchy as put forth by James I. *Edward II* thereby participates in the contemporary dialogue concerning absolutism and parliamentary prerogative between king and parliament, while its posthumous publication during the Exclusion Crisis indicates its relevance for the similar debate between Charles II and his parliaments concerning his prerogative to name James II as his successor. Cary diverges from the traditional Protestant national historiography of Britain to advance a theory of nationhood based on an eclectic synthesis of political theory—both English and continental—that prioritizes the importance of the common good.

Criticism on Cary's *Edward II* has traditionally privileged the longer of the two printed versions of 1680, the folio *History of the Life, Death, and Reign of Edward II*. Discussion of the much shorter octavo version, *The History of the Most Unfortunate Prince,* has always been speculative and dismissive: it is treated either as a redaction of the longer version made by a later publisher or as a spurious early version. The importance of the octavo, and its relationship to the folio, are taken up by Jesse Swan and Margaret Reeves, respectively. Jesse Swan provides a detailed postpublication history of the 1680 octavo. His discussion accentuates its importance as a witness to the literary work of Cary, as an independent production with an independent aim, rather than as a redaction of the longer 1680 folio text, and illustrates the perils of trusting later editions, beginning with the version of *The History of the Most Unfortunate Prince* included in *The Harleian Miscellany* (London, 1744–1746). As Swan argues, the textual apparatus and other editorial interventions in these later editions introduce many misleading readings, solidify the erroneous attribution to Henry Cary, perpetuate the belief that the octavo was a redaction of the folio, and further, obscure the fact that the preface to the octavo was written by Sir James Hayes in 1680 and *not* by William Oldys in 1744. Swan demonstrates that commercial and bibliographical forces have led to the misrepresentation of the 1680 octavo since 1744, and describes the effect that this has had on twentieth-century scholarship on *Edward II*.

In the mid-1990s, the late Jeremy Maule discovered two manuscript versions of Cary's history of Edward II, which both enhance and complicate our understanding of the history's function and readership. The earlier, shorter manuscript (Northamptonshire Record Office, Finch-Hatton MS 1) bears some similarity to the octavo version, although it is significantly longer, while

INTRODUCTION 7

the longer manuscript (Fitzwilliam Museum, MS 361) and the 1680 printed folio exhibit a high degree of similarity to one another. Both manuscripts are in the same scribal hand and come from similar paper stock. In this volume, Margaret Reeves takes up Maule's arguments, convincingly linking all four versions to Elizabeth Cary and providing a linguistic comparison which shows that the two printed versions are neither expanded nor consolidated versions of one another, but rather two separate and distinct histories emanating from two additional, nonextant, sources. In successive surviving versions of the history, Reeves analyzes the shifts in tone and wording of Cary's preface to the reader (in which Cary explains that the history was written "to owtronne those wearie howers"), attributing the greater emphasis on Cary's emotional distress in the earlier manuscript's preface to the fact that she had just publicly converted to Roman Catholicism, resulting in the loss of financial support and familial bonds. The transformation of Cary's historical narrative of Edward II from the manuscript that informed the octavo version (no longer extant), to the Finch-Hatton manuscript, to the Fitzwilliam manuscript, indicates that Cary was an active reviser of her own work, and that her history was known and available to her contemporaries in at least two different manuscript versions long before its 1680 publication(s).

★★★★★

Cary's most influential work in her own lifetime was a translation of one of the key religious polemical treatises of the early seventeenth century, Jacques Davy du Perron's *Replique à la résponse du Serenissime Roy de la Grand Bretagne* (Paris, 1620). Cary's translation of the first part of this tome, *The Reply of the Most Illustrions Cardinall of Perron to the Answeare of the Most Excellent King of Great Britaine* (Douay, 1630), was part of a multilingual dialogue between du Perron and various Protestant intellectuals that began its printed life in 1611 with a letter from Isaac Casaubon (writing on behalf of James I) to du Perron, and ended in 1664 with the publication of a new edition of the English translation of Pierre du Moulin's 1627 answer to *Replique*, titled *The Novelty of Popery, opposed to the antiquity of true Christianity. Against the book of Cardinal Du Perron*. Cary entered the debate at a time when interest in an English reformed and Catholic Church was high among her irenical, Arminian friends: the Gallican (French Catholic) Church was a useful model because of its delayed and partial adherence to the reforms of the Council of Trent (1545–1563) in 1615.

Cary's translation, which appeared in print shortly after two retorts to *Replique*—Pierre du Moulin's *Nouveauté du Papisme* (1627) and Lancelot Andrewes' *Two Answers to Cardinall Perron* (London, 1629)—and in between two new French editions of du Perron's *Replique*, in 1622 and

1633, earned her a reputation in Rome as a Catholic scholar.[10] The translation gained attention from her family and friends as well, including her husband, her daughters, her son Lucius and his friend William Chillingworth, her friend James Clayton, and most likely Queen Henrietta Maria herself.[11] *Life* notes that most copies of this tome were seized and burned by command of the archbishop of Canterbury upon their arrival in England from Douai, but that "some few copies came to her hands" (141). It is likely that six surviving presentation copies of *Reply*, all containing precise emendations and bound in fine morocco with remnants of blue silk ties, were among these few copies. Five of these include a tipped-in engraving of du Perron with a laudatory quatrain written in manuscript, and four of these five also contain a tipped-in manuscript sonnet addressed to Henrietta Maria.[12]

Karen Nelson situates Cary's translation within the religious controversies in England in the late 1620s and 1630s, when English Protestants were increasingly dismayed by a visible and vocal Catholic population in England, by Charles's French-Catholic queen, whose chapel was frequented by English Catholic courtiers, and by the growth of English Catholic colleges and monasteries on the continent. Nelson compares *Reply* to other works of controversy that were published at the same time, and explicates *Reply*'s voluminous preliminary material and the last section of the translation, which treats the necessity of the Roman Catholic Church's schism with the Eastern churches. The fact that the translation closes with an argument for the king to submit to the pope's spiritual authority, as England's earlier kings had historically done, while maintaining his temporal authority, suggests that Cary was aware of a softening, or at least a more neutral stance, toward Catholics, and that she timed her translation to influence those people who might be sympathetic to a revival of James I's irenical aspirations for a reformed Catholic Church.

Cary was also a controversialist in her own right. *Life* describes "the best thing she ever writ" as a now-lost treatise disputing the Protestant beliefs of her son Lucius, second Viscount Falkland. R. W. Serjeantson addresses the question: What would this treatise have discussed, and how does it relate to the larger debates authored by her son and his friends, the Catholic convert Walter Montague and the Protestant-Catholic-Protestant William Chillingworth? Serjeantson untangles the manuscript and print culture of religious controversy in early modern England to show Cary's critical influence on many well-known works of controversy, and celebrates her as an author of original controversy, arguing that the context for Chillingworth's epic *Religion of Protestants* (Oxford, 1638) was precisely the one that Cary herself was involved in: the controversy between Isaac Casaubon/James I and du Perron.

Mariam, Edward II, and *Reply* are not the only surviving fruits of Cary's pen. The popular epitaph on the Duke of Buckingham that begins "Reader, stand still and look, lo here I am," attributed to Cary in two contemporary manuscript sources, is consistently linked in poetical miscellanies to a 44-line elegy beginning, "Yet were bidentalls sacred." Nadine Akkerman examines the relationship between the epitaph and elegy and makes a convincing argument for Cary's authorship of both texts. After ruling out other possible authors—John Eliot, Richard Weston, and William Juxon—Akkerman offers a close reading of the elegy, written less than a year after Cary penned *Edward II,* another text that addresses the dangerous consequences of royal favoritism while giving the accused an opportunity to speak for himself. Akkerman highlights the contradictions and ambiguities of the poem, particularly its simultaneous defense and condemnation of Buckingham's actions, reading it against other satirical poems relating to Buckingham's 1628 assassination and in the context of miscellanized elegies in general.

★★★★★

Part IV of this collection looks at Cary's legacies: her patronage in Dublin and the literary legacy that she passed on to her children, many of whom went on to circulate their own work in manuscript and print. Deana Rankin's chapter on Cary and Ireland begins with Gaveston's banishment to, and return from, Ireland, as recounted in *History of the Life, Reign and Death of Edward II.* Cary spent approximately four years in Dublin (September 1622–July 1626), where her husband served as Lord Deputy of Ireland from 1622 to 1629. Her time there marks an important juncture in her life, Rankin argues, for it was when Cary began pursuing a public life and began moving and thriving between cultures and religions. She named her newborn son after the patron saint of Ireland, taught herself Irish, conversed with Irish Catholics, started a glorified sweatshop in which poor Irish children became apprentices in spinning and weaving, and became a patron to the Catholic Richard Bellings, who dedicated *A Sixth Booke to the Countesse of Pembrokes Arcadia* to her in 1624. Rankin reads Belling's dedication and work against the political and religious climate in Dublin and London and alongside other dedications to Cary, considering the possibilities of her involvement "at the first birth" of Belling's narrative. The conclusive vision of reconciliation provided by Belling—Amphialus returning from banishment to be restored to grace and to marry and rule alongside Queen Helen of Corinth—perhaps reflected cautious optimisim among the Catholic Old English, who strove to be reintegrated into Irish civil and military life, a liberty denied them in the aftermath of the

Eliźabethan Wars. Belling's ending to Sidney's romance, dedicated to Cary, was consistently appended to all subsequent editions of *Arcadia* from 1627 onward.

Finally, Marion Wynne-Davies introduces us to the writings of four of Cary's children—Lucy, Anne, Patrick, and Lucius—exploring the ways in which they were influenced by, and negotiated around, Cary's attempts to convert them to Roman Catholicism. Both Cary herself and *Life* created a familial discourse that placed spiritual faith above family ties. Yet, Wynne-Davies notes, other writings by Cary's children reflect the tensions created by this dislocation. Their adherance to a dialectic of wordly inheritance and spiritual choice is common to religious discourse of the early modern period in general, and yet they enact it in unique ways. Wynne-Davies explores the language in the obituaries of Lucy and Anne, Anne's free translations of the psalms, Patrick's religious and secular poetry, and Lucius' poetry and his anti-Catholic treatises, including *A Discourse of Infallibility*.

★★★★★

Cary's sixteen surviving letters (fifteen autograph letters, one letter copied out by her husband) are perhaps her most overlooked writings. Letter writing was an established literary genre in early modern England and Cary was master of the form, relying upon rhetoric, casuistry, friendships, and political and religious alliances to shape her pleas and responses to her husband, to the Privy Council, and even to the king. Though she had little bargaining power, her carefully worded explanations and appeals garnered the attention and response of her recipients. She deflected her husband's vitriolic condemnation of her as a bewitched, conniving, and spendthrift wife by portraying herself as an obedient wife and subject who was merely following her conscience. While many other noblewomen wrote carefully calibrated petitionary letters in the early Stuart period, Cary took extraordinary risks with the tone of her letters, deploying wit, sarcasm, and passion under circumstances in which humility and respect might have been more circumspect. She concludes a letter to Secretary of State Sir Francis Windebank by appropriating his earlier attempt to insult her: "If the seruice of a collapsed lady; as you called hir, may bee of use to you, you shall euer comand hir" (the word "collapsed" refers to both sexual and religious misconduct).[13] In a letter to Charles I, she chastizes him for thinking her so foolish as to believe that her conversion to Catholicism would lead to social advancement:

> I heard by person of quality, that your maiesty was pleased to beleeue, that I altred my ^profession of^ religion, upon some court hopes, but I beseech you,

how wicked soeuer you may censure mee, to bee, (as it is no lesse, to make religion, a ladder to clime by) yet iudge mee, not, so foolish, as to understand so little, in the state, of this time, as to thinke promotion, likely, to come, that way.[14]

But her most biting commentary turns up in a letter to Dudley Carleton, Viscount Dorchester. In April 1629, Cary had learned from her friend Elizabeth Knollys, Countess of Banbury, that Lord Dorchester had been offended by the "impatience" and "incivility" of a letter Cary had written to him. In her follow-up letter to him, Cary recommends that he speak further with Lady Banbury so that he fully understands the extent of Cary's "miseryes." She blames the tone in her "incivil" letter on her incorrect belief that Dorchester had colluded with her husband in delaying her allowance, and does "acknowledge my mistakinge." Instead of then referring to herself in the deferential generic terms appropriate to a petitionary letter in which the sender hopes to regain the sympathy of her addressee, she seeks to instruct him in the social and moral responsibilities of nobility by invoking a classical anecdote:

> I am no scholler my lord, but I haue heard of a poore woman in macedon, that was much bolder upon a delay, with a great kinge, yet in that plaine age it was not excepted against.[15]

Cary's self-deprecating assertion that she is "no scholar" is followed by a reference to Plutarch's story of the poor old woman who tugged at Philip of Macedon's gown as he walked down the street, begging him to listen to her.[16] When he answered that he did not have time, she cried out to him, "Leave, then to be no king." Philip of Macedon was so disturbed by her outburst that he immediately returned to his palace and for many days devoted himself to listening to suits and petitions, beginning with the poor old woman. Cary cites this story to soften the perception of her own boldness and to invoke the spirit of that "plain age." By drawing parallels to another king and another period in history (as she does in *Edward II, Mariam,* and *Reply*), she utilizes history, like many of her contemporaries, as a rich source of successes and failures that, in the retelling, can guide not only her own actions, but also the actions of her readers.

NOTES

This collection of essays has been germinating for some time, inspired by a symposium on Elizabeth Cary organized by the late Jeremy Maule, fellow of Trinity College, Cambridge, in June 1996. Jeremy and I had hoped to coedit a volume based on the papers presented there. Since his death in 1998, Cary studies have continued to grow, and thus I have added additional contributors to reflect the current state of scholarship in the twenty-first century. I am grateful to the contributors for making this volume possible; to Richard Kuhta, Librarian of the Folger Shakespeare Library, for granting me sabbatical leave to edit it; to Kathleen Lynch and Jesse Swan for providing valuable advice on the Introduction; and to Quindi Franco for patiently waiting for me to finish it.

1. Editions and/or facsimiles of four printed works—*The Tragedie of Mariam, Faire Queene of Jewry* (London, 1613), the two versions of Cary's history of Edward II (London, 1680), and her translation, *The Reply of the Most Illustrious Cardinall of Perron to the Answeare of the Most Excellent King of Great Britaine*—are readily available, as are her letters and the 1645 biography, *The Lady Falkland her Life*.
2. "The mirror of the Worlde translated Out of French into Englishe by E T," dedicated to Cary's uncle, Sir Henry Lee (Bodleian Library, Dep. d. 817). It belonged to the seventeenth Viscount Dillon, who gave it to Burford Parish in 1925; it was deposited at the Bodleian by the vicar of Burford in 1991 and is generally restricted to microfilm or photocopy consultation. Lesley Peterson's "Source and Date for Elizabeth Tanfield Cary's Manuscript *The Mirror of the Worlde*," *Notes and Queries* 249 (2004): 257–263, argues that this translation was of *Epitome du theatre du monde* (Antwerp: Christopher Plantin, 1588), but her evidence is not conclusive.
3. *Mariam*'s existence in manuscript was noted by Sir John Davies in 1612, when he made Cary a joint dedicatee, along with Lucy, Countess of Bedford, and Mary Sidney, dowager Countess of Pembroke, of *The Muses Sacrifice*. In stanza 18 of "The Epistle Dedicatory" he writes: "Thou makst Melpomen proud, and my Heart great / of such a Pupill, who, in Buskin fine, / With Feete of State, dost make thy Muse to mete / the Scenes of Syracuse and Palestine" (sig. [★★★3^v]). Palestine is the setting of *The Tragedy of Mariam*, while Syracuse refers to the setting of another play by Cary, now lost.
4. *Life*, 214, 114, 213. All references to *Life* are to *Lady Falkland: Her Life*, in *Elizabeth Cary, Lady Falkland: Life and Letters*, ed. Heather Wolfe (Cambridge, England, and Tempe, AZ: RTM Publications and Arizona Center for Medieval and Renaissance Studies, 2001).
5. *Life*, 110, 135, 141. Among her verses on the Virgin Mary were some "verses made on the Anuntiation of our Blesed Lady, and directed to my Lady of Banbury" (Elizabeth Knollys).
6. *Life*, 106, 111.
7. See Heather Wolfe, "The Scribal Hands and Dating of *Lady Falkland: Her Life*," *English Manuscript Studies 1100–1700* 9 (2000): 187–217; Wolfe, "A Family Affair: The Life and Letters of Elizabeth Cary, Lady Falkland," in *New Ways of Looking at Old Texts III*, ed. W. Speed Hill (Tempe, AZ: Arizona Center for Medieval and Renaissance Studies, 2004), 97–108; Judith H. Anderson, *Biographical Truth: The Representation of Historical Persons in Tudor-Stuart Writing* (New Haven: Yale UP, 1984); and Ruth Morse, *Truth and Convention in the Middle Ages: Rhetoric, Representation, and Reality* (Cambridge: Cambridge UP, 1991).

INTRODUCTION   13

8. For an account of the seductive possibilities of biographical criticism, see Stephanie Wright, "The Canonization of Elizabeth Cary," in *Voicing Women: Gender and Sexuality in Early Modern Writing*, ed. Kate Chedgzoy, Melanie Hansen, and Suzanne Trill (Keele, Staffordshire: Keele UP, 1996), 55–68.
9. The dedicatory sonnet of *Mariam*, signed "E.C." and addressed to Cary's sister-in-law, "my worthy sister, Mistress Elizabeth Cary," makes reference to her husband's being abroad: "For when my Phoebus' absence makes it night, / Whilst to th'Antipodes his beams do bend" (sig. A1^{r-v}). This poem, with the list of characters verso, is only present in the copies at the Huntington Library and the Houghton Library (Harvard). Cancelled stubs are visible in copies at the Eton College Library and the Bodleian Library (Oxford).
10. See letters to Cardinal Barberini, Innocent X, and others in Wolfe, *Elizabeth Cary*, 10–12, letters 96, 100, 106, 111.
11. According to *Life*, Henry Cary's copy of *Reply* "was found in his closet after his death, all noted by him" (151). Clayton, who authored one of the unsigned dedications to her (and to whom she owed £30—her list of debts is printed in Wolfe, *Elizabeth Cary*, letter 33), presented his copy to the Bodleian. Her daughter mentions the translation in several places in *Life* (131–132, 141, 151, 207). Chillingworth's and Lucius Cary's religious writings respond directly to du Perron's arguments (see Serjeantson's chapter). Du Perron converted Henrietta Maria's father, Henri IV, in 1593 (and du Perron's nephew arrived in England in May 1631 as the queen's almoner).
12. Cary acknowledges the queen's role in bringing du Perron to the attention of English Catholics, writing in the manuscript sonnet: "It is your heart (your pious zealous heart)/ That by attractive force, bringes great PERROONE / To leaue his SEYNE, his LOYRE, and his GARROONE:/ And to your handmaide THAMES his guiftes imparte" (ll.5-8, Beinecke Library (Yale), Me65 D925+R4G 1630) and in the printed dedication, Henrietta Maria is "fittest to patronize the making him an English man, that, was before so famous a Frenchman" (sig. ã2^r). The other copies are at Harvard, UCLA, Oxford, Cambridge, and Downside Abbey. See Wolfe, *Elizabeth Cary*, 12–13.
13. Cary to Sir Francis Windebank, ca. June 22–30, 1632, National Archives, SP 16/219/58 (Wolfe, *Elizabeth Cary*, letter 78).
14. Cary to Charles I, May 18, 1627, National Archives, SP 16/63/89 (Wolfe, letter, *Elizabeth Cary*, 19).
15. Cary to Dudley Carleton, Viscount Dorchester, April [ca. 17–30], 1629, National Archives, SP 16/141/78 (Wolfe, *Elizabeth Cary*, letter 47).
16. From Plutarch's life of Demetrius, in *Parallel Lives*. For a contemporary English translation, see *The Lives of the Noble Grecians and Romaines, compared together* (London, 1612), 905. The story also appears in George Buchanan's *De jure regni apud Scotos* (Edinburgh, 1579). See Folger Shakespeare Library, MS V.b.223, fol. 37^v, for a ca. 1609 English manuscript translation of this passage. See George Buchanan, *A Dialogue on the Law of Kingship Among the Scots*, ed. Roger A. Mason and Martin S. Smith (Aldershot: Ashgate, 2004), 173n54, for other sources.

PART I

THE TRAGEDY OF MARIAM

CHAPTER 1

PRIVATE LYRICS IN ELIZABETH CARY'S *TRAGEDY OF MARIAM*

Ilona Bell

According to *The Lady Falkland: Her Life*, Elizabeth Cary valued poetry above all other literary genres. Her biographer-daughter asserts that not only had she "read very exceeding much: Poetry of all kinds, ancient and modern, in several languages, all that ever she could meet," but she also "writ many things for her private recreation, on several subjects, and occasions, all in verse."[1] Despite the fact that the most likely models for Cary's *The Tragedy of Mariam, The Fair Queen of Jewry* were written in unrhymed iambic pentameter with intermittent couplets, Cary's play is writ "all in verse" *and* in rhyme.[2] The iambic pentameter lines, quatrains with alternating rhymes, are punctuated by occasional couplets that produce sonnets, or truncated sonnets, throughout the play.

The first edition of *Mariam* is prefaced by a dedicatory sonnet,[3] and the drama begins with a sonnet spoken by Mariam herself. These two prominently placed introductory sonnets alert the reader to be on the lookout for sonnets to come, and indeed, nineteen of the play's twenty-two scenes contain at least one sonnet. In all there are fifteen monologic sonnets, sixteen composite or multivocal sonnets, two self-contained fourteen-line speeches comprising a complete sonnet, six abbreviated ten-line sonnets, and countless sestets, thirty spoken by the chorus alone. Some of the sonnets are the result of errant couplets thrown in to relieve the relentless march of quatrain after quatrain, but most highlight or demarcate significant moments in the drama. Monologic sonnets introduce, climax, or conclude soliloquies and long self-dramatizing speeches. Composite sonnets offer a protective enclosure for clandestine lovers (Salome and Sileus), conspiring accomplices (Salome and Pheroras), or aspiring suitors (Doris and Antipater). Other composite sonnets heighten and encircle conflicts between characters (Salome and Constabarus; Mariam and Doris; Mariam and Herod; Mariam and her mother; Mariam and Salome). Some sonnet-making couplets climax or conclude long declamatory speeches. Some are the pivot upon which an individual character's conflicting, vacillating thoughts and feelings turn; others summarize or acknowledge contradictory impulses, producing a feeling of oxymoronic stasis or a moment of epigrammatic closure. Others undercut or overturn what has just been said by another character, thereby exposing overly authoritative declarations as one-sided, specious, or tyrannical. Some of the sonnets dramatize historical concerns specific to *Mariam,* but most have significant, and often ironic, links to Renaissance lyric tradition.[4]

The Renaissance lyric has often been seen as the genre most inhospitable to women since by definition and convention it expressed the thoughts and feelings of the male poet or speaker. Yet many English Renaissance sonnets were poems of courtship, usually clandestine courtship, written to be recited or sent by a male poet/lover to his mistress, hoping to amuse her with his wit, to reassure her with his attentiveness to her concerns, and to embolden her with his principled but unconventional code of ethics. By encouraging women to follow their own desires rather than submit to their father's will or their husband's command, poetry of courtship validated female desire, encouraged female agency, and challenged the gender hierarchy upon which the social order rested. When we conceptualize the sonnet lady not as the poet's creation but as his private lyric audience, her responses critique the poet/lover's claims and express an alternative point of view, even as they invite the male poet/lover to consider her female point of view.[5]

Even though many of the greatest English Renaissance poetic sequences were written to and for women whose responses helped shape the genre, the sonnet or lyric sequence typically gives us ready access to only one side of the private lyric dialogue—the male side. The female voices responding to the male poet/lovers' persuasions are difficult to recover or even to imagine because they took place outside the poem—quite literally, on the margins of English literary tradition. The resulting private lyric dialogue, carefully encoded to conceal its most pressing concerns from the larger lyric audience, resembles the closet drama, which also contains a network of private subtexts that would have been accessible to its original coterie audience but that are concealed, or at least partially veiled, from the reading public.

By embedding sonnets—whether as soliloquies, monologues, or lyric dialogues—amid the ongoing dramatic conversation, Cary dramatizes the personal, psychological, and political situations which produced sonnets and which were in turn produced by the dialogues the sonnets initiated or

PRIVATE LYRICS IN *MARIAM* 19

sustained. Although *Mariam* is set in biblical Judea, it dramatizes and interrogates a code of ethics very similar to one that Cary herself confronted as a young woman in early modern England. *Mariam* not only breaks women's silence, reexamining conventional attitudes toward femininity, marriage, and political power, but it also explores the ways in which the female audience influenced male lyric and dramatic tradition.

The play begins by placing us solidly in a woman's world. Herod's mentor, Mark Antony, has died, and Herod has gone to Rome to negotiate with Antony's successor, Octavius Caesar. Everyone, including Herod's wife, Mariam, mistakenly believes that Herod has been killed by Caesar. The first scene presents Mariam alone on stage. Her use of the first-person nominative pronoun and active verb ("How oft have I with public voice run on") in her opening speech claims female agency, female speech, and female liberty even as it foregrounds the female point of view, announcing from the very outset that this play offers a counterpoint to Renaissance literary convention.[6] In scenes 2 and 3, respectively, she is joined by her mother, Alexandra, and then by her sister-in-law and foil, Salome. When Alexandra chastizes Salome, saying "Come Mariam, let us go: it is no boot / To let the head contend against the foot" (1.3.259–60), she echoes Queen Elizabeth's reprimand to the insubordinate 1566 Parliament: "I will deal therein for your safety and offer it unto you as your prince and head, without request. For it is monstrous that the feet should direct the head."[7] Alexandra's appropriation of patriarchal political rhetoric reminds us that Cary chose to begin the play at a time when Judea was, like Elizabethan England, ruled by a woman. Indeed, if as most scholars believe, the play was written between 1603 and 1604, it may well be exploring issues raised by the end of Elizabeth's reign.[8] In scene 4, the first male, Salome's lover, Sileus, appears on stage, followed in scene 5 by her husband, Constabarus, but their words and actions are dominated and determined by Salome's desires. Thus act 1 dramatizes a historical moment when family, government, and society are dominated and controlled by women.[9]

The first two acts introduce one set of characters after another, all of whom are planning or plotting to enjoy their newfound freedom from Herod's tyranny. The sheer number of characters appearing in quick succession and the panoply of unexplained historical events that enmesh and disturb their lives pose a continual interpretive challenge that begins with Mariam's opening speech. As if to flaunt the coded nature of the play's historical allusions, Mariam invokes but does not name Rome's previous ruler, Julius Caesar:

    How oft have I with public voice run on
    To censure Rome's last hero for deceit. (1.1.1–2)

Whereas the typical Renaissance sonnet sequence dramatizes the male voice and male point of view, Mariam's speech foregrounds the female point of view, announcing from the very outset that this play offers a counterpoint to Renaissance literary convention.[10]

As the country's interim ruler during Herod's absence, Mariam has adopted the male role of public speaker. Feeling inadequately prepared for this role, Mariam turns to male rulers as role models, but she boldly criticizes their point of view, implying ever so delicately Cary's own feeling of indebtedness to and distance from her male predecessors, the Petrarchan sonneteers, whose conflicting, contradictory rhetoric provides a source for the drama that is about to unfold. While Caesar's contradictory feelings provide a useful analogy and contrast for Mariam's emotional conflict, the Petrarchan sonneteers provide a model and foil for the play's dramatic conflict, even as Mariam's situation provides a parallel and comparison to Cary's.[11] Mariam thinks back to and through her male predecessors, just as Cary thinks back to and through her male predecessors, the male poets whose sonnets provide a starting point for Mariam's self-exploration.

In her opening sonnet Mariam explores her own concerns through Julius Caesar. Now that Herod's death makes Mariam understand why Caesar mourned Pompey's death, she apologizes for her feminine mistake: "Excuse too rash a judgment in a woman: / My sex pleads pardon, pardon then afford, / Mistaking is with us but too too common" (1.1.6–8).[12] The historical displacement shows not only how inadequate being a woman makes Mariam (and Cary) feel, but also that English literary tradition does not provide a ready form for female self-expression. Mariam's own "self-experience" penetrates, or punctuates, the sonnet she constructs, highlighting the tension between historical precedent and current situation: "Now do I find by self-experience taught, / One object yields both grief and joy" (1.1.9–10). The emphasis on what is happening right "now"—and the word "now" recurs eight times in the first speech alone—reminds us that the closet drama follows the classical unities of time, place, and action. The Elizabethan sonnet and lyric also characteristically dramatize a moment in time, replacing Petrarch's nostalgic memories and cyclical shape with Sidney's, Spenser's, and Donne's forward-straining dramatic immediacy.

Much as Julius Caesar provides Mariam with a historical precedent that allows her to break away from her oppression as a woman, the character of Mariam provides a historical precedent for Cary to interrogate the constraints of her own life and marriage. It is difficult to know to what extent the private allusions to Cary's own desire for greater liberty were perceived by her original private audience when the play was first circulating and probably read aloud to a small literary coterie sometime between

1603 and 1609, but this personal topicality would not have been apparent to the reading public when the play was first published in 1613, just as the veiled subtexts of many Elizabethan sonnets would have been lost on later readers of print or widely circulating manuscripts.

The sonnet per se cannot explain and contain Mariam's feelings any more than Elizabethan poems of courtship can foresee and contain the response of the private female lyric audience. Thus, despite the finality of the couplet in line 14, Mariam's speech continues, seeking tropes and role models to express her complicated thoughts and feelings. Like the typical Petrarchan or Neoplatonic sonnet lady, she prides herself on her virtue and chastity, however constraining they may be; at the same time, she yearns for the freedom and authority enjoyed by the male poet, speaker, and ruler. As a result, she is tormented by vacillating, conflicting feelings. Laboring under the mistaken belief that her husband Herod is dead, she is furious at him for killing her grandfather and her brother, and for leaving orders to have her killed if he should die so that she cannot remarry. Yet at the same time she also grieves for Herod and yearns for the passionate love they once shared: "Why, now methinks the love I bare him then, / When virgin freedom left me unrestrain'd, / Doth to my heart begin to creep again, / My passion now is far from being feigned" (1.1.71–74). This quatrain does not produce a sonnet, and that is appropriate since the Renaissance sonnet is traditionally the voice of male desire, not female desire. Rather, the mutual love that originally brought Mariam and Herod together recalls the passionate reciprocity dramatized in Shakespeare's comedies or Donne's *Songs and Sonnets* where, pace Petrarch, "It cannot be / Love, till I love her, that loves me" ("Love's Deity").[13]

Mariam tries to express her conflicting, shifting feelings through conventional Petrarchan oxymorons, but they cannot adequately express what is particularly female about her experience: the feminine feeling of inadequacy prompted by her lack of rhetorical training and political experience; the conflict between the ideology of female chastity and obedience and the "unrestrained" feelings of "freedom" and "passion" that Herod's courtship aroused; the suffering caused by her marriage to an adoring but controlling, abusive, and murderously jealous tyrant; the knowledge that her private desires, like Queen Elizabeth's, will always exceed and contradict her "public voice." Mariam has adopted Petrarchan rhetoric to express her rejection of Herod, but she longs for the youthful, mutual passion she once enjoyed, the kind of love Cary confers upon the clandestine lovers Pheroras and Graphina.

Pheroras, having been forced to betroth himself to an infant cousin, is delighted that Herod's death will finally enable him to marry the woman he loves—a woman who also loves him. Though not an inspired lyricist,

Pheroras uses the language of Renaissance love poetry—"Graphina's brow's as white, her cheeks as red" (2.1.40)—to extol the value of freely chosen, mutual love and to claim that he deserves as much freedom to choose his wife as Herod himself exercised in marrying Mariam. Pheroras wants Graphina to join him in a lovers' dialogue like Romeo and Juliet, who express the inspirational thrill of falling in love by spontaneously composing a perfect Shakespearean sonnet together. Elizabethan poetry of courtship depends upon an answering response; similarly, Pheroras's first speech ends with a question and a plea that encourage Graphina to speak up: "Why speaks thou not, fair creature? Move thy tongue, / For silence is a sign of discontent: / It were to both our loves too great a wrong / If now this hour do find thee sadly bent" (2.1.41–44). Like Elizabethan poets/lovers who are his literary (but not historical) predecessors, Pheroras needs to know that his mistress not only returns his love for her but is now prepared to act on her love for him.

Like the impassioned but decorous lovers in Shakespeare's plays, Pheroras respects Graphina's desire to remain a virgin before marriage to protect herself from social disgrace, but like the lovers in Donne's poems of consummated, elevated, clandestine love, they are clearly drawn together by both body and mind. Indeed, when Salome later scorns Graphina's lack of "beauty," "birth," and "mind," Pheroras defends her physical and intellectual attractions with equal force:

> Mine eye found loveliness, mine ear found wit,
> To please the one, and to enchant the other:
> Grace on her eye, mirth on her tongue doth sit,
> In looks a child, in wisdom's house a mother. (3.1.15–18)

Graphina is usually dismissed as a conventional, subordinate woman, a one-dimensional character whose dutiful silence serves as a foil for Mariam's outspoken independence, but carrying on a clandestine courtship in defiance of Herod's will and secretly marrying a prince without official permission are acts of courageous boldness, not of subservience. Still, Pheroras's and Graphina's dialogic love language does not openly challenge the gender hierarchy as Donne's lovers do when they "forget the he and she" ("The Undertaking"), or when they "prince enough in one another be" ("The Anniversary"). It is also true that Graphina acknowledges her silence and professes her obedience: "Except your lowly handmaid's steadfast love / And fast obedience may your mind delight" (2.2.70–71). When one looks more closely at her words, however, it becomes clear that Graphina is expressing "obedience" not to Pheroras's male supremacy but to his previous request that she too should express her thoughts freely in speech. It is her speech, not her silence or obedience, that she hopes will "your mind delight."

With the sole exception of the butler, who appears briefly to attest to Mariam's innocent death, Graphina is the only character who neither utters a monologic sonnet nor contributes to a dialogic sonnet. As a nonaristocratic woman, Graphina has until now been excluded from the literary tradition that would enable her to speak and write in a manner worthy of her mind and wit. But like the young Cary, Graphina has begun a serious course of study to acquire the knowledge she needs to express herself as she would like in speech and also, presumably, in writing, because Graphina's name puns on the Greek word *graphesis* for writing as a silent form of speech. Hence Graphina is less a foil for Mariam than a surrogate for Cary.

The scene ends with three quatrains and a couplet spoken by Pheroras; yet Pheroras's love sonnet—one of only two self-contained sonnets in *Mariam*—clearly emerges from and depends upon the response Graphina has just given. Pheroras eschews the conventional rhetoric of Petrarchan poetry—"I cannot vaunt me in a glorious style/ Nor show my love in far-fetch'd eloquence (2.2.75–76)—in favor of a dialogic poetics of courtship that encourages Graphina to act on her desires, and cherishes her for her willingness to do so: "Come, fair Graphina, let us go in state, / This wish-endearèd time to celebrate" (2.2.85–86).

If Mariam speaks like Petrarch (and for a fleeting moment like Donne) while pretending to act like Laura, and if Pheroras's and Graphina's dialogic love language sounds more like the lovers in Shakespeare's comedies, Spenser's *Amoretti*, or Donne's *Songs and Sonnets* than like Petrarch, Mariam's and Graphina's foil and nemesis, Salome, speaks and acts more like a combination of Iago and Astrophil, whose "Desire still cries, give me some food," who envies Sidney's alter ego, the parrot Sir Phip, for nestling in Stella's bosom and nibbling on her lips, and who steals a bite himself when he finally gets permission to kiss. Perhaps because Stella/Penelope Rich, like Salome, is already married, Astrophil continues to be oppressed and is finally stymied by the conflict between virtue and desire. By contrast, Salome casts her scruples to the wind:

> But shame is gone, and honour wip'd away,
> And Impudency on my forehead sits:
> She bids me work my will without delay,
> And for my will I will employ my wits. (1.4.293–96)

Rather than the traditionally demure sonnet lady, Salome chooses the role of boldly unconventional poet/lover. Being a woman, she eschews the sonnet form in this scene because it does not provide a ready model for the expression of female desire (significantly, this is one of only three scenes that does not contain a sonnet). Salome will no more submit her desires to the structural constraints of the fourteen-line sonnet than she will submit her will to the ethical and legal codes that deny women the freedom given to men. Indeed, Salome expressly repudiates Judaic law, which gives men but not women the right to divorce: "I'll be the custom-breaker: and begin / To show my sex the way to freedom's door" (1.4.309–10). Presumably, that is what Astrophil wishes Stella would say; moreover, it is what Queen Elizabeth did even if she never acknowledged it. It is also what *A Letter sent by the Maydens of London, to the vertuous Matrones & Mistresses of the same, in the defense of their lawfull Libertie* (1567) urged all Elizabethan women to join them in doing, as the very title proclaims.[14]

Like Pheroras and Graphina, Salome and Sileus enjoy a fully mutual love: "He loves, I love; what then can be the cause / Keeps me [from] being the Arabian's wife?" (1.4.297–98). Like many Elizabethan poets/lovers (including Sidney, Donne, Gascoigne, Whythorne, and Daniel) who used enigmatic, allegorical poetry to negotiate clandestine marriage contracts or extramarital love affairs, Salome urges her lover, Sileus, to join her in rejecting the social, ethical, and legal codes that would prevent them from fulfilling their desires. Yet Salome's love language proves less liberating than one might expect. In claiming the right to speak and act like a man, Salome appropriates the domineering authority of the Petrarchan poet/lover—which, significantly, Pheroras does not do. Like Donne's lovers, whose "true plain hearts do in the faces rest" ("The Good Morrow"), Pheroras treats Graphina as another desiring subject who shares his liberation and returns his loving gaze: "This blessed hour . . . hath my wished liberty restor'd, / And made my subject self my own again. / Thy love, fair maid, upon mine eye doth sit" (2.1.6–9). By contrast, Salome represents herself as desiring subject ("When I on Constabarus first did gaze"), but reduces her lover to the mirror of her desires, rendering him the "object to mine eye" (1.4.275). Like the traditional Petrarchan poet, Salome assumes that the whole world shares her admiration for her beloved's physical beauty: "Whose looks and personage must [all eyes] amaze" (1.4.276). Sileus is perfectly willing to be objectified and controlled by Salome; he is pleased to be "deified, / by gaining thee" (1.4.327).

When Salome's husband, Constabarus, approaches, Salome brusquely says, "Begone Sileus," and he dutifully submits to her "command": "Farewell, but were it not for thy command, / In his despite Sileus here would stand" (1.4.373–74). Sileus refers to himself in the third person, for his subjectivity has been preempted by Salome's agency; by comparison,

Salome apostrophizes herself—"ill-fated Salome" (1.4.277)—because like Iago or Edmund, she aims to be the agent of her own fate.

Sileus's concluding couplet sums up the preceding conversation, producing a dialogic sonnet in which his lines follow and summarize hers. Here, as so often in courtship poetry, the poem's conclusion is determined both by the beloved's response and by external impediments that remain outside the poem and beyond the lovers' control. Instead of claiming the empowerment of a dialogic poetics, Sileus subordinates his will to Salome's desires. Salome is so power hungry that she perpetuates and inverts the inequality of Petrarchan sonnet tradition in order to claim male power and authority for herself. The epigrammatic brevity of Sileus's two-line response signals what his words imply: Salome speaks and acts for them both.

Appalled to find his wife conversing privately with another man, Constabarus complains that Salome's dishonorable behavior wounds not only her but also her husband and society as a whole:

> Oh Salome, how much you wrong your name,
> Your race, your country, and your husband most!
> A stranger's private conference is shame,
> I blush for you, that have your blushing lost. (1.6.375–78).

Sounding like Protestant clergymen who wrote sermons and conduct books denouncing adultery, or Puritan pundits who attacked love poetry for inciting women to immoral behavior, Constabarus utters what the chorus reiterates: to "be both chaste and chastely deem'd" (1.6.394), a woman should never have a private conversation with a man other than her husband.

Constabarus's moralizing ends with an epigrammatic maxim—"Our wisest prince [Soloman] did say, and true he said, / A virtuous woman crowns her husband's head" (1.6.395–96)—that echoes the metaphor Alexandra used earlier to reprimand Salome: "Come Mariam, let us go: it is no boot / To let the head contend against the foot" (1.3.259–60). In both cases the classic political trope appears in a sonnet-forming couplet, implicitly connecting Petrarchan ideology with patriarchal polity that empowers men and subordinates women. Constabarus, the defender of conservative moral and political values, reclaims the trope to its conventional purpose, citing the authority of a male prince and biblical patriarch in order to reassert that the husband is the rightful head of the household, as the male ruler is the rightful head of the state. But Salome is no more willing to be chastened, silenced, or subordinated by Constabarus than she was by Mariam and Alexandra: "Thy love and admonitions I defy. / Thou shalt no hour longer call me wife" (1.6.415–16). Appalled, Constabarus responds that her defiance of traditional gender roles will turn the whole world upside down: "Are Hebrew women now transformed to men? / Why do you not as well our battles fight, / And wear our armour? Suffer this, and then / Let all the world be topsy-turved quite" (1.6.421–24).

On the surface, Constabarus is a "good" character, the upholder of morality and social order. He cherishes Mariam's virtue and wishes to protect her from Salome. He loves Salome despite her infidelity, and tries to protect her from herself: "My words were all intended for thy good, / To raise thine honour and to stop disgrace" (1.6.411–12). Yet Constabarus's sermonizing begins to look considerably less high-minded and more suspiciously self-serving when we recall, first, that his goal is to get Salome (with her access to networks of power) back, subdued to his will and his gain; and, second, that his own love for Salome began as an adulterous liaison (Salome was then married to Josephus). When Constabarus's speech and the scene end with another sonnet extolling the "sweet-fac'd," "innocent," "purest" Mariam, it becomes increasingly clear that Constabarus admires and idealizes Mariam as the ideal of female virtue precisely because he sees her as powerless.

Significantly, Constabarus is the character who forms the strongest male bonds in the play. When he next appears onstage, he is with Babas's sons, whose lives he has saved against Herod's command. Constabarus's friendship with Babas's sons seems to be another sign of his goodness—and an even deeper bond than his marriage—although we soon learn that he protected their lives in the hopes of enhancing his own political power. In act 2 scene 2 Constabarus tries to convince Babas's sons to make their survival known. When they object, arguing that that it would be wiser and safer to wait for a confirmation of Herod's death, Constabarus bullies them into acquiescing by attacking their honor and bravery. The clash of wills, framed by two dialogic sonnets and two separate exchanges of couplets, dramatizes the ways in which the circulation of poems in manuscript among a male coterie comprises a bid for power and patronage.[15]

When Constabarus appears on stage for a third and final time, he is again with Babas's sons, en route to their common execution. Having stopped debating with him, they now serve as his male support group. After giving one final, fleeting, nostalgic tribute to Mariam's virtue, Constabarus utters a violent diatribe against all women:

> You tigers, lionesses, hungry bears,
> Tear-massacring hyenas: nay, far worse, . . .
> You are the wreck of order, breach of laws.
> [Your] best are foolish, froward, wanton, vain,
> Your worst adulterous, murderous, cunning, proud.
> (4.6.316–17, 4.6.331–33)

Constabarus's antifeminist rhetoric recalls those moments in Renaissance sonnet sequences and male lovers' complaints when jealousy, sexual frustration, or rejection reduce even the most witty and endearing poets/lovers to hostility and vituperation.[16]

Constabarus's language is as conventional as it is ludicrous, for he not only contradicts his own praise of Mariam, but he readily sacrifices the entire human race to salve his personal feelings of betrayal: "'Twere better that the human race should fail, / Than be by such a mischief multiplied" (4.6.339–40). Constabarus, who seemed at the beginning of the play to be a good man wronged by an evil, scheming wife, exits the play as a mockery of masculinity whose conventional antifeminist rhetoric is so extreme that it calls into question the code of ethics upon which his conservative gender ideology (and conventional Renaissance poetry) rests.

If the first two acts present a world ruled and dominated by women, the remaining three acts present a world reeling from Herod's return and the reinstitution of tyrannical male power. As the play moves toward its tragic denouement, sonnets and sonnet language become both more pervasive and more painful; rather than expressing harmony and resolution, the couplets, which come one after another, fast and furious, are like volleys in a battle.

When Herod first appears on stage, he expresses his impatience to see Mariam in the language of Renaissance love poetry:

> Thou day's dark taper. Mariam will appear,
> And where she shines, we need not thy dim light,
> Oh, haste thy steps, rare creature, speed thy pace. (4.1.8–10)

Herod's anticipatory thoughts focus almost exclusively on Mariam's physical appearance. The extended, conventional metaphors of sun and light, followed by lengthy comparisons to Roman beauties, culminate in an apostrophe to Herod's own eyes that literally turns Mariam into the "object" or reflection of male desire:

> Be patient but a little while, mine eyes.
> Within your compass'd limits be contain'd:
> That object straight shall your desires suffice. (4.1.33–35)

In her absence Herod imagines Mariam as a distant, idealized Petrarchan lady, but when she actually appears he stops talking *about* her in the language of Petrarchan poetry and begins talking *to* her in the dialogic language of Elizabethan love poetry. Herod's unexpected tenderness and remarkable generosity, his genuine attentiveness to Mariam's feelings, his attempt to elicit smiles and loving words, all recall the happiest moments in *Astrophil and Stella, Amoretti*, or *Songs and Sonnets*. When Herod willingly offers Mariam the active and empowering role that Sidney, Spenser, and Donne grant their private female lyric audience, his dialogic love poetry recalls and confirms the mutual, dialogic love that Mariam herself recalls and yearns for in the play's opening speech. But now Mariam remains glum and unresponsive. Herod, still seeking the kind of love that Shakespeare depicts between Antony and Cleopatra, attempts to cheer her up with offers of wealth and kingdoms:

> What is't that is the cause thy heart to touch?
> Oh speak, that I thy sorrow may prevent.
> Art thou not Jewry's queen, and Herod's too?
> Be my commandress, be my sovereign guide:
> To be by thee directed I will woo,
> For in thy pleasure lies my highest pride. (4.3.95–100)

But Mariam does not respond as Herod thought and wishes she would. She utters one eight-line speech telling Herod she no longer loves him; otherwise she speaks in fractions of lines, or more often in epigrammatic couplets that turn Herod's seemingly endless quatrains into sonnets that are Petrarchan in substance if not in form. Indeed, the Shakespearean sonnet form of quatrains with alternating rhymes capped by a couplet makes the Petrarchan posture seem antiquated and anything but inevitable; meanwhile, the plot strengthens the feeling that Petrarchism is far from desirable.

Having vowed to deny Herod his marital due, Mariam turns herself into a conventional Petrarchan lady, cold but virtuous, and thus condemns Herod to play the role of the unrequited Petrarchan lover. Upset by Mariam's rejection and further discombobulated by the messenger Salome sends with a poison supposedly concocted by Mariam to kill him, Herod leaps to the conclusion that Mariam must be having a clandestine love affair with Sohemus. Mariam can't believe what is happening, and asks, "Is this a dream?" (4.4.184), but Herod doesn't seem to hear her because he has already made up his mind. We know that Sohemus's love for Mariam is a chaste, adoring love, but we also know Mariam has not returned his love. Instead of asking *whether* she loves Sohemus, Herod asks, "Why didst thou love Sohemus?" (4.4.193). She obligingly finishes his pentameter line, and even begins a new quatrain, but her response is so terse and begrudging—"They can tell / That say I lov'd him, Mariam says no" (4.4193–94)—that it makes absolutely no impression on Herod.

At this point, Mariam simply stops talking to Herod, assuming that her innocence and beauty will speak for themselves. However, Herod's monologue goes on and on, fruitlessly bemoaning her betrayal. Despite her presence before him, Herod appears to be composing sonnets for himself or posterity; certainly he is no longer speaking to Mariam the way an Elizabethan poet/lover addresses a private female lyric audience. When he proceeds to punish Mariam's disobedience and alleged dishonor with death, she discovers to her dismay that innocence is no protection against Herod's jealousy and Salome's deceit.

Like Petrarch's love for Laura, Herod's devotion to Mariam is intensified and magnified by her death. Since she can no longer repudiate or criticize him, he can idealize and immortalize her to his heart's content. Mimicking the conventional Petrarchan lover, he praises her eyes, her hair, her skin, but his Petrarchizing seems bitterly ironic—the death knoll for a tradition that objectifies and disembodies the woman it admires and desires from an unattainable distance.

Cary's drama offers a brilliant, scathing exposé of one character and one sonnet posture after another. Constabarus's violent, excessive, antifeminist attack on womankind, uttered to his male coterie, Babas's sons, echoes Petrarchan love complaints gone awry. Herod's equally conventional Petrarchan praise for Mariam, who has quite literally been killed by his self-absorbed, tyrannical love for her, proves as ill advised as it is familiar. Sohemus's attempt to warn Mariam against the dangers of Herod's return culminates in a perfect sonnet soliloquy, idealizing her chaste virtue and eternizing his undying, unrequited love. He predicts that she will undo herself by speaking too freely, but he is mistaken. Mariam says almost nothing; it is her silence rather than her speech that leads Herod to think she is guilty. Salome's mockery of Herod's poeticizing, which recalls Rosalind's deflations of Orlando's arboreal verse or Viola's critique of Orsino's "poetical" wooing, is witty and right on the mark, but it is also reprehensible.[17]

What makes the play at once maddeningly difficult to encapsulate and endlessly intriguing to contemplate is that even the most authoritative declarations and compelling judgments are likely to be undermined or overturned by the next line or a subsequent speech or scene, exposing the characters' limited self-awareness or self-interested manipulations, making it difficult to find any place to rest. The play is rooted in historical events that are only explained after we are completely confused by what we have witnessed because the experience of bafflement, misprision, and constant self-correction is itself central to the play's meaning and purpose. As soon as we think we know what to think, we discover that we were mistaken. Herod was not dead after all. In act 1, the chorus seemed to be criticizing Salome's "wavering mind" (1.6.498), but it was actually criticizing Mariam's "expectation of variety." Herod's anger was not provoked by

Mariam's unbridled speech, as Sohemus predicted it would be, but by her terse refusal to defend herself.[18] Constabarus claims that Babas's first son is a coward "to doubt undoubted truth" (3.3.156), but ensuing events show that one should always be prepared to question "undoubted truth." The final ironies occur at the very moment when our sympathy for Mariam reaches its apex: Mariam is on her way to her patently unjustified execution when she is met and attacked by Herod's first wife, Doris, who complains quite rightly that her life and her son's life were ruined by Mariam's marriage to Herod. Yet even if Mariam is not as pure and innocent as a Petrarchan sonnet lady, that still does not mean that Doris should curse her or that Herod should execute her.

The chorus, which appears at the end of each act, speaks for society at large, subjecting individual characters to the prevailing ideology, including us in its moral lessons: "For if you like your state as now it is, / Why should an alteration bring relief?" (1.6.512–13).[19] In act 3, in what seems to be the ideological center of the play, the chorus declares that "the wife" must reject "all lawful liberties"—both "public speech" and private conversation with any man other than her husband—"for honor's sake." Since it is only in act 3 that the chorus does not use the first-person plural, and since it has no scruples about expressing its views in public, we can infer that it is made up of men who feel that they and their male peers have the right to control their wives, body and mind: "When to their husbands they themselves do bind / Do they not wholly give themselves away?" (3.3.233–34). Blinding itself by being too sure of its judgments, the chorus utters a series of moral prescriptions and judgments in the form of six Shakespearean sestets. While one sestet can be compelling; the effect of six heavily rhymed sestets, each capped by a resounding couplet, following one after another in unrelieved succession, feels heavy-handed and oppressive. The form works in tension with the content, making us yearn to escape from the thudding battery of self-righteous certitude.

If the play has a moral center, it is not the overwrought patriarchal ideology of act 3 but the hermeneutical skepticism of act 2 where the chorus piques us to question the very judgments it utters so authoritatively. Since "the greatest part of us, prejudicate" (2.4.419), the chorus explains, we can only hear what we want to hear: "It [our prejudgment] will confound the meaning, change the words, / For it our sense of hearing much deceives" (2.4.407–8).[20] Here, Cary is brilliantly prescient, forseeing the modern view that language has no single, stable meaning, being inflected not only by the expectations and desires of the speaker but also by the expectations and desires of the listener.

The stage directions include no entrances or exits for the chorus, so the chorus presumably remained on stage throughout. Yet the chorus is as likely as we are to misinterpret what we have just watched or to falsely foretell what we are about to observe. It is only in act 5, after the day's misprisions have come to light, that the chorus acknowledges (at least implicitly) that it too has been prevented by its own prejudgments from hearing or comprehending what the play represents. Now, the very same chorus that castigated Mariam in act 3 for seeking variety returns to marvel that "so many changes are therein contained" (5.1.291), and to remind us "how many" (and the chorus increases the number substantially) "were deceived" (5.1.261) by a single day's events.

At the beginning of the play, Mariam attributed her misjudgment about Julius Caesar to her feminine weakness, but she was wrong. Mistaking turns out to be no more "common" for Mariam and her sex than for Herod, Constabarus, Sohemus, the male chorus, and their sex. Characters, chorus, audience—we have all made one mistake after another: "It [the day's events] will from [us] all certainty bereave / Since twice six hours so many can deceive" (5.1.263–64). The lesson the play leaves us with is that the greatest "wisdom" is the knowledge that "all certainty," all "undoubted truth," ought to be suspect.

Finally, what does Cary's "school of wisdom" have to teach us about this "admirably strange variety" (5.1.292) and its connections to Renaissance sonnet tradition? That we must beware definitive truths, whether the prescriptive truisms uttered by the chorus or the resounding closures reached by sonnets and couplets. Mariam learns that her beauty and virtue could not protect her from Herod's jealousy and Salome's deceit. Herod learns that his loving talk could no more force Mariam to return his love than his regal commands could restore her to life. So too Cary's audience learns that every character in this Senecan closet drama, and every poet/lover in every Renaissance sonnet sequence, expresses only one limited, and thus fallible, point of view; Constabarus has his own reasons for praising his beloved's virtue, beauty, honor, and wit, or for condemning all women as "foolish, froward, wanton, vain." Unless the poet/lover learns to engage in genuine dialogue, his words and actions are in danger of becoming as self-serving and mistaken as Herod's, Salome's, or Constabarus's.

Elizabethan poetry of courtship empowered the women to whom the poems were addressed: not only did the private female lyric audience have the power to accept or reject the poet/lover's proposals, but she also held a privileged position: to critique the poem or to counter the poet's point of view. By writing quatrains with an alternating English rhyme scheme rather than an interlocking Petrarchan rhyme scheme and by interspersing so many sonnet-forming couplets, Cary signals her sympathy with the Elizabethan critique of Petrarchan poetry and ideology. Cary's sonnets provide a dramatic analogue for the private lyric dialogue between

Elizabethan poets/lovers and their mistresses that takes place both inside and beside the sonnet, both in the spaces between the lines and in the spaces between the poems, at the center and on the margins of English literary tradition.

The sonnets scattered throughout *Mariam* comprise a compendium of attitudes toward love, marriage, and women; together, they provide an ironic commentary on Renaissance literary conventions and a searing critique of early modern social conventions. By embedding sonnets, with their conventional tropes and postures, within a narrative frame that both elucidates and questions the attitudes and beliefs that the characters' sonnets enunciate and the chorus's sestets prescribe, Cary invites her audience to question conventional attitudes toward femininity, marriage, and political power, and extends the ways in which the English female lyric audience influenced, critiqued, and helped redefine the lyric genre, making it more dialogic, more complex, and more contestational, giving a remarkably positive twist to Constabarus's remark, "Let all the world be topsy-turvèd quite" (1.6.424).

NOTES

I am grateful to Jesse Swan for encouraging me to speak about Mariam and the poetics of courtship at the 2002 Renaissance Society of America Conference in Tempe, Arizona. This chapter grew out of that talk.

1. Quoted from *The Tragedy of Mariam, The Fair Queen of Jewry with The Lady Falkland: Her Life: By One of Her Daughters,* ed. Barry Weller and Margaret W. Ferguson (Berkeley: U of California P, 1994), 189, 268.
2. *Mariam* is most likely modeled on the Senecan closet dramas of Mary Sidney and Samuel Daniel.
3. This sonnet, dedicated to her sister-in-law, survives in only two of the twenty-two extant copies of the play.
4. For an invaluable study of the English response to Petrarchan poetry, see Heather Dubrow, *Echoes of Desire: Petrarchism and its Counterdiscourses* (Ithaca, NY: Cornell UP, 1995).
5. For a more complete articulation of my argument, see *Elizabethan Women and the Poetry of Courtship*. I am greatly indebted to Nancy A. Gutierrez's groundbreaking essay, "Valuing *Mariam*: Genre Study and Feminist Analysis," *Tulsa Studies in Women's Literature* 10 (1991): 233–250. Gutierrez observes that "*Mariam*, the play, is the sonnet mistress's response to her poet lover; closet drama answers Petrarchan sonnet; female writer redefines a male-engendered literary form" (241). Gutierrez's essay does not consider, however, that *Mariam* is part of a much larger Elizabethan critique of Petrarchan literary tradition.
6. Tina Krontiris, *Oppositional Voices: Women as Writers and Translators of Literature in the English Renaissance* (London: Routledge, 1992), suggests that

Mariam's opening lines "could very well serve as Cary's own apology for assuming the 'publike voyce' of a dramatist" (90).
7. Quoted from *Elizabeth I: Collected Works,* ed. Leah S. Marcus, Janel Mueller, and Mary Beth Rose (Chicago: U of Chicago P, 2000), 98. When Elizabeth was first crowned queen, Parliament debated whether or not to allow her to use the title her father had claimed for himself, supreme *head* of church and state, and decided upon the less symbolically loaded term, *governor.* In 1566, she simply took it upon herself to reclaim the title.
8. Weller and Ferguson explore links between the historical situation of Mariam and Henry VIII's divorce and marriage to Anne Boleyn (30–35) but do not consider the more immediate context of Elizabeth's death and James's succession.
9. In the introduction to *Three Tragedies by Renaissance Women* (New York: Penguin, 1998), Diane Purkiss observes that Cary, Lumley, and Pembroke "saw themselves as close to the center of power and able to influence it" by writing "historical tragedies with clear political overtones" (xx, xviii). Gutierrez points out that "a number of men used this genre as a vehicle for strategic political comment, even protest" (238). Barbara Kiefer Lewalski also stresses the political function of Senecan closet dramas in *Writing Women in Jacobean England* (Cambridge: Harvard UP, 1993), 179–201.
10. Krontiris notes that although there were several contemporary plays about Herod and Mariam, Cary's is "the only one . . . which dramatizes the problem from Mariam's rather than Herod's point of view" (82).
11. There are a number of excellent accounts of Cary's life and work, including: Heather Wolfe, ed., *Elizabeth Cary, Lady Falkland: Life and Letters* (Cambridge and Tempe, AZ: RTM Publications and Arizona Center for Medieval and Renaissance Studies, 2001); Weller and Ferguson's introduction, 3–17; Elaine Beilin, "Elizabeth Cary and *The Tragedie of Mariam,*" *Papers on Language and Literature* 16 (1980): 45–64; and Lewalski.
12. Mariam sounds very much like the inexperienced young Elizabeth Tudor, answering the Commons petition in 1563: "The weight and greatness of this matter might cause in me, being a woman wanting both wit and memory, some fear to speak and bashfulness besides, a thing appropriate to my sex. But yet, the princely seat and kingly throne wherein God (though unworthy) hath constituted me, maketh these two causes to seem little in mine eyes, though grievous perhaps to your ears" (*Collected Works,* 260). For a study of Elizabeth's rhetoric, see Ilona Bell, "Elizabeth I—A woman, and (if that be not enough) an vnmarried Virgin," *Political Rhetoric, Power, and Renaissance Women,* ed. Carole Levin and Patricia Sullivan (Albany: SUNY Press, 1995).
13. *John Donne: Selected Poems,* ed. Ilona Bell (London: Penguin, 2006).
14. See my essay, "*A Letter sent by the Maydens of London*—In Defense of their Lawful Liberty," in *Women, Writing, and the Reproduction of Culture in Tudor and Stuart Britain,* ed. Mary Burke, Jane Donawerth, Linda Dove, and Karen Nelson (Syracuse: Syracuse UP, 2000), 177–192.
15. On the importance of manuscript circulation and the male coterie, see Arthur F. Marotti, *John Donne, Coterie Poet* (Madison: U of Wisconsin P,

1986); Wendy Wall, *The Imprint of Gender: Authorship and Publication in the English Renaissance* (Ithaca: Cornell UP, 1993); and Marcy North, *The Anonymous Renaissance: Cultures of Discretion in Tudor-Stuart England* (Chicago: U of Chicago P, 2003).

16. See, for example, Sidney, *Astrophil and Stella*, Fifth Song; Spenser, *Amoretti*, Sonnet 47; Samuel Daniel, Sonnet 10, printed in the pirated text of his unnamed sonnet sequence, reprinted in *Elizabethan Sonnets*, ed. Sidney Lee, vol. 1 (Westminster: Archibald Constable, 1904), but omitted from the authorized first edition read today.

17. In "Elizabeth Cary, Lady Falkland," *Teaching Tudor and Stuart Women Writers*, ed. Susanne Woods and Margaret P. Hannay (New York: MLA, 2000), 164–173, Weller describes Salome's remarks as "a satire on Petrarchan rhetoric and the lethal contradictions of male infatuation" (168).

18. Although I agree with Catherine Belsey, *The Subject of Tragedy: Identity and Difference in Renaissance Drama* (London: Methuen, 1985), that Mariam is presented as "a unified, autonomous subject," I disagree that Mariam gets herself killed because she "speaks her mind," or that "the play as a whole seems to oscillate between endorsement and disapproval of Mariam's defiance" (171–175). Lewalski points out what Belsey fails to consider: the characters and the chorus who criticize Mariam are themselves undercut by the play as a whole (198).

19. Some critics argue that the chorus expresses Cary's own ambivalence about Mariam's rebelliousness; others are more skeptical of the chorus's trustworthiness. Weller and Ferguson conclude: "The disparity between the moral adages of the Chorus and the experience of the heroine (and perhaps, by extension, the bad fit between conventional wisdom and the experience of all women) seems the very heart of Cary's dramatic vision" (35–38). Similarly, Sandra K. Fischer, "Elizabeth Cary and Tyranny," *Silent But for the Word: Tudor Women as Patrons, Translators and Writers of Religious Works*, ed. Margaret Hannay (Kent, OH: Kent State UP, 1985), describes the chorus as "traditional, almost reactionary in its observations, and certainly not to be heard as the voice of the playwright" (236).

20. It is by now a commonplace to note that the third-act chorus proscribes female authorship, but most critics overlook the larger hermeneutical significance of the second chorus.

CHAPTER 2

MARIAM AND EARLY MODERN DISCOURSES OF
MARTYRDOM

Erin E. Kelly

To note that Mariam at the end of Elizabeth Cary's play is a martyr figure has become a critical commonplace. Following Elaine Beilin's lead, many describe the queen as "an early Christian martyr." Both Margaret Ferguson and Sandra Fischer refer to the queen as Christlike, and Fran Dolan compares Mariam's death to the executions and martyrdoms of Protestant women.[1] However, no one has discussed how Cary's depiction of Mariam fits into the complex history of martyrology, especially in relation to the uses of this genre throughout the early modern period. Attention to these important contexts and intertexts, including possible sources for *The Tragedy of Mariam* not previously analyzed in detail, clarifies the argumentative force of this play. Cary seems aware of other texts that present Mariam as a martyr, particularly those that locate her death within a Christian exegetical tradition as a necessary condition for the coming of Christ. While she is not unique in relying upon this way of reading world history to construct Mariam as a martyr, Cary is innovative among English writers in making the queen such an outspoken individual. This way of representing Mariam, I believe, exposes early modern anxieties about female martyrs evidenced by sixteenth- and seventeenth-century texts. Through her problematic title character, Cary critiques early modern attempts to obscure the rebellious qualities of religious martyrs.

Cary's play figures Mariam's death as a martyrdom by including many of the generic conventions one finds in martyrologies. A messenger who witnesses Mariam's final moments calls the queen "guiltless" (5.1.12), but a martyr is more than an innocent victim.[2] Martyrs were often described going to their executions peacefully, stoically, or even joyfully, thus signifying their special relationship to God; it is in keeping with this tradition that the Nuntio admires how "mildly did her face this fortune bear" (5.1.27). Because religious martyrdom was seen as clearly indicating one's spiritual salvation, it was common for martyrs to offer a prayer of thanks, and the Nuntio reports "after some prayer had said / She [Mariam] did as if to die she were content, / And thus to Heav'n her heav'nly soul is fled" (5.1.84–86). Accepting cruel punishment humbly and holily, Mariam, like the early Christian and Reformation martyrs Brad Gregory analyzes, has the primary characteristic of a martyr, a "willingness to die."[3]

Since the passion of Jesus is the model for all Christian martyrdom— what Donald Kelley calls "*imitatio Christi* with a vengeance"[4]—it is significant that the Nuntio describes Mariam's death as echoing key events in Christ's passion. Like Jesus, Mariam is forced to walk among "a curious gazing troop" (5.1.21) on the way to execution. The rejection of Mariam by her own mother references both Roman soldiers' mocking and Peter's denial of Jesus. Just as Christ's betrayer, Judas, hangs himself, the butler who falsely accuses Mariam of attempting to poison the king is found after the queen's death "upon a tree / A man that to his neck a cord did tie" (5.1.104–05). Mariam's final words suggest Christ's "Father, forgive them; for they know not what they do" (Luke 23:34) as she laments "By three days hence, if wishes could revive, / I know himself would make me oft alive" (5.1.77–78), expressing pity for the king who ordered her execution without understanding the consequences of his actions. Furthermore, this statement presages Christ's resurrection. Although Herod may only long for Mariam's return from the grave after three days, God will actually revive Jesus three days after the crucifixion.

However, the fact that Mariam's execution predates the life of Christ should raise questions about whether she should be called a *Christian* martyr. Early modern religious writers regularly declare that the cause, not the death, makes a martyr; in the eyes of such authorities, a martyr had to die defending the true Christian faith.[5] Mariam is not technically a Christian martyr, for she is not a Christian. However, Mariam was seen as a religious martyr within a Christian tradition of interpreting biblical history. As a member of the family of the Maccabees, Mariam was linked to the mother and sons described in 2 Maccabees 7 who willingly died under torture rather than violate the precepts of the Jewish faith by eating pork and sacrificing to idols. These figures were important models of martyrdom for medieval and early modern religious writers and thus had a significant effect on Christians dying to defend their beliefs.[6] Mariam, as a Maccabee, would likely have been seen as a prefiguration of Christian martyrdom by early modern readers. By presenting Mariam as a martyr,

Cary is not inventing a new persona for this character but rather working within a long tradition of Christian exegesis.

Additionally, by emphasizing that Mariam can be considered the last link to the royal bloodline of the Maccabees, and the final obstacle to Herod's total usurpation of the crown, the play depicts Mariam's death as the link in a historical chain of events leading from the creation of the world to the birth of Christ. A number of early modern texts concerned with Christian historiography identify the transition from the Maccabean reign over the Jewish people to Herod's rule as the period when Jews ceased to be God's chosen people and the way was cleared for the Christ's coming. The key prophecy related to the rise of Herod is Jacob's deathbed statement that "The scepter shall not depart from Judah nor a law-giver from betweene his feet, until Shilo come" (Genesis 49:10), which medieval and early modern theologians took as a prediction of the coming of Christ (Shiloh).[7] Showing that the throne passed from the direct descendants of Judah (Jacob's son and the patriarch of the Maccabees) to someone wrongly called the king of the Jews (Herod) was an important element in narratives that present the birth of Jesus as fulfilling scriptural prophecies.

The most prominent early modern texts that offer such an analysis are translations of the Bible into English. In the Bishop's Bible, the translators precede the books of the Maccabees with "A necessary Table for the Knowledge of the state of Juda, from the beginning of the Monarchie of the Greeks ... until the death and passion of Jesus Christ."[8] The account of how Mariam's family is overthrown appears toward the end of this table:

> Pompey with the armie of the Romanes having taken all Syria, led Aristobolus captive, leaving Hircanus in the priesthood, and Antipater Herodes father governed in Jurie. And the 51 yeere after Herode was proclaimed king, *and the scepter taken from* Juda, Christ our saviour came.
>
> (435ʳ; emphasis mine)

The Bishop's Bible continues this line of thought by prefacing the New Testament with a genealogy of Christ tracking his lineage to David through both Mary and Joseph. The claim to succession falls to Jesus, a descendant of David through Nathan, since "the posteritie failed" of those who had been the rightful kings of the Jews, including the line of the Maccabees (461ᵛ).

Similar concerns about the lineage of Christ are reflected in other bibles. The first printing of the King James Bible begins with thirty-four pages showing "The Genealogies of Holy Scriptures," an elaborate chart that connects Adam and Eve through Abraham, Judah, and David to Mary and Joseph and thus to Jesus. In two places within this family tree, the prophecy of Judah is presented (1–34, esp. 10, 17). Catholic translators offered the same information in a different form. The Douai translation of the Old Testament follows 2 Maccabees with a section entitled "The Continuance of the Church, and Religion in the Sixth Age: from the captivitie in Babylon to the coming of our Saviour." A discussion of Herod and "the Romane Monarchie" comments that he was "the first strange king of the Jews" both because he was appointed king by the Romans and because of his lineage (98–1004). The commentator notes, "In him was fulfilled the prophecie of the Patriarch Jacob, Gen. 49. giving it for a signe that Christ our Redeemer should presently come into this world saying: *The scepter shall not be taken away from Judas. . .til he do come that is to be sent*" (1003). The place of Herod within Christian historiography was well known to early modern readers of religious works, so a text depicting the demise of Mariam's family would inevitably have been read in this context.

Cary's play encourages such a reading by referring to Jewish history related to Mariam's royal lineage.[9] The argument of the play introduces the title character in this context, indicating "*Mariam* had a Brother called *Aristobolus,* and next him and *Hircanus* his Ground-father, *Herod* in his Wives right had the best title." Alexandra makes explicit her family's connection to Judah's prophecy, stating that Herod, an Edomite (a descendant of Esau), has no right to rule and thus his time on the throne "disgrac'd / That seat that hath by Judah's race been [fam'd]" (1.2.89–90). Mariam's harsh words to Salome reiterate this understanding of her ancestral claim, insisting that before she married, "My birth thy baser birth so farre exceld, / I had to both of you [Herod and Salome] the Princesse bene" (1.3.233–34).

Two of the moments in the play most frequently discussed by critics are related to this understanding of Mariam and her kin as rightful monarchs of the Jewish nation. With the play's opening "How oft have I with publike voyce runne on" (1.1.1), Cary not only raises issues about women's public speech but also introduces her title character in the midst of comparing herself to Julius Caesar.[10] Mariam explains that although she once thought the Roman ruler hypocritical for mourning his rival Pompey, she now understands his actions as a genuine mixture of "griefe and joy" (1.1.10) since weeping over Herod seems odd in light of her hopes for her husband's death. Mariam explains Caesar's confusion, saying "You wept indeed, when on his worth you thought, / But joyd that slaughter did your Foe destroy" (1.1.11–12), and thus links her own mixed feelings to a recognition that the "foe" of her family is dead, leaving her unchallenged as rightful queen of the Jews. Similarly, Mariam's rejection of Herod after he returns from Rome is more than an example of defiant female speech. Even as she refuses to be appeased for his slaying of her male relatives, Mariam insists her authority to rule does not come from Herod; she rejects his offer of treasure with the statement "I neither have of power nor riches want, / I have enough nor do I wish for more" (4.3.109–10). These lines do not show the queen demurring that she neither has nor wants power but rather asserting that she does not need what Herod offers because all the riches he can present are already hers by birthright.

For early modern readers of *Mariam,* the title character would not simply *seem* like a martyr at the end of the play. Within a traditional Christian worldview, the story of Mariam would always be the story of a martyr. Her death would not merely appear Christlike but register as a necessary sacrifice that made the coming of Christ possible.[11] Because this understanding of how Herod and Mariam fit into Christian history was ubiquitous, it is not surprising that other early modern authors represent the queen as a martyr. What is curious, though, is that Cary's Mariam is such a troubling and troublesome figure. Other texts of the period show Mariam as a martyr who is a passive victim, while Cary repeatedly depicts her title character as outspoken, defiant, and, at times, conflicted. Comparison of this play to her sources and to other early modern versions of the Mariam story make it clear that Cary is interrogating the early modern discourse of martyrdom in ways that others are not.

Cary makes her Mariam seem more rebellious than does the text recognized as her source, Thomas Lodge's *The famous and memorable workes of Josephus.*[12] Lodge's translation does point out the queen's flaws in terms echoed within Cary's play, indicating "she had a certaine womanly imperfection and natural frowardnesse, which was the cause that she presumed too much upon the intire affection wherewith her husband was intangled; so that without regard of his person, who had power and authoritie over others, she entertained him oftentimes very outrageously" (279).[13] Clearly, this Mariam does not meet traditional expectations for female decorum since she is not silent and obedient.[14] Even so, Lodge's text largely excuses such behavior by following its description of the queen's death with the explanation, "She digested also the losse of her friends verie hardly, according as in open termes she made it known unto the king" (281). Justified by familial affection, the Mariam of this narrative seems to have made a strategic rather than moral error by criticizing her husband for murdering her relatives.

Through the structure of her play, Cary emphasizes Mariam's less attractive qualities. While the Mariam in Lodge's text is locked up with her mother in Herod's castle "as it were in a prison" (277) while the king is away, Cary's Mariam, at the start of the play, seems free to roam, act, and lament. Lodge's queen has some reason to hate Herod since she "supposed that her husband did but dissemble his love" out of desire for wealth and power (277), but Cary's queen only worries that she did not properly appreciate "the tender love that he to Mariam bare" (1.1.32). While Lodge's text indicates that Mariam obeys Herod's command and "came into him; yet would she not lie with him" (279), Cary's Mariam seems to make a more conscious choice to disobey, swearing, "I will not to his love be reconcil'd, / With solemn vows I have forsworn his bed" (3.3.133–34). The chorus criticizes Mariam specifically for sharing these words with Sohemus—even though this wise counselor considers her a "poor guiltless queen!" (3.3.181). Mariam is at fault, according to the chorus, because she fails to keep even her thoughts under the control of her husband, since "in a wife it is no worse to find, / A common body than a common mind" (3.3.243–44). While it might seem impossible that Mariam could follow the chorus's admonitions to govern her thoughts and speak only to her husband, Cary's most wholly original addition to the story of Mariam and Herod, the character Graphina, seems to meet all the expectations for an ideal woman even though she is of much lower social standing than the fair queen.[15]

Even as Cary's play makes Mariam more morally problematic than does Lodge's translation, the play offers a very different vision of the queen than that presented in more widely available versions of the story. Lodge's book is a beautifully produced folio volume of more than 800 pages. As editors of *Mariam* have argued, the playwright might have used a manuscript of the work before its first printing in 1602.[16] Whether she looked at the manuscript or a printed edition, she would have been consulting a large and relatively uncommon volume. Although it was reprinted at least five times in the seventeenth century, the size and presumed cost of the book would have made it less well known than Peter Morwen's *Compendious and most marveilous history of the latter tymes of the Jewes commune weale,* which was printed ten times between 1558 and 1615, seven times before 1600. Its quarto format and relative brevity would have made it a much more accessible text than Lodge's. While it has been known since the eighteenth century that Morwen's text is a translation of a medieval history written by Ben Gorion, it is important to note that Morwen (and his readers) believed that he was translating Josephus. Since Gorion's text was a reworking of Josephus's *Wars of the Jews,* there is some overlap between the texts produced by Morwen and, in part, by Lodge.[17]

In addition to the likelihood that a young Cary would have had access to such an often-printed text, there are hints in *Mariam* that Morwen's work is a source.[18] Following the history of "The state of the common wealth of Jury" (A1ʳ) that runs for several hundred pages is a short treatise entitled "The ten captivities of the Jewes" (Nn2ᵛ). The ninth captivity includes an alternate account of the usurpation of the Jewish throne: "Then raygned one *Herode* the serva[n]t of *Hasmonai* [or Maccabees] who killed his masters, and their whole familye, save one mayde whom he loved" (Nn5ᵛ–Nn6ʳ). While the maid in question is never named, her gruesome fate seems woven into key moments of Cary's play. Despairing that "There is no bodye lefte alive of my fathers house but I alone" (Nn6ʳ), Herod's beloved leaps to her death from the top of his house. The unnamed tragic maid is such an object of Herod's "love" that he stores her corpse "in honeye, and preserved her for the space of seven yeare. There were that sayd he hadd carnall copulation with her after shee was deade" (Nn6ʳ). Herod's obsession with Mariam's body in Cary's play has long been of interest to critics who note that his soliloquy references both Petrarchan tropes and the stage tradition of ranting Herods.[19] Such influences seem to be at work in this speech, but so do necrophilic rumors of Herod's treatment of the last fair maid of the Hasmonean family, especially when Herod questions, "Is't, possible my Mariam should be dead? / Is there no trick to make her breathe again? . . . 'tis sure such things are done / By an inventive head, and willing heart" (5.1.88–93).[20] There is no way to prove conclusively that Cary consulted Morwen's book, but it seems likely that she was familiar with this work.

Morwen presents a conventionally admirable version of Mariam, a queen who is clearly an innocent victim. In Morwen's account, Mariam speaks only when "she sued harde and laye sore upon" (F3ʳ) Herod to appoint her brother priest and when she tells the king's mother and sister they are "unholy & of base birth" (F5ᵛ). With her husband, she is so passive that he realizes something is wrong only because "always she was sadde" (F7ᵛ). When Herod asks that she explain her misery, she responds with a statement that focuses as much on her desire for his love as on his wrongdoing: "Thou haste saide heretofore that thou lovest me above all thine other wives and concubines: yet didst thou will *Joseph* . . . to poison me" (F8ʳ). From the moment Herod condemns her, Mariam utters not a single word. The narrator considers this silence evidence of perfect virtue: "Mariam thus going to her execution held her peace, and looked nether to the right nor to the left: nor yet feared death any thing knowing that she was innoce[n]t in deed and thought, and therefore God would re[n]der her a good reward in the world to come" (G1ʳ). Not only does Herod recognize that he has wrongly killed his wife, but so do the people of Jerusalem, who are troubled by a plague sent as divine punishment for Mariam's death (G1ʳ). With God clearly on her side, Morwen's Mariam is a much more straightforward martyr figure than appears in Cary's play. This story of Mariam fits neatly into a Christian historical narrative that marks the rise of Herod (and the death of his wife) as the downfall of the Jewish monarchy, a context Morwen emphasizes in his introductory epistle, which warns readers to see this transfer of favor as a lesson "to see the better to thine owne waies" (n.p.) or risk having God cease favoring the English nation.

Although it might seem that Morwen is able to make his Mariam so meek because she does not need to function as a stage character, an early modern play presenting her story manages the same effect. Markham and Sampson's *Herod and Antipater* presents Mariam, even in moments when she might be excused for resisting, as perfectly obedient to her husband.[21] The queen not only accepts Herod's explanations of why he killed her relatives, but also apologizes for mourning their deaths, assuring Herod that "in my love to you I buried them / . . . 'tis mine eye / that pitties them, my heart doeth honour you" (1.3.32–35). Ironically, Mariam's obedience is what leads to her downfall. Mariam vows to Joseph by "the bonds of chastity and truth" (1.4.104) to protect her source of information about the king's order to have her killed. However, Herod compels his wife to speak "by that love / Once you did faine to beare me; by that faith / Which should link married couples; by the awe, / Duty and truth of women" (2.1.254–57), and Mariam seems compelled to uphold "chastity and truth" by obeying her husband's command. This perfect compliance with the king's will leads to Mariam's death, an execution figured as a martyrdom by the play's comparisons of the queen to a holy "temple" Herod has profaned. A victim who opposes her monarch only through futile prayers and quiet bravery, the Mariam of this play is a martyr figure who does not trouble social ideals of female decorum.[22]

In comparison to these other texts, it is evident that Cary's Mariam is a curiously ambiguous martyr figure. The voices of other characters help to make Mariam's character seem morally problematic. Doris, Herod's first wife, expresses genuine pain as a rejected spouse fighting for the rights of her son, thus creating the sense that Mariam's marriage is questionable, if not technically illegitimate (2.3).[23] Graphina serves as a model of meek and ideal womanhood who speaks only when ordered to and then takes the opportunity to praise her beloved Pheroras and to worry "That I should say too little when I speak" (2.1.50);[24] in comparison, Mariam's speech seems unruly and unlicensed. The chorus critiques Mariam by repeatedly comparing her to the adulterous Salome, and sometimes implying that she is even worse. Although Salome has disposed of one husband to marry Constabarus (and now hopes to divorce him), it is the queen who is criticized because "Mariam wish'd she from her lord were free, / For expectation of variety" (1.6.518–19). After Salome arranges with Pheroras to reveal information that will lead to the execution of Constabarus, the chorus chooses to comment on how Mariam has damaged her "honour" since she "more than to her lord alone will give / A private word to any second ear" (3.3.232; 3.3.228–29). Although Mariam asserts the virtue of her resolutions to never "man beguile / Or other speech than meaning to afford" (3.3.165–66) and to keep her spirit from being "impure" (3.3.178), the chorus describes her actions as improperly immodest.

But by depicting Mariam as troubling to secular authority and social mores, Cary links her to representations of early modern martyrs. The willingness to die that is necessary for martyrdom had to manifest itself in some way that would expose an individual to persecution. Those who were willing to obey church and secular authorities by attending required religious services might be troubled by occasional run-ins with the law but were unlikely to be executed and thus martyred. Foxe's *Acts and Monuments*, the major martyrology of early modern England, offers many examples of Protestants behaving defiantly as they progressed to martyrdom. Many martyrs reportedly came under scrutiny simply for failing to attend Mass, but others actively proclaimed their beliefs. For example, during the reign of Mary, Richard Woodman was apprehended after publicly chastising a priest (in the midst of performing the Catholic Eucharistic rite) for abandoning the true Protestant teachings he had shared with his parishioners under Edward VI (1875).[25] Similarly, by being loyal to the pope, who had excommunicated the queen, and by setting foot on English soil, Catholic priests acted in defiance of English law. It is on these grounds that William Cecil, Lord Burghley, could argue in his 1583 *Execution of Justice in England* that such priests were executed as traitors, not because of differences in religion.[26]

Female martyrs also engaged in rebellious behavior, not only against priests and magistrates but also against their husbands. Alyce Benden refused to attend a Catholic mass even when "her husband willed her to go to the Church," so he eventually had to admit to the bishop that "he could not deliver her" (Foxe 1872). Although Joyce Lewes "was compelled by the furiousnes of her husband to come to the Church," she defied both priest and spouse by turning her back to the altar (Foxe 1904). The Catholic martyr Margaret Clitherow hid priests without her husband's knowledge; according to her martyrologist, John Mush, she asked her confessor for confirmation that it was permissible in the eyes of God to assist priests "without my husband's consent" (381).[27]

Their steadfastness in faith also led female martyrs into situations where they were required to speak publicly on subjects not conventionally open to discussion by women. Foxe records episodes in which his female martyrs debate theology with bishops and other officials. Anne Askew called attention to the irregularity of such proceedings when she declined to expound on a text of St. Paul, saying, "that it was agaynst saynt Paules lernynge, that I beynge a woman, shuld interprete the scriptures" (Foxe 1206; Bale, *First* D7^v).[28] By explaining her beliefs in such detail orally and in writing, Askew violated her own assertion that "God hath geven me the gyfte of knowlege, but not of utteraunce. And Salomon sayth, that a woman of fewe wordes, is a gyfte of God, Prouer.19" (Foxe 1206; Bale, *First* D4^v–D5^r). Other female martyrs were able to proclaim their beliefs on the way to execution or while standing among flames, occasions when it was highly likely that their speeches would be remembered and written down.[29]

As numerous studies of Foxe's *Acts and Monuments* and lesser-known texts have pointed out, the rebellious speech and behavior of female martyrs often drew condemnation from their persecutors.[30] Because they refused to recant, many of these women were criticized as "obstinate." Frequently, their chastity was called into question. For instance, Rose Allin was called a "whore" for not crying when Catholic authorities held her hand over a flame (Foxe 1898). It was common for officials to connect a woman's ability to defend her faith with sexual impropriety, as when Elizabeth Young's interrogators asked her, "What priest hast thou layn withal, that thou hast so much Scripture" (Foxe 1962), and when Protestant authorities told Margaret Clitherow that "it is not for religion that thou harbourest priests, but for harlotry" (Mush 414).

Remarkably, male martyrologists reveal similar anxieties about the behavior of the women they celebrate. A notable example is the way John Bale and John Foxe handled the fact that Anne Askew left her husband in order to practice her faith. Bale, Askew's earliest commentator, explains at length why her actions were lawful, pointing out that her husband instigated the separation and divorce and that the Bible permits religious women to leave impious spouses (*Lattre* 15^r–15^v/B7^r–B7^v).[31] Foxe deals with the potential difficulty in the story of Askew by downplaying it through a lack of comment and an eventual omission of any details about the martyr's family life. In other cases, Foxe ameliorates the rebellious behavior of female martyrs by characterizing them as the ultimate example of God's strength showing its immense power by manifesting itself in a "weak vessel" (1944).[32] While all martyrs going to their deaths were instances of this dynamic, as Christine Peters argues, "The assumed weakness of women meant their martyrdoms stressed more clearly and impressively that God was working through them."[33] Margaret Clitherow's martyrologist manages her disobedience of her husband in a slightly different way, making abundantly clear that she was perfectly subservient to male authorities—the priests who taught her the truth of the Catholic faith.[34] At the same time, he goes out of his way to present her as the best wife possible, including in his narrative praise from her husband (407).

By creating a Mariam who shares the rebellious qualities of early modern female martyrs, Cary exposes the gender-related anxieties present in accounts of their lives and deaths.[35] For her speech, Mariam is criticized by the chorus as an unruly "wife [who] her hand against her fame doth rear, / That more than to her lord alone will give / A private word to any second ear" (3.3.227–29). For insisting on acting out her values, she is condemned by her husband as devious and unchaste (4.4.175–84). Including in her play such explicit criticism of a figure who was widely recognized within the period as a martyr (and who was typically depicted less problematically), Cary makes clear that to be a martyr one had to be at least somewhat rebellious.[36] Her chorus offers excellent advice about social behavior but not about the actions of true martyrs. Good wives might "When to their husbands they themselves do bind, / . . . wholly give themselves away" because "their thoughts no more can be their own" (3.3.233–34, 237), but such women could never be like Anne Askew or Margaret Clitherow. Had Mariam followed the advice of the chorus, it seems likely "Long famous life to her had been allow'd" (4.8.664). However, she would then not have become the martyr-figure whose death ushered in the start of the Christian era.

Cary's play came at a crucial time in the history of the discourse of martyrology in England, a moment when it might have seemed necessary to call attention to the rebellious qualities of martyrs. The decades surrounding the turn of the century in 1600 witnessed an official shift from the celebration of martyrs as models of zealous spirituality that might lead to dissent to the use of martyrs to encourage conformity.[37] It is well known that *Acts and Monuments* was a readily accessible text because a 1571 edict required most churches to have a copy that would be available to the public.[38] Despite this endorsement of Foxe's work, many Elizabethan church officials seem to have been uncomfortable with the possibility that it might justify resistance on the part of reform-minded Protestants. As Damian Nussbaum explains in detail, in the 1570s "Foxe's name and reputation remained a prized endorsement that both conformists and Presbyterians claimed for their cause."[39] Eventually, revisions to prefatory materials as well as public references to it by church officials made *Acts and Monuments* seem more a celebration of England as an elect Christian nation than a call for doctrinal change.[40] A marker of this trend was Timothy Bright's 1589 abridgement of Foxe's work. Focusing primarily on the events leading up to the deaths of more recent English martyrs, Bright created a document that stressed Catholic cruelty without expounding upon potentially controversial points of Protestant doctrine.[41]

In the context of this change in the uses of martyrology, female martyrs in particular were often transformed from outspoken proponents of their faith into meek victims. An early example of this dynamic appears in Cecil's *Execution of Justice,* when he refers to the killing of women during Mary's reign to emphasize the viciousness of Catholic persecutors but fails to mention the cause for which these women died (20–21). Also, it is interesting to track changes in depictions of Anne Askew from Bale's early editions of her examinations through Foxe's martyrology to Bright's condensed version and into the seventeenth century.[42] Early representations of Askew make explicit how she openly defied secular and religious authorities on the way to her death. At the end of his version of the first examination, Bale appends "The Ballade whiche Anne Askewe made and sange, whan she was in Newgate," a poem that describes the martyr as an "armed knight" setting out to battle with the world protected by her shield of faith (O4^r). The speaker ends with a critique of state authority, offering a vision of "a roiall trone / Where Justyce shuld have syt" taken up by a cruel tyrant inspired by Satan (O4^v). Clearly, Askew here does not shrink from what might be seen as rebellion. This ballad is missing from Foxe's martyrology, but he does retain in full her lengthy debates with interrogators over church doctrine. Bright's version, however, shortens the section on Askew. While he indicates she "boldly and roundly (with some checke unto the adversaries) made answere" (70/EE3^v), he gives few specific examples of such speech. Still, this is more than can be found in Cotton Clement's 1613 redaction of Foxe's work, which reduces the accounts of martyrs to their dying words, occasional letters, and prayers; of Askew's words, he retains only her prayer, included in both Bale's and Foxe's editions, which begins "O Lord I haue more enemies then there bee haires on my head" (170/I1^v).[43] The last unique text that purports to present the words of the martyr exists in a printed broadside from 1624, "A Ballad of Anne Askew intituled I am a woman poore and blind," in which she compares herself to Mary Magdalene, unable to recognize Christ without his help.[44] This transformation of Askew from a warrior ready to fight to the death to a blind woman who refers to herself as already burned to ashes parallels the change in the mainstream English Protestant discourse of martyrdom across the sixteenth and seventeenth centuries.

Countering this trend, the Mariam of Cary's play serves as a reminder that martyrs are always rebellious. It insists that to assume all outspoken women are unchaste and immoral is to make the same error as the chorus, equating Mariam's carefully considered critique of her husband's actions with Salome's willful adultery and murderous plots.[45] To demand all women be silent, chaste, and obedient is to make them like Graphina, potentially victims but never possibly martyrs. Cary's play signals how it should be read against the grain of the chorus's moralistic advice with its final lines: "This day's events were certainly ordain'd, / To be the warning to posterity / . . . / This day alone, our sagest Hebrews shall / In after times the school of wisdom call" (5.1.289–94). Commentators have pointed out that with this speech, Cary calls attention to her authorial virtuosity in transforming the story of Herod and Mariam into a play that perfectly follows the classical convention of presenting a play's action in real time.[46] Additionally, these lines refer to the biblical Book of Wisdom, a text relevant to the play's key themes of martyrdom and monarchy.[47] While Catholic bibles place this text after the Canticles and Protestant translations include it among the Apocrypha, all versions share the same contents, described in the Douai Old Testament as "an Instruction, and Exhortation to Kinges and Magistrates, to minister justice in the commonwealth, teaching all sortes of virtues under the general names of Justice & Wisdome" (344/Tt3^v). The Book of Wisdom instructs readers how to interpret properly, warning that what seems ignominy in the world might be righteousness in the eyes of God:

> The soules of the just are in the hand of God, and the torment of death shal not touch them. They seemed in the eies of the unwise to die: and their decease was counted affliction: and that which with us is the way, is destruction: but they are in peace. And though before men they suffered torments, their hope is ful of immortalitie.
>
> (3:1–4)

This passage seemed to Catholic translators so pertinent to the condition of martyrdom that they glossed it "for albeit Martyrs seme in the eyes of the unwise to dye, or to be extinguished, they passe indeed into eternal, and unspeakable glorie" (347^r/Vu2^r). Cary's reference to wisdom in the last line of the play calls readers' attention to the need to see beyond the surface of earthly events.

In the preface to his translation of Josephus's works, Thomas Lodge similarly picks up on this idea in a discussion of how to read history. Like many other early modern historians, Lodge thinks individuals and societies can benefit from history's positive examples of great virtue and negative models of corruption (¶3^r). However, he warns, too many readers seek only history that is to their tastes (¶3^r–¶3^v), and too many writers alter or edit historical truth to suit popular expectations or teach particular lessons (¶3^v). Continually pointing out that what is to be gained from the right reading of history is "wisdom," Lodge instructs readers to examine themselves from the perspective of a historian if they wish to be enlightened:

> Whereas the difficultie and difference is a like, to yeeld an upright verdict both of a mans owne, and other mens lives, neither may any man rightly examine another . . . except in equal balance he weigh his own imperfections; it must necessarily follow on both sides, that with the more wisedome, and the greater observation wee ought to entertaine Historie, least our mind like the wind should wander uncertainly, and our devotion should prevent our resolution.
>
> (¶3^r)

Through the chorus's condemnatory speeches, Cary shows her readers what happens when one "reads" history only through the lens of his or her own biases. While these evaluations of Mariam parrot conventional advice about women's behavior, they also preclude the martyrdom of Mariam, which seemed essential to those who read her death as a step toward the coming of the messiah. The judgments of the chorus serve as an implicit critique of the martyrologists who celebrate female martyrs while simultaneously apologizing for and erasing the very qualities that made them martyrs. Cary's heroine differs from the martyr-figures presented in other early modern versions of the story of Herod and Mariam, but she is one the playwright teaches her audience to read through the lens of "wisdom," in a way that exposes the discontinuities and contradictions in early modern discourses of martyrology.

NOTES

Support for the research for this project was provided by an American Association of University Women American Dissertation Fellowship and a Nazareth College Faculty Research Grant. Special thanks are due to the Centre for Studies in Religion and Society at the University of Victoria, British Columbia, for offering the space and collegiality that made it possible for me to finish this project during the year I spent as one of their visiting research fellows.

1. See Elaine V. Beilin, *Redeeming Eve: Women Writers of the English Renaissance* (Princeton: Princeton UP, 1987), 170; Margaret W. Ferguson, "The Spectre of Resistance: *The Tragedy of Mariam*" in *Staging the Renaissance*, ed. David Scott Kastan and Peter Stallybrass (New York: Routledge, 1991), 235–250, esp. 244; Sandra K. Fischer, "Elizabeth Cary and Tyranny, Domestic and Religious," in *Silent But for the Word,* ed. Margaret Hannay (Kent: Kent State UP, 1985), 225–237, esp. 235–236; and Frances E. Dolan, "'Gentlemen, I Have One More Thing to Say': Women on Scaffolds in England," *Modern Philology: A Journal Devoted to Research in Medieval and Modern Literature* 92, no. 2 (1994): 157–178, esp. 162–165.
2. Parenthetical references to Cary's play follow *The Tragedy of Mariam,* ed. Barry Weller and Margaret Ferguson (Berkeley: U of California P, 1994).
3. See Brad Gregory, "The Willingness to Die," in *Salvation at Stake* (Cambridge: Harvard UP, 1999), chapter 4.
4. Donald Kelley, "Martyrs, Myths, and the Massacre: The Background of St. Bartholomew," *American Historical Review* 77, no. 5 (1972): 1323–1342, esp. 1328.
5. Augustine's statement "not the punishment, but the cause, makes a martyr" was cited by numerous early modern authorities attempting to distinguish martyrs from heretics. For a discussion of this idea, see Gregory, 87, 140–141. Laurie Shannon notes the oddity of calling Mariam a *Christian* martyr in "*The Tragedie of Mariam:* Cary's Critique of the Terms of Founding Social Discourses," *English Literary Renaissance* 24, no. 1 (1994): 135–153, esp. 141–142.

MARIAM AND DISCOURSES OF MARTYRDOM 49

6. Gregory offers numerous examples that show how paradigmatic the Maccabees were to all Christian denominations (123).
7. This quote is taken from the King James translation of the Bible (*The Holy Bible* [London, 1611], STC 2216); other translations interpret this passage similarly but render it differently. The Douai OT states: "The scepter shall not be taken away from Judas, and a duke out of his thigh, til he do come that is to be sent" ([Douai, 1609/10], STC 2207). Subsequent references to these texts appear parenthetically.
8. *The Holy Bible* (London, 1584), STC 2141; subsequent references appear parenthetically.
9. For comments on the play's dynastic concerns, see Danielle Clarke, "'This Domestic Kingdome or Monarchy': Cary's *The Tragedy of Mariam*," *Medieval and Renaissance Drama in England* 10 (1998): 179–200, esp. 185–188; Rosemary Kegl, "Theatres, Households, and a 'Kind of History' in Elizabeth Cary's *Tragedy of Mariam*," in *Enacting Gender on the Renaissance Stage*, ed. Viviana Comensoli and Anne Russell (Urbana: U of Illinois P, 1999), 135–153, esp. 146–147; and Shannon, 137.
10. Central to many studies of Cary's play is examination of Mariam's "public voice." See Catherine Belsey, *The Subject of Tragedy* (New York: Routledge, 1993), esp. 164–174; Dolan, 164–165; Naomi J. Miller, "Domestic Politics in Elizabeth Cary's *Tragedy of Mariam*," *SEL: Studies in English Literature 1500–1900* 37 (1997): 353–369, esp. 366.
11. Others have described Mariam as a figure who somehow prefigures Christ but emphasize different narratives. For example, Beilin notes that Cary's source, Lodge's translation of Josephus, has marginal dates that construct history as a countdown to the nativity. See also Lyn Bennett, "'Written on my tainted brow': Woman and the Exegetical Tradition in *The Tragedy of Mariam*," *Christianity and Literature* 51, no. 1 (2001): 5–28; and Dympna Callaghan, "Re-Reading Elizabeth Cary's *Tragedie of Mariam*," in *Women, "Race" and Writing in the Early Modern Period*, ed. Margo Hendricks and Patricia Parker (New York: Routledge, 1994), 163–177.
12. A. C. Dunstan and W. W. Greg identify this source in "Note on the Source, Date, and Authorship of the Play" in *The Tragedy of Mariam* (London: Malone Society/Oxford UP, 1914), xiii–xv.
13. Sections of Lodge's translation excerpted on pages 277–282 of Weller and Ferguson's *Mariam* are cited parenthetically from that edition. Other sections of Lodge's work are cited from Josephus, *The famous and memorable workes of Josephus* (London, 1602), STC 14809.
14. Suzanne Hull's collection of women's behavior manuals lays out the formula that women should remain "chaste, silent, and obedient"; see *Chaste, Silent, & Obedient: English Books for Women 1475–1640* (San Marino: Huntington Library, 1982). While recent scholarship has shown that these values were perhaps more often violated than perfectly followed, this is still a useful yardstick for the presumed acceptability of a woman's actions.
15. Ferguson, in "The Spectre of Resistance," writes about Graphina as a foil to Mariam who meets idealized expectations for women's behavior, 237–238.

Josephus mentions that Herod's brother fell in love with a servant, but this woman is neither named nor described (592/K2ᵛ).
16. Lodge's text was entered in the Stationers' Register in 1598, so it was presumably completed by that date. See Dunstan and Greg vii.
17. Parenthetical references are to Peter Morwen, *A compendious and most marueilous history of the latter tymes of the Iewes commune weale* (London, 1558), STC 14795. For more information about Morwen's book and the relationship of Lodge's translation to this work, see my "Jewish History, Catholic Argument: Thomas Lodge's *Workes of Josephus* as a Catholic Text," *Sixteenth Century Journal* 34, no. 4 (2003): 993–1010.
18. Callaghan identifies Morwen's translation as "an earlier version of the Herod-Mariam story" (n29) that Cary might have seen, but she does not identify influences on the play.
19. See Weller and Ferguson's discussions of Herod in their introduction, esp. 22–23, 40–41.
20. Clarke also sees Herod's wish to have Mariam appear as "necrophiliac desire" (196), but she does not link this idea to Morwen's text.
21. References here are to *The True Tragedy of Herod and Antipater,* ed. Gordon Ross (New York: Garland, 1979). A number of plays tell the story of Herod and Mariam, but only Cary's, Markham and Sampson's, and Massinger's survive from the early modern period; for a full list, see Maurice J. Valency, *The Tragedies of Herod and Mariamne* (New York: AMS Press, 1966).
22. Similarly, Massinger's *Duke of Milan* (first printed in 1623), which uses the story of Herod and Mariam as a source for its romance plot, presents its Mariam character as a more passive and thus less ambiguous victim than does Cary's play.
23. Clarke indicates Doris raises questions about Mariam's marriage because Herod's first wife met expectations for a good, English Protestant woman (185).
24. On Graphina's silence and speech, see Andrew Hiscock, "The Hateful Cuckoo: Elizabeth Cary's *Tragedie of Mariam,* a Renaissance Drama of Disposession," *Forum for Modern Language Studies* 33, no. 2 (1997): 97–114.
25. I use the term "Foxe" as a shorthand reference to *Acts and Monuments* but realize that there were numerous other contributors. See John King, "Fiction and Fact in Foxe's *Book of Martyrs,*" in *John Foxe and the English Reformation,* ed. David Loades (Aldershot: Scolar, 1997), 12–35, for a brief history of the martyrology. Parenthetical citations list page numbers from the 1576 edition (STC 11224).
26. William Cecil, *The Execution of Justice in England,* ed. Robert Kingdon (Ithaca, NY: Cornell UP, 1965), 39.
27. References to Clitherow's martyrdom are taken from John Mush, *Life of Margaret Clitherow,* in *The Catholics of York under Elizabeth,* ed. John Morris (London: Burns and Oates, 1891), 331–440.
28. The examinations of Anne Askew were first brought to press by John Bale. References here are to *The first examinacion* (London, 1547), STC 851, and *The lattre examinacyon* (Wesel, 1547), STC 850. For a discussion of these

MARIAM AND DISCOURSES OF MARTYRDOM 51

texts, see Beilin's introduction to *The Examinations of Anne Askew* (New York: Oxford UP, 1996) xv–xxii, xlv-xlix.
29. See Dolan for a discussion linking representations of female martyrs to Cary's depiction of Mariam; see also Karen Newman, *Fashioning Femininity and English Renaissance Drama* (Chicago: U of Chicago P, 1991), 69.
30. For discussions of female martyrs and their martyrologists, see Claire Cross, "An Elizabethan Martyrologist and his Martyr: John Mush and Margaret Clitherow," *Studies in Church History* 30 (1993): 271–281; Peter Lake and Michael Questier, "Margaret Clitherow, Catholic Nonconformity, Martyrology and the Politics of Religious Change in Elizabethan England," *Past and Present* 185 (2004): 43–90; Susannah Brietz Monta, "Foxe's Female Martyrs and the Sanctity of Transgression," *Renaissance and Reformation* 25, no. 1 (2001): 3–22; and Steven Mullaney, "Reforming Resistance: Class, Gender, and Legitimacy in Foxe's *Book of Martyrs*," in *Print, Manuscript, and Performance,* ed. Arthur Marotti and Michael Bristol (Columbus: Ohio State UP, 2000), 235–251.
31. Beilin discusses this matter in her introduction to *Examinations.* See esp.xix.
32. For discussions of this trope, see Christine Peters, *Patterns of Piety* (Cambridge: Cambridge UP, 2003) and Monta.
33. Peters 270.
34. See Lake and Questier and Cross on Mush's roles as Clitherow's confessor, as her martyrologist, and as a priest.
35. Mariam's rebelliousness is discussed by Ferguson, Belsey, and Betty Travitsky, "Husband-Murder and Petty Treason in English Renaissance Tragedy," *Renaissance Drama* 21 (1990): 171–198. Susan Iwanisziw compares Mariam to Foxe's female martyrs and to recusant Catholic wives (113–114); see "Conscience and the Disobedient Female Consort in the Closet Dramas of John Milton and Elizabeth Cary," *Milton Studies* 36 (1998): 109–122.
36. For reasons why Mariam's rebelliousness might have been seen as justified, see Shannon 136; Fischer; Iwanisziw, esp. 109; and Ferguson, esp. 244.
37. For a fuller account of this transition and accompanying debates, see Damian Nussbaum, "Appropriating Martyrdom: Fears of Renewed Persecution and the 1632 Edition of *Acts and Monuments,*" in *John Foxe and the English Reformation,* 178–191, and "Whitgift's 'Book of Martyrs': Archbishop Whitgift, Timothy Bright and the Elizabethan Struggle over John Foxe's Legacy," in *John Foxe: An Historical Perspective,* ed. David Loades (Aldershot: Ashgate, 1999), 135–153.
38. William Haller, *The Elect Nation* (New York, Harper and Row, 1963), 220–221.
39. Nussbaum, "Whitgift's," 142.
40. See Jesse Lander, "Foxe's *Book of Martyrs:* Printing and Popularizing the *Acts and Monuments*" in *Religion and Renaissance Culture,* ed. Claire McEachern and Debora Shuger (Cambridge: Cambridge UP, 1997), 69–92, for a discussion of the implications of various editions of *Acts and Monuments.*
41. This text is listed by the STC under Foxe's name as *An abridgement of the booke of acts and monumentes* (London, 1589), STC 11229.

42. This is a project that Beilin undertakes in her edition of Askew's work. See also Peters and Thomas Freeman and Elizabeth Wall, "Racking the Body, Shaping the Text: The Account of Anne Askew in Foxe's 'Book of Martyrs,'" *Renaissance Quarterly* 54 (2001): 1165–1196.
43. Clement Cotton, *The mirror of martyrs* (London, 1613), STC 5848.
44. Anonymous, "A Ballad of Anne Askew intituled I am a woman poore and blind" (London, 1624), STC 853.5.
45. Many critics compare and contrast Mariam and Salome. See Irene Burgess, "The Wreck of Order in Early Modern Women's Drama," *Early Modern Literary Studies* 6, no. 3 (2001): 6.1–24 (http://purl.oclc.org/emls/06-3/burgwrec.htm); Travitsky, esp.186; and Karen Raber, "Gender and the Political Subject in *The Tragedy of Mariam*," *SEL: Studies in English Literature 1500–1900* 35 (1995): 321–343.
46. See Weller and Ferguson's note for this line as well as Kegl 142–143.
47. Shannon sees these lines as generally indicating the play offers a "lesson" to "posterity, the descendants of a social order, the extension of the Jewish nation into time" (147).

CHAPTER 3

ELIZABETH CARY'S HISTORICAL CONSCIENCE: *THE TRAGEDY OF MARIAM* AND THOMAS LODGE'S JOSEPHUS

Alison Shell

The plot of Elizabeth Cary's closet drama *The Tragedy of Mariam, the Fair Queen of Jewry* has long been identified as deriving mainly from Thomas Lodge's translation of Josephus's *Antiquities of the Jews*. However, it has not so far been considered how instrumental Lodge's approach to Josephus was in determining Cary's own treatment of her source material. Lodge gives voice to a common Renaissance preoccupation, the moral utility of history, and—more unusually—stresses his readers' obligation to interrogate their own lives by actively reflecting upon relevant historical exemplars, both good and bad. He could hardly have wished for a reader more attentive than Cary, and this chapter argues that the close correspondence between her life and her works, so often remarked upon by her commentators, derives largely from her imaginative and—quite literally—conscientious reworking of Lodge's strictures.

Lodge's translation of Josephus first appeared in 1602, with a preface addressed "To the courteous reader, As touching the use and abuse of Historie."[1] It begins by asserting the moral efficacy of historical example: history "hath true proportion and documents for the government of mans life." As so often, this is primarily interpreted as the usefulness of bad example, from which readers must not distance themselves: it is not enough "to sit and learne prevention by other mens perils, and to grow amplie wise by forraine wreckes."[2] Though history itself is irredeemable, Lodge invites his readers to use narratives of historical events both to interrogate their own pasts and to avoid pitfalls in their own futures.

So far, this is reasonably familiar territory in the Europe of the 1600s.[3] Respect was universally paid to the Ciceronian dictum that history could teach the individual valuable lessons and foster virtue, while Plutarch's conception of history as biography reinforced the conception of it as a source of exemplar. The potential moral utility of history was one of the main reasons why it figured so prominently in educational curricula and became a popular form of recreational reading, among women as well as men.[4] The *trattatisti*, a group of sixteenth-century Italian historians, had aimed to foreground questions about the nature and goals of historical writing, and their insights had been influential. The writings of one of their number, Francesco Patrizi, had reached England in predigested form in Thomas Blundeville's *The true order and methode of wryting and reading hystories* (1574).[5] Blundeville commends a leisurely, careful, morally alert reading of history, and a systematic gathering of exemplars for the instruction of others. Around the time Lodge was writing, the translations of Tacitus published in 1591 and 1598 by Henry Savill and Francis Greneway had stimulated further debate about the moral purpose of historical writing.[6] Finally, Lodge's comments should be read against Machiavelli's more politically charged awareness that lessons could be learned from the mistakes made by one's predecessors.[7]

Thus, Lodge is working within a well-established tradition of appropriating history for didactic purposes, but his historiographical emphases are distinctive. It should be said that this is a distinctiveness not entirely his own; he borrows heavily and rather cheekily from an essay by Simon Grynaeus, *De utilitate legendae historiae,* which he might have seen prefacing Arthur Golding's translation of the histories of Trogus Pompeius (1570 ed.).[8] But Grynaeus's sentiments are very much in keeping with Lodge's agenda elsewhere: as Arthur F. Kinney has commented, "What sets Lodge's acts of humanist *imitatio* decisively apart from his predecessors . . . is [their] deliberately reiterative concern with virtuous action in this world as preparation for the beatitudes of the next."[9] Grynaeus and Lodge both have an unusually pronounced religious stress on avoiding sin, and in contrast to the outward-looking notion of history as a means to steer others toward virtue, so characteristic of the early Stuart period, they foreground personal vigilance on the part of the reader.[10] They are, of course, well aware that the historian has moral responsibilities too; as Lodge says, "he that writeth an Historie is the interpreter of those things that are past: whose judgement being depraved, it fareth with him as with the purest and most richest wine, which waxeth mustie by reason of that vessell wherein it is inclosed." Nevertheless, opening a history book sets up a dialogue between author and reader in which ultimate responsibility is passed firmly to the latter. Part of this responsibility comes in selecting from the entire text what is personally appropriate to oneself. Using the analogy of a banquet—or, as we would say, a buffet—Lodge explains how the reader has to survey the dishes on offer, and choose what is most nourishing in terms of his or her personal diet. When the reading of history is embarked upon negligently, calamitous misinterpretations occur. Extending the analogy with diet, Lodge compares careless readers to a bevy of peasants in the recent French uprisings who broke into an apothecary's shop, ate whatever looked appetizing, and so became ill, waxed mad, or died.

Selection is important because correct reading of history demands self-examination, locating a parallel within oneself to every external circumstance the history narrates. Lodge explains: "Thou maist easily conceive, how a historie ought to be read: how mens lives ought in them selves be examined: finally how equal a proportion is required in both." This active self-knowledge is demanded of writers as well. Lodge condemns writers who "set downe such things as are acted, not onely for our profit sake, but to feed their owne humours: and like to certain Architects (by interposing their judgements) doe vainely praise some things, supposing that our imitation should be tied to their pleasure." In yet another reheating of his culinary metaphor, he compares them to "cookes, who rather respect their masters pleasurable taste, then his profit."[11] Though Lodge is writing here of the historian as is conventionally understood, his strictures are very applicable to those who, like Cary, used stories from Josephus or another history as an inspiration for drama, and the points he makes would not have been lost on Cary.

The Tragedy of Mariam is an unusually pure example of the creative writer's response to source material, because that response—within the parameters of Josephus's story—is itself in part the matter of the drama. Historical figures are revivified and interrogated, and their deeds resonate in the effect they have on the contemporary individual. The confrontations of historical characters within the play have knock-on effects well beyond their immediate dramatic circumstances, and carry the expectation that the author, as well as every separate member of the audience, will engage in the debates too. And even within the action of *Mariam*, the past continues to inform the present. Consider the very first words of the play, now very well known:

> How oft have I with public voice run on
> To censure Rome's last hero for deceit:
> Because he wept when Pompey's life was gone,
> Yet when he liv'd, he thought his name too great.
> But now I do recant, and, Roman lord,
> Excuse too rash a judgement in a woman:
> My sex pleads pardon, pardon then afford,
> Mistaking is with us but too too common.

> Now do I find, by self-experience taught,
> One object yields both grief and joy:
> You wept indeed, when on his worth you thought,
> But joy'd that slaughter did your foe destroy.
> So at his death your eyes true drops did rain,
> Whom dead, you did not wish alive again. (l.1.1–14)[12]

The usefulness of the soundbite "public voice" to describe the predicament of the early modern woman writer has tended to obscure other interesting points about these lines; and some of these have to do with Cary's addressing an audience that includes Lodge. Of course, Mariam's voice is not to be identified with Cary's, though it would be too revisionist to deny any connection between the timorous assertions of a pioneer woman playwright and the apologies of her character. But with her reference to "Rome's last hero," Julius Caesar, Mariam is following Lodge's instructions exactly. She is using historical exemplars as a means of quickening her own understanding: "Now do I find, by self-experience taught." And she employs the similarity between historical and experiential fact to discipline herself, again as Lodge suggests: "We may either as partners in what we have past, or observers of future casualties, by presedent events, tie ages to our memories: and prevent our escapes, by survew of other mens repentance, briefly beget experience by sight, or foresight of worldly casualties, and forme a mirror of forepassed errors, to forejudge our future calamities."

As the play proceeds, the way in which the chorus follows and comments upon the action formally echoes the two-stage process of reading and moral digestion which Lodge urges upon his readers. The chorus to act 2 again engages in historical speculation, discussing how one may assess rumour objectively; and another exemplar comes in the chorus to act 3. Julius Caesar is again alluded to, this time pointing toward the occasion when he divorced his wife Pompeia for being mentioned in connection with a scandal, despite the fact that there was no evidence decisively implicating her. Plutarch quotes him as saying that "I thought my wife ought not even to be under suspicion," and the pronouncement became proverbial in contexts of political rectitude, female chastity or—as here—both:[13]

> 'Tis not enough for one that is a wife
> To keep her spotless from an act of ill:
> But from suspicion she should free her life,
> And bare herself of power as well as will. (3.3.215–8)

In a manner typical of the interplay between *Mariam* and Cary's daughter's memoir of her mother, a similar moral imperative can be glimpsed in a passage from the latter: "She did allways much disapproue the practice of satisfying ones self with their conscience being free from fault, not forbearing all that might haue the least shew, or suspicion, of vncomlynesse, or vnfittnes."[14] As many critics have pointed out, *Lady Falkland: Her Life* is a source that needs to be read with care because of its hagiographical agenda; but this, in turn, needs qualification.[15] Hagiographies written from personal recollection are certainly likely to minimize their subject's lapses, but one should not assume that virtue is featureless, and such texts can provide potentially excellent evidence of the moral and religious ideals most valued by their subjects—in this case, the high standards of marital duty that Cary set for herself—and the distinctive ways in which they set about achieving them. Even if no memoir survived, we can hardly ignore the question of how Elizabeth Cary's gender and marital status would have affected her writing, when looking at her work.

In recent years, criticism of *Mariam* has gone through two stages. The first, pointing out the inexact but striking analogies between the personal circumstances of heroine and author, has been succeeded by scepticism about autobiographical readings of *Mariam*: Dympna Callaghan, for instance, has criticized those who posit the play "as an allegory of events of Cary's rather turbulent life."[16] Yet while this is a level-headed and understandable attitude, the biography still keeps intruding itself into critical consideration; and this need not be a bad or an ahistorical thing if one is careful to distinguish between autobiographical and autodidactic.

"Autobiographical" is usually taken to mean that the material is drawn from or inspired by events in the author's own life, and has no particular moral charge. Though "autodidactic" overlaps with the first term, two of its emphases are very distinctive. First, it privileges the exemplarity both of characters and of individual situations: one incident or character trait can have a particular moral utility to the reader, without a point-by-point correspondence being necessary. As Virgilio Malvezzi had suggested in his *Discourses upon Cornelius Tacitus* (trans. Sir Richard Baker, 1642), examples taught by their "suggestive and analogical persuasiveness, not an absolute likeness with any event or person"; the writer depends on the reader's powers of inference.[17] Secondly, autodidacticism demands parallels between past and present tenses, principally to set the imaginative agenda for future action: the kind of active moral vigilance that Lodge enjoins. I have argued elsewhere that *Mariam* is an autodidactic text—in other words, a text that shows the author constructing models of how to behave that may echo subsequent events in that author's biography—and that it makes perfect sense to consider life and works together, providing one does not conflate the two.[18] However, that discussion viewed the play in relation to Cary's conversion, rather than considering, as this chapter does, the way that autodidacticism itself was inspired by how Renaissance historians exhorted their readers. In the above quotations, Lodge instructs Cary and all his readers to select from history the material that is most conducive to profitable self-examination and modeling of future conduct; he, at any rate, seems positively to invite biographical interpretations of any work inspired by his edition of Josephus, and though his preface seems never to have been quoted by any of the previous critics who have identified autobiographical elements in the play, it seems to demand a reassessment of their claims.

Supposing *Mariam* to have been written from autodidactic motives, the place to start is not the biography—though clearly this does transmit evidence of Cary's behavior as shaped by prior moral demands. One needs to take the play first, and go for the largest exemplarities and admonitions. Mariam is the central and most obvious—though not the only—site for this kind of moral identification of writer with character. Lodge says, in his generally positive picture of Mariam, that "she defaulted somewhat in affabilitie and impatience of nature" and that she "presumed upon a great and intemperate libertie in her discourse" (399)—much picked up on in the play, where Mariam's tendency to speak out is criticized not just by Herod, but by the chorus as well.[19] Faults are perhaps more likely to arrest the autodidactic reader than virtues; to seek to remedy one's faults was virtuous, too great a consciousness of one's own virtues engendered pride. Mariam's faults, especially her frowardness of discourse, are likely ones for Cary or any woman writer of the time to reproach herself with; and despite some idealizing traits in Cary's portrait of Mariam, the characterization is decidedly more negative than in many early modern retellings of the story.[20]

This is reinforced by a typology that focuses on names. Cary is not alone, of course, in employing typology as an autodidactic device. Both tight and loose forms of biblical typology were used by early modern writers: the tight form being where Old Testament types are fulfilled in New Testament antitypes, and the loose form where historical similarities were perceived between biblical characters and a host of other texts and events.[21] And they could easily become tools of self-interrogation—as Barbara Lewalski has said of seventeenth-century literature, "Typological symbolism became . . . an important literary means to explore the personal spiritual life with profundity and psychological complexity."[22] As usual with historical adaptation, one is dealing with points of intersection more often than with point-to-point similarities.

Where is it being employed in *Mariam?* Most of all, it surfaces in the name and character of the heroine. "Mariam," "Miriam," and "Mary" are forms of the same name—to some extent, forms used interchangeably by Lodge as well as by other biblical commentators and writers on Jewish history. Thus, the name of Herod's queen is bound to suggest comparisons both with Moses's sister Miriam and with the Blessed Virgin Mary—characters who were, in any case, often compared to each other.[23] Both Cary's Mariam and the Virgin Mary are repositories of orthodoxy: Mary through giving birth to Christ, Mariam because she gives Herod the best title to the Jewish throne by virtue of her descent and his marriage to her. The echoed nomenclature points up how the mother of Christ can be seen as representing God's chosen people in propria persona.[24] Miriam too is a guardian of the faith when she is responsible for Moses's being found in the bulrushes by the Pharaoh's daughter, and suggests successfully that Moses's mother be hired as his wet-nurse.[25] Jeremiah sees Miriam as the personification of Jerusalem;[26] and Mariologists would have noticed the connection between Miriam and Mary. Both biblical women are likely models for a pious woman writer, though one must distinguish between Mary's private song of praise, the Magnificat, and the more public creativity of Miriam when she hymns the victory of the Israelites over the Egyptians.[27] Within Counter-Reformation commentaries, there was a tradition of talking up Miriam's poetic abilities: for instance, Cosma Magaliano praises her for her fervent leadership of the Israelites' worship, and sees her as a model for all religious writers.[28]

But it is at the point where Mary and Miriam begin to diverge that Cary's own conscience comes most into the equation. As mentioned above, Mariam is condemned for being prone to detraction, and her disparagement of Herod is seen as completely in character by both Josephus and Cary. This is a fault Miriam shares—perhaps not coincidentally, since the biblical anecdotes about Miriam may well have helped to shape Josephus's account of Mariam. Both women suffer for speaking out—God punishes Miriam with leprosy when Miriam and Aaron criticize Moses's marriage to a Cushite woman in Numbers 12, and Mariam's life becomes forfeit when, in act 4 scene 3, she condemns Herod's assassination of her family members. But in both cases their remonstrations are linked with a concern for cultic purity, since Moses's marriage is seen as endangering this, and the murdered members of Mariam's family can be seen as fitter inheritors of the Jewish throne than Herod himself.[29]

Both stories, therefore, portray the outspoken female protagonist as at least having a good case, presenting the reader with something more complicated than a straightforward condemnation of female backbiting. Even after her punishment by God, Miriam's question, "Hath the Lord indeed spoken only through Moses?" (Numbers 12:2), never quite goes away; and recent feminist scholarship across the disciplines has seen the recovery of Miriam's voice within Old Testament studies, paralleling the reemergence of *Mariam* onto the Renaissance landscape.[30] Maureen Quilligan has argued that *Mariam* "exposes the bodily costs of female public speech," while Rita Burns has noted how Aaron, who plays a full part in criticizing Moses, is not struck with leprosy like his sister; and against Phyllis Trible's comment that for Miriam "the price of speaking out is severe," one can set Sohemus's: "Unbridled speech is Mariam's worst disgrace, / And will endanger her without desert."[31] Though one must be sensitive to all the possible contemporary meanings of "disgrace," its main connotation here appears to be "ungracefulness" rather than "shame," since Sohemus rightly predicts that this trait will endanger Mariam without her deserving that danger. But if so, hers is an ungracefulness that does lead to public ignominy, with her offence against female discretion ultimately counting for more than the point she makes.[32]

Though Cary's use of the Numbers story is unusually sophisticated, Miriam's fate was often used by early modern writers as a warning to detractors or, as Henry Ainsworth declared, a reminder that church leaders should refrain from "ambition and vain glorie."[33] An even more suggestive reference occurs in a letter from Lord Vaux to Elizabeth, Lady Montagu, in the 1580s, in which Vaux disclaims rumors that he has criticized the treatment he received during his detainment at her house.[34] Objecting that he has learned from the biblical exemplar of Miriam not to engage in detraction, he nevertheless goes on to accuse Lady Montagu of speaking with undue aggressiveness to him on matters of religion when he was last in her company, expressing wonder that "you beynge of suche modestie, and w[i]thall so oft reedinge [th]e scriptures: wolde so sharpely reason w[i]th mee, and [tha]t in [th]e presence of yo[u]r husbande." While justifying himself against what he claims are untrue accusations, he is clearly expecting an apology from her for a more palpable offence, indulging in unfeminine behavior—and the exemplar of Miriam is explicitly evoked as a way of turning the tables.

The force of Cary's play derives in large part from her use of history as a means of merciless self-interrogation. She was hardly the only early seventeenth-century English writer to do this: a number of critics have observed, for instance, that Bacon's portrait of Henry VII in his history of the reign, written after Bacon's fall from grace, contains elements that can be read as an admission of personal failure. This has sometimes been said lightly, and sometimes as a prelude to observing that Bacon was consciously or unconsciously projecting himself onto his protagonist:[35] Judith Anderson has observed that Henry VII is even made to speak in characteristically Baconian syntactical patterns.[36] It seems most likely that this is a conscious construct; Bacon was using his history to praise statesmanlike qualities, and any statesman-historian would identify a continuum between abstract precept, biographical example, and elective personal behavior. As Bacon himself commented, "History and experience I consider to be the same thing."[37] But when Bacon considers Henry VII's avarice, there are also decided autodidactic elements. Bacon wrote his history during the period when he was out of political favor, having been impeached for taking bribes, and it has been recognized as part of an attempt to make a comeback.[38] For all readers, the history is a demonstration that political wisdom outweighs incidental vice; for those readers in the know, it would have been read as an admission of failings as well as an apologia; while for Bacon, the writing of it must have been undertaken in the hope of reparation, and have entailed a kind of public confession.

If this was a common method of historical reading and writing, was there anything different about Cary's deployment of it? Giving minute, conscientious attention to speaking or acting out of turn is one of the coping strategies most visible in early modern woman writers, and the way that the act of speaking is so compellingly identified with detraction in *Mariam* gives the play a highly individual emphasis that it is tempting to call "gendered." But Cary's actively moral reading of Mariam's story, employing affective techniques very like those recommended by Lodge, caused her to take on a historian's authority in turn, and ask her readers to apply similar techniques to her own text, in the ceaseless alternation of writer and reader, precept and example. Here, it may be worth stressing the sheer fervor of the imaginative participation recommended by historians. Plutarch's *Morals,* translated by Philemon Holland, appeared in 1603, the year after Josephus; like Lodge on history, the book stresses that imaginative writing must not be read passively. The mind is not a vessel that needs only to be filled up, but a pile of kindling that needs a match to "ingender in it a certain inventive motion"; to read passively is to warm yourself at a neighbor's fire, and never think to ignite one yourself.[39] Lipsius's is perhaps the weightiest justification in the early modern era of this subjective imaginative interpretation of historical narrative.[40] History, he claimed, is to be seen less as a continuous narrative than as a series of analogical relationships, interactively exploiting the tension between similarity and distance. Words, sentences, and actions have a double meaning, as act and as reference. The Lipsian subject constitutes himself in relation to historical exemplars, and Lipsius's understanding [41]of historical interpretation has been described by David Halsted as "a movement along the lines of similarity that link a present moment to an incident or situation in the past." Thus, it is Lipsius, Lodge, and a whole company of voices that lie behind the chorus to act 5 of *Mariam,* with its claim that the play is a lexicon of moral exemplars:

> This day's events were certainly ordain'd,
> To be the warning to posterity:
> So many changes are therein contain'd,

So admirably strange variety.
This day alone, our sagest Hebrews shall
In after times the school of wisdom call. (5.1.289–94)

Critics are right to be wary of too easy an assumption that all early modern women's writing is more or less autobiographical, since this can be patronizing—and, what is worse, dated. But, in placing Cary's work in the Renaissance tradition of conscientiously engaged historical commentary, as practiced by both men and women, this chapter has attempted to make a case for revisiting the debate in her case. This trend is visible in some other recent commentaries on Cary's work: Joan Parks, for instance, remarks of *Edward II* that "there can be little doubt that Cary was exploring her own situation through that of the historical queen [Isabel]," but that it would be reductive to ignore the public, political significance of Cary's history on the strength of that.[42] A stimulating recent discussion of *Mariam* by Alexandra G. Bennett invokes the notion of performativity, seeing the play as posing a "vivid distinction between Mariam's or Salome's inner convictions or desires and their outer conduct" and thus revealing "the ways in which women could fabricate public characters and adapt those personae to their environments."[43] Using the potential ambiguity of Cary's motto "Be and seem" as a starting-point for exploring the relationship between femaleness and theatricality as well as between Cary's life and art, Bennett evokes "the integrity of an individual self over which the changeable mask and/or mirror of social performance can and must be fitted."[44] Though Bennett displays a keen understanding of how *Mariam* brings history and personal experience into conscious dialogue through the operations of exemplarity, and her case is in some ways analogous to the one presented above, her argument risks misrepresenting how Cary, or any conscientiously engaged reader of either sex, would have consciously wanted to refine their own characters through active engagement with the past—not just for form's sake, but because they wished to discover their best self in the process.

Lodge would surely have approved of historical exegesis so near the bone, though he could have objected that the moral is evasive—after all, *Mariam* is about what happens when exemplarities clash. The play sets high ideals of marital submission on one end of the scales, on the other the hard case of how one should behave if one's husband is an absolutist tyrant; it goes out of its way to condemn detraction, but also makes the audience ask what alternative Mariam has to speaking out, and stresses her altruistic motives for doing so in a way that is not necessarily true even with more positive depictions of the character.[45] Straining over the gaps between political virtue and ideals of femininity, twisting its heroine between irreconcilable demands, *Mariam* demonstrates a thoroughly

ELIZABETH CARY'S HISTORICAL CONSCIENCE 63

baroque torsion on the part of its author—one reason why it is such a dynamic text to read and teach—and it is hard not to recognize the same type of agony in the historical character handed down to us by Cary's daughter in her account of her mother's life. Perhaps, after all, we may have paid too little attention to the relationship between Cary's life and works, rather than too much.

NOTES

Patrick Collinson, Katharine Dell, Arnold Hunt, the late Jeremy Maule, Lisa Richardson, and Heather Wolfe were of great help at various stages in the composition of this essay. Material from this paper was delivered at colloquia at Cambridge and Warwick universities, and I would like to thank the audiences on each occasion for their kind interest and feedback.

1. *The famous and memorable workes of Josephus* (1602), sig. ¶iii–iv^r (the Epistle to the Reader, from which all quotations are taken). For recent discussions of Lodge's Josephus, see Erin Kelly, "Jewish History, Catholic Argument: Thomas Lodge's *Workes of Josephus* as a Catholic Text," *Sixteenth–Century Journal* 34, no. 4 (2003): 993–1010, and Arthur F. Kinney, *Humanist Poetics: Thought, Rhetoric, and Fiction in 16th-Century England* (Amherst: U of Massachusetts P, 1986), 418–419.
2. This contrasts with Lodge's letter to William Trumbull of November 22, 1609 (quoted and discussed in Kinney, *Humanist Poetics* 390) in which he discusses history as a means toward self-reformation. Kinney points out the concordance of Lodge's views here with those expressed by the Greek historian Polybius, who stresses the relative painlessness of learning lessons from history. See Polybius, *Historia*, trans. W. R. Paton, Loeb Classical Library (Cambridge, MA: Harvard UP, 1937, this ed. 1975), 1.35.7—10, 98–99.
3. See Timothy Hampton, *Writing from History: The Rhetoric of Exemplarity in Renaissance Literature* (Ithaca, NY Cornell UP, 1990). On the place of history in the Renaissance curriculum, see Paul F. Grendler, *Schooling in Renaissance Italy, 1300–1600* (Baltimore: Johns Hopkins UP, 1989), 255–263.
4. See D. R. Woolf, *Reading History in Early Modern England* (Cambridge: Cambridge UP, 2000), 104–108. On women's recreational reading of history, see Louise Schleiner, *Tudor and Stuart Women Writers* (Bloomington: Indiana UP, 1994), 179.
5. See its dedication (sig. A2^v), and Hugh G. Dick, "Thomas Blundeville's *The true order and methode of writing and reading hystories* (1574)," *Huntington Library Quarterly* 3, no. 2 (1940): 149–170.
6. See J. H. M. Salmon, "Seneca and Tacitus in Jacobean England," in *The Mental World of the Jacobean Court*, ed. Linda Levy Peck (Cambridge: Cambridge UP, 1991), chap. 10.
7. See Paul Oscar Kristeller, *Renaissance Thought and the Arts* (Princeton: Princeton UP, 1990), 28.

8. For other occurrences of Grynaeus's essay, printed as a preface to early modern editions of classical historians or within early modern historiographical collections, see *Biographie universelle . . . nouvelle édition,* vol. 17 (Paris: Madame Desplaces/ M. Michaud, 1857), s.v. "Grynaeus."
9. Kinney, *Humanist Poetics* 364.
10. On the historian as counsellor, see D. R. Woolf, *The Idea of History in Early Stuart England: Erudition, Ideology, and "The Light of Truth" from the Accession of James I to the Civil War* (Toronto: U of Toronto P, 1990), chap. 5; and on moralistic reader-response, see Woolf, *Reading History,* 104–105.
11. The 1602 reading, "expect," is altered in later editions to "respect."
12. This is identified by Marta Straznicki and Richard Rowland as indebted to Montaigne's *Essais* 1.37: see the supplement to the introduction in *The Tragedy of Mariam,* ed. A. C. Dunstan with W. W. Greg, Malone Society Reprints (1914: this edition Oxford: Oxford University Press, 1992), xxv. On *Mariam*'s debt to Montaigne, see William M. Hamlin, "Elizabeth Cary's *Mariam* and the Critique of Pure Reason," *Early Modern Literary Studies,* 9, no. 1 (2003): 2.1–22 (http://purl.oclc.org/emls/09-1/hamlcary.html).
13. The story is told in Plutarch, "Life of Julius Caesar" (from *Lives,* trans. Bernadotte Perrin, Loeb Classical Library (Cambridge, MA: Harvard University Press, 1919, this ed. 1994), X:464–467).
14. Transcription adapted from Heather Wolfe, ed., *Elizabeth Cary, Lady Falkland: Life and Letters* (Cambridge and Tempe, AZ: RTM Publications and Arizona Center for Medieval and Renaissance Studies, 2001), 118–119.
15. See the discussion in Wolfe, *Elizabeth Cary,* 64–85.
16. Dympna Callaghan, "Re-reading Elizabeth Cary's *The Tragedie of Mariam, Faire Queene of Jewry,*" in *Women, "Race," and Writing in the Early Modern Period,* ed. Margo Hendricks and Patricia Parker (London and New York: Routledge, 1994), 165. For other critiques of the autobiographical approach, see Stephanie Hodgson-Wright, "The Canonization of Elizabeth Cary," in *Voicing Women: Gender and Sexuality in Early Modern Writing,* ed. Kate Chedgzoy, Melanie Hansen, and Suzanne Trill (Keele: Keele UP, 1996), 55–68; Marta Straznicky, "'Profane Stoical Paradoxes': *The Tragedie of Mariam* and Sidnean Court Drama," *English Literary Renaissance* 24, no. 1 (1994): 104–134; and Laurie J. Shannon, "*The Tragedie of Mariam:* Cary's Critique of the Terms of Founding Social Discourses," *English Literary Renaissance* 24, no. 1 (1994): 135–153. For a typical autobiographical reading, see Tina Krontiris, *Oppositional Voices: Women as Writers and Translators of Literature in the English Renaissance* (1992: repr. London: Routledge, 1997), chap. 3. Barbara Lewalski summarizes different views in *Writing Women in Elizabethan and Jacobean England* (Cambridge, MA: Harvard UP, 1993), 190–201.
17. This is one of the main arguments in Malvezzi's *Discourses upon Cornelius Tacitus* (summary from John M. Wallace, "Dryden and History: A Problem in Allegorical Reading," *English Literary History* 36 (1969): 265–290).

18. Alison Shell, *Catholicism, Controversy and the English Literary Imagination, 1558–1660* (Cambridge: Cambridge UP, 1999), chap. 4.
19. For Lodge's treatment of the story of Mariam, see *Workes*, 384, 387–388, 396–399, 589–590. Mariam's frowardness is commented upon in the margin on 398. However, as Catherine Belsey points out, the play makes it clear that Mariam's downfall is brought about by her specific defiance of Herod, rather than her general tendency to criticize. See Belsey, *The Subject of Tragedy: Identity and Difference in English Renaissance Drama* (London and New York: Methuen, 1985), 173.
20. See below, pp. 45.
21. See Earl Miner, ed., *Literary Uses of Typology from the Late Middle Ages to the Present* (Princeton: Princeton UP, 1977).
22. Barbara Lewalski, "Typological Symbolism and the Progress of the Soul in 17th-Century Literature," in Miner, *Literary Uses*, 79–114 (quotation from 81).
23. See David Lyle Jeffrey, ed., *A Dictionary of Biblical Tradition in English Literature* (Eerdmans: Michigan, 1992), 515. Though the Old Testament itself is not unambiguous, Miriam is traditionally referred to as Moses's sister: see Rita J. Burns, *Has the Lord Indeed Only Spoken through Moses? A Study of the Biblical Portrait of Miriam*, Society of Biblical Literature Dissertation Series 84 (Atlanta: Scholars Press, 1987), chap. 4. Cary's spelling may indicate that she is particularly stressing comparisons between her heroine and Miriam: in both his text and his index, Lodge usually spells Miriam as "Mariam" (referring to her as "Mary" at her death, 81), while Herod's queen is spelt "Mariamne" (a common, and probably the most usual, form elsewhere). "Miriam" is the Hebrew form of the name, "Mariam" the Greek (for a contemporary gloss, see Henry Ainsworth, *Annotations upon the second book of Moses* (this ed. 1617), sig. L3b).
24. Lodge even includes a countdown to Christianity in the margins of his translation: Kelly's, "Jewish History, Catholic Argument", argues that he is consciously returning to the Catholic tradition of using Josephus for biblical commentary (1000).
25. Miriam is seen by at least one twentieth-century scholar as a priestly figure: Burns, *Has the Lord*, chaps 3–4. However, Phyllis Trible argues that Miriam later functions as a means by which Mosaic orthodoxy is contested: "Subversive Justice: Tracing the Miriamic Traditions," in *Justice and the Holy: Essays in Honour of Walter Harrelson*, ed. Douglas A. Knight and Peter J. Paris (Atlanta: Scholars Press, 1989), 99–109.
26. Exodus 2 and 15; Jeremiah 31:4.
27. Exodus 15:20–21; Luke 1:46–55.
28. Cosma Magaliano, *Commentarii in canticum primum Mosis* (1619), 122. In her tract *A mouzell for Melastomus*, Rachel Speght uses the exemplar of Miriam to argue that women should be allowed to sing God's praises. See *The Polemics and Poems of Rachel Speght*, ed. Barbara Kiefer Lewalski (New York and Oxford: Oxford UP, 1996), 19.

29. Numbers 12. "Cushite" has sometimes been glossed as "Ethiopian": see Burns, *Has the Lord,* 68 (chap. 3 gives a general discussion of the episode). The incident may be obliquely recalled in the episode in *Mariam* where Mariam criticizes Salome's racial origins (discussed in Callaghan, "Re-reading *Mariam,*" 173).
30. Two essays in part three of Athalaya Brenner, ed., *A Feminist Companion to Exodus to Deuteronomy* (Sheffield: Sheffield Academic Press, 1994) give a full account of the issues, discussing the possibility of latent sympathy for Miriam within the text: Phyllis Trible, "Bringing Miriam out of the Shadows," 166–186, and Naomi Graetz, "Did Miriam Talk Too Much?," 231–242. See also the articles cited above in footnotes 23 and 25.
31. Maureen Quilligan, "Staging Gender: William Shakespeare and Elizabeth Cary," in *Sexuality and Gender in Early Modern Europe,* ed. James Grantham Turner (Cambridge: Cambridge UP, 1993), 208–232 (quotation 228); Burns, *Has the Lord,* 72; Trible, 176; *Mariam,* 3.3.183–184.
32. Identifying conscious transgression of the silent feminine ideal has become a commonplace within critical commentary on Renaissance-women's writing. For a recent discussion relating to Cary, see Karen Raber, *Dramatic Differences: Gender, Class and Genre in the Early Modern Closet Drama* (Newark and London: U of Delaware P and Associated University Presses, 2001), 153–156.
33. Henry Ainsworth, *Annotations upon the fourth book of Moses, called Numbers* (1619), sig. O3^r.
34. British Library, Add. MS 39828, fol. 59b (October 23, 1581).
35. Jonathan Marvil, for instance, believes Bacon unconsciously shaped Henry VII's character to take on lineaments similar to his own. See Marvil, *The Trials of Counsel: Francis Bacon in 1621* (Detroit, MI: Wayne State UP, 1976), 156ff. (esp. 194).
36. Judith H. Anderson, *Biographical Truth: The Representation of Historical Persons in Tudor-Stuart Writing* (New Haven: Yale UP, 1984), chap. 10, esp. 176, 202.
37. *De Augmentis,* in *Works,* ed. James Spedding et al. (London: Longman & Co., 1857–1874), 8:408.
38. See, most recently, Lisa Jardine and Alan Stewart, *Hostage to Fortune: The Troubled Life of Francis Bacon* (London: Gollancz, 1998), chap. 17.
39. *The philosophie, commonlie called the morals written by Plutarch* (1603), 63. See John M. Wallace, "'Examples Are the Best Precepts': Readers and meaning in Seventeenth-Century Poetry," *Critical Inquiry* 1 (1974–1975): 273–290.
40. The arguments in this paragraph are summarized from David Halsted, "Distance, Dissolution and Neo-Stoic Ideals: History and Self-definition in Justus Lipsius," *Humanistica Lovaniensia* 40 (1991): 262–274.
41. Halsted, 263.
42. Joan Parks, "Elizabeth Cary's Domestic History," in *Other Voices, Other Views: Expanding the Canon in English Renaissance Studies,* ed. Helen Ostovich, Mary V. Silcox, and Graham Roebuck (Newark and London: U of Delaware P and Associated University Presses, 1999), quotation from 187. Meredith Skura argues for "intriguing resemblances" not only between

Cary and Isabel but between Cary and Edward in "Elizabeth Cary and Edward II: What Do Women Want to Write?" *Renaissance Drama*, no. 27 (1996): 79–107. The 1996 edition was published in 1998. See also Margaret Reeves's essay in this collection.
43. Alexandra G. Bennett, "Female Performativity in *The Tragedy of Mariam*," *SEL: Studies in English Literature 1500–1900* 40, no. 2 (2000) quotations from 306.
44. The motto is mentioned in Wolfe, *Elizabeth Cary*, 118. See also Shari A. Zimmerman, "Disaffection, Dissimulation and the Uncertain Ground of Silent Dismission: Juxtaposing John Milton and Elizabeth Cary," *English Literary History* 66 (1999): 553–589.
45. In Thomas Bentley's *The Monument of Matrones* (1582), for instance, an angelic Mariam reproaches Herod with his decree concerning her execution in the event of his death. See "Seventh lampe of virginitie," in *The Early Modern Englishwoman: A Facsimile Library of Selected Works*, Series 3, selected by Colin B. Atkinson and Jo B. Atkinson (Aldershot: Ashgate, 2005), 323. Cary's Mariam is much less self-interested in her upbraidings of Herod, which refer to the death of her kinsmen rather than threats to her own person.

PART II

EDWARD II

CHAPTER 4

"ROYAL FEVER" AND "THE GIDDY COMMONS": CARY'S *HISTORY OF THE LIFE, REIGN, AND DEATH OF EDWARD II* AND THE BUCKINGHAM PHENOMENON

Curtis Perry

This chapter seeks to recover the political engagements implicit in Elizabeth Cary's *History of the Life, Reign, and Death of Edward II* (written ca. 1626–1627; printed 1680). Cary's *History* not only appropriates a genre of writing—Tacitean or political history, assumed to be a masculine preserve until much later—but it takes up a political fable, the story of King Edward II (1284–1327), that had already become deeply entangled with Jacobean and Caroline political controversy and that had obvious parallels with recent events in the public, political sphere.[1] The *History*'s engagement with contemporary current events has to do, of course, with the furor surrounding George Villiers, duke of Buckingham, whose career as court favorite to both James I and Charles I had made him the focal point of intense and sometimes violent political animosities by 1626. More precisely, Cary's *History* explores what I am here calling the Buckingham phenomenon: the meaning of the duke's career within the larger context of the controversy it occasioned. In response to the violent animosities and increasingly polarized political discourse of early Caroline England, Cary recasts the story of Edward II and his favorites in such a way as to anatomize the consequences of immoderate favoritism, showing how the intemperance of King Edward's affections leads to a scenario in which only unbalanced and immoderate responses are possible.

Cary's text responds, specifically, to the political conflicts laid open and exacerbated during 1626, when King Charles found himself needing to dissolve Parliament in order to stave off an attempt to impeach his favorite. Buckingham had been the great favorite of the second half of the reign of King James, and his perceived domination of the king's attention had generated a great deal of animosity among those who blamed him for administrative corruption and for encouraging James's irenic, diplomatic approach to Spain and the Palatinate. After the breakdown of negotiations over the proposed Spanish match for Prince Charles, Buckingham enjoyed brief popularity as a leading proponent of military opposition to Spanish interests. But the embarrassing failure of the naval expedition to Cadiz in 1625—organized by Buckingham in his capacity as Lord Admiral—helped to rekindle smoldering animosities and to renew concerns about the corruption and incompetence of the duke's administration. The first Caroline parliaments were dominated by efforts to redress grievances associated with the duke, and when Charles dissolved the Parliament in 1626 he issued a declaration chastising the "intemperate passions" displayed by the House of Commons in their pursuit of his favorite:

> That House, being abused, by the violent and ill advised passions of a few members of the House, for private and personall ends, ill beseeming publike persons trusted by their Countrey, as then they were, not onely neglected, but willfully refused to hearken to all the gentle admonitions which his Maiestie could give them; And neither did nor would intend any thing, but the prosecution of one of the Peeres of this Realme.[2]

These animosities spread well beyond Parliament, fuelled by newsletters and an avalanche of libels accusing the duke of cowardice, sexual transgressions, corruption, treason, and religious duplicity. Roger Lockyer, the duke's modern biographer, comments ruefully upon the "acute, almost paranoiac, suspicion which every move and gesture of Buckingham generated."[3] The political issues raised by Buckingham's career and the political turmoil it had caused were, by 1627, both complex and urgent; to say that Cary's text involves commentary on Buckingham is therefore only a starting point.

Cary's perspective on Buckingham must have been shaped by her ambivalent relationships with the duke and his family. During the period in which the *History* was written, Cary and her husband, Henry Cary, first Viscount Falkland, a client of the duke, were at odds, quarreling over Cary's formal conversion to Catholicism in 1626. The conversion, in fact, was made public by Buckingham's sister, Lady Denbigh, herself a crypto-Catholic and one of Cary's erstwhile friends. Outraged, Falkland attempted to cut off support to his wife. The letters that Cary wrote during this period seeking assistance elsewhere make reference to her friendship with Denbigh as well as with Buckingham's wife and mother.[4] More generally, as an associate of the so-called Durham House circle in the years leading up to her conversion, Cary is likely to have had a rather immediate interest in the growing conflict between Arminians and Calvinists that helped structure opposition to the duke. Buckingham's opponents accused him of aiding recusants and pointed suspiciously to the Catholic sympathies of his kinswomen, Cary's associates.[5]

As this thumbnail sketch suggests, Cary had a great deal of contact with Buckingham and his family and a real but complicated stake in the controversies surrounding him. I think it is plausible to suggest, as Louise Schleiner has done, that Cary wrote her *History* in order to help herself cope with "the enormously painful position of having to depend on Buckingham's relatives and subordinates."[6] I think it equally plausible, however, that she was interested in exploring the politics of favoritism for reasons beyond her personal entanglements with the duke and his family.[7] Buckingham was at the center of urgent political debate in 1626–1627, and anyone with an interest in England's future had to be concerned with him one way or another. Thus, Cary's text is interested in the corruption of favor, but also in the rhetorical duplicity of favoritism's opponents and—most of all—in the disfiguring influence of what Charles referred to as the age's "intemperate passions."

★★★★★

The story of Edward II is one of the most frequently retold historical tales of the English Renaissance. Cary, who read "History very universally, especially all ancient Greeke, and Roman Historians" and "all Choniclers what soever, of her owne Country," presumably was familiar with many versions of the story.[8] Cary was a dedicatee of Michael Drayton's, and so had likely read his versions of the story, and since Francis Hubert's verse history of Edward II (first composed in the 1590s and published in editions of 1628 and 1629) circulated in manuscript during the 1620s, Cary may have seen it as well.[9] Alongside these documentary sources, we might note that by 1626, the connection between Buckingham and the favorites of Edward II had taken on something of a life of its own in the culture's political imagination. The various invocations of this parallel add up to something like a nonliterary source that can help to explain both Cary's choice of material and her handling of it.

In the spring of 1621, Buckingham was compared to Edward II's favorite, Spencer, in an explosive session in the House of Lords. The speaker was Sir Henry Yelverton, a former attorney general with a history of conflict with Buckingham. He had been called to testify earlier about his role in the granting and enforcement of a controversial patent on gold and silver thread supported by Buckingham's brother. As efforts to redress grievances in the patent system came increasingly to focus on Buckingham's pernicious influence, Yelverton was resummoned at the request of the favorite's enemies to add further testimony about this patent and another on Inns granted to the notorious monopolist and Buckingham associate Sir Giles Mompesson. As was probably expected, Yelverton defended himself by blaming Buckingham, and added that the favorite should have "read the articles against Hugh Spencer in this place, for taking upon him to place and displace officers."[10]

The comparison caused an uproar and occasioned a heated debate about its meaning. Though some of Buckingham's opponents attempted to downplay the slander, King James felt himself implicated and expressed as much in no uncertain terms: "If he Spenser, I Edward 2, for theise are relatives, King and people, Master and servant, Father and sonne, and to reckon me with such a Prince is to esteeme me a weeke man and I had rather be noe kinge then such a one as Kinge Edward the 2nd."[11] In fact, James described any hesitation to punish Yelverton as an act of disobedience analogous to the revolt of Edward's peers: "If you sensure him [Yelverton] you doe well, but if you doe not you judge me and never any Monarch will be judged by his Nobility; noe more will I. For if you may judge of my honor you may depose me."[12] Yelverton was subsequently censured, fined, and imprisoned.

There is considerable evidence to suggest that this episode became notorious, not least because Yelverton's carefully circumscribed parallel was understood by contemporaries to invoke the whole sordid story of Edward II as a vehicle for understanding Buckingham's corrupting influence. Where Yelverton's comparison had alluded only to a specific parliamentary censure, contemporary accounts of the episode tended to retell it in more general and inflammatory terms. John Chamberlain wrote to Dudley Carleton, for example, reporting that Yelverton "indeavored to cast many aspersions upon the Lord of Buckingham and his regall authoritie (as he termed yt) . . . further comparing these times in some sort to those of Edward the second wherin the Spensers did so tirannise and domineer."[13] Here, as in other contemporary reports, Yelverton's parallel is treated as a general comparison between the Jacobean present and the reign of Edward II, and the attack on Buckingham becomes more vivid and damning.[14]

Tensions in the early Caroline parliaments of 1625 and 1626 brought back memories of the failure of the Parliament of 1621. There is considerable evidence, moreover, that Yelverton's parallel was remembered and that the story of Edward II and his disastrous favorites remained an important part of the imaginative vocabulary with which Buckingham's enemies conceptualized his pernicious influence on king and nation. In a speech prepared for the Parliament of 1625 (but apparently never delivered[15]), Robert Cotton and Sir Robert Phelips discuss how grievances like the ones associated with Buckingham had been handled in the past. Not surprisingly, Edward II and his favorites figure prominently in the piece's discussion of precedent:

> It was noe small motive to the Parliament H: 3 to banish the King's halfe Brothers for procuringe to themselves soe lardge proportion of the Crowne lands to the Kinges want.
> Gaveston & Spencer for doeinge the like for themselves & followers in Ed. 2. time, both exiled.[16]

Gaveston and Spencer are mentioned again in a discussion of ministers banished for engrossing "the person of the Kinge from his other Lords."[17]

This speech also bears some more specific signs of the cultural memory of Yelverton's controversial participation in the attack on Buckingham in 1621. Its brief enumeration of corrupt patents under Buckingham includes gold and silver thread—the patent about which Yelverton had been called upon to testify in 1621—and its discussion of corrupt patronage and the selling of titles recalls the same parliamentary censure of Spencer alluded to by Yelverton four years earlier:

> If worthie persons have byn advanced frely to places of greatest Trust, I shalbe gladd. Spencer was condemned in the 15 Ed. 2. for displaceing good servants about the Kinge, and puttinge in his freinds and followers. Not leaveinge way either in the Church or Commonwealth to any before a fine was paide to him or his dependants.[18]

These choices, I think, demonstrate a degree of continuity between attacks on Buckingham in 1621 and 1625.

Cary's *History*, much of which was probably written after Buckingham's parliamentary difficulties had been further exacerbated by the fiasco of 1626, draws upon this broad comparative framework. But in assessing the meaning of this ongoing political debate as a nonliterary source for Cary's work it is important to remember that Yelverton's notoriety—and thus the meaning of his inflammatory parallel—was decidedly mixed. To supporters of Buckingham, Yelverton's outburst was symptomatic of a dangerous trend toward seditious popularity. And this too was remembered during the contretemps of 1626. We see this, for instance, in a strikingly paranoid anonymous letter drawn up in support of Buckingham toward the tail end of the Parliament of 1626, after formal charges against him had been delivered.[19] This letter, from "Ignoto," treats opposition to Buckingham as a conspiracy fomented for the sake of mischief by duplicitous cadres of "King-haters."[20] Unchecked "Parliamentary discoursings," the letter opines, are "the certain symptoms of subsequent Rebellions, Civil Wars, and the dethroning of our kings," and so much of the document is taken up with enumerating the various seditious groups eager to attack the king through Buckingham.[21] Suggestively, Yelverton is one of only a handful of contemporaries mentioned by name as a censured malcontent eager to bring down the duke.[22] In fact, Yelverton had made efforts to reconcile himself to Buckingham by 1626, but this letter makes it clear that he was still remembered as a symbolic figure as a result of the outspokenness that got him censured in 1621.

Instead of remembering Yelverton's parallel as a useful way to understand Buckingham's corruption, "Ignoto" recalls his speech as exemplifying a brand of seditious criticism of favorites designed covertly to attack the monarchy and foment open rebellion. This recollection of Yelverton's speech recalls James's own shocked response to the parallel between Buckingham and Spencer, for James too understood Yelverton's implied comparison between Buckingham and Spencer as an attack upon his own administration and treated hesitation to punish Yelverton as analogous to open rebellion. This alternative version of Yelverton's parallel supplies the explicit conceit of a royalist response to Yelverton's outburst that seems to have been written for manuscript circulation in 1621. This tract, entitled "Observations concerning Sir Henrie Yelvertons Charge, his Answere thereunto, and his defence of that Answere in this present Parliamente," elaborates upon James's reaction by drawing a comparison between Yelverton's supporters and the rebellious subjects of Edward II himself:

> Observe, that this defence of Sir Henry Yelvertons, if hee might have Complices for his purpose, might prove as pernitious as the Archbishop of Canturburie his Theame att the deposition of King Edward 2d in Westminster being this Vox Populi Vox Dei. Oh take heede of Popularitie in a Monarchie: For though the Kinge had bene noe better then a Devill, yet neither his Barons, nor his Sonne, nor his Wife ought to have rebelled against him.[23]

Whereas for some Yelverton's parallel had implied criticism of Buckingham and commentary on corrupt favoritism, the author of these "Observations" sees it as a harbinger of dangerous popularity and rebellion. Elsewhere, the author of the "Observations" compares the disingenuousness of Yelverton's self-defense to the famous episode in the story of Edward II in which the king's execution is ordered in an unpunctuated Latin letter that could also be interpreted as a stay of execution. Yelverton, like the author of the unpointed letter, seeks both to attack the king and deny his intentions. Lest anyone miss the point of this comparison, the author of the "Observations" adds: "Read the interpretation of this Storie in Stowes Chronicle of Edward 2d, & marke the events, that followed upon this divelishe Amphibologie."[24]

Part of the utility of the Edward II story—one reason, that is, for its popularity throughout the Elizabethan and early Stuart period—is its complex and easily reversible political moral. It can be a story about the corruption of kingship and about unruly rebellion. In the wake of Yelverton's inflammatory outburst, and again as conflicts surrounding Buckingham deepened at the start of Charles's reign, the story of Edward II was reread simultaneously as a warning about the dangers of either domineering favorites or unruly popularity and unbridled speech. The contest over the meaning of the Edward II story thus runs parallel to the increasing polarization of late Jacobean and early Caroline political culture. Taking up the history of Edward II as Cary did therefore means inheriting a deeply contested story whose meaning is already entangled with contemporary political conflict and which had recently been adapted for simultaneous commentary upon different aspects of the turbulence surrounding the controversial duke of Buckingham.

★★★★★

In keeping with the recent history of this rich and contested political fable, Cary's version of the Edward II story is everywhere eager to engage, invoke, parallel, and comment upon key issues—favoritism, its corruption, the monarch's culpability, resistance, and rebellion—dredged up by the recurring conflicts surrounding Buckingham under both James and Charles. This is especially true of the folio version of the text which, in marked contrast to the shorter octavo version (also printed in 1680), sets the actions of its major players amid a world of court corruption designed to evoke concerns about Buckingham's monopoly of patronage and the politics of access.[25] For example, in the octavo version of the narrative, Edward's decision to recall Gaveston from banishment is motivated simply by passion and a pig-headed desire to assert his authority by "running in a direct train of opposition against his Predecessor's will."[26] The folio, by contrast, supplies an "oyly" tongued chamber page who advises the king to assert himself.[27] This, as the text makes clear, conflates criticism of Edward's own corrupted will with analysis of the way a monarch's errors can be magnified by the very institutions that govern access to him. The corrupting page has the king's ear because of his position in the chamber, and the text is explicit about the way corruption and the politics of access reinforce one another: "Court-corruption ingenders a world of these Caterpillers, that, to work their own ends, value not at one blow to hazard both the King and the Kingdom. The Errour is not so properly theirs, as their masters, who do countenance and advance such Sycophants" (9). Since Buckingham's power stemmed from his control of the Jacobean bedchamber, this version seems designed to locate the story of Edward II squarely within a world of corruption associated in the popular imagination with Buckingham himself. Once in power, Gaveston spreads corruption by replicating Edward's errors in judgment and choosing his servants "as his Master chose him." "Hence," the folio argues, "flew a world of wilde disorder" (20). This perspective broadens the scope of the text's concerns, showing how the court's "Caterpillers" are spawned. The folio version is likewise much more interested than the octavo in enumerating the cunning policy of Spencer, and it does so in ways that again treat the story as a refraction of concerns with Buckingham's monopoly of access and domination of patronage: "His first work is employ'd to win and to preserve an able party. To work this sure, he makes a Monopoly of the King's ear" (51).

Perhaps the single best example of the heightened topicality of the folio version is the account of Spencer's censure in the Parliament of White Bands (so called because of the liveries worn by the barons' yeomen guards). Where the octavo version of the story passes over this episode in two short sentences, the event is given four full pages in the folio, where it includes a long speech from Edward to the Parliament and a full enumeration of the charges brought against Spencer. Each of these embellishments, moreover, is designed specifically to remind readers of the controversy surrounding Buckingham in general, and specifically of the attempt to impeach him in the parliament of 1626. Edward's speech, to give one striking example, is a defense of prerogative and *arcana imperii* that nicely encapsulates the royalist response to Parliamentary attacks on Buckingham:

> Actions of State you may not touch but nicely, they walk not in the Road of vulgar Knowledge; these are high Mysteris of private workings, which foreright eyes can never see exactly . . . So grave a Senate should not be the meeting where men do hunt for News to feed their malice. Nor may you trench too near your Sovereigns actions, if they be such as not concern the Publick: You would not be restrain'd that proper freedom, which all men challenge in their private dwellings: My servants are mine own, I'll sift their errours, and in your just complaint correct their Vices. Seek not to bar me of a free election, since that alone doth fully speak my Power: I may in that endure no touch or cavil, which makes a King seem lesser than a Subject. (59)

The enumeration of specific charges against Spencer in the folio likewise seems designed to resonate with the fact that charges had been brought against Buckingham in the Parliament of 1626. First, Spencer is accused of using his influence to make corrupt appointments in the judicature and the church. The former undermines the law, since corrupted judges will accept bribes (an issue much in debate since 1621, when Buckingham's enemies in the House of Commons successfully challenged Francis Bacon). The latter of course alludes to Puritan opposition to Buckingham's church patronage. Spencer, like Buckingham, is also accused of selling titles, dominating royal patronage, and engrossing the "Royal ear" (62). Finally, the Parliament's objections that "Setling the strengths and Military Provision in the command of One so much insufficient, must open the way to foraign loss, or domestic mischief" (62) transparently reflects widespread concern about Buckingham's mismanagement of the admiralty. We might think of these charges against Spencer by comparison with Dr. Turner's famous queries in Commons in March of 1626.[28] These questions, which set the agenda for the House's inquiries, likewise accused the duke of weakening the realm's naval power, encouraging recusancy, selling titles, and monopolizing royal patronage to the detriment of the administration. It would have been hard for even a marginally informed reader to miss the topicality of Cary's account.

Asides on the pitfalls of royal misrule and favoritism are interlaced throughout the folio version of the text, and they often seem carefully designed to comment directly on early Caroline current affairs. The following piece of advice from Cary seems a remarkably bold and direct commentary on contemporary events, for instance, given the fact that Charles had just blocked parliamentary procedures against his favorite:

> If the tye of Duty and Allegeance preserve the Obedience to the Crown inviolate, let him beware that is the Prime Instrument, or Seducer; for he must be persecuted with implacable hatred, which ends not until he be made a Sacrifice to expiate and quench the fury, or the endangering of his Master by his unjust Protection. It is no less proper for the Majesty and Goodness of a King, in case of a general Complaint, to leave those great Cedars to the trial of the Law, and their own purgation; this makes known the integrity and equality of his Justice, which should not be extended to the grubbing up of Brambles and Shrubs, while monstrous Enormities of a greater height and danger scape unlopped. (158–159)

As with the Parliament of White Bands episode, added commentary of this kind directs the reader to contemporary analogy and signals Cary's interest in points of contact between the story of Edward II and recent turmoil over the politics of favoritism.

For all of its striking specificity of application, however, Cary's *History* is not designed to be read as a roman à clef. Parallels evoked with different persons or with recent political configurations sometimes overlap, and similarities between the actions of Cary's characters and contemporary events are sometimes conceived episodically rather than in terms of the narrative as a whole. In several cases, aspects of Cary's text seem designed to allude simultaneously to recent Caroline politics as well as to Jacobean political configurations. Though Cary's narrative clearly draws parallels between the reign of Edward II and the reign of James I (and thus between Isabel and Anna of Denmark, Gaveston and Somerset, Spencer and Buckingham), these overlap with the text's refraction of more contemporary events.[29] When Cary's Spencer rises to prominence, for example, his handling of Isabel is reminiscent of Buckingham's relationship with both Anna and Henrietta Maria:

> The *Queen,* that had no great cause to like those Syrens, that caus'd her grief, and did seduce her Husband, he [Spencer] yet presumes to court with strong professions, vowing to serve her as a faithful Servant. She seeing into the quality of the time, where he was powerful, and she in name a Wife, in truth a Hand-maid, doth not oppose, but more increase his Greatness, by letting all men know that she receiv'd him. To win a nearer place in her opinion, he gains his Kindred places next her person; and those that were her own, he bribes to back him. (52)

This detail (omitted in the octavo) seems to allude simultaneously to what Barbara Lewalski calls Anna's "course of politic accommodation" with her husband's favorite and also to the fact that Buckingham had indeed installed his own kin (and Cary's closest allies)—his mother, wife, and sister—into Henrietta Maria's bedchamber as part of his attempts in 1626 to neutralize that queen's hostility.[30]

Similarly, though Cary's Gaveston may recall James I's earlier, Scottish favorite Somerset (he is a foreign favorite whose influence, though decried, seems comparatively benign next to the machinations of his native successor who already knows the "plain-song of the State" and is thus more dangerous [51]), complaints about Gaveston's domination of patronage in the first portion of the book would probably have reminded readers more vividly of recent complaints about Buckingham's monopoly of royal patronage: "No man may now have the King's ear, hand, or purse, but he's the Mediator; his Creatures are advanc'd, his Agents fourish, and poorest Grooms become great Men of Worship" (27). The *History* is allusive in multiple ways in that it is animated by the renewed and heightened political conflicts of 1625–1627 but shaped—as were the reactions of many early Caroline observers—by the experience of conflicts over favoritism that unfolded during James's reign.

Cary is in fact quite cagey about the relationship between Jacobean scandal and the persistence of Buckingham's monopoly of royal favor in the newly formed court of Charles I. On the one hand, the text's descriptions of Edward's inability to control his passionate affections draw upon a tradition of criticism of James I's irresponsible favoritism. It was James, much more than Charles, who seemed to contemporaries to be in the thrall of favorites such as Somerset and Buckingham. The *History*'s insistence upon the sheer besottedness of Edward would likely have pointed readers back to James, and Cary points out quite early on that Edward "could not have been so unworthy a Son so noble a Father, nor so inglorious a father of so excellent a Son, if either Vertue or Vice had been hereditary" (2). This seems designed to draw a distinction between James's flawed nature and Charles's own, as if to exonerate Charles from the sins of his father. On the other hand, the text alludes specifically to conflicts exacerbated by Charles's continuing support for Buckingham, and the summative commentary at the end of Cary's history welcomes this application fairly overtly:

> If the Masters actions be never so pure and innocent, yet if out of affection he become the Patron of the Servants misdemeanours and insolencies, by protecting or not punishing, he makes himself guilty, and shares both in the grievance and hatred of the poor distressed Subject ... he that will read the History of our own, or those of Forreign Nations, shall finde a number of memorable Examples, which have produced Deposition of Kings, Ruine of Kingdoms, the Effusion of Christian Blood, and the general Distemper of that part of the world, all grounded on this occasion. (141)

This rather ominous-sounding admonition seems aimed directly at Charles I, whose personal style, as contemporaries noted, was far more ceremonial and decorous than that of his father, but who nevertheless had just sheltered Buckingham from the grievances of subjects by dissolving Parliament to avoid his impeachment. Cary may be returning to a story easily associated with the passionate favoritism of James I, but she is clearly interested in Charles as well. This is in keeping with the kind of cumulative exemplarity that the Edward II story seems more generally to have had, as a link between opposition to Buckingham in 1621 and 1626. We might say that Cary's *History* responds to very recent events, but it does so in a broadly allusive manner that draws on Jacobean as well as Caroline history and reflects an interest in the way the same deep problems and conflicts can recur in different configurations. Edward's reign parallels James's, and *both* cast light upon problems bedeviling Charles's.

Though several episodes allude fairly directly to concerns about Buckingham, at least one is laid out in such a way as to allude to concerns about Buckingham's opponents. This comes early on, as the peers, "whose noble hearts disdain'd to suffer basely" at the favorite's hands, decide to "feel their Soveraign's pulses" in order to gauge the depth of his devotion to his unworthy minion (22). They are contemplating open rebellion, but approach the king with great delicacy. Lincoln, accordingly, addresses the king as follows:

> See here (my Liege) your faithful though dejected servants, that have too long cry'd ayme to our Afflictions; we know you in your self are good, though now seduced; the height is such, we fear a coming Ruine. Let it not taint your ear to hear our sorrow, which is not ours alone, but all the Kingdoms, that groan and languish under this sad burden. (22)

Though we are supposed to agree with its enumeration of the problems Gaveston has caused, there is something duplicitous in the way this speech is set up here. For one thing, professions of faithful service ring hollow when coming from subjects who have just resolved "to cure the State" of the king's errors "or make the Quarrel fatal" (22). For another, there may be some tension between the profession of public interest and the sting of personal affront that motivates the peers. Most jarring, though, is the rhetorical attempt to separate the king's virtue from the vice of his seducer—"we know you in yourself are good, though now seduced"— which comes across as an empty formula in the context of Cary's narrative, with its clear emphasis on Edward's accountability. One simply does not accept that Lincoln—speaking on behalf of the peers—believes this, especially since he expresses the opposite sentiment a few pages later: "Your Soveraign cares not how long the State be gutted, so he may enjoy his wanton Pleasures" (34).

From the perspective of Buckingham's supporters and perhaps Charles himself, the duke's enemies used this same disingenuous rhetoric to cloak a deeper and more troublingly rebellious animosity to the monarchy itself. In his 1626 letter, "Ignoto" lashes out at those who, like Lincoln, claim that attacking the favorite stems from loyalty to king and nation. Instead, the letter opines, the nation's unrest is "stirred up and maintained by such, who . . . seek the debasing of this free Monarchy; which because they find not yet ripe to attempt against the King himself, they endeavor it through the Dukes side."[31] As parliamentary attack on Buckingham intensified in March of 1626, Charles I also expressed the belief that attacks on the favorite were really veiled attempts to "wound the honour and government of himself and his father."[32] The rhetoric that Cary puts in the mouths of the peers at this point in the text would have been more likely to seem disingenuous then than now, I think, since in the overheated political debates of early Caroline England such disclaimers accompanying attacks on the favorite were so frequently denounced. The opening of Lincoln's speech is designed to be legible as the rhetoric that rebellion uses to cloak itself in the mantle of public interest. This in turn makes available a parallel between the barons' hollow protestation of loyalty and the kind of self-protecting speech excoriated as "divelishe Amphibologie" in Yelverton and his allies.

For the most part, the resistance of the peers would seem to be justified in Cary's eyes. But the questionable nature of Lincoln's address to Edward II is an example of the folio's heightened interest in the ambiguities of political motive. To some degree this is a formal development, a result of the folio's long dramatic speeches that of necessity focus attention on character and motivation. But the text's interest in the duplicity of political posturing runs deeper than that. When, after Edward's deposition, Mortimer takes the lead in securing his execution, Cary's text goes out of its way to underscore the enigmatic quality of Isabel's motivation: "The Queen, whose heart was yet believed innocent of such foul Murther, is, or at least seems, highly discontented" (151). The octavo version of this exchange omits this quality of willful enigma, painting the queen as merely innocent: "The Queen, whose Heart was yet innocent of so deep a Transgression, was deeply and inwardly troubled with this unhappy Proposition" (octavo, 71). It is suggestive of the tenor of the times that the folio's more overt topicality should be accompanied by this increased interest in the ambiguity of political motive. It is as if the closer the text comes to mirroring contemporary conflicts, the more it reflects the mutual suspiciousness characteristic of the moment's political paranoia.

★★★★★

In order to understand Cary's nuanced response to "the violent and ill advised passions" swirling around Buckingham during the early years of Charles's reign, it is necessary to attend to the larger conceptual architecture underpinning her historical narrative. The *History,* as I have argued elsewhere, is structured by Cary's interest in the centrifugal movement of immoderate passion outward from the breast of Edward II, so that we see personal misrule translated into political corruption fuelled by the intemperate ambition of his favorites, and this translated in turn to civil conflict in which Mortimer, the queen, and their rebellious followers become unruly passion's avatars.[33] Instead of seeing individual characters as Cary's focal points, it is useful to think of the text's narrative as organized primarily around passion's charge as it moves from from king to court to realm.

This narrative structure is counterintuitive to modern readers since it subordinates character to theme, but it is actually a conventional early modern conceptualization of political unrest, legible in other writers whose interest in the politics of passion, like Cary's, was derived from classical and neo-Stoic sources. There are similarly centrifugal narratives of passionate misrule, for example, in Sackville and Norton's court drama *Gorboduc* (in which the disorderliness of passionate rivalry moves outward from the royal family to civil war) or Jonson's *Sejanus* (in which the immoderate passions that originally fuel court corruption eventually find expression in terrifying mob violence). In fact, Cary's interest in the centrifugal movement of disorderly passion is very much in keeping with the kind of reading that she grew up on, at least according to her filial biographer. She is said to have admired Seneca and indeed to have translated his moral epistles at a young age, and also to have read broadly in classical and contemporary history.[34] The conceptual world of *The History of the Life, Reign, and Death of Edward II* seems to me to owe a great deal both to Seneca and Tacitus in its interest in material causes of historical events, in its aggressive paralleling of contemporary controversies, and in its Stoic emphasis upon the way failures of self-government find symptomatic expression in broader political unrest.

The *History* falls into three parts. The first of these, comprising the period of Edward's infatuation with Gaveston, is preoccupied with the king's inability to regulate his passions, a moral weakness that Cary characterizes as "Royal Fever" (16). This moral weakness makes him vulnerable to Gaveston's charms, but also makes him generally prone to respond to challenges in an irrational and violent manner. Immoderation equals tyranny, as the king's failure of self-government translates into failures of government: "It is a very dangerous thing when the head is ill, and all the Members suffer by his infirmity" (44). The second portion of the text, which runs roughly from the death of Gaveston to the invasion of Isabel's supporters, shifts the focus from the operation of "Royal Fever" to its primary symptom, the cunning ambition of the favorite. This portion of the story, which alludes most pointedly to complaints about Buckingham, tends to treat the favorite Spencer as the agent of misrule, relegating the king's corrupted will to a secondary position. Spencer is here characterized as a figure of passionate and greedy ambition incapable of remaining within moral compass, and the king as a besotted bystander content to let his favorite prey upon his subjects. The final portion of the narrative focuses upon Isabel's "unruly conquest" (124) of England and on the violence of "the giddy Commons" (123). Isabel's actions, in this part of the story, savor "more of a savage, tyrannical disposition than a judgment fit to command" (129), and she unleashes the "heady monster Multitude" who "never examine the Justice, or the dependence, but are led by Passion and Opinion" (121). This savage denouement is the logical culmination of a narrative that moves systematically from an "unnatural Civil War" (8) played out within Edward's own breast to civil war played out in earnest on the soil of England.

This conception of the meaning of the story encapsulates Cary's complex reaction to the controversy surrounding Buckingham and helps make sense of its moral ambiguities. On the one hand, the *History* is quite consistent about blaming England's troubles on the king's personal misrule and the predation of his favorites. Cary treats the latter as a symptom of the former, but in general this anatomy of unrest would probably have appealed to those opponents of Buckingham who saw him as another Spencer. On the other hand, the clear condemnation of rebellion at the end of the text resonates with the fears of those who felt that attacks on the favorite were disingenuous forerunners of more dangerously antimonarchical attitudes tending toward open rebellion and the overthrow of the monarchy itself. Criticism of the duke notwithstanding, the increasingly outspoken and sometimes violent opposition he provoked seemed equally worrisome. In October 1626, for example, Buckingham's coach was demolished by a mob of sailors upset over lack of pay. This was not the first such outburst, and a guard was subsequently appointed to keep watch over the duke's house.[35] Cary's narrative allows for a double perspective in which both the king and the rebels are wrong because each is impelled by rebellious passions, and this in turn functions as a sophisticated and balanced response to a perceived political crisis.

If Cary's narrative structure is designed to anatomize the destructiveness of immoderate passions, it does so at the expense of consistent characterization. Edward II is proactive during the first portion of the text and rather passive during the second part. Spencer, who is completely monstrous during the second section of the text, dies valiantly at the hands of Isabel in the final section (129–130). The barons are mostly depicted in a positive light during the first two-thirds of the *History,* but are represented by the ambitious and violent Mortimer during the last portion. And Isabel, who is a highly sympathetic character capable of mastering her passions during the section of the text that is primarily concerned with Spencer's predation, is seized by ambition and finally becomes a tyrant. Since criticism of the *History* has hitherto focused predominantly on the character of Isabel, the change in her character has been the subject of some debate. Gwynne Kennedy, whose study of the representation of women's anger is among the more perceptive readings of the *History,* notes that Cary revises her source material to emphasize Isabel's cruelty in the last portion of the text. But, as Kennedy also notes, critics interested in Isabel have tended to downplay the character's transformation, finding it difficult to reconcile the vengeful Isabel with the more positive figure earlier on.[36] This difficulty dissolves as soon as one realizes that the transformation of Isabel is a function of the text's larger narrative logic.

Kennedy points out that the furious and violent Isabel of the *History*'s final section embodies a stereotypical notion of female moral weakness according to which women were thought to be capable of violence because they were overly susceptible to passion.[37] But in this regard, too, Isabel's misrule can be seen as the symbolic culmination of a centrifugal progress that begins with the king's own "effeminate disposition" (13). Effeminacy, understood this way, is likewise associated in the text with the king's sodomitical desire (Gaveston and Spencer are each described as his Ganymedes [4, 54]), and the link is clear if we recall that in the early modern period "sodomy represented desire unfettered, appetite ruling the mind rather than ruled by it. Sodomy was less about desiring men than about desiring everything."[38] Effeminacy describes failed self-government, which is in turn associated with other failures of government, so that for instance it is Edward's "effeminate weakness" (24), that prevents him from dealing forcefully with the rebellious barons.

One effect of the text's pervasive interest in the gendered language of passion, though, is to put pressure on the difference between gender as a biological fact and gender as a symbolic language. Cary seems specifically interested in the gap between these ways of thinking about gender, and the dissonance becomes prominent in the final section of the *History*. Cary sums up her condemnation of Isabel for the execution of Arundel by opining, rather dismissively, that "we may not properly expect Reason in Women's actions" (130). Though this seems to ratify the link between effeminacy and passion, it sits uneasily within a text that has also shown Isabel acting quite rationally under extreme pressure. Here is Cary on Isabel just before the latter's journey to France: "Reason . . . o'ercame her Sexes weakness, and bids her rather cure, than vent her Passion" (90). This could simply be another of the text's inconsistencies of character, but my sense is that Cary is here manufacturing this uneasiness to comment on the vacuity of gendered language for passion in a world dominated by rebellious monsters. What does it mean, the text seems to be asking, to treat Isabel's passion as typical for a woman if it is also seen as symptomatic of a world destabilized by the unruliness of the men at the top?

One way to think about this dissonance would be to say that the interrogation of the terms of the gendered language of virtue in *The History of the Life, Reign, and Death of Edward II* inverts and extends the analysis of gender undertaken in Cary's much earlier and better known *Tragedy of Mariam*. That play, as Laurie Shannon has brilliantly described, puts pressure on the implicit gendering of constancy as a masculine, political virtue by examining the predicament of a heroine who would seek to embody it in the face of political and domestic tyranny.[39] This text, by contrast, scrutinizes the gendering of moral inconstancy through its characterization of Isabel, a woman who becomes stereotypically "effeminate" only insofar as she gets caught up in passionate imbalance that is already characteristic of the predominantly masculine public sphere. I think it is possible, along these lines, to read Cary's *History* in feminist terms as an attempt to intervene in the discourses governing the gendering of virtue. But in order to read the text in this way—that is, to gain access to Cary's sophisticated thinking about gender—we must also learn to factor in her complex response to the political milieu in which she wrote and lived.

NOTES

1. Devoney Looser's study of early women historians, *British Women Writers and the Writing of History, 1670–1820* (Baltimore: Johns Hopkins UP, 2000), begins its narrative in 1670.
2. *A Declaration of the True Causes which moved His Majestie to Assemble, and After Inforced Him to Dissolve the Two Last Meetings in Parliament* (London, 1626), 19–20.
3. Roger Lockyer, *Buckingham: The Life and Political Career of Geoge Villiers, First Duke of Buckingham 1592–1628* (London: Longman, 1981), 359.
4. Cary's letters are available in *Elizabeth Cary, Lady Falkland: Life and Letters* ed. Heather Wolfe (Cambridge and Tempe, AZ: RTM Publications and Arizona Center for Medieval and Renaissance Studies, 2001).
5. After Buckingham's assassination in 1628, Cary may have written an epitaph for him that appears in numerous manuscript collections of the period. See Nadine Akkerman's chapter in this volume.
6. Louise Schleiner, *Tudor and Stuart Women Writers* (Bloomington: Indiana UP, 1994), 189.
7. Compare Meredith Skura, "Elizabeth Cary and Edward II: What Do Women Want to Write," *Renaissance Drama* ns 27 (1996): 79–104.
8. Wolfe, *Elizabeth Cary*, 212.
9. See Virginia Brackett, "Elizabeth Cary, Drayton, and Edward II," *Notes and Queries* ns 41 (1994): 517–519.
10. Samuel Rawson Gardiner, ed., *Notes of the Debates in the House of Lords*, (London: Printed for the Camden Society, 1870), 48.
11. Lady De Villiers, ed., "The Hastings Journal of the Parliament of 1621," *Camden Miscellany* 20 (London: Printed for the Camden Society, 1953), 33.
12. De Villiers, 33.
13. N. E. McClure, ed., *The Letters of John Chamberlain*, 2 vols. (Philadelphia: American Philosophical Society, 1939), 2:369.
14. For further discussion and more examples see Curtis Perry, "Yelverton, Buckingham, and the Story of Edward II in the 1620s," *Review of English Studies*, ns 54 (2003): 313–335.
15. Kevin Sharpe, *Sir Robert Cotton, 1586-1631: History and Politics in Early Modern England* (Oxford: Oxford UP, 1979), 177–180.

16. Sir John Eliot, *An Apology For Socrates and Negotium Posterorum*, 2 vols., ed. Alexander Grosart (privately printed, 1881), 1:145. I have silently expanded some abbreviations for clarity.
17. Eliot, 1:147.
18. Eliot, 1:145.
19. The letter is reprinted in *Cabala, Sive Scrinia Sacra* (3rd ed., London, 1691), 255–257. See also Richard Cust, *The Forced Loan and English Politics, 1626–1628* (Oxford: Clarendon Press, 1987), 20–22.
20. *Cabala*, 257.
21. *Cabala*, 256.
22. *Cabala*, 256.
23. For a transcription of this document, see Perry, "Yelverton," 313–335. I quote here from 335.
24. Perry, "Yelverton," 334.
25. See Barbara Kiefer Lewalski, *Writing Women in Jacobean England* (Cambridge: Harvard UP, 1993), 317–318.
26. *The History of the Most Unfortunate Prince King Edward II* (London, 1680), 4. Subsequent citations will be given parenthetically.
27. E. F. [Elizabeth Cary, Lady Falkland], *The History of the Life, Reign, and Death of Edward II* (London, 1680), 9. Subsequent citations will be given parenthetically.
28. For Turner's questions see *Proceedings In Parliament, 1626*, 4 vols., ed. William B. Bidwell and Maija Jannson (New Haven: Yale UP, 1991–1996), 2:261–62, 268. For the articles of impeachment brought against Buckingham see 1:463–77.
29. On these parallels see Lewalski 204–205, and Schleiner, *Tudor and Stuart Women Writers*, 189.
30. Lewalski, 205; Cust, 25. Compare Karen Nelson, "Elizabeth Cary's *Edward II*: Advice to Women at the Court of Charles I," in *Women, Writing, and the Reproduction of Culture in Tudor and Stuart Britain*, ed. Mary E. Burke, Jane Donawerth, Linda L. Dove, and Karen Nelson (Syracuse: Syracuse UP, 2000), 157–173.
31. *Cabala*, 255.
32. Quoted in Cust, 17.
33. See Curtis Perry, *Literature and Favoritism In Early Modern England* (Cambridge: Cambridge UP, 2006), 216–227.
34. See Wolfe, *Elizabeth Cary*, 106, 111, 212.
35. Lockyer, 342–343.
36. Gwynne Kennedy, *Just Anger: Representing Women's Anger In Early Modern England* (Carbondale: Southern Illinois UP, 2000), 93–112.
37. Kennedy, 108.
38. Cynthia Herrup, *A House in Gross Disorder: Sex, Law, and the 2nd Earl of Castlehaven* (New York: Oxford UP, 1999), 33.
39. Laurie Shannon, *Sovereign Amity: Figures of Friendship in Shakespearean Contexts* (Chicago: U of Chicago P, 2002), 70–86.

CHAPTER 5

"FORTUNE IS A STEPMOTHER": GENDER AND
POLITICAL DISCOURSE IN ELIZABETH CARY'S
HISTORY OF EDWARD II

Mihoko Suzuki

The History of Edward II was published in 1680, during the Exclusion Crisis, and was attributed to Elizabeth Cary's husband, Lord Falkland.[1] Although scholars now accept the work as having been authored by Cary, it is unlike her more frequently discussed *Tragedie of Mariam* in that it is marked by the difficulty, though not impossibility—as I will argue—of locating a gendered, female author in the text. This difficulty is exacerbated by the genres to which the text belongs—history and political thought, the "public" genres considered to be most inhospitable to women authors in the early modern period.[2]

The genres of history and political thought were inextricably linked in the early modern period, and Cary's *Edward II* follows in this tradition. While Barbara Lewalski has noted that Cary uses historians such as Thucydides, Livy, Sallust, and Tacitus in fashioning her own history, it has not been noted that Cary also explicitly refers to Machiavelli, and, in naming her text a "History," asks that her work be read in relation to other political theorists as well.[3] Jean Bodin says in his *Method for the Easy Comprehension of History* (1565): "History teaches us . . . which laws are most desirable, which state is the best," and devotes his lengthy chapter 6 to discussing the different types of government.[4] In *Clio Unbound,* the intellectual historian Arthur Ferguson observes that political narratives in the early modern period were customarily designated as "histories."[5] Conversely, Stuart political thinkers routinely deployed the histories of Tacitus to advance their antimonarchical position.[6]

The publication of Cary's history in 1680 during the Exclusion Crisis when monarchical prerogative was again under debate and Charles II was under attack for ceding too much power to his mistresses (as Edward II was criticized for being under the sway of his favorites) indicates that its publisher, though not crediting Cary as author, considered it an effective intervention in the contemporary political situation. In examining John Locke in his historical context, Richard Ashcraft has called for a widening of the history of political thought to consider political philosophy along with "political pamphleteering."[7] Following and extending Ashcraft's call, and applauding the recent inclusion of the writings of Christine de Pizan and Margaret Cavendish in the series "Cambridge Texts in the History of Political Thought," I suggest that the history of political thought should begin to include and consider women's political writings, such as Cary's *History of Edward II,* as significant contributions and interventions.

In order to achieve this more expansive understanding of the history of political thought, Cary's text must be placed in the context of canonical texts of political theory in England and on the continent (especially France, to which she maintained a close connection), as well as of lesser-known contemporary interventions, in particular, examples of English Catholic and French Protestant monarchomachy. To this end, I will focus first on Cary's use of and divergence from Machiavelli's *The Prince* and *Discourses,* then will juxtapose Cary's gendered critique of the hierarchical metaphor of the body politic with Christine de Pizan's in *The Book of the Body Politic.* The second part of this chapter will take up Cary's place in the tradition of English political thought that advances limited monarchy, whose chief exemplars are John of Salisbury and John Fortescue, and her relation to late sixteenth- and early seventeenth-century English Catholic and French Protestant proponents of monarchical resistance, with a focus on Robert Parsons and the anonymous *Vindiciae, contra Tyrannos,* which saw many editions and translations between 1579 and 1660, and which was often published as a separately paginated supplement to Machiavelli's *The Prince.*[8]

REVISING MACHIAVELLI

Early in *Edward II,* Cary criticizes Edward's favorite, Gaveston, for falling short of the standard of what she calls "*Machiavilian* States-men," by displaying "publick hatred" and failing to "disguise [his] aims with Vizards, which see and are not seen, while they are plotting." Since "he that will work in State, and thrive, must be reserved," Cary even goes so far as to suspect that her source is inaccurate in stating that Gaveston is Italian.[9] In *The English Face of Machiavelli,* Felix Raab has shown that the general tenor of political writing during the period 1603–1640 was hostile, or at best ambivalent, to Machiavelli, with very few notable exceptions, such as Henry Wright's *The First Part of the Disquisition of Truth, Concerning Political Affaires* (1616), which draws on Machiavelli as a source of sound political wisdom.[10] Needless to say, Raab's 1964 study does not include mention of *The History of Edward II*. Cary's notable departure from the prevailing opinion on Machiavelli may be explained partly by her Catholicism, for she does not share her contemporaries' popular hostility toward Italy and Italians, which were associated with Catholicism. Significantly, it is neither Gaveston, nor even the wily Spencer, the favorite who succeeds Gaveston in Edward's affections, but Isabel, Edward's queen, who exemplifies qualities of Machiavellian statecraft, which perhaps not coincidentally accord with the motto she had inscribed on her daughter's wedding ring, "BEE AND SEEME."[11] By contrast with Gaveston, Isabel "advances her own affairs by all means possible: She courts her Adversary with all the shews of perfect reconcilement" (90). Although Spencer suspected "her Cunning," and although he himself was "as cunning as a Serpent," he "findes here a female Wit that went beyond him" (90–91). For example, Cary praises Isabel's judgment for being "so fortunate" when she "pretend[s] a Journey of Devotion to St *Thomas* of *Canterbury;* which by her jealous Overseers . . . is wholly unsuspected" (91). Isabel's shrewdness enables her to prevail over Spencer, despite her disabling gender, so that Spencer is "thus over-reach'd by one weak Woman" (92). Here Isabel overcomes her disability as a woman but also uses others' expectations of her to her advantage and lulls her adversaries into complacency: as one of them states, "Alas, what can the Queen a wandring Woman compass, that hath nor Arms, nor Means, nor Men, nor Money?" (93). Spencer in fact knows Isabel to be "a Woman of a strong Brain, and stout Stomack, apt on all occasions to trip up his heels, if once she found him reeling" (86–87). By contrast, the king mistakenly and fatally believes his monarchical and patriarchal prerogatives to be unassailable: "The King, a Sovereign, Father, and a Husband, did hope these Titles would be yet sufficient to guard his Life, if not preserve his Greatness; but they prov'd all too weak" (126).

Cary goes on to devote the second part of *Edward II* to the rise of Isabel, beginning with the decline of Edward: "Fortune, that triumphs in the Fall of Princes, like a Stepmother, rests not where she frowneth, till she have wholly ruin'd and o'rethrown their Power, that do precede or else oppose her Darlings" (127). This reference to the famous allegory in *The Prince* of Fortune as a woman who must be mastered by a Prince exhibiting *virtù* exemplifies Cary's use of and departure from Machiavelli. As Hanna Fenichel Pitkin has shown, Machiavelli's text insistently constructs political agency as masculine—in this example of the sexual mastery of

Fortune, as well as in the figuration of Italy as a woman who will welcome a redeeming prince as her lover.[12] While following Machiavelli's gendering of Fortune, Cary's text departs from his representation of a sexual relationship between the masculine ruler and feminine Fortune by calling Fortune a "Stepmother" to Edward and by featuring Queen Isabel as Fortune's "Darling." In thus designating Isabel as a favorite of Fortune, Cary suggests a surprising link between Isabel and Edward's favorites Gaveston and Spencer; this link prepares the way for Cary's severe condemnation of Isabel's exercise of power.

Although Machiavelli considers Fortune's favors to be beneficial to a prince, Cary turns against Isabel after Fortune has shifted from favoring Edward to favoring Isabel: Cary harshly criticizes Isabel's "Tyranny" and her departure from "her former Vertue and Goodness" when she gratuitously insults and exults over Spencer. Cary's criticism of Isabel is not solely based on considerations of realpolitik, as it would be if she were following *The Prince,* but also on ethical considerations: Isabel's ostentatious humiliation of Spencer "savour'd more of a savage, tyrannical disposition, than a judgement fit to comand, or sway the Sword of Justice . . . It was at best too great and deep a blemish to suit a Queen, a Woman, and a Victor" (129). The apposition of "a Woman" and "a Victor" indicates that the two terms are not in contradiction—as they would be in Machiavelli; at the same time, Cary criticizes Isabel for falling short of ethical and political standards.[13]

While Machiavelli provides a framework for Cary's political discourse, Cary departs from his strict gendering of political agency as *virtù* by her focus on Isabel as an exemplum.[14] In *The Prince,* where exempla of male rulers predominate, Machiavelli briefly discusses in chapter 20 Caterina Sforza as a negative example of a ruler who mistakenly trusted in a fortress rather than the goodwill of her own people; their alliance with Cesare Borgia made her vulnerable to his attack. *The Discourses* includes, in addition to a chapter on "How Women have Brought About the Downfall of States" (III.26), another brief, but memorable, account of the widowed Sforza: the "Madonna of Forlì" defended the citadel against attackers who had taken her children hostage and defied them by "expos[ing] her sexual parts to them and said she was still capable of bearing more."[15] Through this striking gesture, Machiavelli reduces Sforza to the fact of her sex and her reproductive function.

While Cary, unlike Machiavelli in his treatments of Sforza, emphasizes Isabel's ability as a ruler, she nevertheless excoriates Isabel's lack of what she calls "female pity" (72), just as she criticized Edward's ruthlessness when he executed his rebellious subjects. Edward's lapse is not only an ethical error but also a political one: "So many excellent lives, so ingloriously lost, had been able to have commanded a victorious Army while it had triumpht in some forrain conquest" (73). By showing how both examples of "Tyranny" have political consequences and contribute to the weakening of the ruler, Cary accomplishes a complex and multifaceted gendered critique of and intervention in Machiavellian political thought.

Despite these explicit references to *The Prince*, the political thought developed in *Edward II* owes more to Machiavelli's *Discourses*. For example, Cary criticizes Edward for following his private will and not being bound by laws or considerations of the common good, in a manner that recalls Machiavelli's excoriation of tyrants for "forsaking virtuous deeds, considered that princes have nought else to do but to surpass other men in extravagance, lasciviousness, and every other form of licentiousness" (I.2, 107). According to Machiavelli, such a state of affairs leads to a revolt of *la moltitudine* and *i potenti;* the governments thus formed are legitimate as long as the people "rule[d] in accordance with the laws" and "subordinate[d] their own convenience to the common advantage," but they soon degenerate to "avarice and ambition"(I.2, 108).

This devolution corresponds closely to the shift in Cary's representation of both Isabel and the masses. Cary initially affirms the worth of the Commons and the legitimacy of their grievance against Edward: "The subjects sensible of the disorders of the Kingdom, and seeing into the advantage which promis'd a liberty of Reformation, make choice of such as for their wisdom and integrity deserv'd it" (58). Calling the Commons a "goodly body," Cary affirms their judgment against Spencer: "*Spencer* is pointblank charg'd with *Insolency, Injustice, Corruption, Oppression, neglect of the publick and immoderate advancement of his own particular*" (61). Yet she later becomes more critical of them as they become unruly and violent: "But the actions of this same heady monster Multitude never examine the Justice, or the dependance, but are led by Passion and Opinion; which in fury leaves no Disorder inacted, and no Villainy unattempted" (122). Significantly, the "giddy Multitude, who scarcely know the civil grounds of Reason" (129), approve of Isabel's cruel actions toward Spencer, of which Cary is harshly critical, as I have already mentioned. Cary further excoriates Parliament for committing "Politick Treason" in deposing Edward: "It ne're was toucht or exprest by what Law, Divine or Humane, the Subject might Depose, not an Elective King, but one that Lineally and Justly had inherited . . . They had just cause to restrain from his Errours, but no ground or colour to deprive him of his Kingdom" (131). This apparently contradictory judgment of the Commons is in keeping with Machiavelli's similar assessment of *la moltitudine:* they can be either benign when bounded by laws and the common good or maleficent if driven by passionate willfulness and private ends. Interestingly, Machiavelli cites

Herod's regret for the execution of Mariam as an example of "reputedly wise princes [who] have put people to death and then wished them alive again" (I.58, 253)—behavior often attributed to and blamed on the masses by monarchists. Of course, coincidentally or not, Cary's *Mariam* features such a repentant Herod.

Both Machiavelli and Cary seek to level the monarch and the commons since both can be driven by will and unbounded by law: Cary even speaks of "Royal Passions" as "rebellious and masterless, having so unlimited a Power" whereby the monarch's "Will becomes the Law; his hand the executioner of actions unjust and disorderly" (140). This leveling tends to subvert the hierarchy implied in the influential metaphor of the body politic, first put forward by John of Salisbury's *Policraticus* in the twelfth century. Cary's innovation, however, lies in linking the claims of a female subject in marriage, in this case Isabel, with the claims of the subjects in the polity. When Isabel appeals to her brother, the French king, for aid against Edward, she speaks in the name of a "distressed kingdom," emphasizing that "'tis not I alone unjustly suffer" (96). She shifts her allegiance here from her husband the king to identify herself as a representative of the English people, who answer her "intentions not . . . to rifle, but reform the Kingdom," by "com[ing] like Pigeons by whole flocks to her assistance" (117–118).

CHRISTINE DE PIZAN AND THE GENDERING OF POLITICAL DISCOURSE

An antecedent to Cary's understanding of equivalences between women and male subjects can be found in Christine de Pizan's *Le Livre de corps de policie*, which was translated into English as *The Body of Polycye* in 1524.[16] Although the volume does not carry Christine's name as author, at the very beginning it prominently announces that it is written from the perspective of a woman: "If it is possible for vice to give birth to virtue, it pleases me in this part to be as passionate as a woman, since many men assume that the female sex does not know how to silence the abundance of their spirits. Come boldly, then and be shown the many inexhaustible springs and fountains of my courage, which cannot be stanched when it expresses the desire for virtue."[17] Whether Cary knew Christine's text in translation or in its French original, her views concerning the polity are remarkably similar to Christine's revision of John of Salisbury's theory of the body politic. In *The Book of the Body Politic*, Christine follows the traditional designation of the prince as occupying the head of the political body, but rather than affirm the hierarchical relationship between the head and other parts of the body, she stresses their interdependence and the indispensability of the lower parts of the body:

> The varied jobs that the artisans do are necessary for the human body and it cannot do without them, just as a human body cannot go without its feet. It would shamefully and uselessly drag itself in great pain on its hands and body without them, just as, he says, if the republic excluded laborers and artisans, it could not sustain itself.
>
> (105)

According to Kate Langdon Forhan, Christine addresses the people themselves in her discussion of burghers, merchants, and artisans, which goes beyond the traditional three orders of warriors, priests, and peasants, revealing a more subtle and detailed knowledge of classes than John of Salisbury.[18]

Cary also displays an interest in the commons and the lower orders of the commonwealth, as I have already mentioned. She deploys the metaphor of the body politic in squarely laying the blame for the "sick State" on "the Head [that] is so diseased" (29), further stating that "when the Head is ill . . . all the Members suffer by his infirmity" (44), thereby repeatedly emphasizing the responsibility of the king to his people. Cary explicitly states this principle of interdependence and reciprocity between king and subject: "The *power Majestick* is or should be bounded; and there is a reciprocal correspondence, which gives the *King* the obedience, the subject equal right and perfect justice, by which they claim a property in his actions; if either of these fall short, or prove defective by wilful errour, or by secret practice, the State's in danger of a following mischief" (68). Christine and Cary agree in recognizing the importance of women and the commons as participants in the body politic, though Christine divides her attention to these two types of subjects by focusing on female rulers in *The Book of the City of Ladies* and on the commons in *The Book of the Body Politic;* Cary, of course, focuses on both types of subjects in *History of Edward II*. Although *The Book of the Body Politic* does not explicitly address the place of women in the polity, Christine's positive characterizing of herself in linking her feminine "passion" to "courage" and "virtue" in authoring the text, together with the book's focus on the importance of the commons, suggests the equivalence of women and the commons.

Unlike Christine's *The Book of the Body Politic,* Cary's *History of Edward II* declines to specify an explicitly feminine perspective; in fact, the publisher's introduction "To the Reader" praises the author, called a "Gentleman . . . every way qualified for an Historian" for "express[ing his] Conceptions in so Masculine a Stile" (A2). Yet I suggest that we can discern a feminine subject position in Cary's wry and deflating use of what we may call "homely" tropes in satirizing male political actions. For example, Cary debunks homosocial alliances among men, specifically the unassailability of the king's favorite, by comparing his followers to sheep: "Where one particular man or faction is alone exalted and onely trusted, his words, be they never so erronious, finde seldom contradiction, and his unjust actions pass unquestioned; all men under him seeking to rise by him, sing the same tune; the Flock ever bleats after the voice of the Bellweather" (75). The king himself is not exempt from this type of satiric debunking: when "a Declaration is sent out to all the Kingdom, that taints the Honour of the Queen, but more [the king's] Judgment. The Ports are all stopt up, that none should follow: a Medicine much too late; a help improper, to shut the Stable-door, the Steed being stoln: but 'tis the nature of a bought Experience, to come a day too late, the Market ended" (94). Here the language of everyday life among the lower ranks serves to demystify kingship and further to link, on the rhetorical level, the queen with the commons. In both instances, the perspective is one that stands outside the world of politics dominated by the king and his male courtiers.

Edward II and Isabel as Exempla

Early modern political treatises used exempla to support explicitly stated political principles, perhaps the most well-known example being Machiavelli's use of Cesare Borgia to support his affirmation of a forceful and resourceful prince. As Timothy Hampton has shown, this appeal to exempla was a prevailing strategy of early modern historiography and literary self-fashioning that was based on—but also at times questioned—the humanist assumption of the authority of the past, especially that of classical antiquity.[19] The Catholic writer Robert Parsons, who in *A Conference about the Next Succession to the Crowne of Ingland* (1594) argued for the legitimacy of the Spanish Infanta as a claimant to the English throne, adduced Edward II as one of the examples of a monarch justly overthrown, along with other kings such as John, Richard II, Henry VI, and Richard III. Resistance theory was an important political tenet of Catholics, especially Jesuits. Unlike Parsons's work, Cary's *History of Edward II* is not overtly a political treatise, but through an analysis of the fall of Edward II, implicitly intervenes in the conversation concerning the monarch's prerogative and the place of the commons in the polity.

In addition, Cary's *Edward II* examines the place of women in politics through the detailed account of Isabel's part in the rebellion against for armed resistance against and deposition of the king and, in certain circumstances, tyrannicide—was elaborated by advocates of Catholic resistance in Elizabethan England. For example, the Jesuit Robert Parsons's *A Conference about the Next Succession to the Crowne of Ingland* (1594) includes a chapter titled "Of Kings lawfully chastised by their common wealthes for their misgouernment, and of the good and prosperous sucesse that God commonly hath giuen to the same," in which he explicates how the divine approval of the assassination of evil kings is indicated by the subsequent accession of good ones, such as Edward III (following Edward II), Henry IV and Henry V (following Richard II), and Henry VII (following Richard III). Taking up the corporate metaphor, Parsons states: "Nothing is more pestilent or bringeth so general destruction and desolation as an evel Prince. And therefore as the whole body is of more authority then the only head, and may cure the head if it be out of tune, so may the wealpublique cure or cutt of their heades, if they infest the rest, seing that a body civil may have divers heades, by succession, and is not bound ever to one, as a body natural is."[30] Cary almost seems to be quoting Parsons in laying the blame for the "sick State" on the "the Head [that] is so diseased" (29), further stating that "when the Head is ill . . . all the Members suffer by his infirmity" (44).[31] The Catholic Parsons, like Cary, notably does not resort to arguments concerning the authority of the pope over secular (or Protestant) rulers in order to support his advocacy of resistance.

Although the anonymously printed *Vindiciae, contra Tyrannos,* by contrast with Parsons's work, was written to justify *Protestant* rebellion against the *Catholic* monarchy of France, it also maintains that the king is the head of the civil body and the people its members. It emphasizes the corporational character of the people in allowing for the many, the *universi,* though not the one, the *singuli,* to resist the king.[32] The argument here accords with Cary's justifying the rebellion against Edward as authorized by the people, as well as her turning against Isabel's own "Tyranny" in the aftermath of her rebellion against Edward, harshly criticizing the queen for overstepping her bounds. Thus the *Vindiciae,* like Parsons's *Conference* and Cary's *Edward II,* bases its theory of resistance entirely on the rights of the community to overthrow a wicked ruler.

Conclusion

Although Cary explicitly mentions only Machiavelli by name, her *Edward II* constitutes a history of political thought, which places in dialogue both English and continental political theorists. Not only does Cary use these political thinkers to shape her historical narrative, her analysis of the fall of Edward II serves as an exemplary narrative through which she tests political theories concerning monarchical prerogative and the claims of the subject. In this respect Cary's history challenged the theory of absolute monarchy as put forth by James I in *The Trew Law of Free Monarchies* (1598). James deployed the corporate metaphor to make the opposite point from the one made by John of Salisbury and later by Cary, affirming the supremacy of the head over the rest of body: "It may very well fall out that the head will be forced to garre cut off some rotten member . . . to keepe the rest of the body in integritie: but what state the body can be in, if the head, for any infirmitie that can fall to it, be cut off, I leaue to the reader's iudgment."[33] His claims of a monarch's independence from the power of the law and his divine right were reiterated in sermons preached before him by William Goodwin in 1614 and before Charles I by Roger Maynwaring in 1627; both sermons were published by royal command.[34]

The History of Edward II thereby participates in the contemporary dialogue concerning absolutism and parliamentary prerogative between king and Parliament. Indeed, its purported composition in 1627 precedes by one year the *Petition of Right* of 1628, "concerning divers rights and liberties of the subject." The posthumous publication of Cary's work later in the seventeenth century during the Exclusion Crisis also indicates its relevance for the similar debate between Charles II and his Parliaments concerning his prerogative to name James II as his successor—though it is ironic in light of Cary's Catholicism that those who supported the Exclusion Bill and thereby would limit monarchical prerogative did so in order to prevent the accession of a Catholic monarch. Although Cary's work is in line with the writings of Catholic resistance theory of the late sixteenth century, as I have shown, it is notable that according to Peter Holmes, Catholic writers, including Parsons, abandoned their earlier positions after 1596 and retreated to nonresistance.[35] Yet it is nevertheless the case that Cary's Catholicism and her close engagement with French religious polemic (she translated Cardinal Perron's attack against James I, for example) go far to explain her divergence from the traditional Protestant national historiography of Britain that defines the nation through negation: as anti-French, anti-Italian, and anti-Catholic.[36] Cary instead advances a different idea of the English nation that is based on an eclectic synthesis of political theory—both English and continental—that advances the importance of the common good.

In addition, the work, in focusing as much on Isabel as on Edward, may also have been intended as political counsel to Queen Henrietta Maria in the tradition of *The Mirror for Magistrates*.[37] Isabel plays as prominent a role as ruler after Edward's fall, and the narrative concerns her own fall as much as Edward's; Cary thus adapts the *de casibus* tradition of deploying negative exempla to advise another French princess, like Isabel, who came to England to be queen. Cary in fact went on to dedicate her translation of Perron's *Replique* to Henrietta Maria in 1630.[38]

Although Buckingham was James's favorite, it was Charles who dissolved Parliament to avoid Buckingham's impeachment. Scholars have recognized Buckingham's correspondence with Gaveston, but they have not given as much weight to Henrietta Maria's potential correspondence with Isabel.[39] Cary's representation of Isabel as a ruler, who through tyrannical misrule squanders the initial support of her people (a trajectory that recalls Elizabeth's shift from a rhetoric of affective identification with the English people that characterized the earlier part of her rule to the tyrannical practices of the 1590s), could serve as a monitory warning to Henrietta Maria. We can thus consider one of the purposes of Cary's *Edward II* to be political counsel to the queen, similar to Christine de Pizan's exhortation to Isabeau of Bavaria to help bring about peace in the civil wars of France.[40] For early in *Edward II* Cary calls attention to the dire consequences of false counsel when a courtier "strives to please, than to advise" and recommends the recall of the exiled Gaveston; by contrast to the "oyly tongue" of this "fawning Orator" (9–10)—that recalls Goneril and Regan's "glib and oylie Art"—Cary's own rhetoric is consistently dispassionate, frequently aphoristic, and thus recalls the essays of James I's counselor, Francis Bacon. Such a perspective brings into focus the gendered subject position of Cary as a writer, who not only participates in the ongoing conversation concerning the relationship between monarchs and the polity, but also represents Isabel as a ruler in her own right, and as an exemplum for Henrietta Maria, who, at the outset of the English Civil Wars, did take political action, seeking to affect the course of the English nation.

Notes

Earlier versions of this essay were presented at the Renaissance Society of America and the Modern Language Association. I thank Arthur Marotti for directing me to bibliography on Catholic political thought; Johann Sommerville for information concerning early modern editions of *Policraticus;* and Pamela Hammons, Frank Palmeri, and Heather Wolfe for offering helpful suggestions for revision.

1. I am discussing in this chapter the lengthier folio (rather than the shorter octavo) version, *The History of the Life, Reign, and Death of Edward II* (1680), which on its title page is attributed to "E.F." and is said to have been composed in 1627. Diane Purkiss, in her introduction to the only modern edition of *Edward II*, has reviewed the various arguments supporting Cary's authorship, concluding that taken together, they constitute a strong case. See *Renaissance Women: The Plays of Elizabeth Cary, the Poems of Aemilia Lanyer* (London: Pickering and Chatto, 1994), xxi–xxx. See also Barbara Kiefer

Lewalski's "Appendix" on the question of the authorship in *Writing Women in Jacobean England* (Cambridge, MA: Harvard UP, 1993), 317–320, and Margaret Reeves's chapter in this volume.
2. Nearly contemporary with Cary's *History*, Richard Brathwait's *The English Gentlewoman* (1631) enjoins women from engaging in "discourse on state matters" (89). Cary's Mariam significantly begins the play by excoriating herself for "run[ing] on" with "public voice" in criticizing Caesar, though Cary as playwright goes on to anatomize the workings and effects of tyranny under the rule of Herod. On political discourse in *Mariam*, see Karen L. Raber, "Gender and the Political Subject in *The Tragedy of Mariam*," *SEL: Studies in English Literature 1500–1900* 35, no. 2 (1995): 321–343.
3. Lewalski, 203. See also Elaine Beilin, "Elizabeth Cary, *The Tragedy of Mariam* and History," in *A Companion to Early Modern Women's Writing*, ed. Anita Pacheco (Oxford: Blackwell, 2002), 136–149.
4. Jean Bodin, *Method for the Easy Comprehension of History*, tr. Beatrice Reynolds (New York: Columbia UP, 1945), 13–14.
5. Arthur B. Ferguson, *Clio Unbound: Perception of the Social and Cultural Past in Renaissance England* (Durham: Duke UP, 1979), 10. Ferguson cites John Hayward's *Henrie IIII* (1594) and Francis Bacon's *Henry VII* (1623) as examples.
6. See Alan T. Bradford, "Stuart Absolutism and the 'Utility' of Tacitus," *Huntington Library Quarterly* 45 (1983): 127–155.
7. Richard Ashcraft, *Revolutionary Politics and Locke's "Two Treatises of Government"* (Princeton: Princeton UP, 1986). See also his "Political Theory and the Problem of Ideology," *Journal of Politics* 42, no. 3 (1980): 687–705.
8. The French translation was published in 1581 and a partial English translation (of the "fourth question") in 1588; the English translation of the complete text did not appear until 1648. The modern editor of *Vindiciae* attributes this work to Phillippe de Mornay and Simon Languet. *Vindiciae, contra Tyrannos: or, Concerning the Legitimate Power of a Prince over the People, and of the People over a Prince*, ed. and trans. George Garnett (Cambridge: Cambridge UP, 1994), lxxxiv, lxxxvi–vii, lxxvi.
9. *The History of the Life, Reign, and Death of Edward II, King of England, With the Rise and Fall of his great Favourites, Gaveston and the Spencers* (1680), 26. Further references in text.
10. Felix Raab, *The English Face of Machiavelli: A Changing Interpretation 1500–1700* (London: Routledge and Kegan Paul; Toronto: U of Toronto P, 1964), 90–91. For a more recent account of "English Machiavellianism," see Victoria Kahn, *Machiavellian Rhetoric From the Counter-Reformation to Milton* (Princeton: Princeton UP, 1994).
11. *The Lady Falkland her Life*, in Heather Wolfe, ed. *Elizabeth Cary, Lady Falkland: Life and Letters* (Cambridge and Tempe, AZ: RTM Publications and Arizona Center for Medieval and Renaissance Studies, 2001), 118.
12. Hanna Fenichel Pitkin, *Fortune is a Woman: Gender and Politics in the Thought of Niccolò Machiavelli* (Berkeley: U of California P, 1964), esp. chaps. 1 and 6.

13. Lewalski, however, stresses Isabel's positive role and states that her "guilt is minimal" (*Writing Women*, 207). This may be because she considers Isabel to be a projection of Cary herself (208). Donald Foster, like Lewalski, considers Isabel to be a sympathetic representation of a suffering woman, with whom Cary identified, particularly in the parallel between Isabel's abduction of Prince Edward and Cary's own abduction of her children ("Resurrecting the Author: Elizabeth Tanfield Cary," in *Privileging Gender in Early Modern England*, ed. Jean R. Brink, Sixteenth Century Essays and Studies, vol. 23 [1993], 172–173). Tina Krontiris explains Cary's "severe condemnation" of Isabel by reference to the author's "strong views on the subject of cruelty" and its violation of Christian ethics (*Oppositional Voices: Women as Writers and Translators of Literature in the English Renaissance* [London and New York: Routledge, 1992], 96–97). Gwynne Kennedy attributes Cary's judgment of Isabel once she attains power to Isabel's "negative emotions, particularly anger and revenge." She concludes, however, that "Cary's text passes a lenient sentence on Isabel" ("Reform or Rebellion?: The Limits of Female Authority in Elizabeth Cary's *The History of the Life, Reign, and Death of Edward II*," in *Political Rhetoric, Power, and Renaissance Women*, ed. Carole Levin and Patricia A. Sullivan [Albany: SUNY Press, 1995], 213, 215).
14. Karen Raber, "Gender and Property, Elizabeth Cary and *The History of Edward II*," *Explorations in Renaissance Culture* 26, no. 2 (2000): 213, examines tyranny and the relationship between "kingship, absolutism, and manhood," thereby focusing on Edward rather than Isabel.
15. Niccolò Machiavelli, *The Discourses*, ed. Bernard Crick (Harmondsworth: Penguin, 1970), III.6, 419. Machiavelli recounts this story—albeit in a much less graphic fashion—also in the *Florentine Histories*, Book 8, chapter 34.
16. William Caxton, who translated Christine's *Fais d'armes et de chevalrie* as *The Book of Fayttes of Armes and of Chevalrie* (1489), indicates in the epilogue that Henry VII commissioned him to translate and publish the work for the benefit of his arms-bearing subjects.
17. Christine de Pizan, *The Book of the Body Politic*, ed. and trans. Kate Langdon Forhan (Cambridge: Cambridge UP, 1994), 3.
18. Kate Langdon Forhan, "Polycracy, Obligation, and Revolt: The Body Politic in John of Salisbury and Christine de Pizan," in *Politics, Gender, and Genre: The Political Thought of Christine de Pizan*, ed. Margaret Brabant (Boulder, CO: Westview Press, 1992), 44.
19. Timothy Hampton, *Writing from History: The Rhetoric of Exemplarity in Renaissance Literature* (Ithaca, NY: Cornell UP, 1990), 298–299.
20. Samuel Daniel, *The Complete Works in Verse and Prose*, ed. Alexander B. Grosart (New York: Russell and Russell, 1963), 5: 201–202.
21. Christopher Marlowe, *Edward the Second*, ed. Charles R. Forker (Manchester and New York: Manchester UP, 1994), 5.3.36.
22. Dympna Callaghan considers the two versions of *Edward II* by Marlowe and Cary as representing a crisis of sovereignty that "hinges on a juxtaposition between representations of femininity and homoerotic masculinity" in "The

Terms of Gender: 'Gay' and 'Feminist' *Edward II*," in *Feminist Readings of Early Modern Culture: Emerging Subjects*, ed. Valerie Traub, M. Lindsay Kaplan, and Dympna Callaghan (Cambridge: Cambridge UP, 1996), 282.
23. Cary would most likely have encountered the 1595 edition published in Leiden by the Plantin Press, of which three copies are held by the British Library.
24. John of Salisbury, *Policraticus*, ed. and trans. Cary J. Nederman (Cambridge: Cambridge UP, 1990), 126.
25. Elizabeth Poole, *A Vision: Wherein is manifested the disease and cure of the Kingdome* (1648), 6. Poole, however, counselled against executing Charles.
26. Glenn Burgess, *The Politics of the Ancient Constitution: An Introduction to English Political Thought, 1603–1642* (University Park: Penn State UP, 1992), 6–7, 77, sees Fortescue as an important early figure in the development of the advocacy of the primacy of the English Constitution and common law, which was taken up in the Jacobean period by Edward Coke and John Selden during Parliament's struggle against James I.
27. John Fortescue, *On the Laws and Governance of England*, ed. Shelley Lockwood (Cambridge: Cambridge UP, 1997), 21.
28. Both Salisbury and Fortescue had close connections with France, as did Cary: Salisbury was educated in Paris and in Chartres under Peter Abelard and was bishop of Chartres; Fortescue, in exile from England, wrote his treatise in France.
29. On "the problem of tyranny" in the *Policraticus*, and John of Salisbury's various discussions of tyrannicide, see D. E. Luscombe and G. R. Evans, in "The Twelfth-Century Renaissance," *The Cambridge History of Medieval Political Thought c.350–c.1450*, ed. J. H. Burns (Cambridge: Cambridge UP, 1988), 328–329.
30. Robert Parsons, *A Conference about the Next Succession to the Crowne of Ingland* (1594), 38. Arthur F. Marotti characterizes Parsons as "the polemical nemesis of English Protestantism" and the author of antigovernment propaganda during the threat arising from Mary Stuart's claim to the throne and attempted invasions of England by the Spanish Catholics, in *Religious Ideology and Cultural Fantasy: Catholic and Anti-Catholic Discourses in Early Modern England* (Notre Dame, IN: U of Notre Dame P, 2005), 11, 48.
31. Also worth noting along with Parsons's text is *Leicester's Commonwealth* (1584), a Catholic polemic against Elizabeth's favorite, significant in light of Cary's own Catholicism and the focus on the pernicious effect on the polity of royal favorites in *Edward II*. See *Leicester's Commonweath: The Copy of a Letter Written by a Master of Art of Cambridge (1584) and Related Documents*, ed. Dwight C. Peck (Athens and London: Ohio UP, 1985). This work was republished in 1641, owing to its approval of resistance, according to J. H. M. Salmon, *French Religious Wars in English Political Thought* (Oxford: Oxford UP, 1959), 82. Peter Holmes, who attributes the work to Parsons, also considers it as an articulation of "a defence of the right of resistance," in *Resistance and Compromise: The Political Thought of the English Catholics*

(Cambridge: Cambridge UP, 1982), 131, 134. I would further suggest that the text held significance for the public hostility against Charles I's favorite, Thomas Wentworth, Earl of Strafford, who was executed on a bill of attainder on May 12, 1641.
32. *Vindiciae*, 59–60.
33. King James VI and I, *Political Writings*, ed. Johann P. Sommerville (Cambridge: Cambridge UP, 1994), 78.
34. William Goodwin, *A sermon preached before the Kings most excellent maiestie at Woodstocke* (1614); Roger Maynwaring, *Religion and alegiance: in two sermons* (1627). See J. P. Sommerville, *Royalists & Patriots: Politics and Ideology in England 1603–1640*, 2nd ed. (London and New York: Longman, 1999), 42, 121.
35. Holmes, 205–207.
36. On English national identity from the Spanish Armada in 1588 to the Glorious Revolution in 1688 as based on a foundation of anti-Catholicism, see Marotti, 9.
37. None of the "tragedies" in the original 1559 edition of *The Mirror for Magistrates* concerns female protagonists. While the 1563 edition included Edward IV's mistress, Jane Shore, and the 1578 edition added Eleanor Cobham, Duchess of Gloucester (who was accused of practicing witchcraft and exiled), neither of these female exempla were rulers, nor do they concern issues of sovereignty as the great majority of male exempla do.
38. Krontiris argues that the stronger and more assertive voice found in *Edward II* and the *Reply* (than in *Mariam*) derives from Cary's religious dissidence, which "encouraged Cary's own critical propensity by teaching her how to challenge officially imposed beliefs" (101).
39. Danielle Clarke addresses the question of Cary's ties to the Buckingham faction, especially, to the duke's sister, the Countess of Denbigh, and Cary's authorship of his epitaph, and concludes that these relations do not rule out a critical representation of Buckingham through Gaveston and her investigation of the problem of court favorites in *Edward II*, in *The Politics of Early Modern Women's Writing* (London and New York: Longman, 2001), 172. Karen Nelson, "Elizabeth Cary's Edward II: Advice to Women at the Court of Charles I," in *Women, Writing, and the Reproduction of Culture in Tudor and Stuart Britain*, ed. Mary E. Burke, Jane Donawerth, Linda L. Dove, and Karen Nelson (Syracuse: Syracuse UP, 2000), 157–173, suggests that Cary's work participates in the genre of mothers' manuals and women's advice tracts, whose intended audience included the queen, among other women at the Caroline court. I diverge from Nelson, who considers Cary's Isabel as offering a "handbook of behavior" (158) for her readers.
40. John Guy, "The Rhetoric of Counsel in Early Modern England," in *Tudor Political Culture*, ed. Dale Hoak (Cambridge: Cambridge UP, 1995), 292, argues that "the term 'counsel' . . . underpinned not only the assumptions, but also some of the most important practices and political structures of the Tudor and early-Stuart policy . . . 'counsel' ranked high among the paradigms and traditions which inform public discourse and shaped political institutions."

CHAPTER 6

A BIBLIOGRAPHICAL PALIMPSEST: THE POST-PUBLICATION HISTORY OF THE 1680 OCTAVO, *THE HISTORY OF THE MOST UNFORTUNATE PRINCE KING EDWARD II*

Jesse G. Swan

At once expressly relegated to the status of a derivative document and implicitly elevated to the status of an authoritative source, the small octavo publication entitled *The History of the Most Unfortunate Prince King Edward II* (London, 1680) has been more used than considered. From its original editor through its subsequent eighteenth- and nineteenth-century editors, the 77-page pamphlet was seen as a sensational yet cogent critique of monarchical excess, especially in the selection, promotion, and maintenance of disreputable and malefic royal administrators or "favorites." Discovered, as is claimed on the title page and in the preface, among the papers of a notable early Stuart privy councillor, Henry Cary, first Viscount Falkland and Lord Deputy of Ireland, the highly moralizing story of the misery effected by Gaveston and Spencer on Edward II and his realm was thought to provide, in 1680, a singularly potent yet loyal warning about contemporary monarchical practice. In the eighteenth century, it was thought to contribute to the commercial promise of the eight-volume *The Harleian Miscellany: or a collection of scarce, curious, and entertaining pamphlets and tracts as well in manuscript as in print, found in the late earl of Oxford's library* (London, 1744–1746). In the twentieth century, the pamphlet came to the interest of literary historians, first as a contributory source documenting the history of the development of modern biography in English and then as a contributory source documenting the history of literature by women in

English. In both of these latter efforts, the octavo has been cast by most as a document derivative of a longer, related version of the history of Edward II also published in 1680, a folio entitled *The History of the Life, Reign, and Death of Edward II*, even as many of its unique features inform bibliographical as well as critical interpretations of the folio, notably those supporting the attribution of the folio text to Elizabeth Cary.

While most commentators attenuate the merit of *The History of the Most Unfortunate Prince*,[1] a few uphold the pamphlet's value as an important witness to the literary work of Elizabeth Cary. However, these upholders have offered either underdeveloped views, especially in relation to those arguing for the octavo's derivative status, or confounded ones. Of the latter, the most suggestive is that of Donald W. Foster. Although obscured by his aesthetics and, according to Randall Martin, his "confused teleology . . . belittling Cary's [supposed] 'excessive borrowing' from and 'tinkering with' her husband's [supposed] work,"[2] Foster endeavors to show that the differences between the octavo and folio texts suggest an elaboration of the octavo's text into that of the folio's, rather than a reduction of the folio's text into that of the octavo's.[3] If Cary worked from the manuscript that is represented by the octavo publication to arrive at the manuscript that is represented by the folio publication, as Foster advances, then the text of the octavo edition assumes a generative and thereby important status, especially for those interested in Cary's life and work.

Supporting the view that the 1680 octavo text is not a shortened version of the 1680 folio text are the facts of its publication. As I detail elsewhere, the manuscript informing the octavo text was brought to the press, independent of the folio text, by Sir James Hayes, who authored the octavo's preface.[4] Jeremy Maule's discovery of two manuscripts of Cary's *Edward II*, one bearing an indirect relationship to the octavo text and the other to the folio text (and discussed in Margaret Reeves's chapter in this volume), provide important evidence about the evolution of the various stages of Cary's writing. Unlike the folio and Fitzwilliam MS 361, and like Finch-Hatton MS 1, the octavo lacks the identification of authorship ("E.F."), and, uniquely, it lacks the author's letter to the reader.[5] Hayes, the second husband of Rachel (Hungerford) Cary, dowager Viscountess Falkland, was motivated to publish the octavo manuscript not only because of his kinship to the Cary family, but also because of personal, political, and financial conditions. A further case for the nonderivative status of the octavo can be made through an examination of the frontispieces: instead of using a frontispiece portrait of Edward II, as does the folio version, the octavo presents one of the king's father, Edward I.[6] In redacting an expensive folio into a cheaper octavo for profit or increased propagandistic circulation, even the most cynical of venal literary pirates would find this brash, if not simply counterproductive. The bibliographical evidence indicates that the octavo publication was a hasty, even slipshod, affair conducted for localized purposes, just as the publication of many such pamphlets was. Those localized purposes, however, did not include cheap commercialization of a coveted, elite-class luxury (such as a folio edition), which is the explanation that has been propagated most pervasively since 1935. The octavo publication was independently pursued and executed, derived from a manuscript remarkably different from that used for the more carefully prepared folio.

As an important, potentially authoritative source contributing to further appreciation of Cary's writing, the text of *The History of the Most Unfortunate Prince* needs to be established. The pre-publication history has been treated; here the post-publication history will be elaborated. Critics have tended to privilege Thomas Park's edition of the octavo in the 1808 *Harleian Miscellany* over William Oldys's edition of the octavo in the 1744 *Harleian Miscellany*, both because the 1744 *Miscellany* has received limited bibliographical attention, and because the 1808 *Miscellany* was reprinted in facsimile in 1965 and is therefore most widely available. Unfortunately, Park, the editor of the 1808 *Miscellany* (reprinted in 1965), uses Oldys's 1744 *Miscellany* edition of *Edward II* as his copy-text, and takes great liberties with it, with no reference to the original 1680 publication. The 1744 edition, by contrast, is based upon the copy of the octavo in the famous library purchased by the bookseller Thomas Osborne.[7] The 1808 *Harleian Miscellany* has also contributed to the erroneous, originally tentative and hypothetical, attribution of the pamphlet to Henry Cary by giving the impression of approbation. Accordingly, in order to uncover the clearest representation of the manuscript underwriting *The History of the Most Unfortunate Prince,* an account of the editions of the pamphlet from 1808 back to 1680 is required. Such an account reveals the basis of many erroneous views of the pamphlet and, complemented by the pre-publication history, permits the manuscript author's text to emerge.

In uncovering the palimpsest-like layering of editorial inscriptions, the first fact to highlight is that owing to apparent interest in the early nineteenth century, there were two separate, but simultaneous, publications of *The Harleian Miscellany* in 1808—one economical and the other scholarly.[8] In what was to be the final volume, the publisher of the economical 1808 octavo version, Robert Dutton, apologizes for having to publish a further volume, owing to "the difficulty of ascertaining with precision in the commencement of printing the exact quantity it would make, in a size in which it has never before appeared" (558). The editor of this edition has been incorrectly identified as John Malham, despite the fact that his contemporaries do not acknowledge the *Miscellany* as his editorial work.[9] The assumption that Malham edited the work probably arises from the fact that he provides and signs the preface, but it is also this preface that further substantiates the reticence to attribute the editorship to Malham. In the preface, Malham offers fulsome praise for the unnamed editor: "The credit of the editor has been long established, as fully qualified for so important a task, as that of examining with minute attention every sheet before it is committed to the press, in addition to the printer's usual habit of correctness" (A3–A3^v). Since publishers and printers engaged in the sort of textual emendation that is realized in this edition, and since the editor is unnamed, but the printer specifically referenced, it is most likely that it was commonly understood that Dutton was honored by Malham with the title of editor in his prefatory testimonial. The textual emendations introduced in the version of *The History of the Most Unfortunate Prince* included in the 1808 Dutton *Harleian* depart from its 1744 copy-text in a number of stylistic ways: the edition regularizes the use of capital letters, limits the use of italics to Latin words, eliminates the two-column format, and occasionally alters the punctuation. Two other emendations are of special note: first, the parentheses on the title page, surrounding "supposed to be," silently disappear, thereby softening the emphasis on the tenuousness of the attribution of authorship; second, through its markers for paragraphs and quotations, it makes the last sentence of Dutton's preface appear to be of a piece with the last quotation from Hayes's 1680 preface.[10]

The other, more elaborate and scholarly 1808 edition of *The Harleian Miscellany* was considerably edited and annotated by Thomas Park and published by John White, John Murray, and John Harding. This is the edition reprinted in facsimile in 1965 and widely available in libraries. Thomas Park was an eminently respected antiquarian and bibliographer, consulted extensively by, among others, Sir Egerton Brydges and George Steevens; and praised by Robert Southey with the following judgment: Park's "knowledge of English bibliography, and English poetry in particular, have never been surpassed."[11]

Although Park is to be commended for the carefulness exhibited by his edition of the *Miscellany*, especially in signaling his own contributions to the text, such fastidiousness is also the basis of serious misrepresentation, however unintentional. Park's meticulousness is of a decidedly, if not strictly, material, even documentary cast, as opposed to an abstract or idealist kind.[12] Even in his less strictly documentary editing, such as when he feels "enabled to correct the antiquated text" of the 1744 edition with reference to the pamphlets' original publications, or such as when he "amend[s] the obsolete punctuation" and spelling of tracts printed after "the accession of our first James to the throne; as our most fastidious antiquaries, it is presumed, will hardly wish for any later specimens of uncouth and obsolete spelling," Park upholds the sovereignty of documents.[13] That is, he makes emendations only when he feels that documentary evidence shows that Oldys, the 1744 editor, was in error, or based upon the universal understanding that punctuation and spelling (what would come to be called "accidentals" by New Bibliographers), are immaterial, a position that has been both challenged, and advanced, repeatedly.[14]

A concern over documentary integrity is most obviously manifest in Park's decision to reproduce the entire collection as a miscellany, rather than to rearrange it according to a more logical principle (such as by topic or date), and in his faithful bracketing of editorial comments, "which lapse of time or change of circumstance sometimes rendered essential."[15] Bracketing his notes is crucial, since his edition presents William Oldys's 1744 edition, augmented by new notes. Park thus reproduces, after the "Advertisement" and "Table of Contents," the 1744 introduction, which indicates that "most of the pieces . . . will be introduced by short prefaces, in which will be given some account of the reasons for which they are inserted."[16] These short introductory prefaces, unless otherwise noted with square brackets, are presented as authored by the 1744 editor, William Oldys.[17]

The effect of Park's materialist editing is intended to be the arousal of hermeneutical confidence in the simplicity of the document representing the texts of the various authorities involved in its creation and transmission. Accordingly, a reader of Park's edition would be given to understand that there are three authorities for *The History of the Most Unfortunate Prince:* Henry Cary, William Oldys, and Thomas Park. In the first three pages (67–69), for instance, the following is presented: the title; a bracketed bibliographical note, which refers to a bracketed explanatory note at the foot of the page; a horizontal rule; the preface, all in italics except for the Latin on page 68; a horizontal rule on page 69 separating the preface from the history; then the first six paragraphs of the history. A reader understands the title to be authored by Oldys, the bracketed notes by Park, the preface, in italics as opposed to the roman of the main text, by Oldys, and the history by Henry Cary, Lord Falkland. A reader might think that Oldys takes some portion of the title, probably the first, from his source document, but the precise composition of the title was to arouse little, if any, concern.[18]

Even as Park's edition preserves the parentheses that originally accentuated the tenuous authorial attribution in the title, it makes the parentheses seem either odd or punctiliously faithful to an archaism, and further, it makes the false attribution appear to have the approbation of both Oldys and Park. The implied approbation is achieved through the careful insertion of bracketed notes by Park and the implied authorship of the preface. The bracketed notes provide bibliographical, historical, and critical commentary, suggesting authoritative consideration. If Park is suspicious, he notes the nature of his suspicion. Further, Park's notes bring together the original 1680 octavo and folio editions, suggesting that Park takes them both to be authored by Henry Cary, even though such a belief moves him wrongly to conclude against Oldys in the following way: "The diction throughout [the octavo presented in the miscellany] seems to have been much modified by Mr. Oldys, according to the averment of the folio edition: for the octavo has not been met with" (67, n. 1). Noting such negative curiosities when he thought they existed and associating the 1680 folio with the 1680 octavo, in a way that Oldys never does—even in the *Catalogus Bibliothecae Harleianae,* where he easily could have and might be expected to, if he thought the two publications were associated, bibliographically or authorially[19]—Park neither thinks that anyone other than Henry Cary authored the history in folio or octavo, thereby implicitly endorsing the editorially comment-free parenthetical ascription of authorship, nor that anyone other than Oldys authored the preface only found in the octavo.[20] That is, Park believes, in associating the folio and octavo, that Oldys modified his source text considerably, and, in effect, that Oldys reduced the text from the folio version into the version he prints, which is the octavo, complemented by a preface Oldys prepared, as he did and was to do for most of the other pamphlets included in the *Miscellany.* Park would have doubted his conclusion that Oldys redacted the folio, no doubt, had he been able to consult a copy of the octavo, since Oldys's edition is clearly an edited version of the octavo. Further, had he consulted the octavo, he would have realized not only that Oldys edited the text of the history as it appears in the octavo, but that he did not author the preface, since the preface appears in the 1680 octavo. He would have realized further, if perhaps somewhat reticently, that Oldys misrepresented, quite willfully, it seems, the authorship of the preface in his 1744 publication.

But for his 1808 edition, Park does not consult the 1680 octavo edition of *The History of the Most Unfortunate Prince,* and his consultation of the folio does not appear to have influenced his editorial decisions. Park's edition presents Oldys's edition in a modernized form, sometimes in ways that continue to make simple sense, at other times in less immediately explicable ways. Alterations in punctuation as well as mechanics, such as those of spelling, capitalization, and use of apostrophes, and the employment of quotation marks rather than italics for signaling speeches as well as for signaling epithets, such as in the historical references to "The White Battle" (74) and "The Parliament of White Bands" (76), continue to represent recognizably modern preferences and pose no significant problem, except for the strictest advocate of diplomatic editing.[21] Inexplicable alterations are few, but include the apparently random introduction of italics (e.g., "The melancholy apparitions of this *loth to depart*" [69] and "My *Queen!* (quoth he)" [93], which also introduces the exclamation point in place of a comma) and dashes (e.g., "that seldom use to fight for nothing.—Time hath at last brought" [86] and "before he could avoid or resist it.—The writers differ mainly" [94]). Explicable but quite unnecessary are a few substantive changes, such as eliminating the word "whole" at the top of page 80, which in the original serves to emphasize; changing "terms" into "forms" on page 76, which renders a less idiomatic expression today as well as in the pattern of the octavo's colloquialism; and the insertion of the first "to" in the following sentence describing the queen's reaction both to being rejected by her brother, the king of France, and to receiving Mortimer's passionate response to the news of the rejection: "This makes her temporize, and cunningly to seem to provide for a voluntary return, which might prevent that danger" (85).[22] Finally, one phonologically driven alteration seems to be an obvious correction: at page 91, Park changes "once" to "one's" to produce, "Howsoever, it is the more innocent and excellent way, to offend in the better part; and rather to let the law, than one's own virtue and goodness to be visibly deficient and disesteemed." However, when considered in relation to the 1680 octavo and folio as well as the manuscript witnesses, the seemingly clarifying emendation actually deprives readers of potentially suggestive possibilities.

Although Park's 1808 edition bears many formal marks of critical and bibliographical authority, it actually introduces many misleading readings and implications. Many of these inform erroneous assumptions, speculations, and arguments about the 1680 octavo proffered in later criticism. Of equal significance, Park's edition, because it is an edition of an edition, and so uses the 1744–1746 volumes for its copy-text, adds a layer of editorial inscription onto the original pamphlets. In addition to its own modernizing layer, in the case of *The History of the Most Unfortunate Prince,* the overlaying of editions has also misrepresented the authorship of the preface, which has gone a long way in affirming the original misrepresentation of the authorship of the history, even as it has left the traces of its misrepresentation.

To understand what Park did and why, it is important to understand what Oldys did before him, especially in regard to the preface, but also to the main text. The son of a civil lawyer, also named William Oldys, and his mistress, Ann, Oldys was parentless by the age of 15. Acquiring an education through his mother's bequest, Oldys collected, considered, edited, and wrote various works, drawing the attention, eventually, of Edward Harley, the second Earl of Oxford, for whom Oldys became literary secretary in 1738. Oldys had acquired a reputable name by then, as editor of Sir Walter Ralegh's *History of the World* (1736), which included an elaborate, well-received biography of Ralegh by Oldys. Upon Harley's death in 1741, Thomas Osborne, who had connections to Oldys, partly through having published his *The British Librarian,* purchased the earl's library with the intention of selling the books for the best profit possible. It is in this effort that Oldys joined Osborne and Samuel Johnson to produce the sale catalog and *The Harleian Miscellany*. Oldys, not unlike Johnson, was quite apt for the employment, and certainly he needed the remuneration.

Unfortunately, no "body of men are more uniform and eager" than eighteenth-century booksellers "in taking advantage of [authors' and scholars'] necessities, who, like Johnson, are reduced to a dependence on their favour," as William Shaw, one of Johnson's early biographers, characterizes people like Osborne.[23] Indeed, it is in relation to the production of *The Harleian Miscellany* that we have one of the sensational stories indicative of Johnson's character. The *Miscellany,* which Oldys was primarily responsible for, was instituted only as "another scheme to help Osborne recoup his investment in the Harleian Library," an investment that was not realizing the returns Osborne, "the sharp businessman," had contemplated.[24] In response to Osborne's repeated and "most illiberal" reprimands about allegedly slow work, as William Cooke tells it,

> Mr. Johnson heard him for some time unmoved; but, at last, losing all patience, he seized up a large folio, which he was at that time consulting, and aiming a blow at the Bookseller's head, succeeded so forcibly, as to send him sprawling to the floor: Osborne alarmed the family with his cries; but Mr. Johnson, clapping his foot on his breast, told him "he need not be in a hurry to rise; for if he did, he would have the further trouble of kicking him down stairs."[25]

Haste for profit, and a coarse environment, pressured Oldys in his work for Osborne, and these circumstances account for why he would select the sensational story of *The History of the Most Unfortunate Prince* for inclusion in the first volume of *The Harleian Miscellany,* and why he would represent the preface as his own work.

As indicated in both the printed proposal to potential subscribers and the introduction to the first volume, the procurement of subscriptions was the motivating force behind the planning and publication of *The Harleian Miscellany.* The *Proposals for Printing, by Subscription, The Harleian Miscellany* attempted to garner subscriptions by affecting an antiquarian and scholarly demeanor. In order to remedy the problem of the ephemeral quality of pamphlets, which has retarded the empirical and efficient accumulation of knowledge, the *Proposals for Printing* announces that the

> obvious Method of preventing these Losses, of preserving to every Man the Reputation he has merited by long Assiduity, is to unite these scattered Pieces into Volumes, that those, which are too small to preserve themselves, may be secured by their Combination with others.[26]

By contrast, the introduction to the first volume effectively drops the antiquarian and scholarly pretense in favor of a commonsense appeal to the mass market. In anticipating the criticism that the *Miscellany* is not arranged according to topic, for example, the introduction forthrightly explains that "by confining ourselves for any long time to any single subject, we shall reduce our readers to one class, and, as we shall lose all the grace of variety, shall disgust all those who read chiefly to be diverted" (1744, vol. 1, vii). So, even though the *Miscellany* is not arranged chronologically or topically, it is selected and arranged with a purpose: the titillation of its browsers.

Anyone considering the purchase of the first volume of *The Harleian Miscellany* would naturally consult the table of contents, after, perhaps, having consulted the proposal. The table of contents is more provocative than the proposal, if only because it is more specific and detailed. The proposal provides about two double-columned pages of "Heads" or topics to be included in the collection: "Agriculture . . . Algebra . . . Funds and public Credit . . . *Jews* . . . Jesuits . . . Mines and Minerals . . . Quakers . . . Slaves and Slavery . . . Suicide . . . University . . . Witchcraft, Sorcery, etc." The first volume, by contrast, gives, on the first page of the table of contents alone, several specific works on socially polarizing topics, all related to government and religion. Complementing treatises giving support, in various ways, to limited, constitutional monarchy and the rights of Parliament (such as James I's *Vox Regis: Or, the Difference between a King ruling by Law, and Tyrant by his own Will; with a Declaration of the English Laws, Rights, and Privileges,* which Oldys saw as advice unwisely ignored by James II) and treatises designed to gratify anti-Catholic sentiment (such as *The Plots of Jesuits* and *The Protestants' Doom in Popish Times*), *The History of the Most Unfortunate Prince King Edward II* would appeal to readers variously prurient, habitually jealous, and drawn to cruel and exceptionally perverse executions of violence. Such sensational appeal seems all the more intentional when one notices that the story of Edward II immediately follows *Machiavel's Vindication of Himself and his Writings.*

Saltiness, however, is not the only reason for including *The History of the Most Unfortunate Prince* in the first volume. More usefully, the 1680 pamphlet came with a fully crafted preface, a preface that could easily be made to appear to be the work of the 1744 editor, William Oldys. This ready-to-use preface was an efficient way of fulfilling the promise in the introduction to *The Harleian Miscellany* that "MOST of the Pieces, which shall be offered in this Collection to the Publick, will be introduced by short Prefaces, in which will be given some Account of the Reasons for which they are inserted,"[27] especially in light of the pressure being applied by the publisher, Osborne. That Oldys meant for the readers to take the preface to *The History of the Most Unfortunate Prince* to be by him is clear from the other prefaces of the first volume as well as the editorial changes and additions Oldys made to the preface.

Like the preceding prefaces in the *Miscellany,* the italicized preface to *The History of the Most Unfortunate Prince* is presented as an explanation of the historical significance of the pamphlet, including its continuing relevance. Despite being considerably longer than the preceding ones, it departs from the style of the octavo edition and conforms to the style of the other prefaces, which were authored by Oldys, in numerous ways, including in its altered pattern of capitalization, spelling, and punctuation. Even more indicative of Oldys's desire to represent the preface as his own, rather than as Sir James Hayes's, though, are the additions and deletions. For instance, in the first sentence, Oldys transforms the original "*got him such an Esteem with King* James, *(who for his great Learning and Sagacity is stiled* The English Solomon) *that he thought him a Person*" (A2) into "*got him such an Esteem with King* James the First, *that he thought him a Person*" (64 [wrongly designated 66]). Similarly, Oldys deletes "*with which I shall conclude*" from Hayes's introduction of the long quote of Sir Winston Churchill (octavo A3ᵛ; Oldys 65), because he adds, following the long quote, a concluding sentence for the preface: "*A dreadful Example, both to* Prince *and* People, *that usurp unlawful Methods to accomplish their unjust Intentions*" (66). Unlike the penultimate long quote, which Hayes had extracted from Richard Baker, the final long quote from Churchill is highlighted with an open single quotation mark at the beginning of each line, which also highlights the fact that the last sentence of the preface is not part of the quote, but from Oldys, since it lacks the open quotation mark for its new line.[28] Without consulting the original octavo, and in the context of the *Miscellany's* announced and usual practice, a reader could only conclude that the entire preface was by the editor, when, actually, only some changes and the last sentence were. Indeed, this is exactly how the 1793 selected edition and how Park presented the preface.[29]

Whatever our feelings about an editor misrepresenting himself and his texts in the way Oldys did with the octavo *The History of the Most Unfortunate Prince* in the first volume of *The Harleian Miscellany,* given the document and the circumstances, the misrepresentation is entirely, and easily, comprehensible. Similarly understandable, if unfortunate, is Park's considered judgment over 60 years later, since he was providing an edition of Oldys and since he had not been able to consult an original copy of *The History of the Most Unfortunate Prince.* Park understood the preface to have been authored by Oldys and the text of the history "to have been much modified by Mr. Oldys, according to the averment of the folio edition: for the octavo has not been met with" (67n1). Park also understood the original pamphlet, following a notation he references in Antony à Wood, "to have been published when the press was open for all books that could make any thing against the then government" (67n1).³⁰

It is this set of erroneous textual representations and potentially relevant contextual speculations that informed, over 125 years after Park, Donald Stauffer's consideration of the 1680 octavo and folio publications in his 1935 essay "A Deep and Sad Passion," encouraging him to think the octavo was a shortened redaction of the folio. Because Stauffer consulted a copy of the octavo in the Bodleian Library (Bod. Wood 234), as well as one or more copies of the folio (including probably Bod. Mason E. 115),³¹ he knows the preface to *The History of the Most Unfortunate Prince* is of a piece with the 1680 publication, and not authored by Oldys, and that the folio is, indeed, considerably more elaborate than the octavo. In bringing the two editions together as he does, Stauffer not only overtly defames Samuel Johnson and William Oldys,³² he also silently aligns himself with the scholarly Park. Although Stauffer knew Oldys did not redact his publication from a folio, as Park surmised, Stauffer continued to think of the octavo as redacted from the folio, with nothing more to substantiate such a theory than a feeling, derived perhaps not entirely self-consciously from Park. In order to achieve his purpose, Stauffer did not need the octavo to be a shortened redaction of the folio; such a condition was just the simplest way to draw on the octavo in order to associate the folio with the Cary family, while simultaneously being able to discount the relevance of the textual representation transmitted by the octavo. Because the octavo, in *The Harleian Miscellany*, was much more known than the folio, which had seen only one reissue in 1689, Stauffer felt that the folio was "more rare," and because the folio is clearly more elaborate, considerably more complex, and substantially more dramatic, Stauffer wanted to use it for his essay on the "deep influence of drama upon historical biography" (291). One scholar-editor, Park, had already proposed that the octavo was a redaction of the folio; Stauffer could, and did, simply join that scholar, with some alteration, in order to take from the octavo what he needed for his interpretation of the folio.

Commercial, bibliographical, and literary purposes operated to misrepresent *The History of the Most Unfortunate Prince* after its initial publication in 1680. A desire on the part of critics involved in the recovery of writing by early modern Englishwomen to have stable, singular, and user-friendly texts has, at least partly, contributed to the further misrepresentation of the octavo.³³ However, by simultaneously appreciating the accumulated patina and reconsidering the text of the elutriated octavo, we can account for much of the history of the reception of *The History of the Most Unfortunate Prince* as well as begin to consider some further possibilities for the text represented by the original publication, especially in relation to the workings of Cary. As a document independently published from a manuscript found in the Falkland household among the old papers of the first Viscount Falkland and husband of Cary, the text of the history should be related, either positively or negatively, to the other witnesses or states of the history of Edward II attributed to Cary.

While this is not the place for an extended consideration of the octavo text's relation to that of the folio and the two known manuscripts, it is instructive to consider an instance suggestive of the development of the text from that represented by the octavo to that of the Finch-Hatton manuscript, the Fitzwilliam Museum manuscript, and the folio. The instance is one in which the octavo's post-publication history also contributes, and it is one that contributes to the history of the development of modern perspective and, consequently, forms of consciousness.

In perhaps the most dramatic section of the text, regardless of the state or version, Mortimer presses Isabel to agree to the murder of Edward II.[34] The versions are of varying lengths and detail, but all contain clearly demarcated speeches forming a dramatic dialogue between Isabel and Mortimer. Less demarcated or more mixed is the text surrounding the clearly delineated speeches. That is, the text moves among various narrative perspectives and between narrative and dramatic modes on either side of the speeches that form a dramatic dialogue. The fluidity of the movement evokes various effects in each instance, but only Park reduces the fluidity into relatively circumscribed, modern units of narrative and drama. For instance, as the text approaches the speeches forming a dramatic dialogue, Park provides the following rendition (the quote begins with a reference to the protracted deliberations about the problems associated with keeping Edward II captive, which were described in the sentences immediately preceding):

> On this, Mortimer falls to the matter roundly, and tells the Queen plainly, "That there is no way left to make all sure, but absolutely to take away the cause, and to leave the party by Edward's death hopeless, that, by his life, sought to make a new combustion." (93)

Except for the word "That" and the past tense form "sought," the sentence as presented by Park provides a nice bit of dramatic exclamation, introduced by objective narration. The dramatic exclamation is created by the introduction of open and close quotation marks and the editorial insertion of commas between "this" and "Mortimer," between "that" and "by," and between "life" and "sought." Park follows Oldys in the insertion of the commas, but he is the one to introduce the quotation marks. The original octavo presents the same sentence as follows:

> On this *Mortimer* falls to the matter roundly, and tells the Queen plainly, That there is no way left to make all sure, but absolutely to take away the

Cause, and to leave the Party by *Edward*'s death hopeless, that by his life sought to make a new Combustion. (71)

The sense of the narrator communicating, in her own tone and rhythms as she summarizes, is lost in Park's rendition, just as is the multiplicity of consciousness implied by the text. Given that this passage is only one short paragraph away from a clearly demarcated dramatic speech (that of Edward II to an insolent attendant) and only one short paragraph before another (Isabel's first to Mortimer), it would not be unreasonable to understand the author to intend the presentation as realized in the 1680 octavo, whatever a reader's reaction to it. The other documents—the folio and the two manuscripts—elaborate this sentence into many sentences, and they do so not by straightening out the narrative perspective or delimiting more rigidly narrative and drama, as Park does, but by elaborating the mixed perspective and mixed mode, thereby accentuating the sense of a narrator's presence.[35]

If this narrator be Cary, and if we care about Cary, such textual moments are richly valuable. Such texts are also important, however, for those who do not necessarily care about Cary, since they give further evidence of the incipient, inchoate literary expressions of modernity, even as they also give evidence of fully developed expressions of early modernity, expressions sometimes quite alien to contemporary readers. The only way to appreciate these early modern texts is to understand both how they have been transmitted to us and, as much as is possible, how they were created and understood before their transmission over the centuries.[36] For Cary and the history of Edward II, this requires further study of the 1680 octavo as an important text in itself as well as a text representing an important, perhaps primary, relation to her ongoing work on her story of the life of Edward II, work that occupied at least a year of her own life.[37] Coupled with the publication conditions of the 1680 octavo, the postpublication history indicates that the best document for representing the early modern as well as authorial text of *The History of the Most Unfortunate Prince King Edward II* is the octavo published in 1680, even as the postpublication history is valuable in elucidating the source of many of the erroneous suppositions concerning the 1680 octavo, the 1680 folio, and the rich texts of the history of Edward II and of Elizabeth Cary.

NOTES

Of the many people I am happily, even if considerably, obliged to, here I would like to acknowledge two most gracious, and singularly elegant, librarians, Marilyn Wurzburger and Julian Roberts, and two scholars who have been more generous and more the true friend than anyone, certainly I, could possibly deserve, O M Brack, Jr., and Elena Levy-Navarro. I further acknowledge the University of Northern Iowa, for a competitively awarded sabbatical, and responsibility for any error.

1. To be precise, the cases used in the title are as follows: THE HISTORY *of the most unfortunate Prince* King EDWARD II.
2. *Women Writers in Renaissance England* (New York: Longman, 1997), 161.
3. Esp. see note 38 of Foster, "Resurrecting the Author: Elizabeth Tanfield Cary," in *Privileging Gender in Early Modern England*, ed. Jean R. Brink. Sixteenth Century Essays & Studies 23 (Kirksville, MO: Sixteenth Century Journal Publishers, 1993), 141–173. For a review of criticism in relation to the status of the 1680 folio and octavo editions, see the Bibliographical Note (188–190) in Jesse G. Swan, "Towards a Textual History of the 1680 Folio *The History of the Life, Reign, and Death of Edward II* (attributed to Elizabeth Cary, Lady Falkland): Understanding the Collateral 1680 Octavo *The History of the Most Unfortunate Prince*," in *New Ways of Looking at Old Texts, III,* ed. W. Speed Hill (Tempe, AZ: Arizona Center for Medieval and Renaissance Studies and Renaissance English Text Society, 2004), 177–190.
4. For details of Hayes and his authorship of the octavo's preface and publication of the octavo, see Swan, "Towards a Textual History."
5. The confidence of the folio attribution is suggested by it being rendered on the title page in red ink, and not being altered by the printer in any copy, including corrected copies of the folio. The use of red ink to ornament and accentuate also imitates the manuscript it represents, as suggested by Fitzwilliam MS 361.
6. The Huntington Library copy preserves the portrait. For the portraits of Edward I and Edward II used in the octavo and folio editions, see *Baziliologia A Book of Kings: Notes on a Rare Series of Engraved English Royal Portraits from William the Conqueror to James I. Published under the above Title 1618,* by H. C. Levis (New York: Grolier Club, 1913).
7. For Osborne, see O M Brack, Jr., "Osborne, Thomas (*bap.* 1704?, *d.* 1767)," *Oxford Dictionary of National Biography* (Oxford: Oxford University Press, 2004) [hereafter referred to as *ODNB*].
8. The fact of two separate publications of *The Harleian Miscellany* in 1808 often seems to be overlooked. See, for instance, Barry Weller and Margaret W. Ferguson in their Selected Bibliography to *The Tragedy of Mariam, The Fair Queen of Jewry with The Lady Falkland: Her Life, by One of Her Daughters* (Berkeley, CA: U of California P, 1994), 317.
9. As an example of the misattribution of Malham as editor, the Library of Congress catalog notes that the 1808 *Harleian Miscellany* is "A reprint of the first edition, chronologically arranged by J. Malham." Aside from the fact that this edition of *The Harleian Miscellany* is a haphazard chronological arrangement (as its preface admits), neither Malham's contemporary biographer, Frederic Shoberl, nor his *ODNB* biographers, Gordon Goodwin and S. J. Skedd, assign it to him. (For Shoberl, see [John Watkins and Frederic Shoberl], *A Biographical Dictionary of the Living Authors of Great Britain and*

Ireland [London: Printed for Henry Colburn, 1816], 218.) Further, *The Harleian Miscellany* is not included in the list of Malham's work that concludes his obituary in *The Gentleman's Magazine* (1st ser. 9 [1821]: 568–569). A more truly chronological edition of *The Harleian Miscellany* is a selection printed in 1793 for C[atherine] and G[eorge] Kearsley, widow and son of George Kearsley (for widow and son, see Trevor Ross, "Kearsley, George (c. 1739–1790), bookseller," *ODNB*).

10. Other points of modernization are not pursued in the Dutton 1808 edition, such as spelling and indentation. This edition provides open and close single quotes throughout the preface, except for lacking a close quote for the last quotation.
11. The quote is from W. P. Courtney, rev. John D. Haigh, "Park, Thomas (1758/9–1834), antiquary and bibliographer," *ODNB*.
12. For commentary on the distinction between idealist and documentary bibliography, the following are suggestive: Peter Shillingsburg, *Scholarly Editing in the Computer Age: Theory and Practice*, 3rd ed. (Ann Arbor, MI: U of Michigan P, 1999) and G. Thomas Tanselle, *A Rationale of Textual Criticism* (Philadelphia: U of Pennsylvania P, 1992).
13. Quotes are from Park's 1808 edition, vol. 1, "The Advertisement" (a3^{r-v}), except for the last quote, which comes from vol. 9, "The Editor to the Reader" (6). The collation of the editions indicates that Park emends the spelling for more than just those tracts added in his two supplemental volumes.
14. For a brief history of bibliography and accidentals, complemented by a polemic against altering accidentals, see Hershel Parker, "Regularizing Accidentals: The Latest Form of Infidelity," in *Proof: The Yearbook of American Bibliographical and Textual Studies*, vol. 3., ed. Joseph Katz (Columbia, SC: U of South Carolina P, 1973), 1–20.
15. Quote from Park's 1808 edition, vol. 1, "The Advertisement" (a3^v).
16. Quote from Park's 1808 edition, 1:xviii. See below for the quotation of this passage from the 1744 publication.
17. Park understands that Oldys performed the editing, as he makes clear in his advertisement for the volume and his notes for *The History of the Most Unfortunate Prince*.
18. See note 20 for some discrepancies in representing the title.
19. In addition to Osborne and Johnson, the classicist and non-juror Michael Maittaire is sometimes thought to have contributed to the sale catalog, *Catalogus Bibliothecae Harleianae* (London: Thomas Osborne, 1743–1745) (e.g., Margaret Clunies Ross and Amanda J. Collins, "Maittaire, Michael," *ODNB*), but it is clear from an analysis of the *Catalogus* that Maittaire did not contribute to the work but, rather, was drawn upon, somewhat unfairly, and made to serve as "the compilers' whipping boy" (see Thomas Kaminski, "Johnson and Oldys as Bibliographers: An Introduction to the Harleian Catalogue," *Philological Quarterly* 60, no. 4 [1981]: 439–453, qtd. from 443. Kaminski clarifies and elaborates notes regarding Maittaire made by Allen T. Hazen, *Samuel Johnson's Prefaces & Dedications* [New Haven, CT: Yale UP, 1937], 43–44). Both folio and octavo history of Edward II are listed

in volume 1, within a dozen pages of each other, and within the category "History of England, from the Conquest to the Reformation," separated into the subcategories, folio and octavo.

20. Park's thinking about the octavo and the folio dated back to the time he was editing Horace Walpole's *A Catalogue of the Royal and Noble Authors of England* (1758); included in *The Works of Horatio Walpole, Earl of Orford* (London: Printed for G. G. and J. Robinson and J. Edwards, 1798; reprinted and introduced by Peter Sabor [London: Pickering & Chatto, 1999]; edition by Park published in London by John Scott in 1806). In his 1806 edition of *Royal and Noble Authors,* Park introduces bracketed notes, much as he would come to include in *The Harleian Miscellany.* To Walpole's listing of the octavo *History of the Most Unfortunate Prince* in *Royal and Noble Authors,* a listing that provides only the first part of the title and indicates that Anthony à Wood "ascribes it to Mr. Henry Cary" (ed. Sabor 1:500), Park appends the following bracketed note: "[*Containing several rare passages of those times, not found in other historians. Found among the papers of, and *supposed* to be writ by the right hon. Henry viscount Faulkland, some- | time lord-deputy of Ireland.' Wood says this was published when the press was open for all books that could make any thing against the then government, with a preface to the reader by sir James Harrington. Ath. Oxon.]". For the part in which Park provides more from the title, which he presents in double quotation marks, gone are the parentheses surrounding "*supposed* to be" and introduced, at least to Oldys's 1744 edition, is the italic type for "*supposed*" (the original 1680 has much in italic, including all of "(*supposed to be*)"). For his reference to Wood, a reference that he received from Walpole, but does not acknowledge, it is imperative to note that Wood does not identify the author of the octavo preface as "sir James Harrington" (see Swan, 182). This is Park's speculation, a speculation that he drops for his 1808 *Harleian Miscellany* notes. In 1808, Park repeats his 1806 note about Wood's speculation as to why the octavo was published, and he adds his speculative relation of the octavo's derivative relation to the folio. These erroneous speculations by Park have made their way into scholarship on Walpole. Allen T. Hazen, in *A Catalogue of Horace Walpole's Library* (New Haven, CT: Yale UP, 1969), notes that Walpole, in *Royal and Noble Authors,* "quotes, apparently from Wood, the title as it appears in the octavo, but he himself seems to have owned only the folio" (7). Hazen makes a connection that his author, Walpole, did not make—a relation between the octavo and the folio—but that Walpole's editor, Park, did make. Like Stauffer, and perhaps knowing of Stauffer, Hazen follows Park's erroneous speculations regarding the octavo and folio versions of the history of Edward II, giving to later scholarship the further sense of authoritative approbation.

21. For the two historical epithets, Park also provides explanatory notes, both referencing, simply, "Rapin," which refers to Paul Rapin de Thoyras, an appropriate source for glosses to a text critical of monarchy.

22. Park also presents the narrative voice, speeches, and dialogues in a way different from his base text, Oldys's edition of *The History of the Most Unfortunate Prince* (see below).

23. William Shaw, *Memoirs of the Life and Writings of the Late Dr. Samuel Johnson, 1785*, in *The Early Biographies of Samuel Johnson*, ed. O M Brack, Jr., and Robert E. Kelley (Iowa City: U of Iowa P, 1974), 156.
24. See Paul Baines, "Oldys, William (1696–1761), herald and antiquary," *ODNB*, and Brack, "Osborne," *ODNB*.
25. William Cooke, *The Life of Samuel Johnson, LL.D.* 1785, in Brack and Kelley, eds., *Early Biographies*, 97–98. James Boswell's report corresponds to Cooke's, even while insisting on its own superiority (*Boswell's Life of Johnson*, ed. R. W. Chapman [London: Oxford UP, 1953], 112). Sir John Hawkins, in *The Life of Samuel Johnson, LL.D.*, relays the story similarly in order to justify an even more contemptuous and emotional characterization of Osborne and Johnson's misfortune in having to suffer such a person (1787; rpt. in *Johnsoniana* 20 [New York: Garland, 1974], 151).
26. *Proposals for Printing, by Subscription, the Harleian Miscellany* (London: 1743), A2. For Johnson's authorship of the central part, "An Account of this Undertaking," to which I refer and from which I quote, see J. D. Fleeman, "Johnsonian Prospectuses and Proposals," in *Augustan Studies: Essays in Honor of Irvin Ehrenpreis*, ed. Douglas Lane Paley and Timothy Keagan (Newark, DE: U of Delaware P, 1985), 215–238.
27. 1744, 1:viii; see above for Park's presentation of this passage.
28. The final quote, from Churchill, is the only one to be indicated with the single, open quotation marks at the beginning of the lines.
29. Park provides a close, single quotation mark and does not begin a new line for the last sentence.
30. Park draws this speculation in Wood from the passage Walpole references, *Works* (ed. Sabor), 500.
31. Stauffer does not identify the folio copy or copies he used, though he does note the octavo copy he consulted: "In the same Bodleian volume with the 1680 quarto [*sic*] *Edward II* is bound a 'Life and Reign of Richard II,' 1681, which is hostile to Charles II" (294, n. 5). This is Bodleian MS Wood 234, in which there are penciled notes about the history of Richard II to the effect that it is hostile to Charles II.
32. Stauffer states inaccurately, at one point: "Although William Oldys and Samuel Johnson reprinted in the Harleian Miscellany a rare and curious tract, they overlooked a book more rare and more curious, published the same year, of which their own was a shortened redaction" (295).
33. See, for instance, Kim Walker, *Women Writers of the English Renaissance* (New York: Twayne, 1996), 139–145.
34. Edward's queen is commonly called "Isabella," as in Marlowe, but both the octavo and folio texts render her "Isabel," even as both usually simply refer to her as the queen. The octavo refers to the queen as Isabel on page 5, while the folio refers to the queen as Isabel on pages 18 and 102. The manuscripts also render "Isabell" (e.g., Finch-Hatton MS 1, 19; Fitzwilliam MS 361, 260).
35. See the folio, 151; Fitzwilliam MS 361, 377; Finch-Hatton MS 1, 180–181.

36. For two examples of this critical viewpoint, see Roger Chartier, *The Order of Books,* tr. Lydia G. Cochrane (Stanford: Stanford UP, 1994), and D. F. McKenzie, *Bibliography and the Sociology of Texts* (Cambridge: Cambridge UP, 1999).
37. Finch-Hatton MS 1 is dated January 7, 1626; Fitzwilliam MS 361 is dated February 2, 1627; and the folio is dated February 20, 1627.

CHAPTER 7

FROM MANUSCRIPT TO PRINTED TEXT:
TELLING AND RETELLING THE *HISTORY OF
EDWARD II*

Margaret Reeves

This chapter explains the relationships between four texts—two in manuscript and two in print—each of which presents a version of the history of King Edward II of England. All of these texts have been linked either directly or indirectly to Elizabeth Cary, and each one consists of a prose narrative that recounts the story of the troubled reign of this early fourteenth-century king who was murdered shortly after he was deposed in 1327 by his wife, Queen Isabel, and her reputed lover, the baronial magnate, Roger Mortimer. A longstanding controversy over questions of authorship and source texts has existed in recent scholarship on Cary in relation to two of these narratives, both of which were printed in 1680: *The History of The Life, Reign, and Death of Edward II*, a folio volume, and *The History Of the most Unfortunate Prince King Edward II*, an octavo published contemporaneously with the folio.[1] The octavo's title page indicates that the history was found, we can assume in manuscript, "among the Papers of, and (supposed to be) Writ by the Right Honourable Henry Viscount Faulkland," Cary's husband. Whereas a consensus has been reached among Cary scholars that she composed the folio (which is attributed to "E.F." on the title page and preface), some are reluctant to attribute authorship of the much shorter octavo to her.[2] These debates have recently been complicated by the discovery of two manuscript histories of Edward: "Edwarde The Seconde: His Rainge and deathe wth the ffall of those too his greate ffavorites Gauestone and Spencer," dated "Janu^y: 7°. 1626," and "The Rainge and deathe off Edwarde the Seconde: The highe and ffall of his too greate ffavorites Gaveston and Spencer," bearing the date "Fe: 2°. 1627" and author's initials "E.F." on its title page (fol. 4ʳ).[3] Although no scholarly analysis of the manuscripts has yet been published, they have been linked to Cary through the work of the late Jeremy Maule.[4] In demonstrating that a precise pattern of relationships links these four texts, I will argue that questions about textual precedence and identification of the source for the printed texts can be answered by positioning all four texts in relation to one another as pieces of an intriguing bibliographical puzzle. Moreover, I will demonstrate that this positioning points directly to Elizabeth Cary as the author of all four texts.

One issue that has received considerable attention in Cary scholarship on *Edward II* is the problem of precedence. The question as to which of the two printed histories of Edward II, octavo or folio, is the source for the other arises because these two texts have much in common. A comparison of the forms of expression used in the opening sentences to each version illustrates the nature of these similarities. The octavo begins as follows:

> EDWARD the Second, born at Carnarvan, was immediately after the death of Edward the First his Father, crowned King of England. (1)

The opening sentence of the longer, folio version repeats the exact wording of all of these phrases, but the sentence itself is comparatively longer:

> **EDWARD the Second**, eldest Son of Edward the First and Elenor the vertuous Sister of the Castilian King, **was born at Carnarvan**; and in the most resplendant pride of his age, **immediately after the** decease **of his** noble **Father, crowned King of England.** (1; emphasis added)

The words and phrases in bold highlight the similarities in vocabulary and syntax between octavo and folio. Missing from the octavo are the adjectival phrase following "Edward the Second," an adverbial phrase following the main predicate, and the adjective "noble" as a descriptor for "Father," and one additional change in vocabulary occurs with the replacement of the word "death" with "decease." Nevertheless, the two initial sentences remain comparable in choice of principal words as well as word order. This is a pattern that applies to these two narratives as a whole: commonalities in expression and syntax are sufficiently comprehensive to suggest that some relation exists between them, but whether the folio is an expansion of the octavo or the octavo a redaction of the folio has been a matter of dispute.

Much energy has been expended by critics in an effort to determine which text—folio or octavo—can be assigned precedence, because they both bear the publication date of 1680, and were likely published within a couple of months of each other, if not at the same time. Donald A. Stauffer, whose 1935 article was the first to attribute authorship of the folio to Cary, argues that the octavo is an abridgment of the folio devised by the printer after the longer work appeared. Most critics, following Stauffer, have assumed that only one manuscript—that being the source for the folio version—ever existed, and that this longer folio volume was printed first.[5] Barbara Kiefer Lewalski, Louise Schleiner, and Meredith Skura concur with Stauffer's view in proposing that the octavo is a redaction or condensation of the folio.[6] In his earlier work on Cary, Jesse Swan supported this argument for the folio's precedence by referring to the dates on which the texts were entered into *The Term Catalogues*. The folio is recorded in the Michaelmas *Term Catalogue*, which appeared in November 1679, whereas the octavo is recorded in the Hilary *Term Catalogue*, which appeared three months later, in February 1680.[7] Such assumptions about the folio's precedence have contributed to doubts about Cary's authorship of the octavo.

Moreover, a further difference between the two versions complicates the discussion: several passages appear in the shorter, octavo version that are not present in the folio. For example, the closing paragraph of the octavo begins with the observation that Edward "found the Climacteric year of his Reign before he did expect it" (77). The folio contains neither this phrase nor an exact approximation of its sentiment, nor does the word "climacteric" appear anywhere in that text. If the octavo were a redaction of the folio, the origin of this and other anomalous passages remains open to question, for they demonstrate that the octavo is not simply a condensed version of the longer text, and invite speculation that these passages may have been invented by the printer. On the other hand, if the folio is an expansion of the octavo, the question of attribution for the considerable additions to the shorter text would then need to be addressed. As a result, these differences are sufficient to have complicated recent attempts to specify the precise relationship between the two printed texts and to settle questions of attribution. Until the recovery of the manuscripts, this question of which came first—octavo or folio—continually threatened to collapse into a futile debate in the order of chicken-or-egg primacy.

Another factor complicating, and likely fueling, this debate was a reluctance among scholars to attribute authorship of the octavo to Cary. Indeed, Lewalski argues that "it seems impossible that Elizabeth Cary could or would have produced this version."[8] On the other hand, a considerable number of critics have presented convincing arguments attributing authorship of the folio to Cary.[9] These arguments can be summed up as follows: although scholars have debated the exact nature of the relationship between the folio and octavo, obvious similarities in title, subject matter, and wording, together with the coincidental timing of their publication, have encouraged critics to combine the evidence provided by the respective printers of the two texts in order to identify the author. The octavo is an important piece of the puzzle because information provided by the publisher links it directly to the Falkland family. No such information is provided by the printer of the folio, but the marked similarity between the two texts illustrated above has suggested to scholars that these works share a common source. Although no authorial signature is noted on the octavo, the folio's title page and preface identify the author by the initials "E.F." So where the octavo establishes the author's family connections, the folio narrows it down. These initials help to identify which member of the Falkland family composed the source manuscript for the folio, because as Lewalski points out, no one else among Viscount Falkland's family, including his children and grandchildren, bore the initials E.F. other than Cary, and her signature on the title page of an earlier work takes precisely this form, as Lewalski also observes: *The Tragedie of Mariam, the Faire Queene of Iewry*. Written by that learned, virtuous, and truly noble Ladie, "E.C."[10] In addition, critics have noticed that E.F.'s claim in the folio's preface to have composed it in one month is similar to the claim regarding the speed with which she is said to have produced *The Reply of the Most illvstriovs Cardinall of Perron*, a translation of Perron's work addressed to James I.[11] The claim that "[o]ne woman, in one Month" translated "so large a booke" appears in an unsigned commendatory poem, although undoubtedly the claim originated from Cary.[12] Further arguments based on Cary's treatment of female subjectivity in *The History of Edward II* favor attribution of the folio to a woman writer rather than to one of the male members of the Falkland family. Lewalski demonstrates that *The History of Edward II* shares a common theme with *The Tragedie of Mariam* by exploring the predicament of a queen who, as the wife of a tyrant, is subjected to both domestic and state tyranny. This treatment of Isabel is, as Lewalski, Tina Krontiris, and Joan Parks demonstrate, more extensive, sympathetic, and complex than any previous Elizabethan or Jacobean history of Edward II.[13] Finally, the sentiments expressed in the folio's prefatory address to the reader, in which the author claims she wrote in order to "out-run those weary hours of a deep and sad Passion," have been linked to the circumstances of Cary's life prior to February 1627/28.[14] Several critics have argued that her difficult personal situation during the late 1620s—her eldest daughter had died giving birth to Cary's first grandchild, who also died, and she had alienated her husband and thereby impoverished herself by converting to Catholicism—was more in keeping with the stated motivation of the preface than that of any other member of the Falkland family at that time.[15]

Anxiety over the question of authorship is evidenced by the fact that nearly every single critic who discusses the folio version of *The History of Edward II* prefaces his or her analysis with a consideration of attribution, which suggests that the material evidence of manuscript versions of these histories of Edward will prove a welcome contribution to Cary scholarship. Indeed, one of the most recently published articles on this folio situates the question of authorial identity as the focus of its analysis of the notion of literary property.[16] The one opponent to the prevailing view attributing authorship to Cary is the historian D. R. Woolf, who insists that both the octavo and folio were composed at the time of their 1680 publication. Woolf claims that the content of these works pertains more closely to the historical context of publication than the early Stuart period, and that the pretense of historicity is a "bogus" claim made by the printers of both the 1680 octavo and folio volumes.[17] The contention that these two works have application to the early 1680s is in and of itself convincing; their subject matter—a licentious king and the influence of royal favorites—are relevant to problems associated with the reign of Charles II. Concerns about the undue influence of Charles's mistresses and the problem of the succession, especially pertaining to the Duke of York's suitability for the English throne, were hotly disputed, which is probably why the printers chose to publish the folio and octavo at that time. In this respect, Woolf's argument for their applicability to a 1680s context is irrefutable, but his denial of Cary's authorship of these texts rests on what we now know is an erroneous assumption—that no source manuscripts for these texts ever existed. These are the debates on relationships between the octavo and the folio as they now stand: the folio is accepted as Cary's, whereas the status of the octavo remains in limbo.

However, now that two manuscripts have been located, questions of textual precedence and the structure of relationships between scribal and printed texts can be addressed. Certainly, no such chicken-or-egg quandary exists with respect to the manuscripts, because both are dated, with the earliest manuscript, the Finch-Hatton, positioned by virtue of its stated date of completion of January 7, 1626/27, as an underlying text for the second, lengthier narrative found in the Fitzwilliam manuscript, completed one year later. As material objects, these two manuscripts bear the marks of consanguinity. They are composed in an identical scribal hand,[18] and the watermarks on the paper used in both manuscripts appear, from my examination, to be identical.[19] In addition, decorative ornaments on the title pages of the manuscripts are strikingly similar (see figures 1 and 2). Every page in both the Finch-Hatton and Fitzwilliam documents is ruled with reddish-brown double lines that frame the text block on all sides and create a dedicated area for glossing in the outer margins. In the case of the Finch-Hatton manuscript, the marginal ruling is repeated on the vellum binding, which is decorated with a set of double, gold-embossed borders. In addition, the pages of this earlier manuscript have gilt edges, so that the Finch-Hatton is packaged as a fair copy. To a lesser extent, the same claim can be made for the Fitzwilliam manuscript, although its presentation is slightly less elaborate, for it includes the reddish-brown marginal rulings, but its contemporary brown morocco binding lacks the gold-embossed lines that appear on the binding of the earlier manuscript.[20] Commonalities in content, form, and presentation identify the manuscripts as closely related texts, although there is a marked difference in length, with the earlier, Finch-Hatton manuscript estimated to be approximately 37,000 words, and the later, Fitzwilliam, consisting of 54,000 words. These differences in length and thus content can be understood as a function of the author's elaboration as well as revision of her text.

In fact, a direct relationship between these two manuscripts can be demonstrated with reference to narrative content by drawing on passages similar to those quoted above for the comparison of the octavo and folio. The opening sentences of the respective manuscripts demonstrate their close kinship. The Finch-Hatton manuscript begins as follows:

> Edwarde, the Seconde, borne at Carnarvan; In the pride of his Adge was Imediatly after the decease off Edwarde the ffirste, his noble ffather crowned Kinge of Englande. (1)

The opening sentence of the Fitzwilliam manuscript is markedly similar in content, as the emboldened words below illustrate, although it is longer:

> **Edwarde the Seconde**, elldest Sonne of Edward, the firste, and Elleanor the vertuous Sister, of the Castilian King was **borne, at Carnaruan**, and **In the** most resplendente **pride, of his adge, Immediatlye after the decease,** of **his noble ffather, crowned Kinge of Englande**. (1; emphasis added)[21]

The word order in the Fitzwilliam version more or less mirrors that in the Finch-Hatton, although the insertion of additional information on Edward's parentage occasions the shift of the participial phrase "borne at Carnarvan" from its position as modifier of the subject in the Finch-Hatton sentence to its position within the predicate in the Fitzwilliam sentence, with that shift also occasioning a shift forward of the auxiliary verb "was." The structure of the sentence remains the same, with the finite verb in the first version ("Edwarde . . . was . . . crowned") transformed into a compound verb in the second ("Edwarde . . . was borne

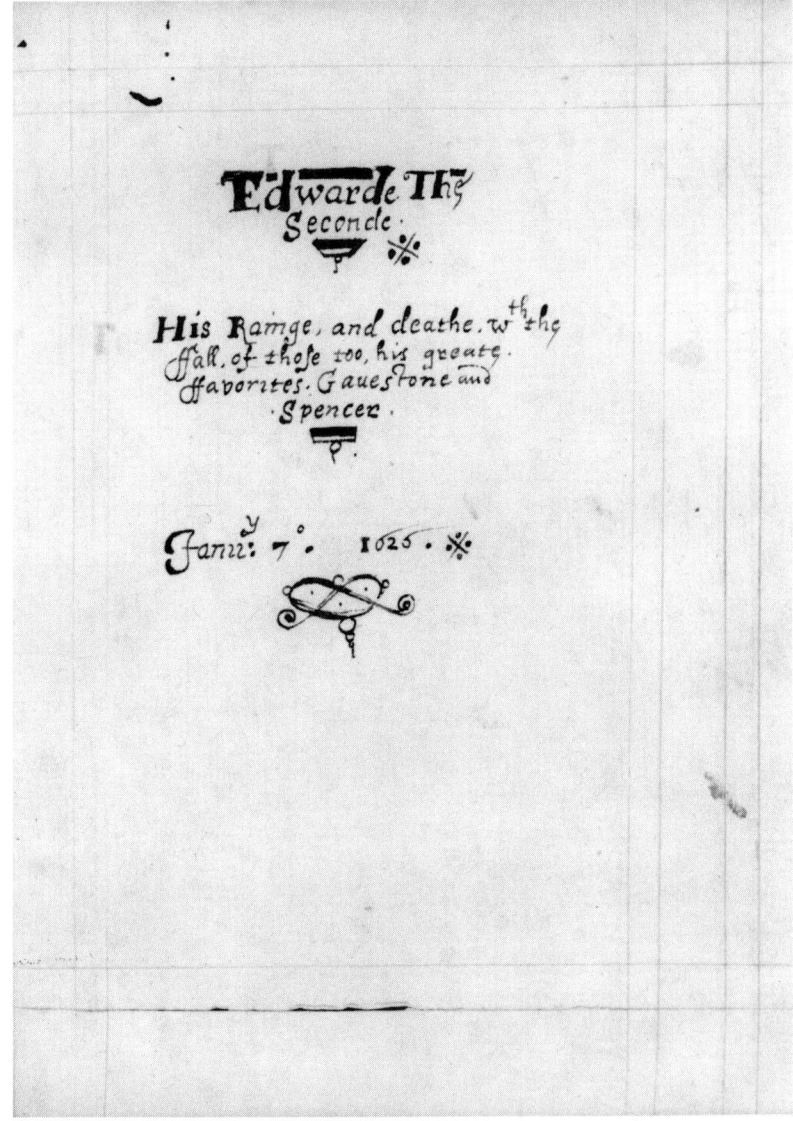

Figure 1 Title page, "Edwarde The Seconde: His Rainge and deathe." Northamptonshire Record Office, Finch-Hatton MS 1. Reproduced by permission of the Northamptonshire Record Office.

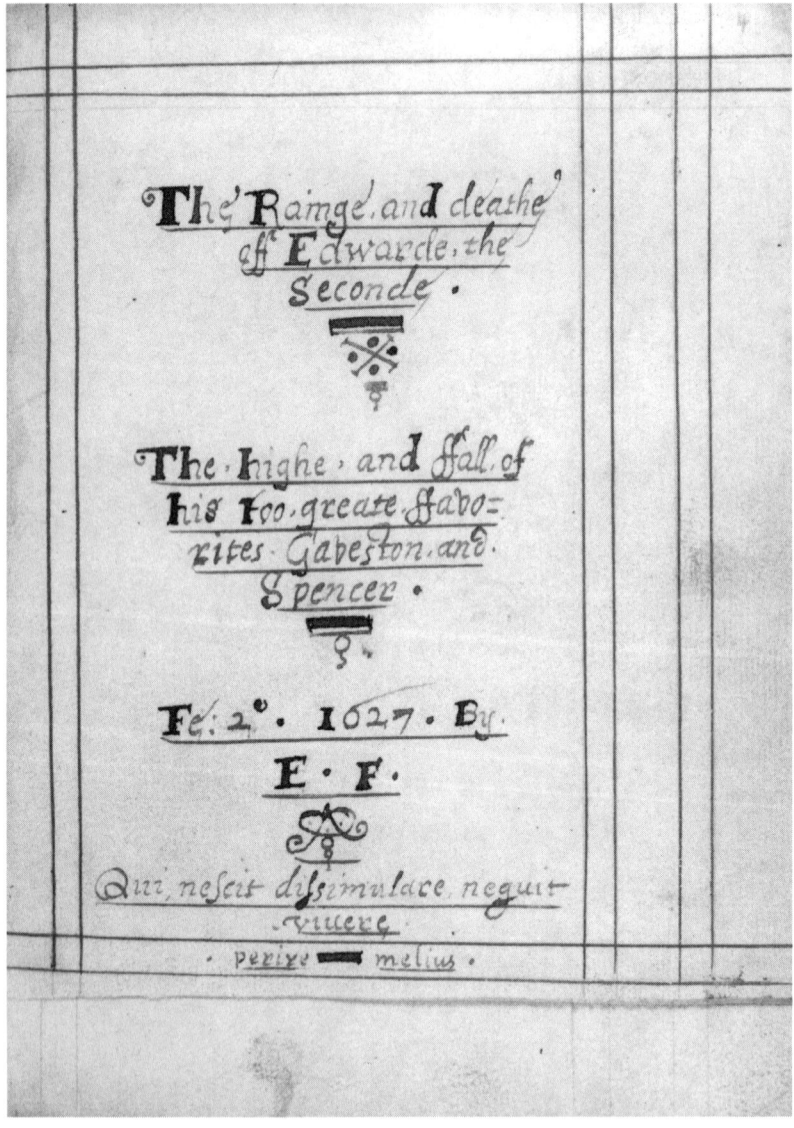

Figure 2 Title page, "The Rainge and deathe off Edwarde the Seconde." Fitzwilliam Museum, Cambridge, MS 361. Reproduced by permission of the Syndics of the Fitzwilliam Museum, Cambridge.

at Carnaruan, and . . . crowned"). Thus, the opening sentence of the Fitzwilliam manuscript elaborates on the information presented in that of the Finch-Hatton, with these two sentences exemplifying a pattern that is typical of the manuscripts as a whole, with one crucial qualification. The Fitzwilliam is not simply an expanded version of the historical narrative presented in the Finch-Hatton manuscript, because some sentences have been completely restructured, with the not unexpected consequence that on various occasions, some portions of text appearing in the first version have been omitted from the second. In some cases, this occasions a slight shift in meaning. For example, in its commentary on Edward's relations with Gaveston, the Finch-Hatton manuscript states:

> Corruption in Nature, is in it self dangerous, but when, it is confirmde by practise And hath gained a second habbitt off his Imperfection, requires a More then ordinary care, to bringe it to a perfect reformation. (3–4)

Three aspects of the relationship are mentioned here: the danger of corruption, the problem of habitual practice, and the hope of reformation. The revision that appears in the Fitzwilliam manuscript restates with considerable adjustments in wording only the first two of these aspects:

> To well he knewe, how difficulte a thinge It was to Inuerte, the course off Nature, especiallie beinge confirmde by continuance of practise, and Made habituarie by custome. (6)

The Fitzwilliam revision intensifies its criticism of the first aspect of Edward's passion for his favorite, transforming it from a form of *corruption in* nature to an actual *inversion of* nature; the rewording of the second aspect enhances clarity through a more elegant and concise articulation of the problem of habitual practice, but with the sense expressed in the Finch-Hatton version retained. Most importantly, however, the third aspect—the possibility of correction with "a More then ordinary care" with its potential for "a perfect reformation"—is not incorporated into the revision presented in the Fitzwilliam text (the omission of this third aspect is a point to which I return below). Although beyond the scope of this study, a closer, comparative analysis of these two manuscripts, as these brief examples demonstrate, is needed to consider the impact of the changes Cary made to that initial version.

Having established the close kinship between the two manuscripts, I now wish to position each of these manuscripts in relation to the two texts printed in 1680. If we accept the arguments for attribution of the folio to Cary, we can attribute authorship of the Fitzwilliam manuscript to her as well, for the folio reproduces almost the entire text of the Fitzwilliam manuscript with few omissions, as is illustrated by a comparison of the opening sentence of the folio with that of the Fitzwilliam manuscript, both of which are quoted above. Aside from differences in spelling and punctuation, the two sentences are identical, and this pattern applies, for the most part, to the document as a whole. There are minor differences occasioned by the transition from an early seventeenth-century manuscript into a late seventeenth-century printed text, such as changes made by the printer to the title and title page, updating of orthography and page layout, and the insertion of the publisher's address to the reader. Two other changes have particular significance. At the end of the preface of the Fitzwilliam manuscript, Cary asks her readers "If so yo^u hapte to veiwe It, taxe not my errors. I my self confess them, Who meant not yo^u should Iudge, till I Amend Itt wch ere it Liue in publicke, I doe promise" ("To the Reader," fol. 6^r). This statement simultaneously anticipates and deflects any criticism should the text be printed without the author's knowledge. In so doing, Cary registers an awareness of the boundaries between alternative forms of publication current during the early modern period, acknowledging a potential reader's scrutiny should the work circulate in manuscript, yet reserving the right of final revisions prior to the narrative's entry into a more public domain of print culture, a right she never exercised.[22] The omission of this last phrase of the preface is the most substantial of the editorial revisions to the text of "Rainge and deathe off Edwarde" made by the printer of the 1680 folio.

A second substantive change occurs on the title page, probably due to the printer's erroneous reading of a superscript "o" as a zero rather than as an abbreviation for the Latin ordinal number *secundo* in the date on the manuscript's title page of "Fe: 2°. 1627" (fol. 4^r). The printer has inserted only the year, 1627, on the folio's title page, and prints the erroneous date of "20 Feb. 1627" at the end of the preface, an error that by its nature suggests that the printer was working either from this particular document or a closely related copy. Although other changes in wording, word form, orthography, paragraphing, and punctuation occur throughout the manuscript, for a text of this length, these changes do not seriously undermine the veracity of the claim that the printer makes on the folio's title page that the text was "Printed verbatim from the Original." As a result, all of the scholarly arguments attributing the folio text to Cary apply equally well to the Fitzwilliam manuscript, with the added dimension of concrete evidence of a dated manuscript, thus refuting Daniel Woolf's claim that such a document could not exist.

Perhaps the most important piece of evidence to emerge from the recovery of the manuscripts is that like the Fitzwilliam, the Finch-Hatton manuscript also contains a preface alluding to the author's situation and state of mind when she composed it (see figures 3 and 4). Its similarity to the Fitzwilliam preface serves as concrete evidence in favor of Cary's authorship of the Finch-Hatton manuscript. The Fitzwilliam preface includes reference to the author's motivation, for she wrote "to owtronne, those wearie, howers of, a deepe, and sad passion," a phrase that is, by now, familiar to readers of the folio, for this preface is reprinted in that 1680 text. The preface to the earlier manuscript makes similar reference to the author's personal situation. Here, Cary also writes "to owteronne, those wearie howers, of a sadde, and deepe passion," the words "sadde" and "deepe" positioned in reverse order in this earlier preface. In addition, her claim in the Finch-Hatton preface, remarkable as it seems, that "what tenne daies wrought, yo^u may peruse in one, wch may Informe yo^u, and excuse my errors" suggests that she began it in late December 1626 and finished it in early January 1627 (the manuscript's date of "Janu^y: 7°. 1626" reflects the early modern English convention of beginning the new year on March 25 (Lady Day) rather than on January 1). This claim places the composition of this narrative about sixteen months after the death of Cary's daughter and granddaughter in August 1625, and almost immediately after she converted to Catholicism on November 14, 1626.[23] Where the "sadde and deepe passion" may pertain to the loss of her daughter and the daughter's child during childbirth, the additional emphasis in the Finch-Hatton preface on her distressed state of mind at the time of writing may gesture to another, more immediate cause, for at that time she was subject to harsh criticism from her family and friends for converting to Roman Catholicism. She explains: "Such workes requier, a quiet mynde, and Leasure both wch to me, I doe confess, are strandgers." More stress is placed in this preface than in the later Fitzwilliam version on her state of emotional distress at the time of writing. This is understandable given that the second narrative was composed more than a year after the Finch-Hatton manuscript (in February 1627/28). The greater emphasis in the earlier preface on the author's state of mind produces a marked defensiveness in tone:

> Some passadges remarkeable, may rake. If yo^u recente them, the rest maye seeme, to make, the story fuller. Lett Crittickes moralise, or Iudge their fancye. I wright, to please the truthe, not humor others. And In that sense, yo^u may, partake, my Labors.

The rather curious mixture of apology and aggression here accords well with her situation during the time of the manuscript's composition. By the time she revises this preface for the Fitzwilliam manuscript, her apology takes a

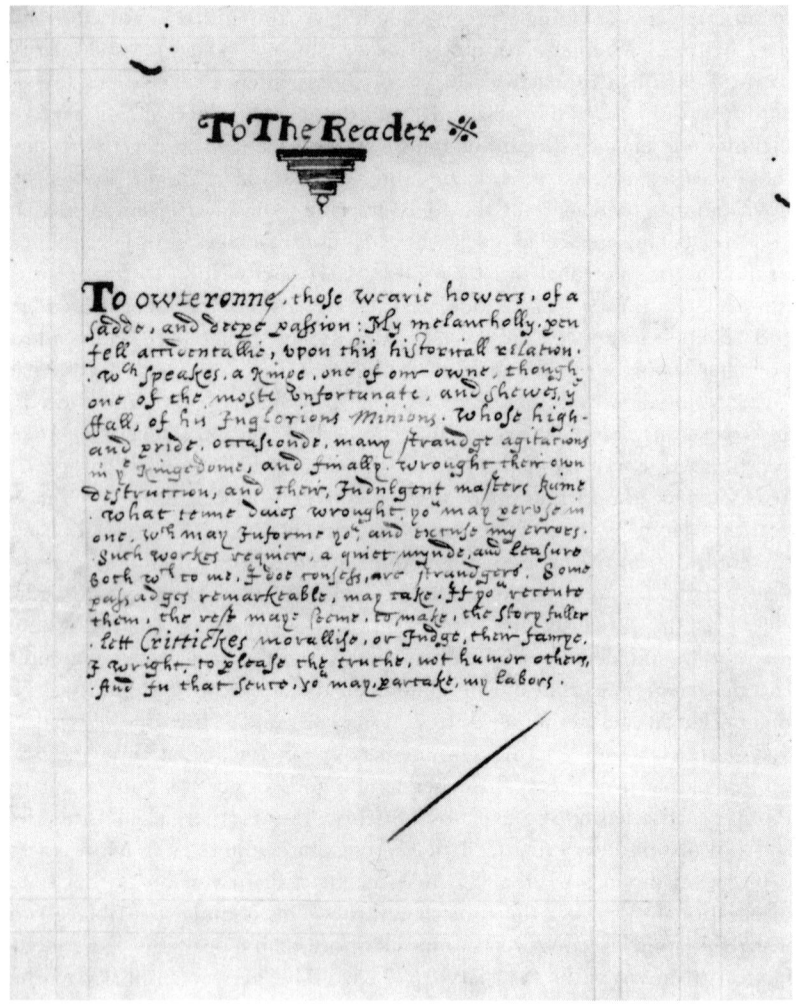

Figure 3 "To The Reader," "Edwarde The Seconde: His Rainge and deathe." Northamptonshire Record Office, Finch-Hatton MS 1. Reproduced by permission of the Northamptonshire Record Office.

more philosophical form: "I strive to please, the truth, not tyme, nor feare I censure. Since at the worste, twas, but one monthe mispended. W^{ch} cannot promise, ought in right perfection." Not only is the tone less defensive, the challenge encoded in her refusal to "humor others" in the Finch-Hatton preface is softened here to a refusal to please a more abstract quantity, "tyme." In addition, Cary claims to have taken triple the amount of time—one month as opposed to ten days—in preparing the revised version of Edward's

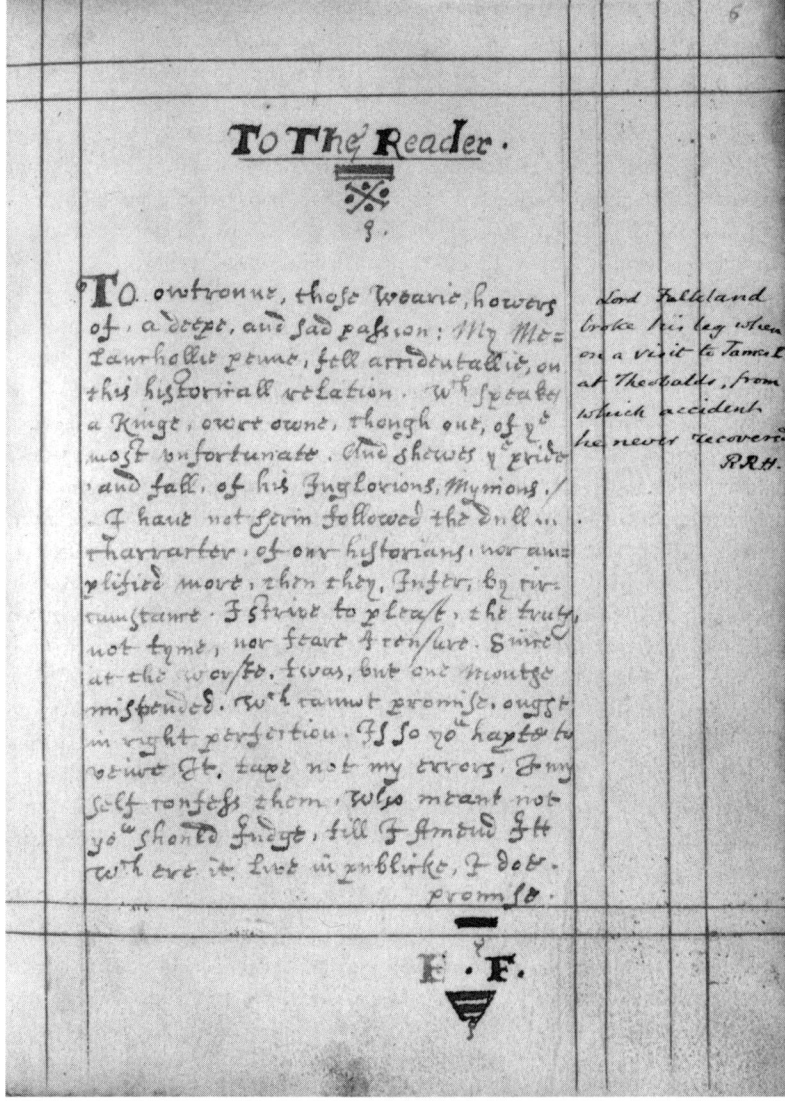

Figure 4 "To The Reader," "The Rainge and deathe off Edwarde the Seconde." Fitzwilliam Museum, Cambridge, MS 361. Reproduced by permission of the Syndics of the Fitzwilliam Museum, Cambridge.

history that appears in the Fitzwilliam document. Thus, the arguments summarized above that are derived from Cary's personal situation and based on a composition date of February 20, 1627/28, noted in the folio apply equally well, if not better, to the earlier rather than the later manuscript.

Although not in itself sufficient to establish a stemma, the above linguistic analysis can be used to propose a tentative, genealogical formulation, proceeding from the earliest, Finch-Hatton manuscript, to the longer, revised Fitzwilliam manuscript or a copy thereof, and finally to the folio volume printed in 1680. Moreover, despite the fact that no authorial initials signal authorship of the Finch-Hatton manuscript, its connection to the Fitzwilliam manuscript, given the similarities in scribal hand, paper, title pages, and prefaces, is beyond question, so that the initials "E.F.," by virtue of this close kinship, refer to the earlier, Finch-Hatton manuscript as well.

This leaves us with one remaining but important piece of the puzzle, that being the octavo, for this is the text that links the entire set of narratives directly to the Falkland papers, and thus, to Cary. The above comparisons between the opening sentences of the printed texts and the two manuscripts are again relevant here. The pattern of similarities and differences between the initial sentences of the manuscripts roughly approximates the same pattern that is evident when the opening sentences of the octavo and folio are compared, and this replication of apparent relationships between each pair of texts points to the answer. Although the folio appears to extend and elaborate on the text of the octavo, we now know that the folio incorporates the revisions made by Cary when she rewrote her history of Edward II in January 1627/28, transforming the shorter, Finch-Hatton manuscript into the longer, Fitzwilliam text. Moreover, rather than being a condensed version of the folio, as some have argued, the octavo is, more plausibly, positioned in close relationship to the Finch-Hatton manuscript instead of the folio. The similarities in wording that we see between the octavo and the folio, as demonstrated earlier, are instead a function of their having a common ancestor, although they are related to that ancestor in different ways. This identifies a potential source for those anomalous phrases that appear in the octavo but not in the folio, because the wording in these passages can be found in the Finch-Hatton manuscript. For example, the passage quoted above from the Finch-Hatton manuscript on the subject of Edward's relations with Gaveston does appear in the octavo in a more concise version that nevertheless retains the Finch-Hatton manuscript's commentary on all three aspects of that relationship:

> A corruption in Nature, that by practice hath won it self the habit of being ill, requires a more than ordinary care to give it reformation. (2–3)

The consideration of the third aspect of Edward's relations, proposing that the hope of reformation could be achieved with "more than ordinary care," is expressed here in nearly identical form to that in the Finch-Hatton, the absence of the qualifier "perfect" being the only substantive difference between the two versions. A second example is equally revealing. The apparently anomalous comment in the last paragraph of the octavo, cited above, remarking on the foreshortening of Edward's final year on the throne, also appears in the Finch-Hatton manuscript. Like the octavo, the Finch-Hatton manuscript observes in its closing remarks that Edward "founde the Clymaterick yeare of his rainge much sooner then he expected" (195). The octavo's printer certainly did not invent these anomalous segments, as some scholars have assumed. These examples typify the close relationship between the octavo and the Finch-Hatton manuscript, and it is necessary to clarify the relationship between the octavo and the Finch-Hatton as well as that between the folio and the Fitzwilliam texts because these anomalous passages have raised doubts among scholars about Cary's authorship of the octavo.

Having established that a close relationship exists between the octavo and Finch-Hatton does not, however, confirm that the latter is the source manuscript for the former, because the differences between these two texts are not negligible—the octavo (ca. 21,000 words) is much shorter than the Finch-Hatton manuscript (ca. 37,000 words)—and a more precise understanding of the relationship between them is needed. On the one hand, it is possible to position the Finch-Hatton as an underlying source for the octavo, the text drastically reduced at the time of its publication. On the other hand, if the Finch-Hatton is not the source for the octavo, we must consider the possibility of a fifth version of *The History of Edward II,* with the octavo having derived from that now-lost manuscript, the one "found among the Papers of, and (supposed to be) Writ by the Right Honourable Henry Viscount Faulkland." Jesse Swan's recent identification of the publisher of the octavo as Sir James Hayes indicates that this second scenario of a lost manuscript serving as the source text for the octavo is the more likely option. As Swan demonstrates, Hayes had access to the Falkland papers as a result of his marriage to Rachel Hungerford Cary, widow of Henry Cary, the fourth Viscount Falkland. Swan's research on Hayes helps to support the hypothesis that this manuscript (found by Hayes but no longer extant), rather than the Finch-Hatton document, is the source for the octavo.[24] It is possible, therefore, to propose that this lost manuscript can be positioned as a kind of missing link from which the contents of both the octavo and the Finch-Hatton manuscript are derived.

The transformation of the historical narration of Edward II's reign from the Finch-Hatton version to that recorded in the Fitzwilliam establishes Cary as a reviser of her own work. It is now evident that for Cary, rethinking and rewriting the history of Edward II was an ongoing process. The Finch-Hatton manuscript is most likely an expanded revision of the now-lost octavo manuscript, with the Fitzwilliam manuscript an even lengthier revision that is very close indeed to the folio text. Therefore, the Finch-Hatton and Fitzwilliam manuscripts can be situated as intervening texts between the octavo and folio. Clearly, the 1680 folio and octavo publications are separate printed versions of two different manuscripts, with the two printed works connected to each other not by the actions and emendations of a printer, but because the source manuscripts upon which they are based establish that connection. Together, these five texts—four extant and at least one lost manuscript—form a pattern of relationships characterized by complex ties of consanguinity in their composition, and by their interdependent status as pieces of evidence upon which a solid case for attribution to Elizabeth Cary can be made. If she is the author of any of the texts, then she is the author of *all* of them, without question, even if the narrative printed in the octavo ranks as merely a primitive ancestor to the much more elaborate version published in the folio. The status of the two manuscripts as pieces of material evidence, or, to borrow Robert Darnton's words, as "hard nuggets of irreducible reality,"[25] has played a crucial role in confirming these relationships, allowing my analysis to move beyond the measure of textual content in order to engage with this intriguing bibliographical puzzle.

Notes

I wish to thank Heather Wolfe for her assistance and advice provided so generously while I was working on these manuscripts, and again while I was revising—and rethinking—my argument in this essay. I also thank those who provided feedback on an earlier version of this paper presented at a session on "Women in the Archives" for the December 2004 MLA annual conference in Philadelphia, especially to Elizabeth Hageman, session organizer, and to Margaret Ezell, commentator. In addition, I am grateful to those who commented on earlier versions of this study, including Brian Corman, Melba Cuddy-Keane, Mary Nyquist, and Kelly Quinn, and more recently, Heather Campbell, Jane Couchman, Elizabeth Cohen, Hugo de Quehen, Joan Gibson, and Agnes Juhász-Ormsby. I also wish to thank the Atkinson Faculty of Liberal and Professional Studies at York University for funding this project in the form of travel grants so that I could examine the manuscripts in the archives of the Northamptonshire Record Office and the Fitzwilliam Museum in Cambridge, England, during the summer of 2004, and then present my findings at the MLA.

1. *The History Of the most Unfortunate Prince King Edward II. With Choice Political Observations on Him and his unhappy Favourites, Gaveston & Spencer: Containing Several Rare Passages of those Times, Not found in other Historians. Found among the Papers of, and (supposed to be) Writ by the Right Honourable Henry Viscount*

Faulkland, Sometime Lord Deputy of Ireland (London: Printed by A.G. and J.P. and are sold by John Playford, at his Shop near the Temple-Church, 1680); and *The History of The Life, Reign, and Death of Edward II. King of England, And Lord of Ireland. With The Rise and Fall of his great Favourites, Gaveston and the Spencers. Written by E.F. in the year 1627. And Printed verbatim from the Original* (London: Printed by J.C. for Charles Harper, at the Flower-de-luce in Fleet-street; Samuel Crouch, at the Princes Arms in Popes-head-Alley in Cornhil; and Thomas Fox, at the Angel in Westminster hall, 1680). Facsimiles of the 1680 folio and octavo are reproduced in Margaret W. Ferguson, introduction to *Works by and Attributed to Elizabeth Cary*, vol. 2 of *The Early Modern Englishwoman: A Facsimile Library of Essential Works, Part 1: Printed Writings, 1500–1640*, ed. Betty S. Travitsky and Patrick Cullen (Aldershot: Scolar Press, 1996). Electronic versions of both folio and octavo are available at the *Brown Women Writers Project* website at http://www.wwp.brown.edu. Passages quoted from the folio and octavo are taken from the facsimiles and are noted in parentheses in the text. A critical edition of the folio and octavo by Jesse Swan is forthcoming in the Ashgate series, *The Early Modern Englishwoman, 1500–1750: Contemporary Editions.*
2. The text of the folio runs to approximately 54,000 words, and that of the octavo to approximately 21,000 words. I summarize these debates below.
3. "Edwarde The Seconde: His Rainge and deathe wth the ffall of those too his greate ffavorites Gauestone and Spencer," dated "Janu^y: 7°. 1626" on its title page (fol. 1^r). Cataloged as Finch-Hatton MS 1, Northamptonshire Record Office, Northampton, England, and hereafter referred to as the Finch-Hatton manuscript; and "The Rainge and deathe off Edwarde the Seconde: The highe and ffall of his too greate ffavorites Gaveston and Spencer," bearing the date "Fe: 2°. 1627" and author's initials "By E.F." on its title page (fol. 4^r). Cataloged as MS 361, Fitzwilliam Museum, Cambridge, England, and hereafter referred to as the Fitzwilliam manuscript. I have modernized the punctuation in the titles of both manuscripts.
4. Jeremy Maule discovered these manuscripts during the 1990s, and presented a paper on the Finch-Hatton manuscript entitled "Twice Murdered? Elizabeth Cary's *Edward II* (1626) and its Bibliographers" (paper presented as a guest lecture at the Centre for Reformation and Renaissance Studies, Victoria College, University of Toronto, November 2, 1995). Drawing on the work of Maule, Heather Wolfe called attention to these manuscripts in a bibliographical listing of extant manuscripts by Cary in *Elizabeth Cary, Lady Falkland: Life and Letters* (Cambridge and Tempe, AZ: RTM Publications and Arizona Center for Medieval and Renaissance Studies, 2001), 494.
5. Donald A. Stauffer offered the first and still one of the most convincing arguments for attribution to Cary in his article, "A Deep and Sad Passion," in *Essays in Dramatic Literature*, ed. Hardin Craig (Princeton: Princeton UP, 1935), 295.
6. Barbara Kiefer Lewalski, *Writing Women in Jacobean England* (Cambridge: Harvard UP, 1993), 317; Louise Schleiner, "Lady Falkland's Reentry into Writing: Anglo-Catholic Consensual Discourse and Her *Edward II* as Historical Fiction," *The Witness of Times: Manifestations of Ideology*

in *Seventeenth-Century England,* ed. Katherine Z. Keller and Gerald J. Schiffhorst (Pittsburgh, PA: Duquesne UP, 1993), 285n10; Meredith Skura, "Elizabeth Cary and Edward II: What Do Women Want to Write?," *Renaissance Drama* ns 27 (1996): 83.

7. Jesse Swan, "Elizabeth Cary's *The History of the Life, Reign, and Death of Edward:* A Critical Edition" (PhD diss., Arizona State University, 1993), 193 and 229n111; and Edward Arber, comp., *The Term Catalogues, 1668–1709 A.D.; with a Number for Easter Term, 1711 A.D.: A Contemporary Bibliography of English Literature in the reigns of Charles II, James II, William and Mary, and Anne,* vol. 1 (London: Professor Edward Arber, 1903), xi. An entry in the *Term Catalogues* does not necessarily indicate the precise date of a book's appearance in bookshops. Arber explains that whether or not the book had been published when that term's catalog appeared depended on the book's licensing date, size, and how far the printing had progressed when the catalog itself was produced. For this reason, Arber explains, books listed in the Michaelmas *Term Catalogue,* which was published in November, often bear the date of the subsequent year on their title pages, as is the case with *The History of Edward II.* Thus, it is also possible that a book dated 1680 could have been printed prior to the end of 1679. See Arber, vol. 1, xi and 368.

8. Lewalski, 318. Schleiner agrees with Lewalski but transposes the printers of the two versions, incorrectly listing John Playford as the printer of the folio, when, in fact, his name is noted only on the octavo volume. He is listed as the octavo's bookseller, but is likely also one of its printers, who are identified as "A.G. and J.P." This difference, which may seem minor, indicates both the energy with which scholars have approached the question of precedence and also the confusion that has arisen as literary historians have attempted to identify the precise relationship between these texts.

9. The most comprehensive of these arguments have been presented by Lewalski, Skura, Stauffer, and Karen Raber, "Gender and Property: Elizabeth Cary and *The History of Edward II,*" *Explorations in Renaissance Culture* 26, no. 2 (2000): 199–227.

10. Lewalski, 318. Cary's *The Tragedie of Mariam* was printed in 1613, although editors of a modern edition argue that it was probably written before 1609. See Barry Weller and Margaret W. Ferguson, eds., *The Tragedy of Mariam: The Fair Queen of Jewry with The Lady Falkland Her Life: By One of her Daughters* (Berkeley: U of California P, 1994), 5–6. Cary's husband had not yet been elevated to the rank of Viscount Falkland when *The Tragedie of Mariam* was written, but after 1620 she signed her letters "Efalkland," so her use of the initials "E.F." on "Rainge and deathe off Edwarde" is consistent with her epistolary signature at that time of her life. Wolfe indicates that Cary changed her signature again in 1632 to "'EM Falkland' instead of 'E Falkland' to emphasize the name 'Maria,'" the confirmation name she assumed subsequent to her conversion to Catholicism. See Wolfe, 33. For examples of Cary's epistolary signature, see the letters transcribed in Wolfe, 299, 300, and 302.

11. Both Lewalski and Schleiner make this point. See Cary, trans., *The Reply of the most illvstriovs Cardinall of Perron, to the Ansvveare of the most excellent King*

of Great Britaine, by Jacques Davy du Perron (Dovay: Martin Bogart, 1630), a translation of *Réplique à la Response du Sérénissime Roy de la Grand Bretagne* (Paris, 1620). See Lewalski, 320 and 201; and Schleiner, 285n10.

12. This poem is composed in Latin with an English translation inserted directly underneath it. See "The same in English," a translation of "*In Lavdem Nobilissimæ Heroinæ,*" in *The Reply,* sig. c2ᵛ.
13. Lewalski, 179. Some qualification of this last point is necessary with respect to Marlowe's *Edward II,* however, because the length and form of Cary's narrative give her more scope and textual space with which to develop and portray Isabel's character. That Cary chooses to do this, however, and that she explores and reflects on Isabel's motivations, supports Lewalski's claim that this evident interest in a female perspective may be another factor pointing to the author's gender. Skura challenges this argument for its essentialism, yet her claim that the more sympathetic representation is of Edward rather than Isabel is unconvincing. See Skura, 87–92. For comparison to other Renaissance histories of Edward II, see Lewalski, 203–204, and Skura, 81–82. For comparisons to other representations of Isabel, see Tina Krontiris, "Style and Gender in Elizabeth Cary's *Edward II,*" in *The Renaissance Englishwoman in Print: Counterbalancing the Canon,* ed. Anne M. Haselkorn and Betty S. Travitsky (Amherst: U of Massachusetts P, 1990), 137–153; and Joan Parks, "Elizabeth Cary's Domestic History," in *Other Voices, Other Views: Expanding the Canon in English Renaissance Studies,* ed. Helen Ostovich, Mary V. Silcox, and Graham Roebuck (Newark: U of Delaware P, 1999), 176–192.
14. The folio's preface is dated "20 Feb. 1627" (sig. A2ᵛ). I address the discrepancy between this date and that on the Fitzwilliam manuscript below.
15. See Lewalski, 203; Schleiner, 210; Skura, 90; Stauffer, 313–314; and Weller and Ferguson, 7.
16. See Raber, n11. Skura's earlier article is also, in fact, an argument for attribution, but she moves well beyond reference to biographical circumstance to arguments based on content and Cary's place in Renaissance literary and political culture.
17. D. R. Woolf, "The True Date and Authorship of Henry, Viscount Falkland's *History of the Life, Reign, and Death of King Edward II,*" *The Bodleian Library Record* 12.1 (1985): 440; and Woolf, *The Idea of History in Early Stuart England: Erudition, Ideology, and "The Light of Truth" from the Accession of James I to the Civil War* (Toronto: U of Toronto P, 1990), 285.
18. Wolfe confirms that this is not Cary's handwriting. Private correspondence, November 19, 2002.
19. The watermark is strikingly similar to watermark "NAME.008.1" in *The Thomas L. Gravell Watermark Archive* [http://ada.cath.vt.edu:591/dbs/gravell/default.html (November 16, 2005)], which describes it as the arms of France and Navarre. The mark consists of fleur-de-lis above a pair of shields positioned inside a half-circle of chaining, with an eight-point star centered underneath the chaining. The letters in the countermark are "DVRAN," although Gravell identifies the countermark as "G DVRAN."

20. It must be acknowledged, however, that the gold tooling on the binding and edge gilding could have been done by a subsequent owner. I thank Hugo de Quehen for alerting me to this possibility.
21. In both manuscripts, aside from title pages and prefatory material, the pages on which the historical narrative appears have been numbered by the scribe, and references to the manuscripts are noted in parentheses by that pagination. Thus, both passages just cited appear on the first pages of the respective narrative histories. Quotations from these documents are made by the kind permission of the Northamptonshire Record Office and the Syndics of the Fitzwilliam Museum.
22. Cary's daughter reports that one of her mother's earliest works, identified in Wolfe's chronology as *The Tragedie of Mariam,* had been stolen from a sister-in-law's chamber and printed, but that Cary had recalled it. See Wolfe, 110. Weller and Ferguson indicate that this play circulated in manuscript prior to its publication in print in 1613. On the distinction between scribal and print publication forms, see Harold Love, *The Culture and Commerce of Texts: Scribal Publication in Seventeenth-Century England* (Amherst: U of Massachusetts P, 1993), 35.
23. These biographical details are reported in "The Lady Falkland Her Life," and listed in the "Chronology" of her life, both of which are printed in Wolfe, 126–140 and xiii–xx.
24. Jesse Swan, "Towards a Textual History of the 1680 Folio *The History of the Life, Reign, and Death of Edward II* (attributed to Elizabeth Cary, Lady Falkland): Understanding the Collateral 1680 Octavo *The History of the Most Unfortunate Prince,*" in *New Ways of Looking at Old Texts, III: Papers of the Renaissance English Text Society, 1997–2001,* ed. W. Speed Hill (Tempe, AZ: ACMRS and RETS, 2004), 177–190. Maule indicated in his Toronto lecture that the Finch-Hatton manuscript was owned by Sir Christopher Hatton (1605–1670), its existence in his collection confirmed by an undated index of manuscripts in Lord Hatton's collection compiled by Sir William Dugdale (1605–1686). The index is cataloged as Finch-Hatton 4017, Northamptonshire Record Office.
25. Robert Darnton, *The Great Cat Massacre and other Episodes in French Cultural History* (New York: Basic Books, 1984), 157.

PART III

OTHER WRITINGS

CHAPTER 8

"TO INFORME THEE ARIGHT": TRANSLATING
DU PERRON FOR ENGLISH RELIGIOUS DEBATES

Karen L. Nelson

Elizabeth Cary's translation of Jacques Davy du Perron's *The Reply of the most illustrious Cardinall of Perron to the Ansvveare of the most Excellent King of Great Britaine, the First Tome* was published in Douai in 1630, its impressive red-and-black title paage graced with a printer's mark depicting the seal of the Society of Jesus.[1] This 500-page, folio-sized volume was designed to bring the light of Catholic doctrine to an English population living in semidarkness. While the translation was an enormous exercise in erudition, it is an often-overlooked element of Cary's canon. The translation's protofeminist elements are excerpted for inclusion in anthologies or cited to assist in constructing Cary's biography,[2] but the bulk of the volume goes unread, decidedly neither "literature" nor historical evidence. The attention it garners stems largely from its genesis as the product of a woman's pen. Frances Dolan, who frames the text for the most recent facsimile edition, portrays Cary's project as a lone female Catholic cry in the male Protestant wilderness, one that "attempted to reactivate a polemical war which had peaked in 1616."[3] These characterizations undervalue the scope of Cary's project and its place in religious controversies of the late 1620s and early 1630s. Cary forcefully joined her voice with those of many Catholic polemicists of the period. Because she translated *Reply* and had it published, she was able to extend her contemporaries' critiques of the English Protestant Church to include a specific request that the king recognize the spiritual authority of the pope.

Recent work on English church politics and on events of 1630 allows for a more precise reading of this translation in its cultural context, which in turn indicates that Cary's translation was indeed timely. Anthony Milton traces the ways in which topoi in the religious debates began in the early seventeenth century and continued to evolve and be invoked throughout the 1620s and 1630s.[4] Cary's translation of *Reply* encapsulated these debates in the preliminary matter as well as in the main text, and most convincingly in the final paragraphs of the work, which were constructed ostensibly as a defense of Cardinal Bellarmine but also argued that rulers who publicly acknowledged their devotion toward the pope and the Roman Catholic Church did not, in any way, reduce their own temporal power. Coming, as it did, at a time when peaceful relations were being restored between England and France, and when England was rife with anxiety about a reunification with Rome, the translation's call for religious as well as political reconciliation was quite fraught.

In the first part of this chapter, I assess the Catholic conversation into which Cary inserted her translation in 1630 in order to assert that this treatise was one aspect of an increasingly vocal and visible Catholic community centered in part on Henrietta Maria, one that drew upon the publications and translations of printers on the continent to establish its canonical texts and to bolster itself as a community. Cary's translation of Du Perron was part of that effort, and her treatise is especially notable and significant in ways that I examine in the second part of this chapter. Du Perron's *Réplique* to James I, posthumously published in French in 1620 and in Latin in 1621, served as a catalog of the errors of the English Church and the rightness of the Roman Church. True to the genre of religious controversy, Du Perron exhibited his eminence and learning by dissecting King James's initial defense of the English Church into one- and two-sentence passages that he then examined and countered in one- or two-page (or, in one instance, 131-page) rebuttals. It was a definitive work, similar to Thomas Cartwright's *Confutation of the Rhemists translations, glosses, and annotations on the New Testament* (1618) in its extensive analysis of the opponent's errors and its text surrounded by exhaustive references to biblical and scholarly sources. The *Reply* was itself part of a larger debate, since James had framed his own defense of the English Church as a response to critiques offered by Du Perron and by Isaac Casaubon as early as 1615. Cary made Du Perron's text, and its extensive arguments, available to an English audience that in 1630 was invested in determining the proper religious course to follow. For English Catholics, Cary delineated every stance they might need to know; for English conformists, Cary offered abundant rhetoric that might serve to convert them. Couched as it was in terms of a translation of an argument not against Charles but against his father, Cary muted the ways in which her treatise attempted to correct the English Church's errors. Her strategy was a time-honored one, employed by both Catholics and Protestants, in treatises, catechisms, and in versions of the Bible itself. Nonetheless, this publication was framed with paratext, especially its prefaces, its encomia, and its closing paragraphs, that marked its contents as especially significant for 1630 and for England. Events in the two years prior made this *Reply* reverberate for an audience of English Catholics who hoped for reunion with Rome and for an audience of English Protestants who began to consider such a possibility as a real one.

By constructing Cary as a lone figure of Catholic rebelliousness, Frances Dolan erases a vigorous Catholic population from the English countryside and from the religious debates of the late 1620s and early 1630s. Other historians of the period offer models that contrast with Dolan's and instead center upon the English perception of a rising Catholic threat. Kevin Sharpe, for example, attributes English fears of Catholics in the 1630s to an increasingly visible Catholic population in England. Sharpe notes that by the early 1630s, the actual number of priests and recusants had increased substantially from earlier in the century and suggests that "the ranks of all Catholics (that is including those not yet identified as recusants) may well have surpassed 300,000."[5] Sharpe sees many of the apprehensions about Catholics as centered upon Henrietta Maria and her court, primarily the result of internal politics and policies. She served, in essence, as a lightening rod for English fears, with her chapel that attracted increasing numbers of English courtiers to attend mass publicly.

Other historians trace the source of concern to factors outside England. Jonathan Scott, for example, sets England's fears of Catholicism within the context of a perceived domination by a strengthened continental Roman Catholicism and a weakened English military. Scott argues that while the actual numbers of Roman Catholics in England declined as the century progressed, the English were aware of, and felt threatened by, a resurgence in continental Roman Catholicism over the course of the seventeenth century. Scott observes, "Between 1590 and 1690 the geographical reach of Protestantism shrank from one-half to one-fifth of the land area of the continent . . . The European problem was the counter-reformation advance."[6] Later vantage points of the seventeenth century enable one to perceive its Catholic population as a minority and view the period as one in which the English nation was becoming ever more masculine and Protestant.[7] However, English people in the late 1620s and early 1630s were unaware of that outcome. They instead saw the success of Catholic forces on the continent, the failures of their own abortive attempts to defend international Calvinism at La Rochelle and Rhe, and increasing numbers of practicing Catholics in England, especially at the English court.

The English discomfort with these developments is evident in many contemporary letters and records of the period. John Bruce, in the preface to the *Calendar of State Papers Domestic* for 1629–1630, offers an observation that serves as a useful overview of the concerns of the letters cataloged there: "The treaty [of Madrid] was rendered more palatable to the King by the character of the Ambassador who was employed in the preliminary negotiations . . . The gorgeous pencil of Rubens consecrated a peace, which to the Queen of Bohemia, seemed to be a personal desertion, and to the people of England, an abandonment of the cause of Protestantism, at the very time when, under the leadership of Gustavus Adolphus, it appeared likely to achieve success."[8] That sense of abandonment is clear in the letters of Sir Thomas Roe, for example. Writing from the court of Charles I's daughter, Elizabeth of Bohemia, he reports to Dudley Carleton, Viscount Dorchester, on September 20, 1630, that "From Holland I haue heard that our Ambassador hath directly moued the lords the States to make peace with Spayne . . . How vnseasonable this proposition was in tyme: how opposite our owne ends, though we make peace . . . how vnsauorye to those our friends, that now gaspe for their liberty & Religion."[9] Writing to William Weld on October 29, 1630, Roe noted that "I am Constantly perswaded, by the obseruation of twentye yeares, that all Leagues, and trust with any Papist blinded estate, are Egyptian reedes, and that all those inward Counsells are directed to roote out our Religion and to implant their Ecclesiasticall teaching."[10] English Protestants were concerned that restored relations with France and Spain indicated Charles's willingness to negotiate with Catholics, and would undermine efforts to solidify a continental Protestant alliance against the Hapsburgs and in support of Elizabeth of Bohemia's claims.

Elizabeth Cary belonged to a rather large company of connected, powerful Catholics. Her conversion to Catholicism had been made public by 1626; in 1629, her presence was noted among a large group (estimated at 1400–1500 people) of notable English Catholics making a public pilgrimage on St. Winifred's Day (November 3) to St. Winifred's Well in Holywell, Wales, including the Earl of Shrewsbury, Lord William Howard, Sir Thomas Jarrett, Sir William Norris, Sir Cuthbert Clifton, Sir John Tolbot of Bashshaw, "with divers others knights, ladies, gentlemen and gentlewomen of divers Countries" and roughly 150 priests.[11] Clearly, Catholics were not an enemy hidden within the English state. Their numbers included networks of elite English families and families willing to make public pilgrimages and to host priests in their homes.

While these activities were recorded and an attempt was made to account for those involved, English officials were certainly not proactive in preventing English Catholics from assembling publicly. John D. Krugler cautions that "Catholic as victim" historiography must be complicated, particularly for elite English Catholic families who drew from many methods, particularly family and court connections, to exploit opportunities as they found them.[12] In addition, the growth and mediated success of English Catholics was not confined to England. Continental counter-reform efforts on behalf of English Catholics took many guises in the 1620s and included the stabilization and increase of the English Colleges with the foundation of the Irish College in Rome in 1626 and the foundation of the *Collegium de Propaganda Fide* in 1627. English Catholic women's communities also flourished, with the foundation of communities of English Franciscan nuns in Bruges in 1621, English Benedictine nuns at Cambrai in 1623 and at Ghent in 1624, and the foundation of the Congregation of the English Ladies in Munich, Poor Clares at Aire, and Austin Canonesses at Bruges, all in 1629.[13] Maryland, a colony chartered ostensibly to Christianize the native populations and to provide freedom of conscience for English citizens, especially Catholics, was founded in 1632.[14]

English Catholics were more visible; English exile communities thrived; English Catholic controversial texts flourished. Cary's project was one of many efforts in 1630 to translate, and thus to transmit, Catholic values for an English audience. While much of this literature was published or transcribed on the continent, the sheer quantity made it a force to be acknowledged and countered, as the volume of Calvinist and conformist responses makes clear. A survey of titles in Early English Books Online indicates that, in the two years prior to the publication of Cary's translation, both Catholics and Protestants were heavily engaged in codifying their religious platforms and shoring up their positions, in part by returning to voices of authority from earlier religious debates.[15] Both Catholics and Protestants were offering a wide range of tools to aid religious practice, such as catechisms, psalms, prayers, and meditations. Another important subcategory of these religious materials were "models for living": saints' lives, testimonials of sinners and converts saved, and edifying self-help guides for holy living, with titles such as *A shorte and sure way to heauen, and present happiness. Taught in a treatise of our conformity with the will of God*.[16] Publishers reprinted numerous sermons from "the golden ages" of James and Elizabeth, and especially turned to the prayers of Elizabeth and the sermons of John Preston, Thomas Adams, and Henry Ainsworth.[17] Printers continued to issue many volumes of catechisms, psalms, devotional exercises, and models of virtue. Protestant authors especially used nostalgia for earlier reigns to sharpen their calls for further church reform.

Catholic printers, too, returned to arguments that had their origins in these earlier days, and Cary's choice of Du Perron was a contribution to a vibrant debate that justified Catholicism's essential nature by printing or reprinting, in translation as necessary, the works of earlier divines. Catholic printers canonized the debates from the early seventeenth century in order to justify the positions articulated in the late 1620s and early 1630s.

By reprinting these earlier debates, printers were also able to preserve elements of religious cultural practice on the part of Catholics and Protestants, since both groups perceived these practices as under siege from their opponents. Dorothy Latz observes that for English Benedictine men and women on the continent, "the work of copying, transcribing, translating, composing, and preserving books and manuscripts in their libraries" became a central project, one prompted by "the urgency of handing down to posterity a spiritual treasure in danger of being lost amid persecution . . . in England."[18] Especially for the Catholic community, at least partially underground and in exile, print and manuscript texts played a crucial role in the transmission and preservation of English Catholic customs and culture.

Cary was moved, as were many others in the late 1620s and early 1630s, to promulgate Catholic doctrine for her compatriots. The Epistle Dedicatory to a later translation of Bellarmine, *Of the Eternal Felicity of the Saints* (1638), articulated the agendas behind many of the works emanating from the presses in the Catholic Netherlands and France. These texts are to ensure "a true and *Orthodoxall fayth,* residing in the *vnderstanding,*" and "a deuout and vertuous life, residing in the Will" (sig. A2). Indeed, the majority of the books printed in St. Omer, Douai, and Rouen embarked upon one of two projects: they either offered debates as to the rightness of Catholic doctrine or provided models for the virtuous life, in the forms of saints' lives or practical exercises and instructions.

Cary defined her project as one of the former. She claimed, in her preface to the reader that "To looke for glorie from Translation, is beneath my intention, and if I had aimed at that, I would not haue chosen so late a writer, but heere I saw stored vp, as much of antiquitie, as would most fitlie serue for this purpose" (sig. ã2ᵛ). Her choice of the word "antiquitie" was a loaded one, since both Protestants and Catholics had for almost a century been arguing their position as one justified by its roots in antiquity; she explicitly connected Du Perron's lengthy exposition of right doctrine with these debates, while asserting that her purpose was neither an exhibition of fame nor prowess. The translation belied both of her humble claims: it was clearly an accomplished translation that was itself part of a multipronged defense of the Catholic Church from many quarters, refuting attacks from authorities within the English Church. Cary's work coincided with that of eminent Catholic divines such as Anthony Cade and John Floyd and respected Protestant theologians such as Daniel Featley and Ambrose Fisher.[19] She addressed her translation to Henrietta Maria and Charles; the construction of the work, with its controversial topics and its explicitly royal audience, demanded appreciation for her prowess as translator, for her knowledge of divinity, and for her willingness to disseminate and defend the Catholic faith.

The book's preliminary matter frames it as a direct response to the exigencies of its time. Cary first identified it as a task done quickly and easily in her preface to the reader: "If it gaine noe applause, hee that writt it faire, hath lost more labour then I haue done, for I dare auouch, it hath bene fower times as long in transcribing, as it was in translating." She emphasized, as well, the importance of the text for an English audience. Her goals were twofold: first, to "informe [the Reader] aright"; second, to share the words of this "Ornament" of France with the English, especially those who claimed to be educated in theology and religious doctrine:

> "I will not make vse of that worne-out forme of saying, I printed it against my will, mooued by the importunitie of Friends: I was mooued to it by my beleefe, that it might make those English that vnderstand not French, whereof there are maine, euen in our vniuersities, reade Perron; And when that is done, I haue my End, the rest I leaue to Gods pleasure" (*Reply* sig. ã2^v).

Cary underlined the treatise's centrality to England's proper understanding of church doctrine and at the same time disparaged the care with which those who professed to be authoritative interpreters read and understood the accretion of learning available to them from continental sources. While Cary claimed she would leave the translation's reception to God's pleasure, she dedicated the treatise itself to "Queen Henrietta Maria of Bovrbon, Qveene of Great Brittaine," identifying her first as a daughter of France; second as the wife of Charles; third as a woman. Cary concludes her wish for patronage and protection by remarking, "And last (to crowne your other additions) you are a Catholicke, and a zealous one, and therefore fittest to receiue the dedication of a Catholicke-worke." From the outset, Cary marked her text as one engaged in proselytizing, an effort endorsed by the Catholic fathers—as evidenced by the approbation from the English Benedictine congregation in the prefatory material and the Jesuit insignia on the title page—and entrusted to the care of the "zealous" Henrietta Maria. The rigorous logic of Du Perron's reasoning was especially suitable for members of the university community and was so essential for their understanding of the debates of the day that she would not even feign succumbing to the pressures of friends as justification for its publication.

The encomia that precede the translation emphasize the facility with which it was completed, and the repetitions of these claims point again to the urgency of its publication. In the first, "*In Lavdem Nobilissimæ Heroinæ, Qvae Has Eminentissimi Cardinalis Dispvtatioines Anglice Reddidit,*" the anonymous author began his praise of Cary by emphasizing the quickness and grace of this translation: "*Esse quid hoc dicam, quod in vno faemina mense / Tam varium, doctum, grande crearit opus? / Nonne hoc est ipsam cursu praeurtere lunam / Quae simili spatio circuit omne solum?*" In the English version of the poem beneath the Latin one ("The Same in English"), the metaphors are rearranged to maintain the rhyme scheme: "One woman, in one Month, so large a book, / In such a full emphatik stile to turne: / Ist not all one, as when a spacious brooke, / flowes in a moment from a little Burne?" Cary outraced the moon in the next stanza; her prowess was emphasized, though, in both the Latin and the English.

This theme continues in the second encomium, "To the most noble Translatour," which explores variations of these praises, often as rather backhanded compliments. The writer would have liked to recognize Cary, but the translation of this enormous, complex text had been so easy for her that she merely strained her hand in its transcription: "I would commend your labours and I finde / That they were finis'd with such ease of minde / As in some sence the praise I giue must fall / Vnder the title of Mechanicall, / When those who reade it come to understand, / The paines you tooke were onely of your hand / Which though it did in swiftnesse ouergoe / All other thoughts yet to your owne was slow." The writer also expressed surprise that such a complicated work could come from a woman: "But that a Womans hand alone should raise / So vast a monument in thirty dayes / Breeds enuie and amazement in our sex." Ultimately, though, the writer concluded with unmitigated praise: "Whosoere shall try may spend his Age / Ere in your whole work hee shall mend one Page" (*Reply*, sig. ē3). Both authors of these encomia made these claims of speed in part to underline Cary's skill and erudition. However, the combined effect of these poems and Cary's own introductory material ensured that the reader would realize the freshness of the work, and also demonstrated that the Catholic community of producers of texts recognized the relevance of this transformation of Du Perron's arguments for an English audience in 1630.

The treatise confirmed itself as a catalog of the rightness of the Roman Church and addressed, one by one, the errors of the English Church in chapters such as "Of the Vse of the Word Catholiqve"; "Of the marks of the Church"; "Of the necessitie of communicating with the Catholicke Church"; "Of the indiuisibilite of the Church"; "Of the pretended Corruption of the Church"; "Of the definition of the Church, and in what vnion it consists"; and "Of the vnitie of internall faith." Cary indicated her willingness to insert herself into the political and doctrinal debates of her time in thus translating an argument for Catholicism aimed specifically at the king. To achieve her noble ends, she neither assumed a masculine pseudonym nor hid behind concealing initials. Instead, she advanced her combined political and religious agenda of converting English Protestants by fusing her role as active Catholic polemicist with a persona of passive woman translator. She further muted the threat of the work at hand by reminding her readers that she was merely translating an argument aimed not at the current king but at his father. Nonetheless, she offered an emphatic statement of political and doctrinal propaganda designed to assist efforts to return England to the Roman Catholic fold at a moment when Henrietta Maria, Charles's Catholic queen, was gaining power and gathering a circle of Roman Catholic-leaning women and men around her. Perhaps because scholars have tended to read Cary's translation within the context of the recovery of women's writing, its enormity as an achievement has often gone unremarked. It shared shelf space with Roman Catholic works of similarly all-encompassing scope, such as *A summary of controuersies Wherein the chiefest points of the holy Catholike Roman fayth, are compendiously, and methodically proued, against the sectaryes of this age. By C.V.V.*, published first in 1616 and then in St. Omer in 1623, and *Of the author and substance of the protestant church and religion two bookes. Written first in Latin by R.S. Doctour of Diuinity, and now reuiewed by the author, and translated into English by VV. Bas* (St. Omer, 1621). These tracts run between 300 and 350 pages apiece. The treatise that Cary translated resoundingly articulated Catholic doctrine on countless issues. At a moment when many writers were attempting to direct the course of religious politics in England, Cary's translation is among the most extensive.

The specific ends Cary hoped to achieve were readily apparent in her chapter headings; the table of contents serves as an outline of the central issues in religious controversies of 1630. The first book of *Reply* largely deals with definitions—of Catholics, of the Catholic Church—and with asserting the value of a unified church. These terms and debates had been under discussion when Du Perron and James began their debates in 1615 and recurred over the next twenty years (and beyond). Roman Catholic polemicists were especially invested in defining Catholicism's primacy, and one of their central arguments in the 1620s and 1630s was the antiquity of their religion, a position they successfully defended against all Protestant efforts. Among these polemical titles was Lawrence Anderton's *The Progenie of Catholicks and Protestants* (Rouen, 1633). Its title page offered an abstract of its contents, which illustrates how these primacy arguments were constructed:

> Whereby on one side is proued the lineal Descent of Catholicks, for the Roman Faith and Religion, from the holie Fathers of the Primitiue Church, euen from Christ's verie time vntil these our dayes, and, on the other, the neuer-Being of Protestants or their nouel Sect during al the forsayd time, otherwise then in confessed and condemned Herticks, And al this is conuinced by the manifold and clearest acknowledgements of Protestant Writers, both forrain and domesticks.

Catholic controversialists continued to charge Protestants with weak, illogical arguments of primacy.

One could work through *Reply* with Anthony Milton's *Catholic and Reformed* in hand and show in exhaustive detail the many parallels between Cary's translation and the debates of the day. For example, Milton assesses the ways in which the Eastern Orthodox Church is invoked by Roman Catholics and by English Protestants. While Catholics decried sectarianism and obstinacy, Protestants especially claimed their allegiance with these ancient churches cast out by Rome. Milton observes, "In effect, the more that the position of the Roman church was downgraded, the easier it became for Protestants to reject any 'Protestant' identity and to present themselves merely as 'Catholic'. The Greek, Ethiopian and Russian Churches were therefore increasingly cited against Rome for polemical purposes."[20] Catholics, of course, responded to these assertions; one of *Reply's* projects in defining the word "Catholic" was to refute claims such as these.

The entire fourth section, or "book," the last in the translation, devotes all thirty-three chapters to an assessment of the impact of schism and division within the body of the Roman Catholic Church. Chapters I and II (numbered, of course, with Roman numerals), deal with, respectively, "The Estate of the Easterne Church" and "What the diuision of the Empire hath wrought to the diuision of the Church." Woven through these chapters is a discussion of the errors of the Eastern Churches. Chapter X, "Why the Roman hath cut other Churches from her," argues:

> The most excellent King, may be pleased to remember two things, one that antient authors haue written, that oftentimes for one only word contrarie to Faith, manie heresies haue bene cast out of the bodie of the Church: And the other, that the societies of the *Egiptians* and *Ethiopians* haue not bene excluded out of the Church, for refusinge that which his maiestie call the yoake of slauerie; that is to saie, the Superintendencie of the *Roman* Church, but for hauing imbraced the Sect of *Eutyches*, who with all his partakers, was cutt off from the Church by the Councell of *Chalcedon*; and that euen to this daie, they are all readie, and haue often offerred, to acknowledge the Pope, whom they confesse to bee the Successor of the Prince of the Apostles, if they might be receiued into the communion of the *roman* Church, without obliging them to anathemize *Eutiches* and *Dioscorus*. (*Reply*, 413)

Du Perron and Cary did not invoke Egyptians and Ethiopians at random; both author and translator understood the importance of addressing accusations leveled at the Roman Catholic Church. After this analysis, the passage proceeds to justify the schism with the Greek Church not because the Greeks refused the Roman Church's "yoke of slavery" but because they were obstinate: "This was the true cause of the separation of the Greekes, and not the yoake of slaueries of the *Roman* Church; of the which neither *Ignatius*, nor anie of his Catholicke Predecessors, had euer complayned."

Reply makes clear that these complaints were the fault of these schismatics; all would be forgiven if only the lost sheep would admit their error and return to the Roman fold.

Indeed, Du Perron and Cary sound this note repeatedly throughout *Reply;* its most telling occurrence serves as the conclusion of Cary's translation. Ostensibly a defense of the writings of Cardinal Bellarmine ("Of the writings of the illustrious Cardinal Bellarmin"), the final chapter calls for the king to abase himself before the pope and reunify the church. Du Perron, of course, hoped that James I would prostrate himself before the pope, and Cary's prefatory material reassures Charles I that this text was indeed meant for his father. However, in 1630, this call to the English king to turn to Rome was weighted in ways it had not been in 1620. James I's son was married to Henrietta Maria, sister to the king of France and goddaughter to the pope; from the outset, Protestants had suspected that this alliance was a way for Catholics to make inroads in England. The internal climate of England had shifted; historians of the late 1620s and early 1630s point to the waning, if only temporarily, of Calvinist influences and to England's more neutral stance toward the Catholic Church. Jonathan Scott describes England's complicated religious climate in the early 1630s and observes that many "believed that, after the extraordinary progress of the last ten years, reunion with Rome was now a real possibility."[21] England was not ready to run to Rome; neither was it rejecting Rome with the vehemence that it once had, nor was it seeking alliances with continental Protestants as it had when Du Perron initially wrote his *Reply*.

While Cary had not transformed Du Perron's text, the audience for that text had changed drastically. Readers in the 1630s brought a different understanding of the religio-political situation to these words than when Du Perron left the manuscript at his death in 1618 and when it was first printed in French in 1620 and in Latin in 1621. Du Perron's manuscript responded to James's own work, which as Dolan notes, was written in French in 1615, and then translated into English and published in 1616. When Du Perron and James were embroiled in controversy, James continued to champion Protestant causes and sought a reputation for irenicism. Peter White argues that James saw himself as a peacemaker at the Synod of Dort in 1618–1619 and suggests that one of James's priorities for the Synod was working to preserve the common confession among the Reformed Churches of the continent and of England. His eventual goal was a harmony of confessions between all continental Protestants, including Lutherans.[22]

This final chapter of Cary's translation opens, as do the rest, with "The continuance of the Kings answere." While the comment purports to be the king's words, the editorial voice intrudes, as it has throughout *Reply*, in Du Perron's rendering of it:

> The Cardinall *Bellarmine* himself, I will saie it against my will, but I saie truth, amongst the protectors of the Paricides, holds the rancke of the head of a faction who newlie againe to the end to allure the excellent King hath imployed this argument of wondrous efficacie, to perswade that the Kingdome of *England* belonges to the Pope, and that the kinge of *England* is subiect to the Pope, euen in temporall thinges, and in his Feodary. I omitt the other complaintes of the kinge, and of the *English* Church, as well old as newe, which now haue noe neede of commemoration. (*Reply*, 463)

These interjections continued in the answer as well, where Du Perron continued to dismiss as outside the scope of the discussion topics "temporal rather than spiritual." Since the argument built upon itself, the bulk of the passage follows. At issue is the king's allegiance to a higher authority:

> It sufficeth me for the rest to saie, that himselfe aduertises the Readers that what he propounds of the indirect authoritie of the Pope in temporalls, he propounds it not as a doctrine of faith, and whereof either side must be held vnder the paine of excommunication or anathema by meanes whereof this question should not hinder the reunion of those who desire to returne to the Church. For as for the annuall present that it is written, *England* was wont to make to the *Sea* Apostolicke, if his maiesties Predecessors would by anie marke of publicke acknowledgement testifie their particular deuotion towards saint PETERS Sea that could bring noe more dimunition to their temporall glory, then the submission of *Alexander* the great brought to him when he prostrated himselfe before the high Priest of the *Iewish* lawe; or that of the Empreror *Iustinian* the second, when hee prostrated himselfe in *Asia* before Pope *Constantine,* making this acknowledgment not to men but to God, who saith by the mouth of *Esay* to his Church, whereof saint PETER in his Successors, is the head and visible figure: *Kings shall worship thee with their face on the ground.* Contrarywise it will be found, that the kings of *England,* haue bene more esteemed and feared since then, then euer they were before, Iointlie, that whensoeuer it shall please this great king to make so faire a present to the Church as to giue her his heart and person, I assure my selfe, the Pope will shewe (if these temporall acknowledgments bee displeasing to Maiestie) that it is himselfe as S. PAVL saith, that he desires, and not the things that belong to him. (*Reply*, 463–464)

England's kings had historically been willing to prostrate themselves, joining the most excellent company of Alexander the Great and Justinian the Second. To pay homage to a spiritual authority empowered, rather than weakened, a temporal authority. England's king must remember his spiritual obligations, and in doing so, would fulfill what was prophesied in Isaiah. The church, founded by Peter, defined within this treatise so repeatedly as the one true church, is the spiritual home of the English king. It is only right that the king should rejoin with Rome, pay the homage that is the pope's due, thus humbling himself to his spiritual leader here on earth as he should humble himself before God.

The translation ended with this passage, and also with the note, "The end of the first part." Cary provided only the portion of Du Perron's monumental *Réplique* that she thought essential for her English audience; the closing argument with which she left them was this plea for the king to prostrate himself before the pope and recognize the supreme spiritual authority of the Roman Church. The king could preserve his temporal authority; not only would he lose nothing, but he would also gain, as would the people of England.

While literary critics and historians tend to be dismissive of the work of "mere" translators (as Cary self-deprecatingly identifies herself in the prefatory material), English readers in 1630 would have recognized the formidable nature of her undertaking.[23] Women as well as men used the process of translation to confer upon themselves expertise in areas of divinity at the same time as they contributed to their contemporaries' understandings of religious debates, and these contributions were recognized as efforts worthy of notice. Almost one-quarter of the entries Andrew Maunsell lists in his *First part of the Catalogue of English printed Bookes* (1595) are marked as translations; 130 translators warranted individual entries by name.[24] Nevertheless, translations held a complicated position for sixteenth-century religious writers, as Margaret Hannay acknowledges in a discussion of Mary Sidney's *Psalms*: "Although translation could be seen as a passive, nonthreatening activity appropriate to women, the need to disseminate Protestant doctrine made [Sidney's] translations of Mornay, as of Theodore de Beze and John Calvin, work suitable for even distinguished Protestant writers."[25] Elizabeth Cary shared with these Protestant writers the urgent need to educate English readers and stated her purpose explicitly: "Thou shalt heere receiue a Translation wel intended, wherein the Translator could haue no other end, but to inform thee aright" (*Reply*, sig. ã2ᵛ).

Cary and many of her Catholic contemporaries asserted that they translated these polemics for English audiences who were sympathetic to Catholic doctrine, and audiences for these treatises abounded: English Catholics in the exile communities of Louvain, St. Omer, Spain, and elsewhere on the continent; prelates—Catholic and anti-Catholic—embroiled in controversy in England; English Catholic readers anxious for information and willing to purchase smuggled books; English-speaking Catholics in Ireland. Examples proliferate of the ways in which various people used these polemics in England to convert their friends and family.[26] Certainly Cary claimed conversion as one project, and sustaining embattled Catholics in England as a second, so she clearly imagined a Catholic readership in England. However, her work also served these other communities of readers in different ways. For English Catholics on the continent, for example, such works connected their communities to England and helped them to "keep the faith" by imagining their own position as one of exile rather than of emigration.

The force of *Reply* lay not only in its timeliness, but also in the range of its arguments, encompassing as it did all of the major threads in the controversies of the early 1630s. If one reads it as the reply of a dead French cardinal to a dead English king, its immediacy is somewhat muted—these arguments were old news. As a publication in 1630, though, Cary's translation also highlights the consistency of the Catholic position. The old arguments still carried weight, since England's divines had not yet constructed a definitive response to *Reply*. These arguments, made resoundingly in lengthy treatises such as *Reply,* and in versions directed at a variety of audiences, printed in a range of lengths and genres, created an environment of agitation, of print noise, that contributed to the English sense of increasing Catholic solidarity. Charles granted, in 1632, a charter to the Catholic Cecil Calvert, Lord Baltimore, for the Palatinate of Maryland. While one cannot make a causal link between the explosion of Catholic controversial literature and the founding of this Catholic plantation, the general clamor of these publications, ranging as they did from sensationalist tract to learned tome, may have contributed in some way to permitting a member of the English Catholic elite an opportunity to establish a colony where Catholics and Protestants could coexist under the banner of freedom of conscience.

Notes

1. Two modern facsimile editions exist for this treatise. It appears in *Recusant Translators: Elizabeth Cary, Alexia Grey,* ed. Frances E. Dolan, Early Modern Englishwoman, part 2, vol. 13 (Aldershot: Ashgate, 2000), and in *English Recusant Literature 1558–1640,* vol. 248 (London: Scolar Press, 1975) [STC 6385]. In subsequent references to the treatise, the title is shortened to *Reply*.
2. See, for example, Betty Travitsky, ed., *The Paradise of Women: Writings by Englishwomen of the Renaissance* (New York: Columbia UP, 1989), 219–220; Tina Krontiris, *Oppositional Voices: Women as Writers and Translators of Literature in the English Renaissance* (London: Routledge, 1992), 99–100; and S. P. Cerasano and Marion Wynne-Davies, eds., *Renaissance Drama by Women: Texts and Documents* (London: Routledge, 1996), 45.
3. Dolan, "Introduction," *Recusant Translators,* x.

4. Anthony Milton, *Catholic and Reformed: The Roman and Protestant Churches in English Protestant Thought, 1600–1640* (Cambridge: Cambridge UP, 1995).
5. Kevin Sharpe, *The Personal Rule of Charles I* (New Haven, CT: Yale UP, 1992), 304–305, cites Martin J. Havran, *The Catholics in Caroline England* (Stanford, CA: Stanford UP, 1962), 79–80, for the statistics upon which he bases this argument.
6. Jonathan Scott, *England's Troubles: Seventeenth-Century English Political Instability in European Context* (Cambridge: Cambridge UP, 2000), 29–30.
7. For an extended version of this reading of the seventeenth century, see Dolan, *Whores of Babylon: Catholicism, Gender, and Seventeenth-Century Print Culture* (Ithaca and London: Cornell UP, 1999), especially 7.
8. John Bruce, "Preface," Great Britain, Public Record Office, *Calendar of State Papers, Domestic Series, of the Reign of Charles 1, 1629–1631,* edited by John Bruce (1858, Nendeln, Liechtenstein: Kraus Reprints, 1967), vi. Hereafter abbreviated as *CSP*.
9. National Archives, Kew, SP 16/173/49. In this transcription and the one following, superscript letters are silently lowered and abbreviations silently expanded.
10. National Archives, Kew, SP 16/174/101.
11. *Elizabeth Cary, Lady Falkland: Life and Letters,* ed. Heather Wolfe (Cambridge and Tempe, AZ: RTM Publications and Arizona Center for Medieval and Renaissance Studies, 2001), 341–342.
12. John D. Krugler, *English and Catholic: The Lords Baltimore in the Seventeenth Century* (Baltimore: Johns Hopkins UP, 2004).
13. For more complete discussions of English exile communities, see Christopher Highley, "'Lost British Lamb': English Catholic Exiles and the Problem of Britain," in *British Identities and English Renaissance Literature,* ed. David J. Baker and Willy Maley (Cambridge: Cambridge UP, 2002); Dorothy Latz, "Introduction," *Neglected English Literature: Recusant Writings of the 16th–17th Centuries,* Salzburg Studies in English Literature 92.24 (Salzburg, Austria: Institut für Anglistik und Amerikanistik Universität Salzburg, 1997); Margaret Mary Littlehales, *Mary Ward: Pilgrim and Mystic 1585–1645* (1998, London: Burns & Oates, 2001); Claire Walker, *Gender and Politics in Early Modern Europe: English Convents in France and the Low Countries* (Hampshire: Palgrave Macmillan, 2003).
14. For the details of efforts to claim Maryland "for our Sauior," see Thomas Cecil, *Relation of Maryland, Together with A Map of the Countrey, the Conditions of Plantation, His Majesties Charter to the Lord Baltimore, translated into English,* 1635 [STC 17571].
15. Early English Books Online has made such surveys possible; these generalizations are based upon analyses of searches for the years 1628, 1629, and 1630, with especial attention to records for 1630. Caroline Grambo provided research assistance for this essay by searching for records from 1600 to 1635 for St. Omer, Douai, and Louvain, and by assisting with a number of other database inquiries.

16. STC 21144, authored by Alfonsus Rodriguez, and printed by the widow of Charles Boscard, who printed a number of Catholic texts, many authorized by the superiors, in the 1630s.
17. A keyword search for "sermon" in titles of books printed in 1630 yields 45 titles, with multiple offerings from Arthur Dent (1553–1601?), Antony Fawkner (b. 1601 or 1602; sermons printed in 1630 were preached 1627–1629), Robert Harris (1581–1658; sermons printed in 1630 were preached primarily 1610–1622), John Preston (1587–1628; sermons preached in the 1610s and 1620s), and Humphrey Sydenham (1591–1650; sermons printed in 1630 included some preached between 1622 and 1625, and others dating from Charles's reign).
18. Latz, *"Glow-Worm Light": Writings of 17th Century English Recusant Women from Original Manuscripts* (Salzburg, Austria: Institut für Anglistik and Amerikanistik Universität Salzburg, 1989), 11.
19. Anthony Cade, *A iustification of the Churche of England Demonstrating it to be a true Church of God, affording all sufficient meanes to saluation. Or, a countercharme against the Romish enchantment, that labor to bewitch the people, with opinion of necessity to be subiect to the Pope of Rome,*1630 [STC 4327]; John Floyd, *An apology of the Holy Sea,* 1630 [STC 11109]; Daniel Featley, *The Grand Sacrilege of the Church of Rome,* 1630 [STC 1733]; Ambrose Fisher, *A Defense of the Liturgie of the Church of England,* 1630 [STC 10885].
20. Milton, 379.
21. Scott, 129–130. Scott cites Milton, *Catholic and Reformed,* 61–65, to bolster these assertions.
22. Peter White, *Predestination, Policy, and Polemic: Conflict and Consensus in the English Church from the Reformation to the Civil War* (Cambridge: Cambridge UP, 1992), 179. See also Milton, 407–425, and Nicholas Tyacke, *Anti-Calvinists: The Rise of English Arminianism c. 1590–1640* (1987; Oxford: Clarendon Press, 1990), 87–105.
23. See, for example, Kim Walker, *Women Writers of the English Renaissance* (New York: Twayne, 1996), who writes: "Women were, of course, writing prior to 1560, but much of their work in the early years of the Reformation consisted of religious tracts and translations" (ix); elsewhere, she calls translation a "humble reproductive task" (47).
24. Andrew Maunsell, *The First Part of the Catalogue of English printed Books: which concerneth such matters of Diuinite, as haue bin either written in our owne Tongue, or translated out of anie other language: And haue bin published, to the glory of God, and edification of the Church of Christ in England* (1595), published in facsimile in English Biographical Sources, series 2, vol. 1 (London: Gregg Press, 1965). Maunsell lists approximately 725 translations out of roughly 3150 titles.
25. Margaret Hannay, *Philip's Phoenix: Mary Sidney, Countess of Pembroke* (New York: Oxford UP, 1990), 61. As proof of the womanly passivity of translation, Hannay cites Florio's preface to a translation of Montaigne published in 1603.

26. See, for example, Alison Plowden's description of Olive Porter's activities in *Henrietta Maria: Charles I's Indomitable Queen* (Thrupp: Sutton, 2001), 123–124. Elizabeth Cary's "joy and comfort" from "a Catholic book of devotion" brought to her by "Mr Chaperlin, a very honest Catholic gentleman" is related by her daughter in *The Lady Falkland her Life,* as is the place of the arguments concerning doctrine in her conversion. See *The Tragedy of Mariam: The Fair Queen of Jewry, with The Lady Falkland Her Life: By One of her Daughters,* ed. Barry Weller and Margaret W. Ferguson, (Berkeley, CA: U of California P, 1994), 208–213.

CHAPTER 9

ELIZABETH CARY AND THE GREAT TEW CIRCLE

R. W. Serjeantson

This chapter is about a piece of writing by Elizabeth Cary that no longer exists. It was a contribution to the lively debate over conversion to the Roman Catholic Church that took place in court circles in the middle years of the 1630s. One of Cary's daughters wrote of this "paper of Controversy" that it "was thought the best thinge she euer writ."[1] Cary, a talented linguist, had already distinguished herself as a writer by her translation, published in 1630, of Cardinal Jacques Davy du Perron's *Replique à la response du sérénissime Roy de la Grand Bretagne* (1620). But Cary's authorship of this brief paper establishes her as an even rarer thing in early Stuart England: a woman writer of religious controversy.[2] Although the work itself is lost, something can be done to reconstruct the ground over which it fought and the circumstances in which it was written.

I also have a larger purpose in discussing Elizabeth Cary as writer of religious controversy: to place her back into the intellectual milieu inhabited by her eldest son, Lucius Cary, second Viscount Falkland (1609/1610–1643), and thereby to broaden our sense of what that milieu was. Lucius Cary has long been celebrated as the guiding spirit of the Great Tew, or Falkland, circle: a group of scholars that gathered informally at his house at Great Tew in Oxfordshire in the middle and later years of "that peaceable time," the 1630s.[3] The conception of a "Tew" or "Falkland" circle is a historiographical creation, but it is one with rather venerable roots, since the notion of a group of friends who gathered around Falkland's table and in his library was first given shape by Edward Hyde, Earl of Clarendon (1609–1674), in his *History of the Rebellion* and *Life of Himself*. In these works Clarendon spoke of a *convivium philosophicum* or *theologicum* centered around Falkland at

Great Tew.[4] The most recent scholar of the group, J. C. Hayward, cleaves to the notion, although he states in his published study that it "never met as a circle" and that its "members never thought of themselves as such."[5] While there does seem to be good evidence for such gatherings in the 1630s, then, the case for there being, and for the people concerned retaining, a distinctive philosophy in the years after Falkland's death in 1644—as Hugh Trevor-Roper argued in an elegant and learned essay—is perhaps somewhat slimmer.

No scholar, however, has yet systematically considered Elizabeth Cary's intellectual relations to Falkland and his circle. For Trevor-Roper, "old Lady Falkland" (she was fifty-four when she died in 1639) was "an insufferable blue-stocking," with no role to play in his account of the dangerous path trodden by the Great Tew authors "along the precipitous, crumbling ledge between faith and reason."[6] Yet the path chosen by Cary—a disinherited and impoverished convert, separated by her faith from her husband—was hardly less vertiginous.[7] Moreover, Cary's own intellectual preoccupations can be shown to relate directly to those subsequently developed by the central Great Tew authors: Falkland, and his friend and associate William Chillingworth (1602–1644). These three were closely involved with each other personally. But they were also, as we shall see, mutually concerned with the fiercely debated question of the respective claims to authority of the Church of Rome and of the Church of England. They all read, translated, and contributed to some of the most advanced literature on the subject in the period.

The dominant interpretation of the Falkland circle sees its theology as a rationalistic working-out of tendencies within the Protestant tradition (or, in case of Erasmus, an honorary Protestant tradition), tendencies that for some have even had the Enlightenment as a whole as their ultimate telos.[8] This interpretation has focused on the religious rationalism of Falkland and Chillingworth, and has even spoken of their Socinianism. According to Trevor-Roper, the most effective synthesizer of this account, "The intellectual influences which dominated Great Tew are . . . perfectly clear": Erasmus, Cassander, Philippe du Plessis Mornay, Hugo Grotius, and European Socinianism.[9] Yet while it has sometimes—rightly—been argued that Falkland's interest in religious controversy was connected to his mother's conversion to Catholicism and her subsequent efforts to bring about the conversion of her children, Elizabeth Cary's place in her son's intellectual life has been consistently downplayed.[10]

Here I propose to consider Falkland, Chillingworth, and Elizabeth Cary in the more local context of the controversies between Roman Catholicism and the Church of England that were worked out in later Jacobean and early Caroline England. The preoccupations of Great Tew,

I shall suggest, should be seen as a response to controversial developments in the years between 1611 and 1635 as much as they are the natural working out of any longer-term tradition. These controversies had a strong French dimension. English converts—such as William Chillingworth (briefly), Walter Montagu, and Elizabeth Cary's own children—commonly found their way to France. Moreover, Anglican apologetic was often conducted against members of the Gallican Church in France, and it took place alongside the parallel apologetic endeavors pursued by the Huguenots after the promulgation of the Edict of Nantes (1598).

This chapter therefore has two related goals. Its first task is to look more closely at some of the specific ways in which the intellectual concerns of Elizabeth Cary, her son Falkland, and William Chillingworth were intertwined, and to emphasize these concerns more forcefully than they have been so far. A second task is to consider the intellectual resources on which these concerns drew. Some of these sources have already been identified by other scholars. An important preoccupation of earlier seventeenth-century religious controversy concerned the use and authority of the church fathers. This was an issue that had reached its height in the first third of the seventeenth century in France. As is well known, a key figure in this debate was the Huguenot scholar Jean Daillé (1594–1670). But Daillé's work must in its turn be seen in the context of the great Catholic patristic scholars of those years, a triumvirate of cardinals: Caesar Baronius, Robert Bellarmine, and Jacques Davy du Perron (1556–1618).

It is the last of these figures who brings us back to Elizabeth Cary, for after her formal conversion in November 1626[11] she spent some time translating at least one and perhaps all of the works of Cardinal Du Perron.[12] The fruit of this labor was the publication at Douai in 1630 of the first volume of her translation of Du Perron's lengthy and erudite *Replique* to James I, of which several presentation copies survive.[13] The cardinal's original French volume had first been published in 1620, and was republished in a second and fuller edition in 1622, but an immediate stimulus for the printing of Cary's translation was perhaps the posthumous publication in 1629 of Lancelot Andrewes's animadversions on Du Perron's book.[14] Cary undertook the translation, as her daughter archly wrote, "for the sakes of the scholers of Oxford and Cambridge (who doe not generally vnderstand french)."[15] It is ultimately in the light of Du Perron's book and the controversy that provoked it that we should see the focus of the theological preoccupations of Elizabeth Cary, her son Falkland, and Falkland's associate William Chillingworth.

★★★★★

We need first to consider the personal relations between these three people. Falkland's relationship to his mother does not need to be established, even if the details of their contact in the earlier 1630s bear further investigation. Chillingworth's friendship with Falkland, certainly from 1634 onward, is also well established. Chillingworth's biographers, however, have been rather less willing to acknowledge that he was also well acquainted with Elizabeth Cary. The evidence for this relationship comes from the manuscript, *Life,* that one of her daughters—probably Lucy Cary (1619–1650)— wrote at the English Benedictine convent at Cambrai in 1645.[16] The *Life* allows us to connect Cary, Falkland, and Chillingworth intimately. It tells us that after the death of her husband, Henry Cary, first Viscount Falkland, in September 1633, Elizabeth Cary's "first thoughts were to gett her children to liue with her (which, she desired in order to their being Catholikes)." In this she succeeded, and in the winter of 1633/1634 she even had her son Lucius—who had become second Viscount Falkland on the death of his father—and his younger brother Lorenzo living with her at Drury House in London. While they were there "many of thir frinds, (Oxford scholars and others) came much to her house, and were exceeding wellcome to her."[17] Here, perhaps the life of scholarly exchange that Falkland subsequently pursued at Great Tew was adumbrated in the impurer air of London, at Elizabeth Cary's table. Nonetheless, Falkland's residence with his mother does not seem to have lasted long, and he was no longer living with her when Elizabeth Cary's daughters converted to Roman Catholicism in the early summer of 1634.[18]

William Chillingworth, however, "continually freqvented" Drury House at this time.[19] After obtaining a fellowship at Trinity College, Oxford, in 1628, Chillingworth had been converted to Catholicism in the following year by John Fisher. In 1630 he had gone over to France, most probably to the English seminary at Douai. But by 1631 he had already returned to England, apparently in a state of doubt.[20] These doubts, however, were unknown to Elizabeth Cary, in whose eyes he gained "the greate esteeme of a saint." While at Cary's London house in 1634, Chillingworth was received as a friend, whom the children heard "with an open eare, as a confirmer, and informer in catholike religion." Yet Chillingworth, apparently by now reconciled to the Church of England, was acting as a spiritual double agent, endeavoring to sow seeds of doubt in the minds of Cary's daughters while always professing his Catholic orthodoxy.[21] A letter from Chillingworth to Anne Cary survives to confirm the *Life*'s account of this stratagem.[22] It was only when Elizabeth Cary overheard Chillingworth exclaiming to one of her daughters "against catholikes, and their religion, as founded on lyes" that she turned against him. A debate was arranged between Chillingworth and the Jesuit Guy Holland (1585/1586–1660), at which Chillingworth was provoked into losing his temper and revealing himself. Immediately afterward he was forbidden entry to the house.[23]

The scheming and authoritarian portrait of William Chillingworth given in the *Life* is one that is radically at odds with his conventional reputation, stemming from the nineteenth century, as one of the most prominent incarnations of "rational theology" in England. Neither the account of the humanistic mores of Great Tew by Hayward nor the restrained suggestion made by Orr of the ethical lessons that might be learned from Chillingworth's writings are sustainable if one gives more than the most minimal credit to the Heathcliffian figure that the *Life* portrays.[24] Consequently, neither do. Nor does Kurt Weber, who in his book on Falkland consistently rejected matters of fact and interpretation that the *Life* offered, commonly without adducing any evidence to the contrary.[25] Orr's monograph on Chillingworth equally has little room for the evidence offered by the *Life*, and in one point at least directly misrepresents it.[26] Yet it seems possible to allow that Chillingworth could both have been a fierce disciplinarian who slept lightly (as the *Life* depicts him) and a harbinger of rational religion (as Tulloch and much subsequent literature has prized him for).[27]

It is hard, furthermore, to avoid the suspicion that Falkland had been complicit in Chillingworth's bid to retrieve his sisters from the Church of Rome. By 1634 Falkland had retreated permanently (that is, until his parliamentary and subsequently military career on the king's side intervened after 1640) to the adjacent estates that had passed directly to him from his maternal (Tanfield) grandparents at Burford and Great Tew in 1629—his mother having been cut out of the inheritance on account of her conversion. Once there, Falkland pursued the study of Greek, and also continued to gather Oxford scholars around him in a setting that Clarendon memorably painted as a "college situated in a purer air" and "a university in a less volume."[28] When Falkland's sisters' conversion to Catholicism became publicly evident by their absence from Church of England services, efforts had been made to have Charles I send them to live with Falkland at his house at Tew. But the king—to whom Elizabeth Cary appealed in person—was unwilling to send them unless Falkland desired it, and Falkland was unwilling to be "their Jaler" by holding them against their will.[29]

After his exposure as a Protestant agent provocateur, Chillingworth also retired to Great Tew to act as tutor to Elizabeth Cary's two youngest sons, Patrick and Henry.[30] These boys had returned from school to live with their brother Lucius, both for financial reasons and to protect them from their mother's Catholicism, to which they had already "received great inclinations."[31] As with the daughters, so with the sons, Chillingworth's function was to keep them on the religious straight and narrow, or rather, in the via media. In fact, illness and poverty eventually constrained Elizabeth Cary to send her three daughters to stay with Falkland toward the end of 1635, "to be againe tormented, but, by the grace of God, not hurt, by mr chillingworth." Nonetheless, in a brilliant coup she and her daughters effected the secret removal of the two young brothers from Tew in April 1636, from where they eventually made their way to the English Benedictine fathers in Paris.[32]

There is no question that Falkland's religious preoccupations in the mid-1630s derived part of their stimulus from his status as the noble son of a prominent convert mother whose siblings' faith was constantly being contested for. The *Life,* for its part, ascribes his "good inclination towards religion" to the "conversation of his mother."[33] It is also evident that Falkland was publicly closely identified with his mother's faith. Clarendon recorded that "many attempts were made upon him, by the instigation of his mother . . . to pervert him in his piety to the Church of England, and to reconcile him to that of Rome." Clarendon went on to suggest that the covert removal of Falkland's young brothers from Great Tew "much lessened" his charity toward Roman Catholics. In Clarendon's account, it was the loss of his brothers and the "perversion" of his sisters by his mother that was the occasion of the controversial discourses that Falkland went on to write "against the principal positions of that Religion."[34] John Suckling's well-known character of Falkland in "A Sessions of the Poets" (1637)—"Hee was of late soe gone with divinitie / That he had all most forgot his poetree"—therefore arises directly from his personal situation.[35]

There was also a strong courtly dimension to the attempts to convert Falkland to Roman Catholicism. The presence of a Catholic queen in the English court, Henrietta Maria, provided a focus for the conversion of a number of noble Englishmen and women. Elizabeth Cary, for all that her conversion brought poverty upon her, continued to move in court circles. On January 9, 1633, for instance, Lucius' younger sister Victoria danced the role of Martiro in a performance of Walter Montagu's (1604/1605–1677) masque *The Shepherd's Paradise* that was privately presented to Charles I and the court by Henrietta Maria and her ladies of honor.[36] In 1635 Henrietta Maria wrote a letter of introduction for Elizabeth Cary's daughter Mary to the English ambassador in Spain.[37] Cary herself was buried in Henrietta Maria's own chapel in 1639. Indeed, until her own troubles supervened, Henrietta Maria supported Falkland's siblings in France.[38] Falkland's retreat to Great Tew from London—"the Place He loved of all the World,"[39] according to Clarendon—should also be seen as a retreat from the world of the court, with its strong Roman Catholic accent.

★★★★★

Yet Falkland could not escape the court entirely. In 1635 the same Walter Montagu who had written *The Shepherd's Paradise* converted to Roman Catholicism while on an embassy in Paris. He subsequently wrote a letter to his father, the Earl of Manchester, defending his decision and announcing his intention to join the Oratorian fathers in Rome.[40] This letter became a celebrated document in the English court, where it was handed round and widely copied.[41] When the newly ordained Montagu returned to England in 1637 through the mediation of the papal nuncio and court favorite George Con, he became chamberlain to Henrietta Maria at Somerset House. Montagu clearly knew Elizabeth Cary well, since in late 1638 he wrote a letter to Cardinal Barberini recommending her son Patrick to him.[42] In the meantime Lucius Cary had written (by the end of 1636 at the latest) a reply to Montagu's 1635 letter to his father.[43] In this reply Falkland alluded to his own experience as the son of a known *convertisseuse*: as someone who had "beene sometimes in some degrees mov'd with the same inducements."[44] Falkland's answer to Montagu provided the kernel of his subsequent writings against the claims of the Roman Catholic religion.

Montagu himself did not answer Falkland's semipublic letter to him. But Falkland's own mother did. Elizabeth Cary's response to her son was never printed, and seems now to be lost. The only testimony we have of its contents is from the *Life* written by her daughter:

> She had writ . . . only one paper of Controversy; When Mr Mountague defended that Faith with his pen, for which he hath now the honer to suffer . . . in a letter to his father (in answere to one of his, to him) which was much praised by all; her sonne, writing, in answere to it; she writ somethinge against his answere; taking notice in the beginning of it, of the fullfilling of his prophecy, who sayd; he came not to bringe peace but the sowrd; the sonne being heer against his Father, and the mother against her sonne, where his faith was the qvestion. which paper was thought the best thing she euer writ; and by him it was against, was acknowledged for a sufficient answere to his, though not satisfactory to him, and that it was, certainly, enough to confute a protestant clearly; and to answere it againe, it would be necessary, to goe farther and deny more, then he had done in his.[45]

What form might Cary's answer to her son have taken? We know that she was already well versed in religious controversy, both oral and written. In the 1620s she had frequented the London residence of the bishop of Durham, Richard Neile, who gathered around himself an Arminian "college" at the heart of which were Richard Montague and John Cosin, who discuss their "good talke" with Cary in their correspondence.[46] (Indeed, it was subsequently reported that these men became "sensible of the disgrace which they sustain[ed]" on account of her subsequent conversion.[47])

At Durham House Cary was apparently "diuers times present att the examination, of such beginers, or receavers, of new opinions, as were by them esteemed Hereticks." The *Life* also noted that before her conversion she had read "most that has bene writen" of controversy, including Protestant authors such as Luther, Calvin, Latimer, and Jewel, and also "of their newer Devines of noat whatsoever came forth; and much French of the same matter." After her conversion she read "some" Catholic authors and "did allways continue with leaue to read protestant controvertists."[48] We may perhaps take it that Cary would have been an assiduous reader of some of the modern works that also exercised her eldest son and his friend William Chillingworth, and that this reading would have issued in the one work of controversy that she is recorded as writing.

About the precise contents of her paper against her son we cannot know more than that it took as its epigraph the neatly turned allusion to Matthew 10: "I came not to send peace but a sword. For I am come to set a man at variance against his father, and the daughter against her mother, and the daughter in law against her mother in law. And a man's foes shall be they of his own household."[49] Whether there would have been any other more autobiographical self-consciousness about the endeavor we can only conjecture; it seems likely, given the conventions of the form, that there would not. Hence in order to establish in more detail what sort of arguments Cary's answer would have addressed we need to turn to those works we do have—Montagu's letter and Falkland's reply—to establish what she was undertaking in joining the controversy. As we shall see, her translation of Du Perron would have made her particularly well placed to participate in the debate.

The key point at issue in the controversy between Falkland and Montagu was the question of historical fact raised by the so-called visibility of the Protestant Churches before Luther.[50] Whereas Protestants had precious little claim to a ministry directly linked to the Apostles, the Catholic Church could appeal to the "consent of Fathers, and Councells" for its perpetual visible ministry.[51] Hence Luther was guilty of innovation, and the Protestant Churches generally were guilty of schism. If Elizabeth Cary had defended this point further, she might have drawn on the ninth chapter of Du Perron's *Replique,* which had cited a battery of Augustinian texts to assert the power of the Catholic Church to "bind and loose" (*lier & délier*) its members as an aspect of its perpetuation from apostolic times to the present day.[52]

Falkland's response to this argument raised the question of authority: does the Roman Catholic Church have, as it claimed, sole authority to determine its own doctrine and to identify the errors of other churches that may dissent from it? If indeed it does—if it is actually infallible—then all argument must end there. True Christians must embrace it, and those who do not place themselves beyond the pale of salvation. Montagu had claimed that there was no one point of controverted doctrine between the Church of England and Rome, "whereupon all the rest depended"; and therefore that the factual question of the visibility of Protestantism was the matter which "determined all the rest."[53] Falkland countered this argument by asserting that there was indeed such a fundamental doctrinal question: did Rome have the right to infallibility? Hence he devotes much of the rest of his reply to Montagu to this issue. By denying Roman infallibility Falkland sought to question the entire structure of the authoritative teachings of the Catholic Church. The question of infallibility, moreover, continued to dominate Falkland's other major piece of writing against Catholicism, his *Discourse of Infallibility,* which was written around this time as an extension of this controversy.[54] The *Discourse* develops at greater length several of the arguments that Falkland had made in reply to Walter Montagu.

At this point we might note that it had been the infallibility of the Roman Church that Chillingworth, too, had held up as its chief foundation in the course of trying to undermine the Catholic faith of Elizabeth Cary's daughters.[55] Yet Chillingworth's subsequent book, *The Religion of Protestants* (1638), also written at Great Tew, approached the same issues as Falkland from a slightly different perspective. For Chillingworth, the principal question was that of interpretation. What troubled him about the Catholic claim to infallibility of interpretation over scripture, fathers, and Councils was that it licensed a degree of interpretative freedom that might leave the original texts quite behind. All the Church of Rome needed to do "to establish her tyranny over mens consciences" was to assert the claim to be the "*publique and authoriz'd interpreter*" of Scripture, and to arrogate to itself in addition "the Authority of adding to them what doctrine she pleas'd under the title of *Traditions* or *Definitions.*" It was for this reason that Chillingworth went on, like Falkland, to exhort Rome to "cast away the vaine and arrogant pretence of *Infallibility,* which makes your errors incurable."[56] For the authority of the church, therefore, Chillingworth substituted the authority of the individual conscience guided by reason, working upon the scriptures, which are, he said, older, more unified, and more universal than any church. It is this argument that issues, toward the end of Chillingworth's book, in the famous pronouncement that "The BIBLE, I say, The BIBLE only is the Religion of Protestants!"[57]

The apologetic strategy pursued by Falkland and Chillingworth, however, involved making concessions that were not very welcome to some of their coreligionists—concessions that were hinted at by Lucy Cary when she reported Falkland as saying that to respond to their mother's arguments it would be necessary for him to go further and deny more. Between them,

Falkland and Chillingworth had already denied several of the tenets of the existing Protestant apologetic. They had asserted, for instance, that not all scripture, but only its so-called plain places were to be considered necessary to salvation: "such," said Chillingworth, "as need no interpreter."[58] In this way they could counter the Catholic argument that an authoritative tradition was required to prescribe to those who in the debates were called "simple Persons."

Concessions such as this certainly did develop out of what even Du Perron acknowledged as "la distinction universelle," between things necessary to salvation (*fundamenta*) and things about which Christians could with charity differ (*adiaphora*). This distinction had underlain the efforts of liberal Catholics such as Erasmus and Cassander, and their later Protestant heir, Hugo Grotius, to find a basis upon which the Christian Churches might ultimately be reconciled.[59] One further problem was raised, however, by this strain of apologetic: how did it square with the doctrines taught in Christian antiquity? One Catholic author was sure that it did not. According to Cardinal Du Perron (in Elizabeth Cary's translation), "*Erasmus, Cassander,* and others . . . haue written things which would confound their faces if they were to maintain them before anie that were versed of purpose in the studie of Antiquitie."[60] It was to counter this argument—the argument from antiquity—that Falkland and Chillingworth went furthest, and denied most of all.

★★★★★

Du Perron's *Replique* to James I rested upon a magnificently weighty patristic foundation. Scarcely a margin of his book is not marked with a reference either to one of the fathers of the Christian Church, or to one of the early church historians, or to the judgment of a Council. Few other writers came with so enormous a reputation for learning as did Du Perron. Falkland himself gave him the striking approbation of being "the great, eloquent and judicious Cardinall *Perron,*" for whose "large, and monstrous understanding" even cardinals Bellarmine and Baronius might without disgrace have been "employ'd in seeking quotations."[61]

The only Protestant who could match these scholarly giants of the cardinalate in equal battle was the great Huguenot scholar Isaac Casaubon (1559–1614). James I had persuaded Casaubon over to England in 1610 to perform a comprehensive refutation of Baronius's *Annales Ecclesiastici* (1601–1609). Casaubon only made the first down payment on this task before his death in 1614, with the publication of his *Exercitationes* on the prolegomena and first part of Baronius' ecclesiastical history.[62] Three years prior to this, however, Casaubon had found himself acting as James's

ELIZABETH CARY AND THE GREAT TEW CIRCLE 175

mouthpiece in a debate over the status of the Church of England, which jealously guarded its claim to be both Catholic and Reformed. After Casaubon's journey to England, his old acquaintance Du Perron had written him a letter on the meaning of the name "Catholic." Casaubon showed the letter to James, and James, delighted (as Casaubon wrote) "that yet he knew one Diuine of your side . . . which handling the controuersies of these times, appeared to be of a moderate, and a quiet disposition (*placidum & mansuetum ingenium*)," instructed his *secrétaire* Casaubon to frame an answer that would be owned by the king.[63] This letter was written and sent in 1611, and when Du Perron had it and his original letter published, Casaubon and James felt constrained to bring out in 1612 editions of both the Latin original and an English translation.

It is a quotation from Casaubon's reply to Du Perron, written in James's name, that adorns the frontispiece of Chillingworth's 1638 *Religion of Protestants*—surely an indication of intellectual influence, or at least affiliation, that is also (to echo Trevor-Roper) "perfectly clear," although no one, so far as I know, has commented upon its significance.[64] Moreover, it was Casaubon's reply to Du Perron that provoked the French cardinal into undertaking his *Replique* to James—the book Elizabeth Cary translated, and which itself printed Du Perron's original letter as a preface.[65] Chillingworth had cited Cary's translation of Du Perron in the body of *The Religion of Protestants*.[66] But the epigraph to his famous book signals as clearly as might be wished that a central stimulus for the work was the controversy between Casaubon and Du Perron that had resulted in the cardinal's *Replique* to James.

The text of the Latin epigraph used by Chillingworth was translated in the 1612 English version as follows:

> Hee [James I] commendeth the truth of that speech [of Perron's] that there is no great number of those things which be absolutely necessarie to saluation (*rerum absolute necesariarum ad salutem, non magnum esse numerum*). Wherefore his Maiestie thinketh that there is no more compendious way to making of peace, then that things necessarie should be diligently separated from things not necessarie: that all endeuours might be spent about the agreement in the necessarie, and as touching the not necessarie, that a Christian libertie might be granted . . . And his excellent Maiestie doth hold this distinction to be of such moment for the diminishing of controuersies, which at this time do vexe the Church of God, that he iudgeth it the dutie of all such as bee studious of peace, diligently to explore it, to teach it, to urge it.[67]

This epigraph explains the purpose of Chillingworth's *Religion of Protestants:* to explore, teach, and urge the realm of the necessary. It also, of course, serves to give the authority of James's (and Casaubon's) names to the contentious conclusions that Chillingworth's book draws about minimally necessary *credenda*. In this respect the epigraph also serves an analogous purpose to the powerful battery of names signing the imprimatur that Chillingworth's godfather William Laud insisted the book have: John Prideaux, Regius Professor of Divinity at Oxford; Richard Baily, Laud's chaplain; and Samuel Fell, Lady Margaret Professor of Divinity at Oxford.[68] These names were an attempt to take the sting out of a book that even before its publication was being attacked by its principal target, Edward Knott, as unlikely to be palatable to the generality of Protestants.[69]

Casaubon's passage employs the classic controversialist's tactic of picking up on a point made by one's opponent, and agreeing with it in such a way as to turn it against them. The consequences in this case are turned against Du Perron later in the letter, in reply to the French cardinal's proposal of two rules for governing the use of the fathers in debate. Rather than disagree with them, Casaubon—speaking in the name of James I—acknowledged that the fathers "may have their place." But he went on to argue that "because the controuersies of these daies are not about ceremonies, and other matters of lighter moment (*mediocris momenti rebus*), but about some articles of faith, and opinions appertaining to saluation: therefore his judgement is that above all there be a generall agreement upon this rule, that opinions concerning matters of faith, and whatsoever should be beleeved as necessarie to salvation, ought to be taken out of the sacred Scripture alone."[70]

Now this position was not particularly novel or significant in itself. But it took on a particular importance for Chillingworth. It did so because of the two rules of patristic interpretation that Du Perron had proposed. One of these was that if the fathers spoke not as doctors, but as witnesses, then what they testified to was to be accounted as the doctrine of the church. The other was that patristic consent in a particular age, accompanied by an absence of patristic dissent, should be taken satisfactorily to prove the point at issue.[71] We know that one of the reasons Chillingworth gave at the time for his conversion to Catholicism was the consensus in Rome's favor on the part of the primitive church and the fathers.[72] I would not venture to suggest that Chillingworth was particularly engaged by the implications of these rules, however, were it not that in a later work, *Answer to Some Passages in Rushworth's Dialogues* (after 1640), he cites, in order to deny, Du Perron's two rules in such a way as to suggest that he was closely familiar with them.[73]

Chillingworth—and Falkland too, despite his reputation for deep patristic reading—thus took the debate over the use of Christian antiquity a step beyond the kind of scholarly attack that James I had Casaubon conduct against the historical errors in Baronius's *Annals*. The Tew authors went so far as to assert that use of the fathers in religious controversy was, if not utterly invalid, then at least highly problematic. Their arguments were partly logical, and partly philological. They were logical, insofar as the same problems of interpretation and authority attended the use of the fathers as that of the Bible. And they were philological, insofar as the texts of the fathers were sometimes corrupt and their sense was often uncertain. As Chillingworth put it in the *Religion of Protestants,* "I see plainly and with mine own eyes, that there are Popes against Popes, Councells against Councells, some Fathers against others, the same Fathers against themselves, a Consent of Fathers of one age against a Consent of Fathers of another age, the Church of one age against the Church of another age . . . There is no sufficient certainty but of Scripture only, for any considering man to build upon."[74]

The source of these arguments was no mystery, then or now: they came from a work that formed one of the most thorough and coherent contributions to the several reformulations of historical knowledge and authority that were developed in the earlier years of the seventeenth century. This was the Huguenot Jean Daillé's *Traicté de l'employ des saincts pères, pour le jugement des differands, qui sont aujourd'hui en la religion* (1631).[75] An English translation of Daillé's book was published in 1651 by the keeper of the university library at Cambridge, Thomas Smith.[76] In the preface to his translation, Smith reported the esteem that Falkland had held it in: he used, wrote Smith, "to make a very honourable mention of this Monsieur, whose acquaintance [he] was wont to say was worth a voyage to *Paris.*"[77] Smith went on to state what he himself thought the value of Daillé's work was: "You have here [a] sufficient . . . confutation of *Perrons* book against *K.*[ing] *J.*[ames]."[78] Furthermore, in his *Reply* to Thomas White of *c.* 1636, Falkland had written that his own arguments were "confirmed by consideration of what hath been so temperately, learnedly, and judiciously written by Monsieur Daillé, our Protestant-Perron."[79]

In a recent paper on Daillé, Mario Turchetti has reaffirmed what was thus already clear to Falkland and Smith: that above all other Catholic controversialists it was Du Perron who was the target of Daillé's *Traicté.*[80] Yet this is a further reason to believe that if Daillé's treatise was, as Trevor-Roper (following Anthony Wood) argued, "the germ of Chillingworth's *Religion of Protestants,*"[81] then that germ was fertilized by Du Perron's *Replique* to James—of which Elizabeth Cary had published her translation in 1630.

★★★★★

Behind the writings of the central Great Tew authors, then, lies the challenge offered above all by the works of Cardinal Du Perron. The antagonistic stimulus that his works posed for the writings of Falkland and

Chillingworth has, I think, been insufficiently emphasized in those scholarly traditions that have stressed the search for their Protestant forebears over their Catholic opponents. Du Perron had ultimately set the agenda that Elizabeth Cary would have addressed in her reply to Falkland. To do so, she too might have made that metaphorical voyage to Paris to read Daillé's book, directed against an author she had invested so much energy in translating. Cary's experience as a translator of Du Perron would have helped provide her with arguments to deploy against her son. Unlike the more theologically dangerous Socinian tastes that were often attributed to the Great Tew group—tastes exemplified in Johann Völkel's *De vera religione* (which Guy Holland accused of being the inspiration for the *Religion of Protestants*) and Christopher Potter's 1631 Oxford edition of Jacobus Acontius's *Strategemata Satanae*—Daillé might perhaps have been one of the Protestant controversialists that Elizabeth Cary had "with leave" read.[82] Accounts of the intellectual context of the ideas of the Falkland circle might do well, in short, to place a little more emphasis on the intellectual preoccupations of Elizabeth Cary and above all on her translation of Du Perron; and also to consider Cary as a writer and controversialist in her own right: an author who was engaged by the same questions as the authors of Great Tew, and whose productions helped provoke their own controversial writings.

Notes

1. [Lucy Cary], "The Lady Falkland Her Life," in *Elizabeth Cary, Lady Falkland: Life and Letters,* ed. Heather Wolfe (Cambridge and Tempe, AZ: RTM Publications and Arizona Center for Medieval and Renaissance Studies, 2001), 214 (hereafter, *Life*).
2. There is as yet no Caroline equivalent of Peter Milward, *Religious Controversies of the Jacobean Age: A Survey of Printed Sources* (London: Scolar Press, 1978).
3. John Aubrey, *Brief Lives,* ed. Andrew Clark (Oxford: Clarendon Press, 1898), 1:151.
4. Edward Hyde, Earl of Clarendon, *The Life . . . Written by Himself,* 3 vols. (Oxford: Oxford University Press, 1759), 1:42–43.
5. J. C. Hayward, "New Directions in Studies of the Falkland Circle," *Seventeenth Century* 2 (1987): 19-48 (quotation 19).
6. Hugh Trevor-Roper, "The Great Tew Circle," in *Catholics, Anglicans and Puritans: Seventeenth-Century Essays* (London: Secker and Warburg, 1987), 169, 230. See also David Lunn, *Elizabeth Cary, Lady Falkland (1586/7–1639)* ([Ilford]: Royal Stuart Society, 1977), 2.
7. See further Wolfe, *Elizabeth Cary,* 1–90 (esp. 13–25).
8. Hugh Trevor-Roper, "The Religious Origins of the Enlightenment," in *Religion, the Reformation, and Social Change* (London: Macmillan, 1967), 193–236.

9. Trevor-Roper, "Great Tew Circle," esp. 193–195, 227 (quotation 175). See also Kurt Weber, *Lucius Cary, Second Viscount Falkland* (New York: Columbia UP, 1940), esp. ix; *Life*, 157; and Michael Mendle, "The *Convivium Philosophicum* and the Civil War: A Country House and its Politics," in *The Fashioning and Functioning of the British Country House*, ed. Gervase Jackson-Stops et al. (Hanover: National Gallery of Art, 1989), 289–297, esp. 290–291.
10. For example, by Hayward, "New Directions," 24, 27; Richard Tuck, "Philosophy at the Country House: The Ideas of the Tew Circle," in *The Fashioning and Functioning of the British Country House* ed. Gervase Jackson-Stops et al. (Hanover: National Gallery of Art, 1989), 299–303.
11. On the date of Cary's conversion (November 14, 1626) see Wolfe, *Elizabeth Cary*, 1. Contrast Trevor-Roper, "Great Tew Circle," 201, and Frances Dolan, "Introductory Note," to *Recusant Translators: Elizabeth Cary, Alexia Grey* (Aldershot: Ashgate, 2000), ix.
12. Jacques Davy du Perron, *The Reply of the Most Illustrious Cardinall of Perron, to the Answeare of the Most Excellent King of Great Britaine*, trans. Elizabeth Cary (Douai: Martin Bogart, 1630), *Life*, 132 and 207, suggests that Cary translated all of Du Perron's works, not just the *Reply* to James I that was printed.
13. Wolfe, *Elizabeth Cary*, 12.
14. Lancelot Andrewes, "Stricturæ" and "An Answer to the XX. Chapter," both in Andrewes, *Opuscula* (London: R. B. & Andræa Hebb, 1629).
15. *Life*, 131–132. See also Du Perron, *Reply*, sig. ã2^v.
16. On the authorship of *Life* see Wolfe, *Elizabeth Cary*, 61–62, 87–89; on the date (February–August 1645), see Wolfe, "The Scribal Hands and Dating of *Lady Falkland: Her Life*," *English Manuscript Studies 1100–1700* 9 (2000): 199–204, and Wolfe, *Elizabeth Cary*, 63n132 and 89.
17. *Life*, 151, 156.
18. Wolfe, *Elizabeth Cary*, "Chronology," xvii.
19. *Life*, 165.
20. Robert R. Orr, *Reason and Authority: The Thought of William Chillingworth* (Oxford: Clarendon Press, 1967), 26, 29.
21. *Life*, 165, 166, 165–180.
22. Chillingworth to Anne Cary, [June or July 1634?], in Wolfe, *Elizabeth Cary*, 387–390.
23. *Life*, 176–180.
24. J. C. Hayward, "The *Mores* of Great Tew" (PhD diss., University of Cambridge, 1981); Orr, *Reason and Authority*. See by contrast Wolfe, *Elizabeth Cary*, 60–61.
25. For example, see Weber, *Lucius Cary*, 170, 176.
26. Orr, 34, ascribing to Laud a letter that *Life* (172) suggests was by Chillingworth.
27. John Tulloch, *Rational Theology and Christian Philosophy in England in the Seventeenth Century*, 2 vols, vol. I: *Liberal Churchmen* (Edinburgh: William Blackwood, 1872), 1:95.
28. Edward Hyde, Earl of Clarendon, *The History of the Rebellion*, ed. W. Dunn Macray, 6 vols. (Oxford: Oxford UP, 1888), 3:180.

29. *Life*, 163, 164, and n170.
30. Compare Orr, 30, 34, and Trevor-Roper, "Great Tew Circle," 205.
31. *Life*, 180–181; Stephanie Hodgson-Wright, "Cary [née Tanfield], Elizabeth, Viscountess Falkland (1585–1639)," in *Oxford Dictionary of National Biography*, ed. H. C. G. Matthew and Brian Harrison, 60 vols. (Oxford: Oxford University Press, 2004), 10:429 [hereafter *ODNB*].
32. *Life*, 185, 193–204. See also Weber, 176–181, Wolfe, *Elizabeth Cary*, 16–18, and the King's Bench and Star Chamber examinations in Wolfe, *Elizabeth Cary*, 395–399.
33. *Life*, 157.
34. Hyde, *History*, 3:180, 181.
35. L. A. Beaurline, "An Editorial Experiment: Suckling's *A Sessions of the Poets*," *Studies in Bibliography* 16 (1963): 59.
36. See British Library (BL), MS Stowe 976, fol. 1^r; Wolfe, *Elizabeth Cary*, "Chronology," xvi; *Life*, 155 n147; Thompson Cooper, rev. Edward Charles Metzger, "Montagu, Walter (1604/5–1677)," in *ODNB*, 38:771.
37. Henrietta Maria to Lord Aston, November 17, 1635, in Wolfe, *Elizabeth Cary*, 391.
38. *Life*, 221; Wolfe, *Elizabeth Cary*, 25 and n58; *Life*, 206 and n265.
39. Hyde, *Life*, 41.
40. Cooper, "Montagu," 771. See further Anthony Milton, *Catholic and Reformed: The Roman and Protestant Churches in English Protestant Thought 1600–1640* (Cambridge: Cambridge UP, 1995), 270 and 294n127.
41. BL, MS Harley 6866, fols. 210^r–225^v (including Falkland's reply, fols. 220^v–225^r); other copies are in BL, MS Add. 22591 and BL, MS Add. 29586.
42. *Life*, 211 and n288; Montagu to Cardinal Barberini, December 6, 1638, in Wolfe, *Elizabeth Cary*, 407–408.
43. Falkland's reply to Montagu is mentioned by George Con in a letter of December 11, 1636 (Wolfe, *Elizabeth Cary*, 400 and n252).
44. Lucius Cary, Viscount Falkland, "My Lord Faulklands Answer," in Walter Montagu, *The Coppy of a Letter Sent from France* ([London]: [s.n.], 1641), 21. Cf. BL, MS Harley 6866, fol. 220^v.
45. *Life*, 213–214.
46. *The Correspondence of John Cosin*, ed. G. Ornsby, 2 vols. (Durham: Andrews, 1869), 1:101 (Montague to Cosin, August 26, [1626]).
47. Wolfe, *Elizabeth Cary*, 264–265 (Alexander Cook to James Ussher, November 30, 1626). See also Milton, *Catholic and Reformed*, 85, and generally V. E. Raymer, "Durham House and the Emergence of Laudian Piety" (PhD diss., Harvard University, 1983), esp. 13–51.
48. *Life*, 127, 112; see further Wolfe, *Elizabeth Cary*, 4; *Life*, 213.
49. Matthew 10:34–36 (A.V.). On the significance of this epigraph see further Wolfe, *Elizabeth Cary*, 8–9.
50. Montagu, *Coppy of a Letter*, 7.
51. Falkland, "The Lord of Faulklands Answer," in *Discourse of Infallibility* (1651), 280. Falkland, "My Lord Faulklands Answer," in Montagu, *Coppy of a Letter*, 22, and BL, MS Harley 6866, fol. 220^v, read "or" for "and."

ELIZABETH CARY AND THE GREAT TEW CIRCLE   181

52. Du Perron, *Reply*, 45; Du Perron, *Replique à la response du serenissme Roy de la grand'Bretagne*, 3rd ed. (Paris: Pierre Chaudière, 1633), 40.
53. Falkland, "My Lord Faulklands Answer," in Montagu, *Coppy of a Letter*, 23.
54. Contrast J. I. Packer, *The Transformation of Anglicanism 1643–1660: With Special Reference to Henry Hammond* (Manchester: Manchester UP, 1969), 65, who dates Falkland's *Discourse* to "a year or two before he was killed at Newbury in 1643."
55. *Life*, 169.
56. William Chillingworth, *The Religion of Protestants a Safe Way to Salvation* (Oxford: Leonard Lichfield, 1638), 51.
57. Chillingworth, *Religion of Protestants*, 375–377.
58. Chillingworth, *Religion of Protestants*, 375.
59. Du Perron, *Replique*, 45. See also Richard Tuck, *Philosophy and Government 1572–1651* (Cambridge: Cambridge UP, 1993), 272–276.
60. Du Perron, *Reply*, 447.
61. Falkland, "The Lord of Faulklands Reply," in *Discourse of Infallibility* (1651), 59.
62. Isaac Casaubon, *De rebus sacris & ecclesiasticis* (London: John Bill, 1614).
63. Isaac Casaubon, *The Answere . . . to the epistle of the most reuerend Cardinall Peron* (London: William Aspley, 1612), 1, 5, translating Casaubon, *Ad epistolam illustr. et reuerendiss. Cardinalis Perronij, responsio* (London: John Norton, 1612), 2, 8; Mark Pattison, *Isaac Casaubon 1559–1614* (London: Longmans, 1875), 308.
64. See above, note 6.
65. Du Perron, *Reply*, 11; see also Du Perron, *Replique*, sig. [ãv]ʳ. The account of the origins of Du Perron's book in Dolan, "Introductory Note," x, is erroneous.
66. Chillingworth, *Religion of Protestants*, 345.
67. Chillingworth, *Religion of Protestants*, title page (Latin); English translation from Casaubon, *Answere*, 18–19.
68. See Pierre Des Maizeaux, *An Historical and Critical Account of the Life and Writings of Wm. Chillingworth* (London: T. Woodward, 1725), 137–149 and now Anthony Milton, "Licensing, Censorship, and Religious Orthodoxy in Early Stuart England," *Historical Journal* 41 (1998): 648–649.
69. Edward Knott, *A Direction to be observed by N.N.* ([London?]: [s.n.], 1636); see further Robert Martin Krapp, *Liberal Anglicanism, 1636–47* (Ridgefield: Acorn, 1947), 7, and Orr, 42.
70. Casaubon, *Answere*, 27, translating Casaubon, *Responsio*, 44.
71. Jacques Davy du Perron, *A Letter Written from Paris* ([St. Omer]: [s.n.], 1612), 33; cf. Casaubon, *Answere*, 26.
72. See B. H. G. Wormald, *Clarendon: Politics, Historiography, Religion* (Cambridge: Cambridge UP, 1989), 246, and esp. Orr, 12, 15.
73. William Chillingworth, "An Answer to Some Passages in Rushworth's Dialogues," in *Works* (Philadelphia: Robert Davis, 1840), 746.
74. Chillingworth, *Religion of Protestants*, 376.

75. See esp. Jean Daillé, *Traité de l'emploi des saints Pères* (Geneva: Pierre Aubert, 1632), 291.
76. On Smith, see Paul Hammond, "Thomas Smith: A Beleaguered Humanist of the Interregnum," *Bulletin of the Institute of Historical Research* 56 (1983): 180–194.
77. Jean Daillé, *A Treatise Concerning the Right Use of the Fathers,* trans. Thomas Smith (London: John Martin, 1651), sig. [¶5]^r; repeated by Wood, *Athenae,* 3:91.
78. Daillé, *Treatise,* sig. [¶5]^r.
79. Falkland, *Discourse of Infallibility* (1651), 202.
80. Mario Turchetti, "Jean Daillé et son *Traicté de l'employ des saincts pères* (1632). Aperçu sur les changements des critères d'appréciation des Pères de l'Eglise entre le XVIe et le XVIIe siècles," in *Les Pères de l'Eglise au XVIIe siècle,* ed. Emmanuel Bury and Bernard Meunier (Paris: CERF, 1993), 77.
81. Trevor-Roper, "Great Tew Circle," 185; Wood, *Athenae,* 3:91.
82. Joannes Volkelius, *De vera religione* (Racow: Sebastian Sternacius, 1630); [Henry Hammond], *A View of Some Exceptions* (London: Richard Royston, 1646), 21 (text by Guy Holland).

CHAPTER 10

"READER, STAND STILL AND LOOK, LO HERE I AM": ELIZABETH CARY'S FUNERAL ELEGY "ON THE DUKE OF BUCKINGHAM"

Nadine N. W. Akkerman

Elizabeth Cary's terse epitaph "Upon the death of the Duke of Buckingham" (1628), attributed to her in two sources—British Library Egerton MS 2725 ("An Epitaph . . . by the Countesse of Faukland") and Northamptonshire Record Office ("Epitaph on Buckingham by ye La: Faukland")—has failed to attract much critical attention until now. Kurt Weber, the biographer of Cary's son Lucius Cary, second Viscount Falkland, unequivocally identified the epitaph as hers as early as 1940, but it was never again mentioned until more than five decades later, and then only in a footnote.[1] In 1993, Donald W. Foster located a text in the Beinecke Library that connects Cary's epitaph with a poem of forty-four lines (Osborn Poetry Box VI/28).[2] Subsequent critics have continued to refer only to the short epitaph, however, ignoring the likely relationship between these two texts. The first six lines constitute the epitaph attributed to Cary, and the succeeding forty-four lines, beginning with "Yet were bidentalls sacred," constitute an elegiac poem.[3] This chapter will argue that it is probable that Cary's epitaph ("Reader stand still") and the elegy ("Yet were bidentalls sacred"), reproduced as an appendix at the end of this chapter, were both linked and separated in the course of manuscript transmission, and that Cary is the author of both.

ATTRIBUTION ISSUES

Cary's elegy is plagued by several competing claims for authorship—John Eliot, Richard Weston, lord treasurer, and William Juxon, Weston's successor as lord treasurer—which can be dismissed with relative ease.[4] Margaret Crum's *First-Line Index of English Poetry* proffers John Eliot because the epitaph and elegy appear, in reverse order, in the printed volume *Poems or Epigrams, Satyrs* (London: Henry Brome, 1658), which has introductory verses signed by one "J. E."[5] In fact, *Poems or Epigrams, Satyrs* is not a single-author volume, but a poetical miscellany compiled by someone connected to the universities of Cambridge and Oxford. It includes widely circulated Oxbridge poems such as Richard Corbett's "An Exhortation to Mr John Hamond Minister at Bewdley for the Battring downe the Maypole," which is immediately followed by the elegy in question ("Yet were bidentalls sacred").[6] Apart from the introductory verses, only one poem is signed with the initials "J. E."[7] It is not implausible that a poem written by Cary in 1628 would appear in an Oxford miscellany: her son Lorenzo took his BA from Exeter College, Oxford, in 1630, and her son Lucius's "Great Tew Circle" consisted of many Oxford luminaries, including William Chillingworth, son of the mayor of Oxford and a fellow of Trinity College, Oxford, who, according to *The Lady Falkland: Her Life,* engaged in serious religious debate with Cary and her children in the 1630s.

Crum's attribution to Dr. William Juxon (1582–1663, later Archbishop of Canterbury) is based upon a tenuous subscription to the elegy in a manuscript at the Bodleian (Bod. MS Eng. Poet. e.97): "Docter Juxon (some say) / Nondum constat." Juxon, too, moved within Oxford circles, serving as vice chancellor of the university from 1626–1628. The same scribal hand that attributes the elegy to Juxon, however, also mistakenly attributes another poem in the same miscellany to John Donne.[8] This is not surprising: misattributions were rampant in poetical miscellanies because scribally published poems were rarely signed and easily became detached from the original circumstances of their production.[9]

The attribution to Richard Weston (1577–1635), Earl of Portland, in another manuscript (Bodleian MS Rawlinson Poet. 26) is more difficult to cast aside. Not only was Weston an extreme royalist, but he was also a client of Buckingham's.[10] The duke's influence enabled him to attain the position of lord treasurer in June, shortly before the duke was assassinated, and it seems not impossible for Weston to have written a poem that condemns Buckingham's murder. While the elegy and epitaph are contiguously represented as one poem by the scribe, a different hand ascribes the elegy to Weston and the epitaph to "a Lady." Whereas the attributions to Eliot and Juxon are thus highly questionable, and the attribution to Weston remains unsubstantiated, this chapter brings together sufficient evidence to support the attribution to Cary.

THE ELEGY IN CONTEXT

The elegy centers on Buckingham's murder and the moral implications it arouses. While arranging an expedition for the relief of the Huguenots of La Rochelle, on August 23, 1628, George Villiers, Duke of Buckingham, was stabbed to death. After an initial escape, his assassin, John Felton, turned himself in and was executed. Later, a copy of the House of Commons' remonstrance against the duke, which the House had presented to the king on June 17, two months prior to Buckingham's assassination, was found among Felton's papers. The remonstrance charged that Buckingham's excessive military power had become a threat to the realm: they believed he was conspiring with Catholics on the continent and that he might purposely be lowering the guard of England's coastal defenses.[11] As he had done when Buckingham was impeached by Parliament in 1626, Charles I circumvented the remonstrance by closing Parliament. In 1626, Buckingham's unpopularity, caused by his selling of offices and titles and his shameless promotion of his own kindred, was compounded by his failing military and naval operations. When two years later, Charles I did not attach any consequences to the remonstrance, Felton was convinced that by killing the duke he would serve his country. The duke's assassination was celebrated in a deluge of libelous attacks; Felton was praised, and the duke's death rarely lamented.

Buckingham's assassination, and the trial and execution of his murderer, generated a great amount of politically motivated verse. Cary's elegy heroically counters both the outpouring of contemptuous denunciations of Buckingham as well as the heroic poems celebrating his attacker. More remarkably, the poem answers the "remonstrance" (l.47), as it lends the murdered duke a voice and accuses the accusers. The first four lines identify the speaker as "the mightie Buckingham," which indicates that the king's former favorite is addressing his audience from beyond the grave. Buckingham was a favorite to "two kings," James I and his successor Charles I, yet his murderer, John Felton, was descended from the lower-gentry, "a slave" (l.4). Some of the verses celebrating the duke's murder imagine the duke's assassination to be an example of divine providence. Buckingham humbly and sorrowfully admits that his murder might have been a sudden act of punishment by the hand of God, but if that is the case, so Buckingham argues, then he has been punished enough now that he is dead, and his opponents must let him rest in peace and not disgrace his memory. As he argues, "if this blowe / That strucke me in my height and laid me lowe / Came from the hand of heaven, / lett it suffice / that god required no other sacrifice" (ll.9–12). "Bidentalls," places "struckein with thunder," were after all considered to be "sacred," according to Roman practices (ll.7–8). After the sanctification through the sacrifice of a sheep, in this case through the sacrifice of the duke's life, a bidental was closed off and was never trespassed upon again, or as the speaker puts it, "Ne'er after trampled over" (l.9). Buckingham compares the slander of his memory, then, to sacrilege.

The speaker strongly contests the libelous attacks on his reputation. "As for my fame I clayme and doe not crave / that thou beleeve two kings before aslave," he declares to all the people who trust Felton rather than James I and Charles I (ll.5–6). In an attempt to free himself from slanderous attack, he condemns the mock elegies and libels that were written after his assassination: "Why doe you bruise a Reede; as if your Rodd / could wound me deeper than the hand of God" (ll.13–14), he asks. The alliterative words "Reede" and "Rodd" that are juxtaposed here both have strong biblical echoes. Egypt was called a bruised reed, upon which Hezekiah could not rely if the Assyrians declared war on Jerusalem: "Now, behold, thou trusted upon the staff of this bruised reed, *even* upon Egypt, on which if a man lean, it will go into his hand, and pierce it" (2 Kings 18:21). Not only could it not be trusted for support, it could also do damage. On one level, a rod is associated with anger. God used the Assyrians as an instrument of his anger to reform the Israelites: "O Assyrian, the rod of mine anger, and the staff in their hand in mine indignation" (Isaiah 10:5). On another level, Moses's rod, which turned into a serpent and on another occasion divided the sea (Exodus 4:3 and 14:16), symbolizes God's power invested in man. By turning Moses's humble shepherd's staff into a rod, God committed his authority to man, and the rod therefore symbolizes both divine and human law. In addition, the Hebrew word for rod also means scepter, and thus also symbolizes the authority of the king. Buckingham compares his attackers' hatred toward him, or their use of a rod, then, with the usurpation of God's or the king's authority and power. He likewise condemns the praises written about his murderer: "Why are you not contented with my blood / ffor hate of me why make you murther good" (ll.17–18), he asks rhetorically.

The poem continues with a more direct biblical reference. As is conveniently scribbled in the left margin of the Beinecke manuscript ("Levit: x: ij"), line 23 refers to Leviticus 10:2, the story of Nadab and Abihu, the sons of Aaron who were both devoured by the fire that went out from the Lord after they had offered him a "strange fire" of incense (l.24). The "strange fire" is usually explained as fire that God had not commanded them to offer. God had showed them the way in which they should make offerings. Their disregard of these rules, or "gods proper lawe" (l.22), met with severe punishment. They were punished for idolatrous worship because they did not recognize the difference between holy and unholy, and between clean and unclean, just like those who praise Buckingham's murderer, or so Buckingham and Cary imply. The speaker compares the worship of his murderer, then, to the "straunge fire" Nadab and Abihu offered God (ll.21–25) and which ignited God's anger. Buckingham concedes that he is a scapegoat, but he also implies that the libelers' devotion to his murderer will meet with punishment: "Take heede t'will burne you, t'is adaungerous thinge" (l.25). To praise a murderer who defied the king's wishes could endanger the stability of the laws of the monarchy, the laws of God's representative on earth, the king: "who soe doth blesse a Murtherer kills akinge" (l.26). In other words, the taunting and disrespectful reaction of Buckingham's opponents could jeopardize the monarchy. The powerfully suggestive phrase "who soe doth blesse a Murtherer kills akinge" alludes to the notion that killing a favorite of the king incites hatred toward the king, which is also therefore a form of sacrilege because the king is the representative of God. The line also eerily foreshadows the execution of Charles I in 1649, which might explain why the poem continued to turn up in later miscellanies. It remained topical even after Buckingham was long forgotten.

The author of this intelligent and thought-provoking poem does not acquit Buckingham of all wrongdoing, but charges that the duke cannot be held solely responsible for all the corruption in England. Buckingham himself also questions whether he was thoroughly evil: "Spewes any goodnes in me was I all /Massa corrupta and Stigmaticall /was I all ills?" (ll.31–33). The Latin allusions to Catholic Mass and Christ's stigmata refer to the accusation of the remonstrance, that Buckingham was promoting a Catholic conspiracy. Although many of the poem's readers in the seventeenth century would be inclined to believe that he was a Papist, Buckingham's emotive appeal may sway his audience to think again. The speaker points out that he once had been good enough for those who later turned against him: "those that ript me found /some of my vitalls good some inwards sound" (ll.33–34). He confronts those whose careers he had advanced: "Witnesse those now who needed noe more depend / and those whose Merritts I have made or Raised" (ll.42–43). They hypocritically turned against their benefactor, and accused him of actions from which they had directly benefited. Buckingham is punished for the deeds that he committed out of charity for his friends: "I never lost my selfe but for there sake" (l.48).

Nevertheless, there is one friend who pities him—the poet who abstained from writing mock epitaphs on his death and defended his reputation by writing this elegy: "All doe not mourne in iest theires some one eie / shed teares in earnest when it sawe me die (ll.45-46). The poem's form reveals one characteristic about this elusive author referred to in these last lines: he, or indeed she, was familiar with theatrical devices. The poem written in heroic couplets is not a conventional elegy. It can even be questioned whether it should be called an elegy, because the deceased Buckingham is addressing his audience from beyond the grave. The generic form comes therefore perhaps closest to a dramatic monologue, which suggests that the author was also familiar with writing plays.

Less than a year before the elegy was written, Cary wrote *Edward II*, in which she portrays the king's favorite, Spencer, in such a way that her contemporaries would immediately recognize him as the Duke of Buckingham. The persuasive structural method of both the elegy and *Edward II* is similar. As a lawyer's daughter, Cary defends Isabel's case in *Edward II*. As the narrator states:

> a bare relation of a female passion enforced the cause;
> Which whether true or false was yet in question
> The plaintiff had been heard, but no defendant.[12]

In legal terms, the narrator makes sure that not only is "the plaintiff" allowed to bring his case against Isabel in a court of law, but also that "the defendant," who is being tried, receives a voice through her narrator. In other words, Cary is making sure that Isabel is not merely "quoted in the margins of such a story" (*Edward II*, 223). Likewise, the elegy "Yet were bidentalls sacred" makes sure that not only are Buckingham's adversaries heard, but also that "the defendant," who is being tried, receives a voice. The poem, in contrast to the other poems in which Buckingham is the object, allows Buckingham full subjectivity by making him the speaker. As in *Edward II*, the reader has to pronounce the verdict.

Another comparison with Cary's *Edward II* can be made. The narrator of *Edward II* is, in general, sympathetic toward Queen Isabel; that is, until Isabel's anger clouds her judgment and rational behavior. No other historical narrative emphasizes Isabel's violent nature, and the passage is thus Cary's own invention.[13] Once in control, the virtuous and modest Isabel decisively changes into a vengeful woman. This sudden change does not seem true to the character of the queen. The tone of "Yet were bidentalls sacred" is likewise complex and paradoxical. It criticizes Buckingham's role as favorite, but also defends him by lending him a voice. Like *Edward II*, the elegy warns against blinding hate: "High and revealed malice that canst drawe / heaven out of hell" (ll.21–22). In other words, the author warns that hatred can unexpectedly alter the things one considers most fundamental—indeed, heaven can be drawn out of hell. This sudden change is replicated in the queen's action in *Edward II*. As the narrator in *Edward II*, the speaker of the elegy "Yet were bidentalls sacred" warns of the effects of anger or revenge: "Take heed, t'will burne you, t'is a dangerous thing" (l.25).

The Duke of Buckingham's death was a popular subject for writers, and yet the elegy "Yet were bidentalls sacred" is considerably more complex than the numerous other verses produced on the subject of the duke's murder.[14] It struggles with the moral complications of a murder that was so widely rejoiced:

> Why do you judge me ere the iudgment day
> As if your verdict could gods iudgment swaye
> Why are you note contented with my blood
> For hate of me why make you murther good. (ll. 15–18)

The poem can be connected with a small number of other poems that likewise disapproved of the rejoicings over and implicit legitimatization of Buckingham's murder. Lines 27–28, for instance—"Now I have past the pikes and seen my fate / My princes favour and the peoples hate"—echo the opening lines from an epitaph by James Shirley that circulated widely in manuscript form, "Heere lyes the best & worst of Fate / Two Princes love, the Peoples hate" (Bodleian MS Malone 23, 195).[15] It also shows some familiarities with Owen Feltham's poem on Buckingham, who also uses the image of impact by lightning to describe Buckingham's murder: "I'le pittie yet; at last thy fatall end / Shott like a lightning from a violent hand."[16] Even though Thomas Carew and Sir William Davenant would also take a hostile stance toward Buckingham's attackers, the poets who denounced the murder and the libelous attacks were a clear minority. Since virtually no apologetic verses were produced at the time, the question arises why Cary would have made the decision to act as Buckingham's mouthpiece.

Elegies were not so much written for the deceased as they were for the ones who were left behind, in this case the ladies of the Buckingham family. Arthur F. Marotti has argued that epitaphs, elegies, and epistles that were compiled in manuscript collections had a specific function within a scribal community: "Like verse letters to social superiors, many elegies established or affirmed ties of social, political, or economic patronage; others were composed to declare in-group allegiances of various sorts—to family, to a network of friends and/or colleagues, to a political faction."[17] Even though the poem's tone is at times scornful, Cary's elegy declared first and foremost her allegiance to the Buckingham family.

Cary was extremely well connected at court, both through her maternal uncle, Sir Henry Lee,[18] but especially because of her kinship with the Buckingham family. Henry Cary's sister Frances had married George Manners, the Duchess of Buckingham's uncle, in 1605. It is widely acknowledged that Henry Cary, Elizabeth's husband, was a Buckingham protégé and that they joined forces in the campaign against Catholicism. With the exception of the Countess of Carlisle (Buckingham's mistress), the women in Queen Henrietta's circle were all related to Buckingham. In the years succeeding Cary's conversion, the duke's sister, Susan Feilding, Countess of Denbigh, gradually became the center of the queen's court faction.

Cary would make ample use of her kinship with the Buckingham family to facilitate her children's advancement at court. In a 1635 letter of recommendation for her daughter Mary, whom she desired to become an attendant to the Queen of Spain, she concludes by stressing to the addressee, Lord Aston, that in fulfilling her request he shall "oblige . . . all hir [daughter's] other frends, my lord of Rutland and my lady, hir aunt. My lord of Niewbourg hir unkle, and my lady duchesse Buckingham hir neere kinswoman."[19] Another of her daughters, Victoria, served as maid of honor to Queen Henrietta Maria and performed in masques with her.[20] When the far-reaching consequences of Cary's conversion became apparent, she drew on her powerful connections with the Buckingham women to marshal support. Various Catholic, or Catholic-leaning, ladies of that circle petitioned the king to treat Cary more leniently relieve her from necessities. Karen Robertson suggests that women often supported each other by writing letters when financial rights were violated: "Given married women's limited access to formal structures, they used letters of complaint to announce their need and to mobilize protection."[21] Such a system of support is clearly traceable in the correspondence of the Buckingham women when Cary was cut off from financial means by her husband. For instance, Katherine (Manners) Villiers, Duchess of Buckingham, daughter of the Catholic Earl of Rutland, wrote to Secretary Conway on March 24, 1627:

> My Lord I am to intreat a fauour from you in the behalfe of the poore distressed lady faulkland for I protest her case is very lamentable I desire you will to speake to the kinge that those letters which he sined to be sent to my lady tanfield to keepe her daughter prisner may be stayed[.][22]

The Duchess of Buckingham's short note introduced Cary's own letter to Conway of the same date and subject, guaranteeing that she would be heard. Cary closes this letter:

> I beseech you speake to the duchesse and countesse of Buckingham, about mee, and whatsoeuer you heare of mee, rather beleeue, those noble ladyes,

and my brother and sister barrett with whom I dayly conuerse, then those pestilent seruants of my lords.[23]

On May 18, 1627, Cary sent a letter to Conway that included a petition to the king, which "concernes, no lesse, then the sauinge [her] from steruinge" wherein she wrote that "if [he] second it strongly, to his maiesty . . . [he] shall receaue extraordinary thankes, from all the three ^greate^ ladyes, of my lord of Buckinghams family"—that is, the duke's wife, sister, and mother.[24] The support of these influential ladies granted the discredited playwright a voice.[25]

Spencer, as the Duke of Buckingham's spitting image in *Edward II*, is brought to justice in Cary's history: he is "pointblank charged with insolency, injustice, corruption, oppression, neglect of the public, and immoderate advancement of his own particular" (139). The system of absolute favoritism was finally scrutinized by Parliament in 1628, and much incriminating evidence against the duke was brought forward. On June 13, 1628, the exact day that the House of Commons lambasted Buckingham, John Lambe was murdered by a London mob. A notorious astrologer, Lambe was believed to be able to conjure up apparitions from a crystal glass, and to have accurately predicted several deaths and disasters. A passage in *Edward II* most certainly draws a parallel to Lambe and his practices:

> Some say that he [Edward II] was foretold by a certain magician, who as it seems was his craftsmaster, that this place [Corfe Castle] was to him both fatal and ominous. (223)

While Lambe was repeatedly accused of witchcraft, he was usually acquitted, or else kept in easy confinement where he was still allowed to receive clients. Edward II's meeting with a "a certain magician" in a prison environment certainly points to Lambe. A contemporary pamphlet that describes the life of Lambe recounts an instance where Lambe was found guilty of the rape of an eleven-year-old girl, but was suddenly pardoned by the king's grace.[26] He doubtlessly owed this indulgent treatment to the influence of Buckingham, because the duke and his mother were his most loyal clients. They had consulted him in respect to the insanity of the duke's brother, John Villiers, Viscount Purbeck, in 1622. From then on they employed Lambe, who was by that time also known as "Dr. Lambe," as their personal physician. Dr. Lambe was accused of influencing the fortunes of the duke and the duke's mother with the king through his mastery of sorcery, witchcraft, or black magic. It was alleged that the duke, by means of Dr. Lambe's magic, had not only been able to seduce many virtuous women, but also won the affection of the king. As the speaker of one of the contemporary poems, the duke tries to defend himself from these charges:

> Nor shall you ever prove, by magick charmes
> I wrought the king's affection, or his harmes,
> Or that I need Lambes philters to incite
> Chast ladies to give my fowle lust delight[.][27]

The duke's mother supposedly mastered the black art to aid her son's devilish schemes, an opinion that found utterance in numerous satirical poems about Buckingham. For example, in a poem upon Buckingham's French defeat:

> Could not thy titles scare them? And thy
> Lambe's Protection, safeguard thee from the French rams? . . .
> Could not thy mother's masses, nor her crosses,
> Nor yet her sorceries prevent these losses?[28]

When, in early 1628, Buckingham was attacked in Parliament for abusing his influence at court, the contemporary ballads and poems insisted upon Dr. Lambe's evil influence on the duke.

It is generally assumed that the enraged crowd that killed Lambe, who was known as "the Duke's Devil," committed the act out of the intense hatred it felt for Buckingham. The assassinations of Lambe and Buckingham are inextricably linked, which is reflected in most ballads, pamphlets, and poems describing Buckingham's murder; almost all writings connect the two assassinations. For instance, the following couplet was yelled through the streets by the London mob:

> lett Charles & george doe what they can
> Yet george shall dye like Doctor Lambe.[29]

A contemporary couplet that celebrated Buckingham's murder indeed infers that Lambe's murder led to the murder of the duke:

> The Shepheards struck, The sheepe are fledd,
> For want of Lambe the Wolfe is dead.[30]

These verses show that the growing unpopularity of the duke was also projected upon those who surrounded him. As a lawyer's daughter, Cary takes on Buckingham's case. Her reasons for lending the duke a voice are not entirely altruistic, however. Not only is she defying the libelous attacks out of loyalty toward the Buckingham family, but in a certain sense she is also defending her own interests. The patronage of the Duke of Buckingham

"READER, STAND STILL AND LOOK, LO HERE I AM" 193

had elevated the Carys as members of the new aristocracy, and his unpopularity did not bode well for her family's fortunes.

Cary's relationship with the Buckingham ladies, which she maintained even after the Countess of Denbigh had betrayed her by reporting her conversion to the Duke of Buckingham, was undoubtedly beneficial to her. One can speculate that it must also have advanced her position in the hierarchy of Henrietta's circle. Even though it remains uncertain to what extent Cary's conversion was motivated by the desire to improve her social standing—in a letter to the king, Cary professes that she was not so "foolish" as to "make religion, a ladder to clime by"—the queen's circle certainly empowered her to claim an authorial identity as playwright, poet, and recusant translator.[31] By dedicating her recusant translation *The Reply of the Most Illustrious Cardinall of Perron* to Henrietta Maria, Cary sought acceptance of her work through courtly connections. Moreover, once accepted as an insider belonging to the queen's circle, in all likelihood through the Countess of Denbigh's recommendation, but theoretically still an outsider at court, she could use her literary voice to utter detached criticism of a system of which she was herself a part. The author's unique position allowed her to be sympathetic toward Henrietta Maria and to take a critical stand toward the Buckingham family at the same time in *Edward II*. The continued relationship with the Duke of Buckingham's sister had liberated Cary's authorial voice, and the courtly connections widened the literary circles in which Cary could participate.

Manuscript Circulation and Literary Circles

This chapter will finally show how the elegy can render information about the literary circles in which Cary's work circulated in manuscript form. The Osborn manuscript is not the only contemporary textual source for the epitaph and elegy, and its survival in an array of formats highlights the vicissitudes of scribal publication. The epitaph appears on its own in at least ten different manuscripts,[32] while the elegy appears on its own in at least three manuscripts.[33] The epitaph and elegy are connected in nine different manuscripts and in a printed volume of poems that has hitherto been ascribed to a John Eliot.[34] A full textual history of these poems remains to be written.

Most manuscript versions that include both the epitaph and elegy represent them as a single, unified poem, although their order is sometimes reversed (in the Osborn manuscript, the epitaph is followed by the elegy; in many of the Bodleian versions, the elegy is followed by the epitaph). In two instances, the two parts appear a few pages apart; in another, two separate subscriptions ("finis") imply that they constitute two distinct poems.[35] Elsewhere, the two segments are presented as companion poems: even though the epitaph has a separate heading ("His Epitaph"), the two segments are written in the same hand and ink, and a line-divider, which is used to separate poems throughout the manuscript, comes only after the epitaph (Bod. MS Eng Poet. e.14; also MS Rawlinson Poet. 153 and MS Eng Poet. e.97). In Bod. MS Rawlinson 26 the poem is finished in a different scribal hand that leaves a gap between the elegy and the epitaph but nevertheless recognizes them to be connected; in Bod. MS Rawlinson Poet. 62 the epitaph is indented but the two segments are clearly perceived to constitute one poem. Variations in arrangement and format were not uncommon in the process of scribal publication—describing this phenomenon in the transmission of some of Philip Sidney's most important works, Peter Beal explains: "Some *ur*-examplar was written on separate sheets and, at some stage of copying, got disordered."[36]

The manuscripts in which the elegy and the epitaph circulated, like the printed Eliot miscellany *Poems or Epigrams, Satyrs,* have many Oxford associations. Arthur F. Marotti has argued that women were more active in these "male" centers of scribal publication than is generally assumed:

> Although the keeping of commonplace books was taught to males in grammar schools and the practice of compiling miscellanies and poetical anthologies flourished in all-male social worlds like the universities and the Inns of Court, some women contributed to and/or owned poetical collections. [. . .] In great houses and courtly circles, they had access to and sometimes added poems to manuscript collections.[37]

Regardless of whether one accepts the elegy "Yet were bidentalls sacred" as Cary's, her epitaph "Reader stand still" circulated in the male environment of the University of Oxford. It traveled with a small group of anonymous poems that were defensive of the duke or in any case similarly ambivalent about the celebration of his murder.[38] The miscellanies seem to nurture a set of political and moral values that were shared by the scribal community in which the texts that condemned Buckingham's murder circulated.

Dedications and contemporary references to Cary's writings indicate her Cary's other work—known and unknown—was also circulated in manuscript form.[39] John Davies concluded his dedicatory poem to her in *The Muses Sacrifice* (1612) with a word of warning. Even though the muse Minerva "stands in fear" of Cary "lest she, from her, should get Arts regency," if rather than publishing her writings, she restricted herself to manuscript circulation instead, her writing skills would go unnoticed by future generations:

> Such nervy limbs of art and strains of wit,
> time past ne'er knew the weaker sex to have;
> And times to come will hardly credit it,
> if thus thou give thy works both birth and grave.[40]

This chapter has excavated one poem from the grave. Further research on the social context of the manuscripts in which the elegy was copied could render more information about the literary circles in which Cary's work circulated and might even bring other work to the surface.

Together with the poetry in *The Tragedy of Mariam* and her manuscript poems, which appear in some copies of her recusant translation *The Reply of the Most Illustrious Cardinall of Perron* (1630)—a sonnet "To the Queenes Most Excellent Majesty" and a quatrain to "Jacques Davy"—the epitaph reveals that Cary was an author whose work circulated in manuscript form.[41] While the question of authorship of the elegy cannot be settled conclusively, Eliot, Weston, and Juxon can be ruled out as authors, and there is nothing in the elegy that precludes Cary's authorship. The fact that the epitaph is attributed to her in two sources, and that the epitaph and elegy appear together in ten different sources, including one printed book, further supports her authorship. Additionally, biographical evidence—her kinship relation with Buckingham's sister—makes the attribution plausible and can account for the unconventional decision not to mock the duke but to lend him a voice. Cary had portrayed the Duke of Buckingham in her *Edward II* less than a year before the elegy was written. Thematic and structural correspondence with *Edward II* further strengthens the case that the poem is hers. Like *Edward II,* it counters the mainstream, accepted narratives and lends the accused a voice. If we accept that the poem was written by Cary, it further demonstrates her engagement in the political and literary debates of her time. The numerous dedications to Cary offer us enough traces that indicate that her work was read widely in manuscript form; with the poem on Buckingham we can pick up the trail to make Cary's active participation in literary debates and manuscript culture clearly discernible.

Appendix: The Epitaph and Elegy

Beinecke Rare Book and Manuscript Library, Yale University, Osborn Poetry Box VI/28. Note: the u/v graph is normalized.

> Reader stand still, and looke, loe here I am
> that was of late the mightie Buckingham
> God gave to me my beinge and my breath
> two kings their favours but aslave my death
>
> 5 As for my fame I clayme and doe not crave
> that thou beleeve two kings before aslave
> Yet were bidentalls sacred and the place
> struckein with thunder, was by speciall grace
> Ne're after trampled over, if this blowe

10   That strucke me in my height and laid me lowe
     Came from the hand of heaven, lett it ~~su~~ suffice
     that god required noe other sacrifice
     Why doe you bruise a Reede; as if your Rodd
     could wound me deeper then the hand of god

15   Why doe you judge me ere the iudgment day
     As if your verdict could gods iudgement swaye
     Why are you not contented with my blood
     ffor hate of me why make you murther good
     he that comends the fact does it againe

20   And is the greater Murtherer of the twayne
     High and revealed malice that canst drawe
     heaven out of hell and Checke gods proper lawe
     Nadab and Abihu, that thus accord   [in left margin] Levit: x: ij
     to offer your straunge fire before the lord

25   Take heede t'will burne you, t'is adaungerous thinge
     who soe doth blesse a Murtherer kills akinge
     I now have past the pikes and since my fate
     My princes favour and the peoples hate
     Strange bleareied hatred whose repineinge sight

30   ffeeds all on darkenes and doth hate the light
     Spewes any goodnes in me was I all
     Massa corrupta and Stigmaticall
     was I all ills yet those that ript me found
     some of my vitalls good some inwards sound

35   I had an heart scornd daunger and abraine
     watchinge for honors life in every veine
     Nor was my liver tainted but made blood
     That might have served to doe my country good
     Had you not lett it out, Nor was my minde

40   Soe fixt on gettinge as to make me blinde
     Or to forgett myne honour or my freind
     Witnesse those now who needed noe more depend
     and those whose Merritts I have made or Raised
     will find out some thinge more that may be praised

45   All doe not mourne in iest theires some one eie
     shed teares in earnest when it sawe me die
     And what soever those remonstrance make
     I never lost my selfe but for there sake
     But god forgive them for the rest I say

50   I loved the kinge and Realme aswell as they.

Notes

1. Kurt Weber, *Lucius Cary, Second Viscount Falkland* (New York: Columbia UP, 1940), 28. Weber refers to British Library, Egerton MS 2725, of which the text is as follows:

   An Epitaph upon the death of the / Duke of Buckingham by the
   / Countesse of Faukland
   Reader stand still and see, loe, here I am
   Who was of late the mightie Buckingham;
   God gaue to me my being, and my breath;
   Two Kings their favourers, and a slaue my death;
   Not for my Fame I challenge, and not craue,
   That thou beleeue two Kings, before one slaue.

   Weber mistranscribes "favourers" as "favours" at line 4; he also transcribes "As" at line 5, believing (presumably) that to be the "correct," unaltered reading. However, when examined under ultraviolet light it seems that "As" has been altered to "Not." I am grateful to Prof. Dr. R. K. Todd for examining the Egerton manuscript while visiting the British Library. Barbara Kiefer Lewalski mentions the epitaph in the Egerton manuscript in an endnote in *Writing Women in Jacobean England* (Cambridge: Harvard UP, 1993), 383n5. She, too, makes some minor transcription mistakes, transcribing in line 5 "Not" as "Now", and in line 6 the "K" of "Kings" as a minuscule (even though she transcribes it as a majuscule in line 4) and omitting the comma.
2. Donald W. Foster, "Resurrecting the Author: Elizabeth Tanfield Cary," in *Privileging Gender in Early Modern England*, ed. Jean R. Brink (Kirksville, MO: Sixteenth Century Journal, 1993), 141–173.
3. The elegy has two extra lines in Bodleian MS Ashmole 38 (142): "And for my Death, this Cannott be deny'd / for Caesar and the greatest Henrye Dy'd."
4. For the Eliot, Juxon, and Weston attributions see Margaret Crum, ed., *First-Line Index of English Poetry 1500–1800 in Manuscripts of the Bodleian Library*, 2 vols. (Oxford: Clarendon Press, 1969), item Y209.
5. I am grateful to Prof. Curtis Perry for bringing my attention to this volume.
6. See Crum G161, T1032, A1076, and L222.
7. See Crum S1354, L459, and M451.
8. The poem "On the word Jape in Chaucer" (103–104) is falsely ascribed to Donne. See Arthur F. Marotti, *Manuscript, Print, And the English Renaissance Lyric* (New York: Cornell UP, 1995), 159.
9. See Marcy L. North's extensive analysis of anonymity in coterie culture leading to misattribution in verse miscellanies in *The Anonymous Renaissance: Cultures of Discretion in Tudor-Stuart England* (Chicago: U of Chicago P, 2003), 159–210.
10. For Weston see Michael van Cleave Alexander, *Charles I's Lord Treasurer: Sir Richard Weston, Earl of Portland (1577–1635)* (London: Macmillan, 1975), 4.

11. See James Holstun, "'God Bless Thee, Little David!': John Felton and his Allies," *English Literary History* 59, no. 3 (1992): 513–552.
12. *The History of the Life, Reign, and Death of Edward II. King of England and Lord of Ireland, with the Rise and Fall of his great Favourites, Gaveston and the Spencers* (London, 1680), in *Renaissance Women: The Plays of Elizabeth Cary, The Poems of Aemilia Lanyer,* ed. Diane Purkiss (London: Pickering, 1994), 177. All subsequent references are to this edition and page numbers will appear in the body of the text.
13. See Gwynne Kennedy, "Reform or Rebellion?: The Limits of Female Authority in Elizabeth Cary's *The History of the Life, Reign, and Death of Edward II,*" in *Political Rhetoric, Power, and Renaissance Women,* ed. Carole Levin and Patricia A. Sullivan (Albany: U of NY P, 1995), 211.
14. For example, see the section devoted to the Buckingham assassination in Alastair Bellany and Andrew McRae, eds., "Early Stuart Libels: An Edition of Poetry from Manuscript Sources," *Early Modern Literary Studies* Text Series I (2005). http://purl.oclc.org/emls/texts/libels. A smaller collection of these verses can also be found in F. W. Fairholt, ed., *Poems and Songs relating to George Villiers* (London: Percy, 1850).
15. Although the Osborn text of the elegy reads "Now I have past the pikes and *since* my fate" [my italics] all other manuscripts read "seen." Other sources for Shirley's epitaph are Bodleian, MS Rawl. Poet. 88, 59; British Library, Add. MS 30982, fol. 45^v.
16. Lines 13–14 of Bodleian, MS Malone 23, 132–133. Other known sources for this poem are Bodleian, MS Ashmole 38, 20; Bodleian, MS CCC. 328, fol. 51^v; Bodleian, MS Douce 357, fol. 17^v; Folger, MS V.a.125, fol. 1^r; Houghton, MS Eng. 1278, item 7. Note that Feltham's poem circulated in some of the same manuscripts as the elegy "Yet were bidentalls sacred."
17. Arthur F. Marotti, "Manuscript, Print, and the Social History of the Lyric," in *The Cambridge Companion to English Poetry: Donne to Marvell,* ed. Thomas N. Corns (Cambridge: Cambridge UP, 1993), 52–79 at 65.
18. The poet and personal champion of Elizabeth I, Sir Henry Lee (1530–1610), her maternal uncle—to whom Cary dedicated *The Mirror of the Worlde* (ca. 1598–1600)—was raised by his famous uncle Sir Thomas Wyatt (1503–1542). The fortunes of the Tanfield family seem to have largely depended on its connections with the Lee family. Sir Henry Lee's grandfather, Robert Lee (1483–1538), took for his second wife Lettice Pennyston (1485–1558), widow of Sir Robert Knowles (1485–?). Lettice's son by her first marriage, Francis Knowles (1514–1596), married the daughter of Mary Boleyn (1504–1534), the sister of Anne Boleyn, and became thereby related to Queen Elizabeth. Furthermore, the granddaughter of Lettice Penniston, Lettice Knolles (1540–1634), married successively Walter Devereux, first Earl of Essex (1539–1576) and Robert Dudley, Earl of Leicester (1532–1588), who both figured conspicuously at the court of Queen Elizabeth. See also Roy Strong, *The Cult of Elizabeth* (London: Pimlico, 1977; 1999), 130, for connections of the Lee family.

19. Cary to Lord Aston, National Archives, Kew, SP 16/304/75, in Heather Wolfe, ed., *Elizabeth Cary, Lady Falkland: Life and Letters* (Cambridge and Tempe, AZ: RTM Publications and Arizona Center for Medieval and Renaissance Studies, 2001), letter 89.
20. According to Barry Weller and Margaret Ferguson, eds, *The Tragedy of Mariam: The Fair Queen of Jewry with The Lady Falkland Her Life: By One of her Daughters* Berkeley (University of California Press, 1994), 180. See also Thomas Pestell's poem, "On Mrs Cary or a mayd of Honour" (Bodleian, MS Malone 14, 37).
21. Karen Robertson, "Tracing Women's Connections from a Letter by Elizabeth Ralegh," in *Maids and Mistresses, Cousins and Queens: Women's Alliances in Early Modern England*, ed. Susan Frye and Karen Robertson (New York and Oxford: Oxford UP, 1999), 152.
22. Duchess of Buckingham to Lord Conway, SP 16/58/17, in Wolfe, *Elizabeth Cary*, letter 15.
23. Cary to Lord Conway, SP 16/58/19, in Wolfe, *Elizabeth Cary*, letter 14.
24. Cary to Lord Conway, SP 16/63/102, in Wolfe, *Elizabeth Cary*, letter 18.
25. See Wolfe's treatment of Cary's relationship with the Countess of Denbigh in *Reading Early Modern Women: An Anthology of Texts in Manuscript and Print, 1550–1770*, ed. Helen Ostovich and Elizabeth Sauer (New York & London: Routledge, 2004), 211–214.
26. Anonymous pamphlet, *A Briefe Description of the Notorious Life of John Lambe* (Amsterdam: Theatrum Orbis Terrarum, 1976; photoreprint of the 1628 ed. printed in Amsterdam).
27. Bodleian, MS Malone 23, 113. Printed in Fairholt, *Poems and Songs relating to George Villiers*, 30.
28. BL, Sloane MS 826, fol. 31. Printed in Fairholt, 20–21.
29. National Archives, Kew, SP 16/114/32. Other known sources: Bodleian, MS Tanner 465, fol. 100^r; British Library, Add. MS 22959, fol. 25^v and Sloane MS 1489, fol. 22^r; Cambridge University Library MS, Gg.4.13, 106; National Archives, Kew, SP 16/119/25 and SP 16/119/30.
30. British Library, MS Sloane 826, fol. 185^r. Another known source of this couplet is Bodleian, MS Rawl. Poet. 84, fol. 74^r.
31. Cary to Charles I, National Archives, Kew, SP 16/63/89, in Wolfe, *Elizabeth Cary*, letter 19.
32. British Library (Add. MS 18044, fol. 81^r; Add. MS 29996, fol. 70^v; Add. MS 44963, fol. 40^r; Egerton MS 2026, fol. 12^r); Bodleian Library (MS Don. d. 58, 37; CCC 28, fol. 97^r); Northamptonshire Record Office, MS Westmorland (A) 6.vi.I, fol. 11^r; National Library of Wales, MS 5390D, 429; Harvard University, Houghton Library, MS Eng. 1278, item 15; Folger Shakespeare Library, MS E.a. 6, fol. 3. Like British Library, Egerton MS 2725, the Northamptonshire County Record Office, MS Westmorland explictly attributes the epitaph to Cary; it is headed "Epitaph on Buckingham by ye La: Faukland." The manuscript at the National Library of Wales, however, attributes the epitaph to Richard Corbett.

33. Cambridge University Library, MS Gg.4.13, 109; Leicestershire Record Office, MS DG 9/2796; British Library, Harleian MS 6383, fols. 27ᵛ–28ʳ.
34. The two poems appear together in British Library, Add. MS 25707 (fols. 160ᵛ–161), Add MS 19268 (fol. 32); Bodleian MSS Ashmole 38, 142; Dodsworth 79 (fol. 161ᵛ–162); Eng. Poet. e.97, 57–58); Eng. Poet e.14 (fol. 15r–v); Rawlinson Poet. 153 (fol. 9ᵛ–10); Rawlinson Poet. 26 (fol. 97ʳ⁻ᵛ); Rawlinson Poet. 62 (fol. 35ʳ⁻ᵛ); and in *Poems or Epigrams, Satyrs* (pr. for Henry Brome, 1658), 101–102.
35. The two parts are separated by other poems in British Library, Egerton MS 2725 (fols. 60ʳ and 78ᵛ) and Bodleian Library, MS Malone 23, 134–5, 140). The two parts have separate "finis" subscriptions in Bodleian Library, MS Ashmole 38 (Nicholas Burghe's manuscript compilation).
36. Peter Beal, "Philip Sidney's *Letter to Queen Elizabeth* and that 'False Knave' Alexander Discone," *English Manuscript Studies* 11 (2002): 16. Beal indicates that such a variant ordering and reordering of loose sheets not only occurred with Sidney's *Letter to Queen Elizabeth* but also with the *Arcadia* and possibly with *Certain Sonnets*.
37. Marotti, "Manuscript, Print, and the Social History of the Lyric," 64–65.
38. For a discussion of the Christ Church scribal networks, and the significance of the university scribal communities in general, see Mary Hobbs, *Early Seventeenth-Century Verse Miscellany Manuscripts* (Aldershot: Scolar Press, 1992). I want to thank Dr. Astrid Stilma and Dr. Geert Janssen, who respectively looked at the miscellanies in the British Library and the Bodleian, and took the time to see whether the elegy traveled with the same poems.
39. John Davies of Hereford links her with Lucy, Countess of Bedford, and Mary Sidney, Countess of Pembroke, in the dedication of his own work, *The Muses Sacrifice, or Divine Meditations* (1612). From Davies's dedication it becomes apparent that *Mariam* must have circulated in manuscript form, because he praises the play a year before it was published. Moreover, he mentions another play by Cary, set in Sicily, which is now apparently lost. And, as R. V. Holdsworth points out, a manuscript version of *Mariam* influenced Thomas Middleton's *The Second Maiden's Tragedy* (1611); see R. V. Holdsworth, "Middleton and *The Tragedy of Mariam*," *Notes and Queries* 231 (1986): 379–380.
40. John Davies of Hereford, *The Muses Sacrifice, or Divine Meditations*, (London, 1612) printed in *Readings in Renaissance Women Drama*, ed. S. P. Cerasano and Marion Wynne-Davies (London: Routledge, 1998), 13–14.
41. For the text of "To the Queens most Excellent Majestie," see Germaine Greer, Susan Hastings, Jeslyn Medoff et al., eds., *Kissing the Rod: An Anthology of Seventeenth Century Women's Verse* (London: Virago, 1988), 59, and more recently Jane Stevenson and Peter Davidson, eds., *Early Modern Women Poets* (New York: Oxford UP, 2001). For a list of the manuscript versions of this poem, see Wolfe's introduction to this volume, 13,n.12.

PART IV

LITERARY PATRONAGE AND LEGACIES

CHAPTER 11

"A MORE WORTHY PATRONESSE": ELIZABETH CARY AND IRELAND

Deana Rankin

In the early stages of the 1680 folio version of the narrative *History of the Life, Reign, and Death of Edward II*, the aggrieved English nobles compel the king once more to banish his disruptive favorite, Piers Gaveston:

> A second time this Monster is sent packing, and leaves the Kingdom free from his Infection. *Ireland* is made the Cage must mewe this Haggard, whither he goes as if to Execution. With a sad heart he leaves his great Protector, vowing revenge if he may live to act it.[1]

On the threshold of Gaveston's crossing from England to Ireland, there emerges that great Senecan force which will power the remaining narrative of the *History:* "revenge."[2] It is here a revenge nurtured both by distance and by writing. For the waters between Edward and Gaveston are not quite wide enough to ensure the separation of the lovers, and thus the stability of England. Rather, the Irish Sea swells with a flood of love letters:

> Their Bodies were divided, but their Affections meet with a higher Inflammation. The intervacuum of their absence hath many reciprocal passages, which interchangeably flie between them. The King receives not a Syllable, but straight returns with golden interest.
>
> (24)

The escalation and passion of their correspondence is such that by the time the king manages to weaken the resolve of the confederate nobility, thereby ensuring enough support to bring Gaveston back to London—"upon the wings of Passion, made Proud by the hope of Revenge and a second Greatness"—the stage is set for England's descent into civil war (24).

As Cary penned her *History of Edward II* in England in 1626–1627, her own experience of the Irish Sea, and the distance it opened up, could scarcely have been more different from that of her imagined lovers. In September 1622, she had traveled to Dublin not as exile but as First Lady, consort of Henry Cary, Viscount Falkland, newly appointed Lord Deputy of Ireland. Four years later, in July 1626, she returned home to England with some of her children on a family visit. Shortly after her arrival in London, she made the very public conversion to Catholicism that ensured she would never return to Dublin. For it prompted an immediate estrangement from her highly embarrassed—and firmly Protestant—husband, who was devoting much time to the enforcement of anti-Catholic legislation in James's Irish dominions.[3] In the letters that sped to and from Dublin concerning this particular separation, there was no love lost. Rather, Falkland wrote to engage his friends in the discrediting of his wife at court, claiming, for example, to Viscount Conway, that it was her long history of profligacy—"an impossibility for my Estate to afford that which the wealth of boath the Indiaes cannot supply"—as well as her now publicly evident "serpentine subtlety . . . conjoined with Romishe hipocrasy" that had forced him to send her home to England.[4]

Though scarcely ended, the story of Cary's Irish sojourn was already being refashioned: for Cary had hardly been sent home, and more importantly, she had been anything but a drain on her husband's purse. In fact, her decision to mortgage her jointure in 1622 had enabled Falkland to finance the notoriously expensive post of Lord Deputy. That same decision displeased Cary's father, Sir Lawrence Tanfield, so thoroughly that he immediately disinherited her in favor of her eldest son, Lucius.[5] Cary, it might be said, lost much in Ireland. In what follows, I want to examine what, if anything, she gained.

For too long interest in Cary has been confined to the years before the publication of *Mariam,* and the years after her conversion to Catholicism. Jesse Swan goes so far as to write off 1609–1625 as Cary's "years of childbirth and child rearing," comparing them to "Shakespeare's lost years."[6] In what follows, I want to find a point somewhere between the literary and the confessional from which to review Cary's writings. This point has a geographical location: in the uncertain territory of the cultural exile, the "intervacuum" crisscrossed by the letters of Edward II and Gaveston; somewhere, that is, between England and Ireland. What follows is, in part, an exploration of a much-neglected interlude in Cary's life: her four brief years in Dublin. For it is during this time her earlier perceptions of the borderline between private and public pursuits were challenged; it was in

Dublin that she was shown the possibility of practising both writing and Catholicism in a newly emerging Irish public sphere. And it is on her return to England, where she makes her conversion public, that the second of her achievements listed above becomes clear: her reentry into writing with the penning of that strange *History of Edward II*.

The geographical vantage point I wish to offer for Cary's writings also has further textual implications: it places the reader at a point of intersection between the *History of Edward II*, written *by* Cary and *The Lady Falkland Her Life*, written *about* Cary. On the one hand, the *History of Edward II* is a high-speed, breathless, romance written—as the passage concerning Gaveston illustrates—in a relentlessly dramatic present tense. It is, critics have argued, "an unfinished play or a biography influenced by drama," interpolated with theatrical speeches and vivid scenes of both confrontation and contemplation.[7] The *Life*, on the other hand, is an at times ponderous quasihagiography, composed in retrospect by a convert daughter, to bring to light her mother's lifelong Catholic vocation: textually speaking the *Life* does little justice to the vitality of Cary's own vibrant, dramatic prose. By restoring Cary's Irish connections and experiences to a reading of her work, I hope to suggest ways in which, to coin Seamus Heaney's phrase, this balance of perception might be redressed.[8] In so doing, I hope also to locate Cary at the heart of recent critical reevaluations of seventeenth-century English as a language and a literature that develops through conversations that take place across the Three Kingdoms and to situate her as a writer who moves and thrives between worlds and cultures.[9]

"Yet It Came to Nothinge": Accounting for Cary's Life in Dublin[10]

When it comes to assembling and reviewing the documentary sources that illuminate Cary's time in Ireland, it quickly becomes apparent that—apart from a few glancing, mainly retrospective remarks in Lord Falkland's letters—her daughter's manuscript *Life* remains the essential source: an account of Ireland as brief as it is complex.[11] It seeks to entwine hagiography with biography, to combine an account of Dame Magdalena's soon-to-be converted mother's persistent quest for personal spiritual clarity with a historical overview of Cary's public role as patroness of educational projects for poor Irish children. The story is not one of expatriate distance, but of thorough involvement, of conversation with and interventions into the lives of the inhabitants of her new home: "Being there she had much affection to that nation and was very desirous to have use made of h̶e̶r̶ *what* power she had on any occasion, in theire behalfe, as allso in that of any catholiks."[12] As a mark of her affection, Cary named her newborn son—later editor and arbiter of his sister's manuscript of the *Life* —in honor of the patron saint of Ireland: Patrick.[13] An accomplished linguist, she began her efforts at cultural integration by teaching herself Irish from the Irish-language New Testament, originally produced by the English administration for proselytising purposes.[14] Given that most English administrators and settlers in early modern Ireland tended not only to ignore but also actively to despise the Irish language, this showed remarkable tenacity. Eventually, however—her daughter reports—even Cary was defeated: "It being very hard (so as she could scarce find one that could teach it) and few bookes in it she quickly lost what she had learnt."[15]

The lack of Irish language, however, poses no barrier to spiritual inquiry and conversation, signs of the imminent conversion that Cary's daughter so privileges in her mother's *Life*: "She was ~~allw~~ ever very diligent; when she heard of any that had bene turned protestants, to search out their motives." This diligence leads her to converse with one Nicholas Hackett, a Jesuit priest turned Protestant dean, whom she greatly admires, because he never attacked Catholics in his sermons but "only exhorted to good life."[16] It also leads to Cary's adding another "first" to the story of her life: "In Ireland she grew acquainted with my Lord Inchequin an ~~ca~~ exceeding good catholike, and the first (att least knowing one) she had yet mette."[17] Dermot O'Brien, fifth lord of Inchiquin, shared his family name with the High Kings of Thomond. In spite of their native Irish roots, this Catholic family had proved loyal to the English crown during the Elizabethan wars. It was an example that "did somewhat shake [Cary's] supposed security, in esteeming it lawfull to continue as she was."[18] While her first contact with a 'knowing' Catholic does not quite, yet, lead to her own public confession of faith, it does prefigure that later dramatic moment of conversion, not in Ireland but in another strangely marginal location: the Drury Lane stables of the loyal Irish Catholic, Walter Butler, Earl of Ormond.[19]

Alongside these private conversations, Cary continued to seek the desired connection with Irish public life. Turning to practical social intervention—what her biographer-daughter terms "a great designe"—she established an innovative program of Irish industrial schools: "She tooke of beggar children (with which that country swarms) more than 8 score prentices, refusing none above seven yeare old, and taking some lesse." In the "many romes being filled with little boys and girles, sitting around all att worke" the apprentices produced "broad cloth so fin^e ~~nd~~ and goode (of Irish woole, and spunne and weaved and died and dressed there) that her Lord being Debuty wore it."[20] In spite of that intriguing spelling of "many romes," this offers a vision of Irish industry to gladden the heart of any seventeenth-century English Protestant reader, more accustomed to the relentless detailing of the barbarian Irish and their incurable laziness, propagated by Elizabethan settlers such as Edmund Spenser.[21] While we cannot lose sight of the fact that Cary's "great designe" amounts to a chain of child-labor sweatshops, her project is nonetheless remarkable for the period, not only because it pays constructive attention to the Irish poor, but also because it inspires other leading English settlers to follow her example.[22] For the urban poor continued to be ignored by successive generations of English policy-makers until the moment when they became rebellious therefore demanding a military rather than a social solution. It was over a century later that Jonathan Swift, posing as a Dublin draper, would launch his controversial and vociferous campaign for Irish economic self-sufficiency and, later still, suggest in "A Modest Proposal" yet more radical solutions to the problem of Irish children living in poverty.[23] Thanks to the efforts of his wife, Falkland was already—long before Dean Swift adopted it as his pulpit uniform of colonial nationalism—cutting a fine figure in homespun Irish linen.

"Yet it came to nothing": this utopian vision of happy Irish productivity is cut short when Cary "had great losses by fire and watter (which she judged extraordinary, others but casual)."[24] Cary's parenthetically reported judgment reminds us that this is her daughter's version, a familial narrative of stifled but blossoming Catholicism, told in retrospect. The dynamic of hindsight structures the account as Cary later ("when she was a catholike") reinterprets these losses as "the punishment of God for the childrens going to [the Protestant] church."[25] As a narrative of devotional improvement, the *Life* contrasts starkly with Falkland's waspish complaint to Conway of his wife's "serpentine subtlety" and wasteful extravagance; but both accounts represent Cary's venture as a failure. When read against the grain of these contrastive textual strategies for familial containment, however, Cary's "great designe" emerges as an extraordinary moment of English female action in the Irish public sphere.

This realization should lead us to investigate further the *Life*'s account of Ireland, the apparent detail of its projects, incidents, and conversations, to tease out its elisions and omissions. For the *Life* presents a distorting picture on two counts. Firstly, much attention is directed toward Cary's later Catholic writings: a number of lost saints' lives and her infamous translation of Cardinal Jacques Davy du Perron's *Reply* to James I, dedicated to a fellow female-in-exile, Queen Henrietta Maria.[26] Yet Cary's children pay scant attention to their mother's earlier writing career, and still less to other aspects of her literary life. There is some, tantalizing, reference to further lost work—translations of Seneca's letters, a verse "Life of Tamburlane"— but no mention of any surviving texts.[27] Secondly, and in consequence of this general eclipsing of Cary's secular writing career, while the *Life* takes pains to detail the spiritual contact Cary sought with prominent Irish

Catholics, it fails to mention the specifics of Cary's contact with Dublin literary life. In particular it elides her significant role as "worthy patronesse" not just of poor Irish children, but also of a very particular child of the mind: the first venture into print by a young Irish Catholic author.

"THE FOOTSTEPS OF HIS OBSCURE MISTERIES": ROMANCE, RESOLUTION, AND READING BETWEEN THE LINES[28]

In 1624, *A Sixth Booke to the Countesse of Pembrokes Arcadia written by R.B. Esq* was published in Dublin and dedicated "TO THE RIGHT HONOURABLE, THE truely vertuous and learned La: the Viscountesse of Falkland." The "*R.B. Esq.*" in question was one Richard Bellings, an Old Englishman; that is to say, a Catholic English descendant of Henry II's twelfth-century settlement of Ireland. At first reading, this address might appear to be a standard liminary gesture, courting the favor of the Viceroy's wife, whom the hopeful Bellings terms a "worthy patronesse."[29] Yet the preface also hints both at a more personal involvement, and at the public interventions of this "patronesse" in a larger debate, at once cultural and political, taking place between Dublin and London in the 1620s.

Bellings had trained at Lincoln's Inn, very probably conforming to Protestantism to do so, in order to bypass the ban on Catholic Irish training for the law. It was probably there that he had been schooled in the rhetorical exercise of the imitation and continuation of Sir Philip Sidney's famous romance.[30] Bellings's sequel was tussling with an already canonical text, a thoroughly Protestant tale, narrating Sidney's hopes and despairs of the Elizabethan age.[31] In his dedication Bellings both figures Cary as herself a patron of the arts in Dublin and invokes, beyond her, the leading figure of the literary circle she had belonged to in London: Mary Sidney, member of a dynasty associated in Ireland more with militant policy than poetry.

In 1566, Philip Sidney had briefly joined his father, Henry, in Ireland during his second term as lord deputy, earning early recognition for his later legendary military prowess in the suppression of Irish rebellion.[32] In September 1577, back in England and furious with the Old English Palesmen for bypassing his father and taking a petition directly to the queen earlier that year, Sidney took up his pen to compose his *Discourse on Irish Affairs*. The *Discourse* argued for a military solution to the "problem" of Ireland: a standing army that would enable Elizabeth "by direct conquest to make the country hers, and so by one great heap of charges to purchase that which afterwards would well be countervail the principal."[33] Military conquest would open up the Irish countryside for settlement by English soldiers, and economic stability would soon follow, as both the soldier-settlers and the now fully conquered Irish paid rents to the crown. In this, the son echoes the father, for Henry Sidney saw military garrisons in Ireland as "in effect the only monuments of obedience and nurseries of civility in that land."[34] But the son goes still further, arguing, in a masterly test of loyalty to the crown, that the costs of the initial conquest should be met by the imposition of a cess tax on the most loyal of Elizabeth's Irish subjects, the Catholic Old English.

Invoking Cary as midwife, and beyond her, calling on the Sidneys as guardians to his venture, Richard Bellings, one the most recent generation of Old English, takes up his pen to deliver a remarkably neat and happy ending to the messy romance that Philip Sidney wrote subsequent to the Irish *Discourse*. In so doing he responds to Sidney's hope, expressed in the closing lines of the 1593 *Arcadia,* that the unfinished business of his wandering narrative "may awake some other spirit to exercise his pen in that, wherewith mine is already dulled."[35] From Sidney's list of possible stories, Bellings chooses perhaps the most challenging, and certainly the most controversial: that of Amphialus and Helen. In the course of his *Sixth Book,* Bellings has Sidney's troublesome rebel leader, cast out of civil society as a punishment for his insurrection, restored by the grace of King Basilius to marry and rule alongside the exemplary Queen Helen of Corinth. In time the wicked usurper Tenarus, who has deposed Helen in her absence, repents and is forgiven in the civilized arena of the Arcadian poetry contest. And Sidney's long-deferred marriages are at last, in Bellings's continuation celebrated.

There is, then, a politics as well as a poetics to this romance; both are of closure, for Bellings here stages multiple reintegration. Amphialus, the misguided rebel, is not only reintegrated into civil society, he also takes a throne beside the best of rulers, devoting his life to the prosperity of his country and the education of his subjects, now free from tyranny. In carrying Sidney's late-sixteenth-century disruption forward into seventeenth-century settlement, Bellings was exorcizing not only the ghosts of Philip Sidney, but also those of his father, Henry. And he stages the reconciliation of past divisions in the civic as well as the literary spheres. For the Catholic Old English, the early 1620s were a time of cautious optimism. As they watched England's changing affiliations in Europe, they had every hope that they might be readmitted to the full participation in Irish civil and military life, which had been withdrawn from them in the aftermath of the Elizabethan wars. The 1622 Irish Commission had been charged with investigating the future development of the plantations and suggesting ways in which Ireland could become less of a drain on the English exchequer. The commission's only Old English member,

Richard Hadsor, used his influence to the full, declaring his tribe—in his terms, the "approved Irish of English descent"—ready and willing not only "to discharge the parts of good subjects and commonwealth men but also to take up arms."[36] It was also in 1622 that, largely through the influence of Buckingham, Falkland was appointed lord deputy and arrived in Ireland with the express intention of reenforcing anti-Catholic legislation.[37]

In 1624, when Bellings published his *Sixth Booke,* the swashbuckling, but ultimately ill-fated, Spanish Infanta expedition of Prince Charles and the Duke of Buckingham caused violent anti-Catholic protests on the London streets. But in Dublin, there was quiet jubilation: Falkland was forced to suspend his legislation against Catholic priests and Catholicism was, for a time, openly practised there.[38] Old English hopes of an advocate close to the English throne fell when the Spanish match collapsed, but they were quickly revived when Charles married the French princess Henrietta Maria on his accession. Not only did this marriage promise a close hearing for the Catholic cause, it also gave Ireland sudden strategic importance on the continental stage of the Thirty Years' War. For if the specter of Spanish invasion by way of Ireland had haunted England since the Battle of Kinsale in 1601, the increasingly likely prospect of war between Spain and England rendered Ireland's defense crucial to England's safety. The Old English responded to this crisis with political pragmatism: they began to broker their considerable financial power. In 1625, following Parliament's refusal to approve funds requested by Charles for the defense of Ireland, the Old English repeated the move that had so angered Sidney: they bypassed the Dublin administration to open direct negotiations with Whitehall. It was agreed that twenty-six "matters of grace and bounty"—"The Graces"— would be granted in return for three annual payments of £40,000 to finance defense forces for Ireland, thus ensuring that it would not become a drain on the English continental war effort. The Old English were also, crucially, allowed to enrol in the army.[39] So as Bellings picked up the threads of Sidney's romance, the Old English turned Sidney's ideas for Irish policy on their head. Instead of being the victims of an enforced tax, they volunteered financial support for the king, thereby offering proof of their loyalty as Catholic citizen-subjects.

For Richard Bellings this apparently improved political climate offered golden opportunities for civic participation. Skilled in the use of sword and pen, master of the English language, he considered neither Irishness nor Catholicism a barrier to citizenship any longer. His romance-sequel accordingly refashions the stock imagery of the English colonial enterprise in Ireland, replacing the well-worn tropes of barbarism with visions of civil reconciliation. Thus, for example, Bellings's version of Sidney's rebel leader, Amphialus, first enters disguised as the "Naked Knight":

> With Armour so lively representing nakednesse, wounded in so many places, (where the staunchlesse bloud, in the course the workman had allotted it, seem'd to drop destruction) that many thought a madnesse had possest him (so unarmed, so wounded) to present himselfe in such a tryall, where a surer defence, and a sounder body were more needfull. Before him went sixe, as Savages, bearing the Launces for his first courses.[40]

This artful depiction of nakedness, framed by attendants who appear "as Savages," echoes the repeated performance of civilized wildness in Elizabethan and Jacobean court spectacles. It calls to mind the iconic portrait of Captain Thomas Lee in Ireland: fashionable Elizabethan courtier from the waist up, naked Irish peasant from the waist down.[41] Such images of the dangers of "going native," of the fate of English civilization when it came into contact with Irish barbarism, must have been familiar to Cary, for she and her family had long been on the edges of England's colonial project. Her husband received his knighthood in Dublin in 1599 for his services under Essex in the Irish wars, and Cary herself dedicated her manuscript translation of Abraham Ortelius's *Mirroir du Monde* to Sir Henry Lee, organizer of Elizabeth I's tilts and cousin of the same Thomas Lee who had once posed as an English-Irish "bog-trotter."[42]

Another intriguing possibility of an encounter with such images of the Irish occurs in late 1613, when Falkland took part in the tilt as part of the celebrations surrounding the notorious marriage of James's favorite, Robert Carr, Earl of Somerset, to Frances Howard.[43] There he may have witnessed another controversial part of the proceedings: the dramatic enactment of conquest and civility which is Ben Jonson's *The Irish Masque at Court*. Falkland may not have witnessed the final scene in which the wild Irish first throw off their barbaric mantles, revealing themselves to be civilized English gentlemen well-schooled in courtly dancing, then listen obediently to the Irish bard's English encomium to their royal spectator, James.[44] As a political man, however, Falkland, like Jonson, would have been well aware of the political background to this topical masque. For, even as the Irish were being tamed and silenced in Jonson's masque, elsewhere in London they were proving much more intractable. In a move that both repeated the one that had so frustrated Sidney in 1577 and prefigured events that would so frustrate Falkland a decade later, an Old English delegation had taken the law into their own hands. Bypassing Dublin's Protestant colonial structures of administration, they had traveled to London to make their complaints about political process directly to the king.[45]

Bellings's "naked knight" is, then, a powerfully resonant figure for those, like the Falklands, involved in the troubled world of Irish–English relations. And yet in the *Sixth Booke,* far from being the sign of savagery, the "nakedness" of the knight becomes the key to his redemption. For just after he retires, maintaining his graphic silence, Helen (believed dead) appears bearing a prophecy from Apollo: "Hellen returne, a naked Knight shall finde / Rest for thy hopes, and quiet to thy minde." On being told by the company that a "naked Knight" is present, Helen at first rejects the possibility that he could be the answer to her prophecy since "it cannot be expected that *Apollo* would leave so plaine a way for us to tracke out the footsteps of his obscure misteries."[46] But "obscure misteries" are not Bellings's narrative intention here. The naked Knight is called forth and swiftly abandons suspense, revealing that he is indeed Amphialus, and that he does indeed love Helen. He confesses his part in rebellion to the king, and realizes that the revelation of his identity must bring punishment for his role in "the bloudie tragedy of a civill dissension in his divided State."[47] But Basilius offers forgiveness instead, blessing the union with Helen that will restore the sister-kingdom of Corinth to its former glory. So less than a third of the way through the narrative, the lovers are successfully reunited, Helen's prophecy is fulfilled, and the warrior-rebel is forgiven and reintegrated. Bellings's pattern of restitution and narrative recuperation tells a powerful Old English tale, narrating by analogy their reintegration into the government and history of Ireland. The *Sixth Booke* exorcised Sidney's specters and restored courtly order to the Arcadian world, presenting a repentant Amphialus ready to shoulder the burden of government.

What, then, does Bellings make of Helen of Corinth, the key figure of redemption in this narrative of resolution? She can no longer easily figure, as she did for Sidney, the exemplary Renaissance ruler, Elizabeth I. For in 1624 English queens were proving hard to come by: James's attempt to ensure the Stuart succession through Charles's marriage was not proceeding as planned. It is perhaps fanciful, but not altogether unreasonable, to imagine that Bellings had Cary in mind for the role of this wise ruler-consort. Within the English political sphere, Cary remained a marginal figure; in Ireland, however—figured perhaps as Basilius's sister-kingdom of Corinth—Cary was, as wife to the viceroy, certainly a contender. Moreover, at a moment when the future of the Stuart succession looked uncertain, Cary had not only proved herself as a mother, having just given birth to her eleventh child in Dublin, but had also publicly demonstrated her commitment to the care of Irish children. What was more, this "worthy patronesse" had also been nurturing, if not herself begetting, this very particular child of the mind: Bellings's *Sixth Booke.*

"Priviledged Sanctuarie": Cary's Patronage

If echoes of Cary in the main body of Bellings's text remain elusive, what of the direct address to her in the liminary material? The poet's dedication to his "patronesse," intriguing and tentative, is worth citing in full:

> This sixth Book to the Countesse of Pembrokes Arcadia, at the first birth of it was meant for your Honour. If it containe any thing that is good, that you may justly claim as your own, aswell because it was so auspiciously begun, as that goodness can no where finde a more worthy patronesse. What though it have many faults? yet I hope you will not reject it, both because in its infancie it was vowed to you; and that no where it could have taken a more priviledged Sanctuarie, then is your favourable censure. The desire I had (seeing it was all I could do) to acknowledge your many favours, mov'd mee, when this addition was scarse begun, to intend it for your Hon: and now it is ended, the confidence I have in your well-knowne clemencie, emboldens me to present it to you: for my distrust of my self makes me feare, that as it could be given to none more desirous to excuse the errours of weake well meaning endevours, so your Honour could no where light on a fitter subject for the practise of that virtue, then is this offering of
>
> Your servant
>
> Richard Bellings[48]

Hidden in the folds of this formal and formulaic invocation are tantalizing suggestions of personal contact. Might Bellings be implying Cary's actual presence "at the first birth" of his text—its first public or private reading? Or did she perhaps initiate the project—might the dedication of the *Sixth Booke* to Cary "in its infancie" be evidence of an ongoing literary conversation?

These hints bear some scrutiny in the context of other dedications to Cary, the literary patron. Ten years previously, Sir John Davies of Hereford had dedicated *The Muses Sacrifice* (London, 1612) to the "as well Darlings, as Patronesses, of the *Muses;* LUCY, *Countesse of Bedford;* MARY, Countesse-Dowager of Pembrooke; and ELIZABETH, *Lady Cary,* (Wife of Sr. *Henry Cary:*) Glories of Women." As Dympna Callaghan has argued in her finely nuanced analysis of race and difference in Cary's work, Davies's dedicatory poem trades on the powerful and exotic aspects of Cary's work: the threat she poses to the goddess Minerva, her education in *"abstruse and holy* Tongues," and her reputation as the author of *Mariam:*

> *Thou makst* Melpomen *proud, and my* Heart *great*
> *of such a* Pupill, *who, in* Buskin *fine*
> *With* Feete *of* State, *dost make thy* Muse *to mete*
> *the* Scenes *of* Syraceuse *and* Palestine.[49]

Even though Davies attempts to exert some male control on Cary's art, describing and demarcating her as both a spouse "(Wife of Sr. *Henry Cary:*)" and his own "Pupill," this offers very little resistance to the powerful female alliance of Minerva, Melpomen (the Muse of Tragedy), and Cary herself conjured up in his poem. Cary is firmly planted in the public sphere: given "Feete of State," she is dispatched to dramatize, and thus to domesticate, foreign lands. Twenty years later, the last extant dedication to Cary, published by William Sheares, printer of *The Workes of Mr J Marston* (London, 1633), echoes Davies's invocation of Cary's exotic power and border-crossing reputation. She is "the Mirrour of [her] sex, the admiration, not onely of this Island, but of all adjacent Countries and Dominions, which are acquainted with [her] rare Vertues and Endowments."[50] Avoiding reference to her infamous translation of Perron's *Reply,* Sheares places Cary firmly in England and appeals to her, not as a disseminator of controversial Catholic doctrine, but as a staunch advocate of "Plays."

In relation to the specific context of Ireland, something interesting happens to these tropes of "Vertue and Endowment." In 1622, the English poet William Basse circulated his "To the Right Hon. The Lady Viscountess Falkland, upon her going into Ireland, Two sonnets." Playing with the innuendo of the love lyric, Basse questions her need to leave both the poet and "this amorous land" of England:

> Must needs your anchor taste another sand
> Cause you your praise are nobly loth to heare?
> Be sure your praises are before you there.

Cary's fame confounds and transgresses the borders between England and Ireland, until, in the second stanza, in a distorting echo of the purposeful, passionate exchange of letters between Gaveston and Edward above, Basse offers a perplexing image of the geographical stasis produced by reputation:

> How much your fame exceeds your Caracts sayle:
>   Nay, more than so; your selfe are every where
> In worth, but where the world of worth doth fayle.
>   What boots it, then, to drive, or what to steere?
> What doth the axle or the ore avayle?
>   Since when you ride you cannot part away,
> And may performe your voyage, though you stay.[51]

The possibility that Ireland might live up to its barbarous reputation as a place where "the world of worth doth fayle" is a very gentle alliterative threat, but it nonetheless evokes the uneasy image of being lost at sea, marooned. Stay in England, Basse seems to be saying, and you will at least be in control of, rather than at the mercy of, reputation.

Bellings's Irish dedication moves even further away from English insistences on Cary's exotic, wandering qualities. His images of Cary involved "at the first birth" of the *Sixth Booke,* a constant presence "in its infancie," strike a curiously powerful domestic note. She is both midwife and mother to his work. If we extend the comparison to another interrelated text, Sidney's dedication of the *Arcadia* to his sister, the domesticity of the image becomes more intriguing still: Sidney figured his text as "the child, which I am loth to father," a monstrous birth, and implored Mary to provide "a Sanctuary for a great Offender."[52] Bellings's self-conscious echo of Sidney's "Sanctuary"—"no where it could have taken a more priviledged Sanctuarie, then is your favourable censure"—lacks Sidney's playful, familial tone. Rather, coupled with the invocation of Cary as mother, it appears positively Marian.[53]

Conclusion: "Quoted in the Margent of such a Story"[54]

The chronic shortage of archives has long frustrated scholars of the period in their quest for proof of interconnections between people and projects in Jacobean Ireland.[55] But perhaps here, in the prefatory materials, in the text itself, and in the dialogues between texts and intertexts that Bellings's sequel to Sidney conjures into being, we are beginning to find traces, if not of actual conversations between Bellings and Cary, then at the very least of the kinds of exchange that the poet might have sought with his "worthy patronesse." The echo of these conversations also make themselves heard as Cary returns to England, and to writing, in 1626–1627. We return, then, in conclusion, to our starting point: to the *History of Edward II,* to Gaveston's banishment, and to his reinstatement to favor, the news of which was, Cary writes "scarcely known, before (like an Irish Hubbub, that needs nothing but noise to carry it) it arriv'd in *Ireland* " (24).

In Cary's account of Gaveston's return, the "Irish Hubbub" is oddly dislocated: it travels in the opposite direction to what we might expect, from Edward to Gaveston, from England to Ireland. When Lord Clifford dramatizes the distinction between the exotic Gaveston and the king's new homegrown favorite Spencer thus—"*Nor is this new Lord a* Gaveston, *or naked Stranger, that only talkt, and durst not act his Passions*" (54)—do we find in his verdict a tantalizing echo of Bellings's "naked Knight," of the wandering rebel who earns domestic settlement by recounting his history, rather than by "acting"? Perhaps. But in closing I want not simply to list such possible echoes, but rather to bear in mind this distinction between talking and action, between history and drama, while also revisiting some old questions about Cary's version of the figure who perhaps most closely corresponds to the "worthy patronesse" herself: Queen Isabel.[56]

Certainly it is the new favorite Spencer's predilection for "acting," for the plotting and scheming of the Machiavel, that finally forces Isabel out of the wings to emerge as a full-fledged character in the last dramatic movement of the *History*. Isabel's campaigns against Edward and Spencer show her to be prey to all the stock passions of the stage: ambition, anger, hate. But this Isabel is not, in the end, the vengeful figure of Marlowe's *Edward II*, thoroughly implicated in the plot to murder her husband. In Cary's version, Isabel serves—like Bellings's Helen of Corinth—to resist the worst temptations of tragedy, and so to effect something like closure to the revenge cycle. For Cary carefully distances Isabel from Edward's murder: it is Parliament who makes the decision to intern him, and her lover, Mortimer, can only bring her to acknowledge, not to sanction, what must be done. The queen's final words, before she lapses into silence, are not so much vengeful as elegiac:

> Must Edward dye, and is there no prevention? Oh wretched state of Greatness, frail Condition, that is preserv'd by Bloud, secur'd by Murder! I dare not say I yield, or yet deny it; Shame stops the one, the other Fear forbiddeth: only I beg I be not made partaker, or privy to the time, the means, the manner.
>
> (153–154)

Bound up with this lament is an abdication of responsibility that is also a refusal to know. She begs to be kept ignorant of the coordinates of criminal responsibility: "*the time, the means, the manner.*" In so doing, Isabel denies not only her own agency, but also all possible dramatic suspense around Edward's murder. Her unspoken desire is that the deed should move directly from thought to history; she does not want such knowledge as would enable her to intervene, and so stop the murder from taking place. She wants the king's assassination to be told in a messenger's speech; she wants it as news, narrated in the past tense, a fait accompli.

In the *Life*, Cary's daughter recounts that "After her Lords death [1633] she never wentt to Maskes nor Plays not so much as att the Court though she loved them very much especially the last extreamly" (155–156). It is tempting to read in Cary's self-denial an echo of Isabel's choice in the *History* of narrative over drama. To renounce drama is not, however, to renounce writing: rather Cary produces a closeted drama, one hidden within the narrative folds of a history unfolding in the dramatic present. Previous histories had not served Isabel well. As Cary's narrator puts it, the queen "guilty but in circumstance, and but an accessory to the Intention, not the Fact, tasted with a bitter time of Repentance, what it was but to be quoted in the Margent of such a Story." In plucking Isabel from the "Margent" and placing her center stage, Cary does not so much implicate her in the king's murder, as perform a gesture of resolution worthy of Bellings's romance: she uses her suspenseful art to redress the balance of history.

Cary's brief stay in Ireland deserves more than "to be quoted in the Margent of [her own] Story." Her conversion to the religion she had witnessed flourishing in Dublin prevented her from returning there, and from continuing in the public role she had enjoyed in that city. Those she encountered in Ireland, however, were to remain influential for years to come. Bellings served as Secretary to the Catholic Confederation in the 1640s, and wrote its history in defeat. In the meantime, his sequel proved very successful beyond Irish shores. From the 1627 London edition of Sidney's *Arcadia* onward the *Sixth Booke* was consistently appended to all subsequent editions throughout the early modern period.[57] For Sidney's seventeenth-century readers, the *Arcadia* ended not with Sidney's messy call for more narrative proliferation, but with a vision of reconciliation penned by an Irish Catholic, dedicated to Elizabeth Cary.

Notes

1. [Elizabeth Cary], *The History of the Life, Reign, and Death of Edward II. King of England and Lord of Ireland* (London: Harper, Crouch, and Fox, 1680), 23. For questions relating to Cary's authorship of this history, see Margaret Reeves's chapter in this volume.
2. See Marta Straznicky, "Profane Stoical Paradoxes: *The Tragedie of Mariam* and Sidnean Closet Drama," *English Literary Renaissance* 24, no. 1 (1994): 104–134; John Kerrigan, *Revenge Tragedy: Aeschylus to Armageddon* (Oxford: Clarendon Press, 1996).
3. See Falkland's warnings about Catholic friars in Dublin, January 9, 1624; his proclamation for the banishment of Jesuits, January 21, 1624; and his fears of Catholic rebellion, March 31, 1624, in *Calendar of the State Papers relating to Ireland of the reign of James I, 1615–1625*, ed. Charles W. Russell and John P. Prendergast (London: Longmans, 1872–1880), 455–456, 459–460, 474–478. See also his protests about the installation of recusant magistrates, August 23, 1625; and his fears of Spanish-backed invasion, August 9, 1626, December 20, 1627, in *Calendar of the State Papers relating to Ireland of the reign of Charles I, 1625–(1660)* ed. Robert P. Mahaffy (London: HMSO, 1900–1903), 31, 148–149, 295–296.
4. Falkland to Conway, July 5, 1627, cited in *Elizabeth Cary, Lady Falkland: Life and Letters*, MRTS 230, ed. Heather Wolfe (Cambridge and Tempe,

AZ: RTM Publications and Arizona Center for Medieval and Renaissance Studies, 2001), 293. *Life* insists that Falkland admired his wife's projects, Wolfe, 121–122.

5. Ibid., 117. See also Cary to Conway, March 24, 1627; Cary to Charles I, May 18, 1627 (ibid., 274, 282–283). Falkland claimed his wife was disinherited because of her disobedience and Catholic leanings (ibid., 293).

6. Jesse Swan, "Introduction: The 1680 Folio and Octavo Histories of Edward II by Elizabeth Tanfield Cary, Viscountess Falkland," in *Renaissance Women Online*, a subsidiary component of the *Brown University Women Writers Project*, 1999. By online subscription: http://textbase.wwp.brown.edu/WWO/rIntrosList.html (consulted October 4, 2006).

7. Tina Krontiris, *Oppositional Voices: Women as Writers and Translators of Literature in the English Renaissance* (London: Routledge, 1997), 91.

8. Seamus Heaney, *The Redress of Poetry* (London: Faber, 1995).

9. See my *Between Spenser and Swift: English Writing in Seventeenth Century Ireland* (Cambridge: Cambridge UP, 2005) and John Kerrigan's book on archipelagic English (Oxford: Oxford UP, forthcoming).

10. Wolfe, 120.

11. It occupies just six pages, in Wolfe, 119–125.

12. Ibid., 119.

13. Ibid., 125. James Ussher, Archbishop of Armagh, who preached at the swearing-in of Falkland, campaigned to claim Patrick for the Protestant church, see my *Between Spenser and Swift,* 84–85. See also Alexander Cook to James Ussher, November 30, 1626 in Wolfe, 264–266.

14. William Daniels, trans., *Toimna Nuadh ar dTighearna agus ar Slanagjhtheóra Iosa Criosd...* (Dublin, 1602).

15. Wolfe, 119. On English attitudes to Irish and the shortage of "suitable" (Protestant) teachers see Patricia Palmer, *Language and Conquest in Early Modern Ireland: English Renaissance Literature and Elizabethan Imperial Expansion* (Cambridge: Cambridge UP, 2001).

16. Wolfe, 124.

17. Ibid., 123. See Cary's intriguing double negative: "For Jesuits, To my knowledge, I never saw the face of one in my lyfe, nor intend not to doe." Cary to Falkland, December 25, 1626 (ibid., 272).

18. Ibid., 124. O'Brien died in December 1624, thus dating these conversations to the earlier part of Cary's sojourn.

19. Land disputes with the Protestant branch of the Ormond family had resulted in the imprisonment without trial of Ualtéir na bPaidrín (Walter of the Beads and Rosary), London, 1619–1625. His recent release was connected with the negotiation of "The Graces" discussed below.

20. Wolfe, 272.

21. Edmund Spenser, *A View of the State of Ireland,* ed. Andrew Hadfield and Willy Maley, (Oxford: Blackwell, 1997). For an overview of recent critical explorations of such writing, see my *Between Spenser and Swift,* 1–28.

22. Richard Boyle, first Earl of Cork and his mother-in-law, Lady Alice Fenton both supported the project. See Alexander B. Grosart, ed., *The Lismore Papers* (Series I) 5 vols, II, 87, 93. I am grateful to Heather Wolfe for this reference.
23. "The Drapiers Letters" [1724–1725] and "A Modest Proposal" [1729] in Jonathan Swift, *The Prose Works of Jonathan Swift,* ed. Herbert Davis, 14 vols. (Oxford: Blackwell, 1939–1968), X, XII. See also Robert Mahony, *Jonathan Swift and the Irish Identity* (New Haven and Yale: Yale UP, 1995).
24. Wolfe, 120.
25. Ibid., 121.
26. Elizabeth Cary, trans., *The Reply of the most illustrious Cardinall of Perron, to the Answeare of the King of Great Britaine* (Douai, 1630); Wolfe, 131–132.
27. Ibid., 106.
28. Richard Bellings, *A Sixth Booke to the Countess of Pembroke's Arcadia* (Dublin, 1624), 25.
29. Ibid., 3. See Raymond Gillespie, "The Social Thought of Richard Bellings," in *Kingdoms in Crisis: Ireland in the 1640s, Essays in Honour of Donal Cregan,* ed. Micheál Ó Siochrú (Dublin: Four Courts, 2001), 212–228, and my *Between Spenser and Swift,* 191–229.
30. See John Hoskins, *Directions for Speech and Style* [ca. 1599], ed. Hoyt Hudson (Princeton: Princeton UP, 1935). Other continuations include George Markham, *The English Arcadia* (London, first part, 1607; second, 1613); *The Historie of Arcadia* (anon, ca. 1649); Anna Weamys, *A Continuation of Sir Philip Sidney's Arcadia* (1651). Only Bellings chose to imitate Sidney's Eclogues. See Gavin Alexander, "Five Responses to Sir Philip Sidney, 1586–1528" (PhD diss., University of Cambridge, 1996); Jennifer Klein Morisson, "Readers turned Writers: The Dynamics of the Sequels to Sir Philip Sidney's *Arcadia*" (PhD diss., Yale University, 1997).
31. Blair Worden, *The Sound of Virtue: Philip Sidney's "Arcadia" and Elizabethan Politics* (New Haven and London: Yale UP, 1996).
32. See David J. Baker, "Off the Map: Charting Uncertainty in Renaissance Ireland," in *Representing Ireland: Literature and the Origins of Conflict, 1534–1660,* ed. Brendan Bradshaw, Andrew Hadfield, and Willy Maley (Cambridge: Cambridge UP, 1993): 76–92; Katherine Duncan-Jones, *Sir Philip Sidney, Courtier Poet* (London: Hamish Hamilton, 1991), 108–112; Willy Maley, "Sir Philip Sidney and Ireland," *Spenser Studies* 12 (1998): 223–227.
33. Katherine Duncan-Jones, and Jan van Dorsten, eds., *Miscellaneous Prose of Sir Philip Sidney* (Oxford: Clarendon Press, 1973), 1–13.
34. Henry Sidney in *Letters and Memorials of State,* ed. Arthur Collins (London, 1746), 20–21.
35. Sir Philip Sidney, *The Countess of Pembroke's Arcadia* (London, 1593), 482.
36. [Richard Hadsor], *Advertisements for Ireland* (Dublin, 1923), 5, 50. See Joseph McLaughlin, "Richard Hadsor and the Authorship of 'Advertisements for Ireland, 1622–23,'" *Irish Historical Studies,* vol. 30 (1997): 305–336.

37. Victor Treadwell, *Buckingham and Ireland, 1616–1628: A Study in Anglo-Irish Politics* (Dublin: Four Courts, 1998), 193–194.
38. See footnote 3 above and Jerzy Limon, *Dangerous Matter: English Drama and Politics 1623–24* (Cambridge: Cambridge UP, 1986).
39. See Aidan Clarke, *The Old English in Ireland, 1625–42* (London: Macgibbin and Kee, 1966); Nicholas Canny, *Making Ireland British, 1580–1650* (Oxford: Oxford UP, 2001).
40. Bellings, 19.
41. On Irish knights at the Elizabethan Accession Day tilts see Henry R. Woudhuysen, "Leicester's Literary Patronage: A Study of the English Court 1578–1582" (DPhil diss., Oxford University, 1980). On Lee, and Marcus Geerhardt's 1594 portrait, see the *Oxford Dictionary of National Biography (ODNB)*.
42. Bodleian Library, MS Dep. d. 817. On Henry Lee's diplomacy for Essex, see James Shapiro, *1599: A Year in the Life of William Shakespeare* (London: Faber and Faber, 2005), 316–317.
43. See David Lindley, "Embarrassing Ben: The Masques for Frances Howard," in *Renaissance Historicism: Selections from English Literary Renaissance*, ed. Arthur Kinney and Dan Collins (Amherst: U of Massachusetts P, 1987), 248–264, and *The Trials of Frances Howard: Fact and Fiction at the Court of King James* (London: Routledge, 1993).
44. Charles H. Herford, Percy and Evelyn Simpson, ed., *Ben Jonson*, 11 vols. (Oxford: Clarendon Press, 1925–1952), 7:397–405, (403–404). *A Challenge at Tilt* was staged on December 27, 1613 and January 1, 1614; *Irish Masque* on December 29 and January 3.
45. See James Smith, "Effaced History: Facing the Colonial Contexts of Ben Jonson's *Irish Masque at Court*," *English Literary History* 65 (1998): 297–321.
46. Bellings, 25.
47. Ibid., 31.
48. Ibid., A2^{r-v}.
49. Sir John Davies, *The Muses Sacrifice* (London, 1612), sig. [★★★3^v]; Dympna Callaghan, "Rereading Elizabeth Cary's *The Tragedie of Mariam Faire Queene of Jewry*," in *Women, "Race," and Writing in the Early Modern Period*, ed. Margo Hendricks and Patricia Parker (London: Routledge, 1994), 163–177.
50. The volume was disowned by J. Marston, now an Anglican cleric.
51. Richard Warwick Bond, ed., *Poetical Works of William Basse (1602–1653)* (London: Ellis and Elvey, 1893), 155–156, first included in the unpublished "Polyhymnia," 1622.
52. Sidney, *Arcadia*, 3–4.
53. The Marian vision experienced by Belling's brother, Christopher, was famous in Ireland. See Raymond Gillespie, *Devoted People: Belief and Religion in Early Modern Ireland* (Manchester: Manchester UP, 1997), 140–144.
54. [Cary], *History of Edward II*, 155.

"A MORE WORTHY PATRONESSE" 221

55. A clearer picture is emerging of surviving archives. See, for example, Brian C. Donavan and David Edwards, ed., *British Sources for Irish History, 1485–1641: A Guide to Manuscripts in Local, Regional and Specialised Repositories in England, Scotland and Wales* (Dublin: Irish Manuscripts Commission, 1997).
56. See, for example, Isabel's impoverished exile or the sea storm on her journey to England ([Cary], *History of Edward II*, 109, 116).
57. Bent Juel-Jensen, "Sir Philip Sidney, 1554–1586: A Check-list of Early Editions of his Works," in *Sir Philip Sidney: An Anthology of Modern Criticism*, ed. Dennis Kay (Oxford: Clarendon Press, 1987), 289–314. Annabel Patterson's otherwise excellent study of reading the *Arcadia* neglects this. See *Censorship and Interpretation: The Conditions of Writing and Reading in Early Modern England* (London and Wisconsin: U of Wisconsin P, 1984), 24–43.

CHAPTER 12

"TO HAVE HER CHILDREN WITH HER": ELIZABETH CARY AND FAMILIAL INFLUENCE

Marion Wynne-Davies

CATHOLIC CONVERSION AND THE CARY FAMILY

The primary message of *The Lady Falkland: Her Life* is, of course, that Elizabeth Cary "was a most sound sincere Catholic" who strongly sought "the conversion of others," and, as such, within the Counter-Reformation narrative, was worthy of emulation (270–271).[1] In this context, the account of Cary's life by her daughter Lucy, with annotations by some of her other children, serves as an example to others, and demonstrates that what Cary attempted in her actual life is repeated, by her children, in her textual *Life*.[2] Since the only people Cary converted were her maidservant (*Life* 210) and six of her children, when *Life* records Cary's earnest attempts at conversion, the conclusion is strictly familial and refers back to the extended account of these conversions, which take up almost 90 percent of the text.[3] Indeed, when read as an account of the relationship between Cary and her offspring, *Life* suggests that converting her children to Catholicism dominated any other maternal interests. This chapter sets out to explore the ways in which Cary's children negotiated those discourses of faith and conversion, which had been initiated by their mother, in their own textual productions.

The overwhelming importance of conversion to Cary is repeated throughout *Life*. After her husband died in 1633, Cary "only sought to have her children with her, where they might have more occasion to come to the knowledge of the truth, and better means to follow it"; she "was their mother in faith as well as in nature" (223, 227). However, when four of her daughters (Anne, Elizabeth, Lucy, and Mary) did convert in 1634, they did not inform her beforehand, suggesting that familial intimacy had still not been established fully. Moreover, Cary's main motive for abducting her children seems to have been to deliver them from the threat of being reconverted to Protestantism, or "tormented" as *Life* expresses it, by "Mr Chillingworth."[4] *Life* records how Cary "lived to see six of her children (by God's great mercy) Catholics and out of danger <being> living amongst their Protestant friends might have put them into, being all out of England" (266–267). The six children were Anne (Dame Clementia), Elizabeth (Dame Augustina), Lucy (Dame Magdalena), and Mary (Dame Maria), as well as Henry (Dom Placid) and Patrick.

For the Catholic Carys, the conversion narrative is an essential and dominant aspect of their identity that supplanted any close familial bonds of affection and love. There can be no doubt that the author of *Life,* together with its annotators, readily colluded with her mother in constructing a familial discourse in which spiritual faith and the love of God superseded family ties and affection. At the same time, however, there remains a distinct unease with writing about a mother who left her young children, was reconciled with them primarily to convert them to her own faith, and finally who, through fear of reconversion, exiled them from country, family, and herself. The tensions and dislocations endemic upon this combination of unity and division within the spiritual and familial discourses employed by the Carys was to be replicated in the works of Elizabeth Cary's offspring.

LUCY CARY (DAME MAGDALENA)

The only known extant work composed by Lucy is the *Life* of her mother. Because of its relevance to an understanding of Cary's life and work, this text has been carefully edited in two contemporary editions and has been the focus of critical attention. As such, this chapter only refers to *Life* when it is relevant to a consideration of the works by other Cary siblings. Instead, in order to reconstruct the dominant themes of the Cary family's writings, I consider briefly Lucy's obituary, written by one of her contemporaries at Our Lady of Consolation, Cambrai, after Lucy's death on November 1, 1650.[5] This profile describes Lucy as "an obstinate, haughty, disdainful, sneering lady" before her conversion, after which she led "an obedient, humble life, all the time shee had been in religion without any regard to what she had been or what might have been in the world." Although these terms were common to accounts of conversion and profession, the change in Lucy is credited to her mother, "a woman of an extraordinary piety as will appear in the relation of her life written by a person who knew her very well." This passage is important in several ways since it uncovers a recurring narrative of near-miraculous conversion from material sin to spiritual ideal among the nuns' own self-definitions. For example, the account of the life of Gertrude More, who was a fellow member of the community at Our Lady of Consolation, also represents a worldly and recalcitrant young woman gradually developing into a pious, humble and obedient member of the religious community discussed.[6] Moreover, like the doubled tracings of worldly vanity and spiritual humility in Gertrude's life, the account of Lucy in the obituary stresses immediately that she was the daughter of "Lord Henry Viscount Falkland, sometime Vice Roy of Ireland," but simultaneously discounts what "she had been" in the world of familial hierarchies and aristocratic eminencies. As such, while Lucy is located within a familial discourse of inheritance and political activity, she is also placed within a gendered and spiritual discourse of convent life. This dialectic between a worldly inheritance and a spiritual choice is continually repeated in the religious discourses of the early modern period: in the writings of Catholics and Protestants, as well as in the works of the enclosed orders, the specific community at Cambrai, and in the individual production of Lucy Cary.

ANNE CARY (DAME CLEMENTIA)

The dialectic between spiritual and secular attachments is a commonplace of early modern religious writing and, unsurprisingly, emerges in the writings by, and about, those Cary siblings who undertook an enclosed religious life. While the description of Lucy, noted above, is a classic example of this dialectic, it is the description of her sister, Anne, in the Paris community's House History that provides evidence of the continuation of the specific importance of this concern to the Cary familial discourse.[7] The history records the foundation of the monastery of Our Lady of Good Hope in Paris in 1651 by three nuns from Our Lady of Consolation in Cambrai.[8] Anne was particularly influential in establishing the new community in Paris: her previous court connections facilitated support from the exiled Queen Henrietta Maria and Abbot Walter Montagu; her ability to speak French "in perfection" provided clear and ready communication; and her scholarship allowed her to write the new constitutions necessary for the establishment of the house (House History, fol. 49). The conclusion of this early history of the Monastery of Our Lady of Good Hope describes the "Character, Vertues, and Death" of Anne alongside the lives of the first prioresses of the community (fols. 27, 218–224). A description of Anne's "Nobility & Honourable Rank in the World" is closely followed by an account of her humility and "contempt of herself" once she became a nun (fols. 218–219). Like her mother, however, Anne was a skilled linguist, as her proficiency in French demonstrates, and she is also praised for her "great Wisdom," which was essential to the compilation of the constitutions of the community (fol. 220). The similarity with Elizabeth Cary's *Life* is underscored by their mutual commitment to imparting spiritual faith to others: "Her Confidence in the Divine Providence, was very great, & she desired to imprint it in the hearts of all others" (fol. 221). Moreover, Anne's life quotes "her own words" on the subject, in which she advocates the abandoning of "Temporal Riches" since they "soon fail . . . & like a broken reed fell to the Ground" (fols. 221–222), recalling Cary's rejection of worldly goods described in *Life* (221–222). These key themes—worldly versus spiritual riches and honor, linguistic skill, scholarship and wisdom, and the desire to have a spiritual impact on others—are repeated in the lives of Cary, Anne, and, to a lesser extent, in the obituary of Lucy. There are, however, closer parallels between Cary and Anne since both wrote poetry that adopted a dramatic tone and significantly foregrounded female roles.

A manuscript catalog of the manuscript books belonging to the library of Our Lady of Good Hope lists "eight Collection Bookes" and "The spirituall songs . . . in three parts," all by Anne.[9] The survival of three loose quires of psalm translations in Anne's handwriting in the Archives Départementales du Nord, Lille, which houses part of the archives of the Cambrai community, strongly suggests that these are some of the "spirituall songs" mentioned in the catalog. The first quire contains the end of psalm 69 to psalm 78; the second quire contains the end of psalm 120 to the beginning of psalm 139; and the third quire contains the end of psalm 139 to psalm 149 (one or more quires appear to be missing).[10]

The psalms would have been translated from the Latin Vulgate version, although they are free translations, differing considerably, for example, from those in the English Douai Bible, with which Anne would have been familiar.[11] What is noticeably distinctive about Anne's translations is the adoption of a dramatic voice, especially at the beginning of each psalm. For example, at the commencement of psalm 132 the poetic voice seems to be answering a previously spoken accusation, to which "so" refers—"No Lord thou knowest I doe not so, / And yet thou all my soul dost know"—and this conversational tone is repeated in the following translation, where God is, once again, addressed directly: "Remember Lord the oath I made . . . ." The debate with God continues throughout Anne's translations, as in psalm 140, where she dramatizes her own voice through the use of "I said": "Most holy Lord, thou art my God, I said, / And now's thy time to help, since I have pray'd." Yet the familiar and challenging tone is also varied with a poignant acceptance of human frailty, as in the opening of psalm 142, "My heart just broke. . ." Throughout, Anne incorporates a dramatic voice into her verse translations, thereby producing a vivid and immediate dialogue between the speaker and God. Such stylistic intervention on her part demonstrates that she was aware of early seventeenth-century spiritual verse, but the psalm translations also show a familiarity with dramatic tone, meter, and dialogue that recalls her mother's work, *The Tragedie of Mariam*. Mariam's soliloquies begin with similar bursts of passion against injustice—"How oft have I with public voice run on, / To censure Rome's last hero for deceit—or a bleak self-awareness—"Am I the Mariam that presumed so much, / And deemed my face must needs preserve my breath?"[12] Moreover, it is clear from the layout of one of the psalm translations, psalm 136, that it was intended to be sung, since the chorus appears after the initial verse, "His Mercys have bene ever sure, / And to Eternity endure," and is repeated at the end of each subsequent verse with the prompt, "His Mercys –."[13] This performative aspect might be echoed in the description of her verses as "songs" in the catalog of the Paris nuns.

Anne's verses have a further link with her mother's writing. The alterations to the characters of Mariam and Isabel in *Mariam* and *Edward II*, respectively, expand their roles and present them more sympathetically. No such major alterations are made in Anne's translation of the psalms, but she does include a significant alteration to gender in psalm 71, where the speaker is supposedly King David.[14] The predominant message of the psalm consists of praising God and asking for continued help against the enemy. Anne follows this pattern in asking for help "in my great escape" and against "those who know thee not," but when the speaker, "thy Servant" is described, Anne presents the figure as female: "*she* into thy great Armes was throwne," "*her* who God has left," and "Let *her* who thought thee farre off find thee neere" (italics mine).[15] The Douai translation is not specifically gendered, and the marginal annotation states that the psalm may refer to "King David, or anie other just person."[16] The "just" are categorized systematically throughout the Douai Bible as Catholic, and the annotations as a whole were meant to reinforce Catholic doctrine against Protestantism.[17] Read in these terms, Anne's representation of her own "great escape" (from England) from "those who knew thee not" (Lucius Cary and Chillingworth) echoes the personal and spiritual themes of Cary's *Life* and the Cary familial discourse as a whole. The narrative of individual salvation is thus combined with the common Counter-Reformation narrative of attaining spiritual safety within the church, in order to reinforce the public ideology with personal testament. Parallel patterns of trial, danger, escape, and salvation recur throughout Anne's psalm translations, perhaps the most quasi-autobiographical being psalm 122, which reads like a graphic account of the Cary children's escape:

> Twas ye best news I wish to heare,
> My very soul stood ravisht at my Eare;
> Lets go, they said; Come lets away!

> Already we have tarry'd long enough,
> Now let our speed declare our Love;
> Why should we thus from Sion stay,
> And only be unhappy by our owne delay?[18]

The Douai Bible interprets this psalm as specifically confirming the supremacy of the Catholic Church to which "all nations of the world doe come," once again reinforcing Counter-Reformation policies, which in Anne's translation are reworked and reinforced through a familial context.[19]

Both in her psalm translations and in the account of her in the House History, Anne espouses the dominant elements of the Cary familial discourse. Like other Counter-Reformation Catholics, the necessity for perseverance against the threat of Protestantism and a dedication to salvation are preeminent. In addition, the dialectic of spiritual faith and worldly goods or status is a common element in spiritual biographies and verse, not only in the accounts of Anne, Lucy, and Elizabeth Cary. But more distinctive elements are also evident. Anne's scholarship and skill with languages are emphasized in her life, as they are in that of her mother, and both undertook translations. Dramatic language, the use of dialogue, and the possibility of an envisaged performance also develop as common characteristics. The focus on female experience recurs in the works of Cary, of Anne in her feminizing of the psalms, and of Lucy by choosing to write her mother's *Life*.

Patrick Cary

If the dominant thread of the Cary familial discourse was spiritual conversion, then Patrick represents its failure. He was the elder of the two boys who were kidnapped from Great Tew and transported to France, where, with his brothers and sisters, he made a vow "to enter a Religious life under S. Bennetts habitt."[20] After three years, however, he transferred to Rome where, under recommendation from Walter Montagu, he joined the household of Cardinal Francesco Barberini.[21] Initially Patrick prospered and was granted various pensions by Urban VIII and Henrietta Maria, but with the death of the pope and subsequent political upheavals, Patrick was left, in 1647–1648, with no income and mounting debts. At this point Patrick tried to obtain secular employment in England, although his ambitions proved fruitless.[22] By 1650, however, he had decided to respect his earlier vow, writing to Edward Hyde, Earl of Clarendon, who had been one of his brother Lucius's closest friends, that his ill luck, "Was for nothing else, but in punishment for my neglect of compliance wth my Vowe: and thereupon I resolved to bee clothed without any further delay."[23]

There followed a period of vacillation, which may be traced through the letters exchanged by Anne, who tacitly approved of her brother's vows and Hyde, who supported Patrick in his decision to abandon the religious life.[24] It was during this period at Douai that Patrick contributed his annotations to *Life* and probably composed his own spiritual verse.[25]

Patrick's religious poems are included in a manuscript that also includes secular verse clearly composed after he had left Douai. The work, entitled "Triviall Ballades," are dedicated to "Mrs Tompkins," the daughter of Victoria Cary's husband, William Uvedale, by his first wife, and was completed in 1651. Subsequently, the manuscript was rediscovered by Walter Scott and the poems were first published by him in 1819.[26] The divine poems are, like Anne's of the psalms, translations of Anne, informed by biblical texts, although they are original compositions with the biblical quotes clearly attributed. For example, the first of the divine poems concludes with a quotation from the psalms (55:6), but commences with a much more personal and direct voice:

> Worldly Designes, Feares, Hopes, farwell!
> Farwell all earthly Joyes and Cares!
> On nobler Thoughts my soule shall dwell,
> Worldly Designes, Feares Hopes, farwell!
> Att quiet, in my peacefull Cell
> I'le thincke on God, free from your snares;
> Worldly Designes, Feares, Hopes, farwell!
> Farwell all earthly Joyes and Cares.[27]

Patrick repeats the dialectic between worldly concerns and spirituality found in the writings and "lives" of his mother and two sisters, adding a personal element in which his own "Designes" (plans for political and monetary success), "Feares" (that he will not succeed in these), and "Hopes" (that he will attain a secular position with an income) are abandoned as he accepts that his vow must be fulfilled, "my peacefull Cell." There is, however, a distinct difference in his description of these "Worldly Designes," for unlike Cary, Lucy, and Anne, he describes both the "*Joyes* and Cares" (italics mine) attendant upon a secular life. Such contradictions recur throughout his religious verse, in which Patrick envisages the torments and imprisonment of the faithful soul:

> In a darcke Cave below
> The Conquerour does throw
> His miserable vanquish'd *Foe*.
> Deepe is the Dungeon where that wretch is cast,
> Thither Day comes not nigh;

> Dampish and nasty Vapours doe him blast,
> Yett still his Heart is high.
> His prison is soe straight
> Hee cannot move at will;
> Huge Chaynes oppresse him with their waight,
> Yett has Hee courage still.
> And can I thincke I want my *Libertee,*
> When in such *Thrall,* Hee keepes his *Mind* soe *Free?*[28]

The reference at the end of the poem is to the book of Job (5:4), which provides one identification for the "vanquish'd" Christian soul and his "Conquerour," Satan. However, the image is a recurring one throughout the Bible and in early modern Christian poetry, so that Patrick could equally be drawing upon Christ's temptation in the wilderness and final crucifixion as upon Spenser's description of the Red Cross Knight imprisoned in Orgoglio's dungeon.[29] The question at the conclusion of the stanza, however, implies that Patrick's own "peacefull Cell" may be compared to the "Dungeon" with its "Dampish and nasty Vapours," and that he perceives the enclosed religious life as being in "*Thrall,*" even though he is aware that a free "*Mind*" should be more important than material "*Libertee.*" The final stanza of the poem repeats these spiritual doubts and describes his life as "confin'd" and acknowledges the temptation to leave his current life of "*Restraint,* or *Griefe,* or *Feare,* or *Cold.*"[30] The ultimate welcoming of personal hardship and the enclosed spiritual life described by Patrick's mother and sisters is never achieved. The poems echo the doubts evinced in Patrick's letters to Hyde, and, while they evidence his determined effort to value spiritual hardships over the "Joyes" of a secular life, the self-sacrifice and humility described in the "lives" of the female members of the Cary family never emerge. Interestingly, Anne referred to "worldly desyre" in the letter to Hyde, a parallel noted by the editor of Patrick's poems, who comments that he "had already written these verses and shown them to his sister, or more likely, that the lines reflect ideas they had lately spoken of together."[31] Given the propensity of the Cary siblings to show their manuscript work to others within the family (the *Life* and its contributors, as well as Patrick's verse copies for Lucy Tompkins), it seems likely that Anne had seen the early devotional poetry and had indeed shared the idea of the spiritual and worldly dialectic, although from a more polarized position than that of Patrick.

Inevitably, however, Patrick succumbed to the "Worldly Designes"; partly, it seems, because a diet of fish did not suit him ("the fare (for the first yeare onely fish) in some 3. monthes and a halfe, has cast mee downe into such a weaknesse that I am forc't backe into England").³² He left Douai in September 1650 to live with his sister Victoria at Wickham, the Uvedale family home. Within the space of two years Patrick had married Susan Uvedale, his brother-in-law's niece, and had reconverted to Protestantism. He remained at Wickham with his wife and first child, and it is during this time that he must have composed his "Triviall Ballades."³³ The secular poems are very different in content, form, and tone from the divine verse: the topics are light-hearted, the verses are in the form of ballads with useful notes as to the tune which should accompany them, and the tone is comic. In place of the "Dampish and nasty Vapours" of the cell are "The walls of sweet *Wickham*" and the despised "fish" has been replaced with "Quart" pots of "drincke."³⁴ Yet even in the writing of drinking ballads—an activity Cary would hardly have condoned—Patrick still retains elements of the Cary familial discourse.

Having completely abandoned the spiritual for the "Worldly" in both life and poetry, Patrick does not use religious themes in his secular verse. However, certain elements already identified in the writings of Cary and Anne reappear in the *Triviall Ballades,* where Patrick uses dramatic language and dialogue, focuses on women, and deals with the issues surrounding translation. Indeed, in one of the ballads, "to the tune *But I fancy lovely Nancy,"* Patrick names and commends each of his sisters. The poem begins with an ambiguous, "Surely now I'me out of danger/ And noe more need feare my heart," and a statement that none "Shall subdue my Libertee."³⁵ Read within the context of the poem and its generic tradition, the poetic voice fears romantic entanglements and desires that he will always be at liberty from love. However, read alongside Patrick's divine poetry and in relation to his own history, the poem simultaneously evokes a freedom from holy orders, with a telling repeat of "Libertee," which has been transmuted from the dark imprisonments of the spiritual writing, to the self-ironizing tone of the romantic verse. Patrick's exuberant ballads, with their repetitive manner and tonal simplicity, lack the stylistic sophistication of Cary's dramatic verse and the metrical variety of Anne's translations. While his secular verse participates in the Cary familial discourse, with its allusion to family members, women in general, dramatic language and translation, the lightness of tone and careless versification suggest a conscious distancing from the serious concerns of his Catholic relations. Poetically, Patrick's shift from spiritual to "Worldly designes" denoted a dilution of literary value as he removed himself from the dominant familial concerns. Moreover, while the witty ballads suggest a less troubled existence, Patrick's content was short-lived, for he died shortly after moving to Dublin with his wife and second son, in a further attempt to revive his fortunes.³⁶

Lucius Cary

Of all Cary's children, however, it was Lucius, second Viscount Falkland, who proved most resistant to Cary's attempts to convert him. The convoluted syntax of *Life* in describing Lucius's religious beliefs suggests a clear desire to interpret his contributions to family discussions on religion as sympathetic to Roman Catholicism, but friends such as Edward Hyde, the Earl of Clarendon, make it clear that this was not the case. Hyde notes that:

> Many attempts were made upon him by the instigation of his mother (who was a lady of another persuasion in religion, and of a most masculine understanding, allayed with the passion and infirmities of her own sex) to pervert him in his piety to the Church of England, and to reconcile him to that of Rome.[37]

He goes on to point out that Lucius "declined no opportunity or occasion of conference with those of that religion [Catholicism], and that he treated them with "civility," but that at no time did he contemplate conversion.[38]

Life contextualizes the abduction of the two youngest Cary brothers in terms of a spiritual liberation from Chillingworth's Protestantism, but for the Cary family the spiritual was inextricably bound to the personal and, inevitably, the impact upon Lucius was considerable. *Life* vacillates in its description of Lucius, pronouncing him "a more than ordinarily good son" for welcoming his siblings at Great Tew when asked to by Cary, but castigating him for conspiring with the spying and "skilfully inquisitive" Chillingworth when Cary decides to "steal them away."[39] Hyde's account of Lucius's response to the kidnapping demonstrates that the viscount was equally dogmatic in his spiritual conviction:

> But this charity towards them [Catholic people] was much lessened, and any correspondence with them quite declined, when by sinister arts they had corrupted his two younger brothers, being both children, and stolen from his house and transported them beyond seas, and perverted his sisters: upon which occasion he writ two large discourses against the principal positions of that religion.[40]

The "discourses" Hyde refers to certainly include *A Discourse of Infallibility* (circulated in manuscript and first published posthumously in 1646), which argues, as Weber succinctly sums up: "A reasonable soul has the right to demand that the infallibility of the Church be clearly manifest."[41] While this argument may appear, at times, to be a thoughtful and scholarly intervention into religious controversy, it is, simultaneously, an extensive attack against the Catholic Church, for the key question posed in the treatise is, as Weber points out, "How can the Roman Church convince a rational mind of its infallibility?"[42] Lucius's answer to this self-posed question is long and detailed but his judgment is succinct: "To know whether the Church of *Rome* may erre, (as a way which will conclude against her, but not for her) I seek whether she have erred; and conceiving she hath contradicted her self, conclude necessarily she hath erred."[43] Therefore, since the Catholic Church has erred through self-contradiction, it has failed to prove to the rational mind that it is infallible. Such a summary fails to do justice to Lucius's careful and well-supported arguments, but the important point for an understanding of the Cary family's engagement with religious controversy is that it finally marks the boundary between Lucius and his mother in terms of faith.

At the end of *A Discourse of Infallibility*, Lucius deliberately invites responses: "If indeed any can prove by any infallible way, the Infallibility of the Church of *Rome*, and the necessity under paine of damnation for all men to believe it . . . I will subscribe to it."[44] It is hardly surprising, therefore, that when the treatise appeared in a second edition, in 1660, the title had expanded to include a variety of contributions:

> A Discourse of Infallibility. With Mr Thomas White's Answer to it, and a Reply to him; by Sr Lucius Cary, late Lord Viscount of Falkland. Also Mr Walter Montague (Abbot of Nanteul) his Letter against Protestantism; and his Lordship's answer thereunto, with Mr John Pearson's Preface . . . To which are now added two discourses of Episcopacy by the said Viscount Falkland and his Friend Mr William Chillingworth. (London: William Nealand, 1660)

Montagu's letter in this edition, defending his conversion to Catholicism, had been written to his father in 1635, was circulated widely at court, and was published in 1641 with an answer written by Lucius Cary before appearing again in 1660.[45] Montagu's main argument was that a church cannot exist without a visible form and that therefore, the Protestant Church originating with Luther could not be the true church. Lucius confutes this argument, concluding that neither church had always been visible, but he turns the debate more specifically to the question of infallibility. The theological aspects of Montagu's letter clearly prompted Lucius to respond formally, but his concerns were reinforced by the fact that Montagu was related to him. This link was through marriage, since Lucius's wife, Lettice, was Montagu's cousin, as well as through his own family, via Sir Henry Lee.[46] Certainly, Montagu had close ties with the

Cary family; Victoria had acted in *The Shepherd's Paradise*, and Patrick certainly knew his work, as the mocking reference to "th'*English* of *Watt Montagu*" which was harder "then *French*" reveals. Moreover, Montagu's influence with Henrietta Maria had helped Patrick obtain preferment at Rome, and he was appealed to by Anne when she set about founding the convent of Our Lady of Good Hope in Paris. It is hardly surprising, therefore, that Cary intervened in the debate, writing a reply to her son in defense of Montagu's conversion.

Although Cary's reply to her son appears no longer to be extant, it is possible to surmise what arguments she would have made against him from this brief description in *Life*.[47] *Life* notes Cary's reference, at the beginning of her treatise, to Christ's instructions to the disciples in the book of Matthew: "Think not that I came to send peace on earth: I came not to send peace, but a sword. For I come to set a man at variance against his father, and the daughter against her mother." (Mt 10:34–35). While the introductions and conclusions of Lucius's various theological treatises are unfailingly courteous to his opponents, his mother's reply seems to have been intensely personal, conflating personal and public discourses, even as she denied the importance of the former in comparison with the latter. There are no extant replies by Lucius to his mother's treatise: *Life* suggests that one was intended, but that "to answer it again would be necessary to go farther and dent more than he had done in his."[48] Certainly, the *Life* itself undertakes a further answer to Lucius, although it is more focussed upon *A Discourse of Infallibility* than Lucius's reply to Montagu:

> And another of those that had the like opinions in religion was wont to say that the great conveniency there seemed to be (according to human understanding) of an infallible guide, and the great aptness everyone had to wish there were such a thing, did make them so readily assent <in?> to believe it. (253)

In the margin one of the Catholic siblings has inscribed, "My Br Falkl." In addition, Weber notes that Cary encouraged a further refutation of *A Discourse*, the anonymous *A View of Some Exceptions Which Have Beene Made by a Romanist to the Lord Viscount Falkland's Discourse* (1646).[49] Lucius might have evaded his mother's attempts to convert him to Catholicism, but he nevertheless participated in the dominant familial discourse—faith. Although he appears almost isolated from his mother and siblings in his pursuit of Protestantism, the spiritual conviction and determination of Cary are clearly present in her son, although inverted as in a mirror reflection. Just as *Life* describes Cary's determination to convert her children to Catholicism, so Hyde reveals that the main impetus to write Protestant theological treatises resulted from the kidnapping of his young siblings.

Yet, even before the spiritual rift with his mother, Lucius had attempted to re-create himself as separate and distinct from his blood relatives. In some ways this is summed up by Thomas Triplett in his dedicatory preface to *A Discourse,* where he writes,

> He [Lucius] . . . knowing well how much more glorious it is to be the first then the last of a Noble Family, (Blood without Vertue making Vice but more conspicuous) was so farr from relying upon that empty Title, that He seemed *Ipse suos geniuses Parentes,* to have *begotten* his Ancestors, and to have given them a more Illustrious life, then he received from them.[50]

In the context of the religious discourse, Triplett represents Lucius as devising his own "Vertue" and being the "first" rather than the "last" of the Carys, inferring that the son's Protestantism is superior to the mother's Catholic faith. However, the trope of a parentless child finds a significant parallel in Lucius's poetry and its contemporary reception.

Before his interest in religious doctrine, Lucius, like his brother Lorenzo, participated in the courtly tradition of writing verse. Evidence of Lorenzo's literary activities may be found in a mock elegy, written by John Earle, "An Epitaph on the Living Sr Lorenza Carew," where he is described as spending his time, among the other common activities for gallants, writing,

> verses, that doe stumble worse,
> in Coging, flattering, lying, fleering,
> Jeered by some, and others Jeering.[51]

None of Lorenzo's poetry appears to have survived, although in tone and sophistication, a similarity with Patrick's secular verse seems likely. In contrast, Lucius was taken seriously as a poet, his name being coupled with those of Carew, Davenant, and Suckling.[52] Indeed, Suckling wrote satirically of Lucius that although he was "of late so gone with divinity," his poetic skill would still have allowed him to be Apollo's "priest and his poet."[53] Lucius, however, was also a patron and seems to have created a community of male poets and scholars at his house, Great Tew. As Hyde notes, he gathered together "men of the most eminent and sublime parts . . . who dwelt with him, as in a college situated in a purer air, so that his house was a university in a less volume."[54] This male community at Great Tew, with its emphasis upon faith, culture, and learning, mirrors the female community at Cambrai, with its parallel emphases upon the spirit and manuscript productivity, both scholarly and literary. Even the term "sister" used by Anne, Lucy, Elizabeth, and Mary to signify both faith and blood, is echoed by the use of the term "brother" for those men who congregated about Lucius. One of this group, Abraham Cowley, refers to himself and his companions as Lucius's "younger Brothers."[55] But whereas the women at Cambrai attribute their spiritual inheritance solely to their mother, the men at Great Tew claimed a direct cultural descent from a father, Ben Jonson. The "Tribe of Ben" is a well-known literary designation for those seventeenth-century poets who emulated the verse of Ben Jonson, but for Lucius such literary tribute merged inextricably with poetic themes and autobiographical content. In "An Eglogue on the Death of Ben Johnson [sic], Between Melybaeus and Hylas," a pastoral elegy in which two shepherds lament the death of "that glorious bard," Lucius pays tribute to Jonson, who "did our youth to noble actions raise," although these "his adopted children equall not / The generous issue his own braine begot."[56] Lucius's verse betrays a personal indebtedness to Jonson, which is confirmed by two epistles written to his "father." The first is addressed "To his noble Father, Mr Jonson," and is signed "Your Sonne and servant. Lucius Cary."[57] The second poem is prefaced by a letter again addressed to "Noble Father," and the poem itself presents Jonson in the same terms: "But pardon Father for what I rehearse, / But imitates thy friendship, not thy Verse."[58] Of course, Lucius is adopting a rhetorical strategy in which his verse is dedicated to a "father," and ordinarily such usage could be dismissed as a literary device, much the same as Cowley's claim of kinship with Lucius himself. Yet Hyde's evidence of the closely knit male community of scholars substantiated Cowley's claim of "brotherhood," just as Lucius's well-recorded rejection of his parents and siblings proffers an understanding of his self-(re)creation. Moreover, it is significant that, in the elegy to Jonson, there are two references to mothers: "stern step-dame" and "fierce step-dame."[59] No simple autobiographical reading is necessary here, for the important point is that Lucius eulogizes the father figure, denigrates mothers, and welcomes brothers while he neglects to mention sisters. But ironically, it is precisely Lucius's shadowing of the spiritual with the secular that brings him into a closer alignment with the writings of his brother and sisters. For Anne and Lucy, the dialectic had to be confronted, but faith finally dominated, whereas Patrick's verse, in which he abandons spiritual commitment for secular pleasure, evidences the opposite conclusion. For Lucius, the same divide penetrates his writing—that "divinity" and "poetry" referred to by Suckling—and his faith, whereby he rejects his Catholic family for Protestant friends and remakes his parentage, supplanting his mother with his "father," Ben Jonson, and transposing fellow poets as "brothers" within their male community at Great Tew for his sisters in blood from the Catholic convents in France.

Lucius rejected the discourses of faith and family initiated by Cary and promulgated through her daughters and initially by her son Patrick. But in spite of the vehemence of this denial, Lucius constructed a thematic mirror of his mother's influence, through which Catholic was transmuted to Protestant and female into male influence. In addition, traces of the Cary familial discourse remain intact. Lucius's scholarship and his linguistic proficiency are represented in his "life" by Hyde, just as learning and languages are present in the lives of his mother and sister Anne. Hyde recounts how his friend had decided not to visit London until he had learned Greek, "and pursued it with that indefatigable industry, that it will not be believed in how short a time he was master of it, and accurately read all the Greek histories."[60] He also retained an interest in translation, writing two poems praising his friend George Sandys on his biblical translations, where he comments,

> But so thy illustrious pen reveal'd,
> We see not plainer that which gives us sight,
> Than we see that, assisted by thy light,
> All seems transparent now, which seem'd perplext,
> The inmost meaning of the darkest text.[61]

Similarly, Lucius demonstrates a skill with spoken discourse in his pastoral elegy to Ben Jonson, and he certainly knew of and liked the entertainments of Walter Montagu as well. Lucius fashioned himself as a man without a mother, rejected Catholicism, and distanced himself from his brothers and sisters. The implacable force of familial concerns and the ways in which these are expressed in textual form could not be utterly expelled. The dominant Cary discourses are present in Lucius's writing both via the thematic replication of opposites and in the traces of wider familial concerns.

Conclusion

The aim of this chapter has been to demonstrate the ways in which Cary influenced her children, not only in their choice of faith, but also in terms of their literary productivity. On a basic level, it is clear that in a period in which female authors were uncommon, Anne and Lucy chose to write, paralleling the achievements of their brothers, Patrick, Lucius, and Lorenzo. However, within the broad frame of literary production, certain themes emerge as consistent, in relation to both their mother's interests and their own corresponding activities. The investment in faith and spiritual conversion is paramount. Like their mother, Lucy, Anne, and Patrick (in his devotional poems) espouse Catholicism, while Lucius offers a sharp, but mirroring, focus upon Protestantism. For the Carys this centering of religious conviction in their works is seen through the dialectic of spiritual faith and worldly designs (Cary, Lucy, Anne, Patrick, and Lucius). In addition, parallel interests emerge that align the siblings with their mother. These include: learning and scholarship (Cary, Anne, and Lucius); linguistic skill and an interest in translation (Cary, Anne, Patrick, and Lucius); drama, performance, and the use of dramatic language and dialogues (Cary, Anne, Patrick, Victoria, and Lucius); and a focus upon women and female characters (Cary, Lucy, Anne, Patrick, and Victoria). There were, inevitably, divergences from the overwhelming influence of Cary; for example, Patrick reconverted to Protestantism, and Lucius supplanted his family, both parents and siblings, with a reworked community of male friends and a literary "father," Ben Jonson. Nevertheless, the impact of Cary's ideological and cultural concerns cannot be denied, providing contemporary literary critics with evidence of the way in which early modern women could, and did, influence other writers, albeit within a familial context. There is, however, one final parallel that links Cary to her children, for just as she inspired her daughter to compose *Life*, so are Lucy and Anne commemorated by their religious communities, and just so is Lucius eulogized by his friend Edward Hyde. The Cary siblings were not only adept at repeating and reworking their mother's discourses, but it seems that they were also, like her, able to extend that influence through their ability to inspire others to write about them.

Notes

1. *The Lady Falkland: Her Life*, MS 20H9 in Archives Départementales du Nord, Lille. Editions of the *Life* are: Richard Simpson, ed., *The Lady Falkland, Her Life, from a Manuscript in the Imperial Archives at Lille. Also, A Memoir of Father Francis Slingsby from MSS in the Royal Library, Brussels*. (London: Catholic Publishing and Bookselling Company, 1861); Georgianna Fullerton, ed., *The Life of Elisabeth Lady Falkland, 1585–1639* (London: Burns and Oates, 1883); Barry Weller and Margaret W. Ferguson, eds., *The Tragedy of Mariam: The Fair Queen of Jewry with The Lady Falkland Her Life: By One of her Daughters* (Berkeley: U of California P, 1994); and Heather Wolfe, ed., *Elizabeth Cary, Lady Falkland: Life and Letters* (Cambridge: RTM Publications, 2001). While Wolfe's edition is the most accurate (containing original spellings, for example), unless otherwise noted all references are to the Weller and Ferguson edition (hereafter referred to as *Life*), because the modernized version is more accessible to students of early modern writing.
2. For a discussion of the authorship of *Life* see Wolfe, 87–89.

3. *Life*, 201–272, from "the eldest of two sons" to "for that, [Mary] being the last of her daughters that had a desire to be a nun." The whole text of *Life* runs from page 183 to page 275 of Weller and Ferguson's edition.
4. For a discussion of Chillingworth and his role in the "abduction," see Kurt Weber, *Lucius Cary Second Viscount Falkland* (New York: Columbia UP, 1940), 157–212.
5. Transcribed in Joseph Gillow, ed., "Records of the English Benedictine Nuns at Cambrai, 1620–1793," *Catholic Record Society* 13 (1913), 79–80, from Archives Départementales du Nord, Lille, MS 20H7.
6. See Marion Wynne-Davies, *Women Writers and Familial Discourse in the English Renaissance* (London: Palgrave, 2007).
7. St. Mary's Abbey, Colwich, MS R1, fol. 41.
8. During the French Revolution the Paris nuns came to England and settled in Colwich in 1836, while the Cambrai community moved to Stanbrook Abbey.
9. Paris, Bibliothèque Mazarine, MS 4058.
10. Anne Cary, *Psalms,* Archives départementales du Nord, Lille, MS 20H39. Indeed, the "three parts" mentioned in the Paris list might well refer to a different copy of Anne's psalm translations from those extant at Lille. I have used the current psalm numbering, and not that of the Vulgate and Douai bibles, for the sake of textual comparison with readily accessible bibles. Anne Cary herself numbers her psalms intermittently.
11. Anne would have used the Vulgate Bible since the Council of Trent had, in 1546, determined that it was the authentic version. She would also have had access to the English Douai Bible that had been translated by Gregory Martin (published in 1609–1610). See Gregory Martin, trans., *The Holy Bible* (Rouen: John Couturier, 1635), and F. F. Bruce, *The English Bible. A History of Translations* (London: Lutterworth Press, 1961), 113–124.
12. S. P. Cerasano and Marion Wynne-Davies, eds., *Renaissance Drama by Women: Texts and Documents* (London: Routledge, 1996), 50, 69–70.
13. Anne Cary, *Psalms*.
14. This psalm is numbered 71 in current bibles, 70 in the Douai and Vulgate versions, and 72 by Anne.
15. Anne Cary, *Psalms*.
16. Douai Bible, 128.
17. Bruce, 123–124.
18. Anne Cary, *Psalms*.
19. Douai Bible, 233; psalm 121.
20. Patrick to Edward Hyde, Earl of Clarendon, August 30, 1650 (Bodleian Library, Clarendon MS 40, fol. 169^v). The extensive correspondence exchanged between Patrick, Anne, and Clarendon may be found in Wolfe, 423–442, 446–455, 459–461, and 463–465.
21. Weber, 303–304.
22. Weber, 306–307.
23. Bodleian, Clarendon MS 40, fol. 169^v.

24. Bodleian, Clarendon MS 40, fols. 13–14 and 188.
25. Weller and Ferguson note Patrick's marginal annotations. His poetry is published in Veronica Delaney, ed., *The Poems of Patrick Cary* (Oxford: Clarendon Press, 1978).
26. *Triviall Ballades* (Leeds University, Brotherton Collection, Lt 68). The manuscript contains several hands and appears to have been a general book lent to Patrick by Lucy Tomkins so that he could copy down his poems for her. This presupposes manuscript copies of the religious poetry composed in Douai, which has subsequently been lost. See Walter Scott, ed., *Triviall Poems and Triolets* (London: John Murray, 1918). Further information on the Italianate origins of Patrick's poetic form may be found in Pamela Willetts, "Patrick Cary and His Italian Poems," *British Library Journal* 2, no. 2 (1976): 109–120, and "Patrick Cary: A Sequel," *British Library Journal* 4, no. 2 (1978): 148–160.
27. Delaney, 43–44.
28. Delaney, 51.
29. Edmund Spenser, *The Faerie Queene*, ed. A. C. Hamilton (London: Longman, 1977), 116.
30. Delaney, 51.
31. Delaney, lxxi. See also Bodleian, Clarendon MS 40, fol. 13^{rv}.
32. Bodleian, Clarendon MS 40, fol. 169^v.
33. Weber, 315–320.
34. Delaney, 13 and 15.
35. Delaney, 10.
36. Weber, 320.
37. Edward Hyde, Earl of Clarendon, *The History of the Rebellion and Civil Wars in England*, ed. W. Dunn Macray (Oxford: Clarendon Press, 1888), vii, 221. Macray's edition refers to Hyde's books and section numbers, rather than to the volume and page numbers of the nineteenth-century edition. I have followed this reference system throughout.
38. Hyde, vii, 221.
39. *Life*, 248–249; 146.
40. Hyde, vii, 221.
41. Weber, 226. Weber's detailed account of Lucius Cary's doctrinal position and of Chillingworth's influence on him will not be repeated here, since the thematic concern of this essay is to look at associations within the Cary family.
42. Weber, 226.
43. Lucius Cary, *A discourse of infallibility with Mr Thomas White's answer to it, and a Reply to him* (London: William Nealand, 1660), sig. (a2)^r.
44. Lucius Cary, *A discourse* . . . , sig. [(c4)^v–(d)^r].
45. Walter Montague, *The Coppy of a Letter Sent from France by Mr Walter Montagu to His Father, the Lord Privie Seale, with His Answere Thereunto. Also a Second Answere to the Same Letter by the Lord Faulkland* (London, 1641).
46. Walter Montague's brother, Edward, was related by marriage to Sir Henry Lee, who was in turn the great uncle of Elizabeth Tanfield, Lucius's grandmother.

47. See R. W. Serjeantson's essay in this volume for a full discussion of this lost work.
48. *Life,* 269.
49. Weber, 225.
50. Lucius Cary, *A discourse* . . . , Dedicatory Epistle to Lucius's son, Henry, Viscount Falkland (unpaginated).
51. Quoted in Weber, 44.
52. Weber, 134.
53. Alexander B. Grosart, *The Poems of Lucius Carey, Viscount Falkland* (Miscellanies of the Fullers Worthies' Library, 1871), 26.
54. Grosart, 15–16.
55. Weber, 121.
56. Grosart, 39 and 41–42.
57. Weber, 279–280.
58. Weber, 281–282.
59. Grosart, 38–39.
60. Grosart, 16.
61. Grosart, 86.

BIBLIOGRAPHY: ELIZABETH CARY CRITICISM, BIOGRAPHY, AND TEXTUAL INTRODUCTIONS[1]

Acheson, Kathy. "'Outrage your face': Anti-Theatricality and Gender in Early Modern Closet Drama by Women." *Early Modern Literary Studies* 6, no. 3 (2001): 7.1–16. http://purl.oclc.org/emls/06-3/acheoutr.htm

Akkerman, Nadine N. W. "'Reader, Stand Still and Look, Lo Here I am': Elizabeth Cary's Funeral Elegy *On the Duke of Buckingham*." In *The Literary Career and Legacy of Elizabeth Cary, 1613–1680*, ed. Heather Wolfe, 183–200. New York: Palgrave Macmillan, 2006.

Beemer, Suzy. "Masks of Blackness, Masks of Whiteness: Coloring the (Sexual) Subject in Jonson, Cary, and Fletcher." *Thamyris: Mythmaking from Past to Present* 4, no. 2 (1997): 223–247.

Beilin, Elaine V. "Elizabeth Cary and *The Tragedie of Mariam*." *Papers on Language and Literature* 16 (1980): 45–64.

———. "The Making of a Female Hero: Joanna Lumley and Elizabeth Cary." Chap. 6 in *Redeeming Eve: Women Writers of the English Renaissance*. Princeton: Princeton University Press, 1987.

———. "Elizabeth Cary, *The Tragedy of Mariam* and History." In *A Companion to Early Modern Women's Writing*, ed. Anita Pacheco, 136–149. Oxford: Blackwell, 2002.

Bell, Ilona. "Private Lyrics in Elizabeth Cary's *Tragedy of Mariam*." In *The Literary Career and Legacy of Elizabeth Cary, 1613–1680*, ed. Heather Wolfe, 17–34. New York: Palgrave Macmillan, 2006.

Bennett, Alexandra G. "Female Performativity in *The Tragedy of Mariam*." *Studies in English Literature, 1500–1900* 40, no. 2 (2000): 293–309.

Bennett, Lyn. "'Written on my tainted brow': Woman and the Exegetical Tradition in *The Tragedy of Mariam*." *Christianity and Literature* 51, no. 1 (2001): 5–28.

Berry, Boyd M. "Feminine Construction of Patriarchy, Or What's Comic in *The Tragedy of Mariam*." *Medieval and Renaissance Drama in England* 7 (1995): 257–274.

Brackett, Virginia (Ginger Roberts). *Elizabeth Cary: Writer of Conscience*. Greensboro, NC: Morgan Reynolds Publishing, 1996 [for younger students].

———. "Elizabeth Cary, Drayton, and Edward II." *Notes and Queries* 239 (1994): 517–519.

———. "Sharp Necessities." *Women and Language* 19, no. 2 (1996): 7–13.
Brashear, Lucy. "A Case for the Influence of Lady Cary's *The Tragedy of Mariam* on Shakespeare's *Othello*." *Shakespeare Newsletter* 26 (1976): 31.
Burgess, Irene. "'The Wreck of Order' in Early Modern Women's Drama." *Early Modern Literary Studies* 6, no. 3 (2001): 6.1–24. http://purl.oclc.org/emls/06-3/burgwrec.htm
Calderón López, María Isabel. "Elizabeth Cary's Life and Work Rediscovered: Scepticism and Epistemology in '*The Lady Falkland: Her Life*' and '*The Tragedy of Mariam*.'" PhD diss., Universidad de Cádiz, 2002.
Callaghan, Dympna. "Re-Reading Elizabeth Cary's *The Tragedie of Mariam, Faire Queene of Jewry*." In *Women, "Race" and Writing in the Early Modern Period*, ed. Margo Hendricks and Patricia Parker, 163–177. London and New York: Routledge, 1994.
———. "The Terms of Gender: 'Gay' and 'Feminist' Edward II." In *Feminist Readings of Early Modern Culture: Emerging Subjects*, ed. Valerie Traub, M. Lindsay Kaplan, and Dympna Callaghan, 275–301. Cambridge: Cambridge University Press, 1996.
Cerasano, S. P., and Marion Wynne-Davies, eds. "Introduction to *The Tragedy of Mariam*." In *Renaissance Drama by Women: Texts and Documents*, 43–47. London and New York: Routledge, 1996.
Clarke, Danielle. "Drama and the Gendered Political Subject." Chap. 3 in *The Politics of Early Modern Women's Writing*. Harlow, England and New York: Longman, 2001.
———. "'This Domestic Kingdome or Monarchy': Cary's *The Tragedy of Mariam* and the Resistance to Patriarchal Government." *Medieval and Renaissance Drama in England* 10 (1998): 179–200.
———. "*The Tragedy of Mariam* and the Politics of Marriage." In *Early Modern English Drama: A Critical Companion*, ed. Garrett A. Sullivan, Jr., Patrick Cheney, and Andrew Hadfield, 248–259. New York and Oxford: Oxford University Press, 2006.
Corporaal, Marguérite. "'Moor, She Was Chaste. She Loved Thee, Cruel Moor': Othello as a Starting Point for Alternative Dramatic Representations of the Female Voice." *Comitatus: A Journal of Medieval and Renaissance Studies* 33 (2002): 99–111.
———. "'Thy Speech Eloquent, Thy Wit Quick, Thy Expressions Easy': Rhetoric and Gender in Plays by English Renaissance Women." *Renaissance Forum: An Electronic Journal of Early Modern Literary and Historical Studies* 6, no. 2 (2003). http://www.hull.ac.uk/renforum/v6no2/corporaa.htm
Dolan, Frances E. Introduction to *Recusant Translators: Elizabeth Cary, Alexia Grey*. The Early Modern Englishwoman: A Facsimile Library of Essential Works 1, part 2, vol. 13, ed. Betty S. Travitsky and Patrick Cullen. Aldershot, England: Ashgate, 2000.
———. "'Gentlemen, I Have One Thing More to Say': Women on Scaffolds in England, 1563–1680." *Modern Philology: A Journal Devoted to Research in Medieval and Modern Literature* 92, no. 2 (1994): 157–178.
———. "Reading, Work, and Catholic Women's Biographies." *English Literary Renaissance* 33, no. 3 (2003): 328–357.

Dunstan, A. C. *An Examination of Two English Dramas: "The Tragedy of Mariam"* by Elizabeth Carew; and *"The True Tragedy of Herod and Antipater with the Death of Faire Mariam"* by Gervase Markham, and William Sampson. Konigsberg: Hartungsche Buchdruckerei, 1908.
Dunstan, A. C. with W. W. Greg, ed. Introduction to *The Tragedy of Mariam, 1613*, v–xix. London: Malone Society, 1914.
Ferguson, Margaret W. "Allegories of Imperial Subjection: Literacy as Equivocation in Elizabeth Cary's *Tragedy of Mariam*." Chap. 6 in *Dido's Daughters: Literacy, Gender, and Empire in Early Modern England and France*. Chicago: University of Chicago Press, 2003.
———. Introduction to *Works By and Attributed to Elizabeth Cary*. The Early Modern Englishwoman: A Facsimile Library of Essential Works 1, part 1, vol. 2, ed. Betty S. Travitsky and Patrick Cullen. Aldershot, England: Scolar Press, 1996.
———. "'Running On with Almost Public Voice: The Case of 'E.C.'" In *Tradition and the Talents of Women*, ed. Florence Howe, 37–67. Urbana: University of Illinois Press, 1991.
———. "Sidney, Cary, Wroth." In *A Companion to Renaissance Drama*, ed. Arthur F. Kinney, 482–506. Malden, MA: Blackwell, 2002.
———. "The Spectre of Resistance: *The Tragedy of Mariam* (1613)." In *Staging the Renaissance*, ed. David Scott Kastan and Peter Stallybrass, 235–250. New York and London: Routledge, 1991.
Findlay, Alison, Gweno Williams, and Stephanie J. Hodgson-Wright. "'The Play is Ready to be Acted': Women and Dramatic Production, 1570–1670." *Women's Writing* 6, no. 1 (1999): 129–148.
Fischer, Sandra K. "Elizabeth Cary and Tyranny, Domestic and Religious." In *Silent but for the Word: Tudor Women as Patrons, Translators and Writers of Religious Works*, ed. Margaret Hannay, 225–237. Kent, OH: Kent State University Press, 1985.
Foster, Donald W. "Resurrecting the Author: Elizabeth Tanfield Cary." In *Privileging Gender in Early Modern England*, ed. Jean R. Brink, 141–174. Kirksville, MO: Sixteenth Century Journal Publishers, 1993.
Friedman, Edward H. "El mayor monstruo del mundo and the Subject of Tragedy." *Bulletin of the Comediantes* 53, no. 1 (2001): 129–154.
Fullerton, Georgianna, ed. *The Life of Elisabeth Lady Falkland 1585–1639*. Quarterly Series, 43. London: Burns and Oates, 1883.
Glasscock, Megan. "The Unforgiven in *The Tragedy of Mariam*." *Publications of the Missouri Philological Association* 24 (1999): 20–30.
Glew, Dorothy Fitzgerald. "Introduction: *The Tragedy of Mariam* by Elizabeth Cary, Viscountess Falkland," in *Renaissance Women Online*, a subsidiary component of the *Brown University Women Writers Project*, 1999. By online subscription: http://textbase.wwp.brown.edu/WWO/rIntrosList.html [consulted October 4, 2006].
———. "Elizabeth Cary and *The Tragedy of Mariam*: A Study of Submission and Subversion." PhD diss., Lehigh University, 1995.
Goldberg, Jonathan. "Graphina's Mark." In *Desiring Women Writing: English Renaissance Examples*, 164–190. Stanford: Stanford University Press, 1997.

Goreau, Angelina. "Two English Women in the Seventeenth Century: Notes for an Anatomy of Female Desire." In *Western Sexuality: Practice and Precept in Past and Present Times*, ed. Philippe Ariès and André Béjin, 103–113. Trans. Anthony Forster. Oxford: Blackwell, 1985.

Green, Reina. "'Ears Prejudicate' in *Mariam* and *Duchess of Malfi*." *Studies in English Literature 1500–1900* 43, no. 2 (2003): 459–474.

Gruber, Elizabeth. "Insurgent Flesh: Epistemology and Violence in *Othello* and *Mariam*." *Women's Studies* 32, no. 4 (2003): 393–410.

Grundy, Isobel. "Falkland's History of . . . King Edward II." *Bodleian Library Record* 13, no. 1 (1988): 82–83.

Gutierrez, Nancy A. "Valuing *Mariam*: Genre Study and Feminist Analysis." *Tulsa Studies in Women's Literature* 10 (1991): 233–250.

———. "Why William and Judith Both Need Their Own Rooms." *Shakespeare Quarterly* 47, no. 4 (1996): 424–432.

Hall, Kim F. "Beauty and the Beast of Whiteness: Teaching Race and Gender." *Shakespeare Quarterly* 47, no. 4 (1996): 461–475.

Hamlin, William M. "Elizabeth Cary's *Mariam* and the Critique of Pure Reason." *Early Modern Literary Studies* 9, no. 1 (2003): 2.1–22. http://purl.oclc.org/emls/09-1/hamlcary.html

Hanson, Melanie Ann. "Decapitation and Disgorgement: The Female Body's Text in Early Modern English Literature (William Shakespeare, Elizabeth Cary, Isabella Whitney)." PhD diss., University of Nevada, Las Vegas, 2004.

Heller, Jennifer L. "Space, Violence, and Bodies in Middleton and Cary." *Studies in English Literature, 1500–1900* 45, no. 2 (2005): 425–441.

Hirsh, James. "*A Funeral Elegy*, Shakespeare, and Elizabeth Cary." *Ben Jonson Journal* 7 (2000): 567–588.

Hiscock, Andrew. "'The Hateful Cuckoo': Elizabeth Cary's *Tragedie of Mariam* and the Collapse of Domestic Space." In *The Uses of this World: Thinking Space in Shakespeare, Marlowe, Cary, and Jonson*, 114–141. Cardiff: University of Wales Press, 2004.

———. "The Hateful Cuckoo: Elizabeth Cary's *The Tragedie of Mariam*, a Renaissance Drama of Dispossession," *Forum for Modern Language Studies* 33, no. 2 (1997): 97–114 [an earlier version of the above].

Hogdson-Wright, Stephanie J. "The Canonization of Elizabeth Cary." In *Voicing Women: Gender and Sexuality in Early Modern Writing*, ed. Kate Chedgzoy, Melanie Hansen, and Suzanne Trill, 55–68. Keele: Keele University Press, 1996.

———. "Cary [née Tanfield], Elizabeth, Viscountess Falkland (1585–1639)." In *Oxford Dictionary of National Biography*, ed. H. C. G. Matthew and Brian Harrison. 60 vols. Oxford: Oxford University Press, 2004. 10:427–429.

———, ed. Introduction to *Elizabeth Cary, The Tragedy of Mariam: The Fair Queen of Jewry*, 1–11. Keele University Press, 1996.

Holdsworth, R. V. "Middleton and *The Tragedy of Mariam*." *Notes and Queries* 231 (1986): 379–380.

Hong, Yumi. "[A Study on Renaissance Woman Writer's Self-Fashioning and Writing Strategies, Focusing on Wives' Rebellion in Elizabeth Cary's *Tragedy of Mariam.*]" [In Korean with English summary]. *Journal of English Language and Literature/Yongo Yongmunhak* 47, no. 1 (2001): 37–61.

Hopkins, Lisa. "Women and History: *The Tragedy of Mariam, The Broken Heart* and *Concealed Fancies.*" Chap. 5 in *The Female Hero in English Renaissance Tragedy*. Houndsmills and New York: Palgrave Macmillan, 2002.

Iwanisziw, Susan B. "Conscience and the Disobedient Female Consort in the Closet Dramas of John Milton and Elizabeth Cary." *Milton Studies* 36 (1998): 109–122.

Kegl, Rosemary. "Theatres, Households, and a 'Kind of History' in Elizabeth Cary's *The Tragedy of Mariam.*" In *Enacting Gender on the Renaissance Stage,* ed. Viviana Comensoli and Anne Russell, 135–153. Urbana: University of Illinois Press, 1999.

Kelly, Erin E. "Mariam and Early Modern Discourses of Martyrdom." In *The Literary Career and Legacy of Elizabeth Cary, 1613–1680,* ed. Heather Wolfe, 35–52. New York: Palgrave Macmillan, 2006.

Kemp, Theresa D. "The Family Is a Little Commonwealth: Teaching *Mariam* and *Othello* in a Special-Topics Course on Domestic England." *Shakespeare Quarterly* 47, no. 4 (1996): 451–460.

Kennedy, Gwynne. "Angry Wives: Elizabeth Cary's *The Tragedy of Mariam.*" Chap. 3 in *Just Anger: Representing Women's Anger In Early Modern England*. Carbondale: Southern Illinois University Press, 2000.

———. "Angry Wives as Political Subjects: Elizabeth Cary's *The History of the Life, Reign, and Death of Edward II*. Chap. 4 in *Just Anger: Representing Women's Anger in Early Modern England*. Carbondale: Southern Illinois University Press, 2000.

———. "Feminine Subjectivity in the Renaissance: The Writings of Elizabeth Cary, Lady Falkland, and Lady Mary Wroth." PhD diss., University of Pennsylvania, 1989.

———. "Lessons of the 'Schoole of Wisedome.'" In *Sexuality and Politics in Renaissance Drama,* ed. Carole Levin and Karen Robertson, 113–136. Lewiston, NY: Mellen, 1991.

———. "Reform or Rebellion?: The Limits of Female Authority in Elizabeth Cary's *The History of the Life, Reign, and Death of Edward II.*" In *Political Rhetoric, Power, and Renaissance Women,* ed. Carole Levin and Patricia A. Sullivan, 205–222. Albany: State University of New York Press, 1995.

Krontiris, Tina. "Noblewomen Dramatizing the Husband–Wife Conflict." Chap. 3 in *Oppositional Voices: Women as Writers and Translators of Literature in the English Renaissance*. 1992. Rpt., London: Routledge, 1997.

———. "Reading with the Author's Sex: A Comparison of Two Seventeenth-Century Texts." *Gramma: Journal of Theory and Criticism* 1 (1993): 123–136.

———. "Style and Gender in Elizabeth Cary's *Edward II.*" In *The Renaissance Englishwoman in Print: Counterbalancing the Canon,* ed. Anne M. Haselkorn and Betty S. Travitsky, 137–153. Amherst: University of Massachusetts Press, 1990.

Lawson, Mildred Smoot. "Elizabeth Tanfield Cary and *The Tragedie of Mariam.*" PhD diss., University of Kentucky, 1985.

Levin, Richard. "A Possible Source of *A Fair Quarrel.*" *Notes and Queries* 228 (1983): 152–153.

Lewalski, Barbara Kiefer. "Elizabeth, Lady Falkland, and the Authorship of *Edward II.*" Appendix A in *Writing Women in Jacobean England*, 317–320. Cambridge: Harvard University Press, 1993.

———. "Resisting Tyrants: Elizabeth Cary's Tragedy and History." Chap. 7 in *Writing Women in Jacobean England.* Cambridge: Harvard University Press, 1993.

Lodge, Jeffrey. "The Abuse of Power: Gender Roles in Elizabeth Cary's *The Tragedy of Mariam,*" *Pleiades* 12, no. 2 (1992): 63–75.

Long, Mary Elizabeth. "Reading Female Sanctity: English Legendaries of Women, ca. 1200–1650." PhD diss., University of Massachusetts, Amherst, 2004.

Lucas, Valerie. "Alone of All Her Sex: Elizabeth Cary, the Viscountess Falkland." In *The Renaissance Theatre: Texts, Performance, Design.* Vol. 1, *English and Italian Theatre,* ed. Christopher Cairns, 68–76. Aldershot: Ashgate, 1999.

Luckyj, Chirstina. "Historicizing Gender: Mapping Cultural Space in Webster's *The Duchess of Malfi* and Cary's *The Tragedy of Mariam.*" In *Approaches to Teaching English Renaissance Drama,* ed. Karen Bamford and Alexander Leggatt, 134–141. New York: MLA, 2002.

Lunn, David. *Elizabeth Cary, Lady Falkland (1586/7–1639).* Ilford, Essex: Royal Stuart Society, 1977.

Maguire, Laurie. "Teaching Cary's *The Tragedy of Mariam* Through Performance." In *Approaches to Teaching English Renaissance Drama,* ed. Karen Bamford and Alexander Leggatt, 95–98. New York: MLA, 2002.

Maule, Jeremy. "Twice Murdered? Elizabeth Cary's *Edward II* (1626) and its Bibliographers." Unpublished paper, presented as a guest lecture at the Centre for Reformation and Renaissance Studies, Victoria College, University of Toronto, November 2, 1995.

McIngvale, Elizabeth Anne. "'Birds in Darkness': Early Modern Women, Learned and Learning." PhD diss., University of Mississippi, 2002.

Merrill, Yvonne Day. "'In Silence My Tongue is Broken': The Social Construction of Women's Rhetoric before 1750." PhD diss., University of Arizona, 1994.

Miller, Naomi J. "Domestic Politics in Elizabeth Cary's *The Tragedy of Mariam.*" *Studies in English Literature* 37, no. 2 (1997): 353–369.

Morton, Lynn Mooorhead. "'Vertue Cladde in Constant Love's Attire': The Countess of Pembroke as a Model for Renaissance Women Writers." PhD diss., University of South Carolina, 1993.

Mirkin, Ronnie. "The Portrait of Elizabeth Cary in the Ashmolean Museum: 'Cross Dressing' in the English Renaissance." In *Renaissance Theatre: Texts, Performance, Design.* Vol. 1, *English and Italian Theatre,* ed. Christopher Cairns, 77–106. Aldershot: Ashgate, 1999.

Murdock, Kenneth B. *The Sun at Noon: Three Biographical Sketches: Elizabeth Cary, Viscountess Falkland, 1585–1639, Lucius Cary, Viscount Falkland, 1610–43, John Wilmot, Earl of Rochester, 1647–80.* New York: Macmillan, 1939.

Nelson, Karen L. "Elizabeth Cary's *Edward II*: Advice to Women at the Court of Charles II." In *Women, Writing, and the Reproduction of Culture in Tudor and Stuart*

Britain, ed. Mary E. Burke, Jane Donawerth, Linda L. Dove, and Karen Nelson, 157–173. Syracuse: Syracuse University Press, 2000.

———. "'To Informe Thee Aright': Translating Du Perron for English Religious Debates." In *The Literary Career and Legacy of Elizabeth Cary, 1613–1680*, ed. Heather Wolfe, 147–163. New York: Palgrave Macmillan, 2006.

Parks, Joan. "Elizabeth Cary's Domestic History." In *Other Voices, Other Views: Expanding the Canon in English Renaissance Studies*, ed. Helen Ostovich, Mary V. Silcox, and Graham Roebuck, 176–192. Newark and London: University of Delaware Press and Associated University Presses, 1999.

Pearse, Nancy Cotton. "Elizabeth Cary, Renaissance Playwright." *Texas Studies in Literature and Language* 18, no. 4 (1977): 601–608.

Perry, Curtis. "'Royal Fever' and 'The Giddy Commons': Cary's *History of the Life, Reign, and Death of Edward II* and the Buckingham Phenomenon. In *The Literary Career and Legacy of Elizabeth Cary, 1613–1680*, ed. Heather Wolfe, 71–88. New York: Palgrave Macmillan, 2006.

Peterson, Lesley. "Source and Date for Cary's Manuscript The Mirror of the Worlde." *Notes and Queries* 249 (2004): 257–262.

Poitevin, Kimberly Woosley. "'Counterfeit Colour': Making Up Race in Elizabeth Cary's *The Tragedy of Mariam*." *Tulsa Studies in Women's Literature* 24, no. 1 (2005): 13–34.

Purkiss, Diane. "Blood, Sacrifice, Marriage: Why Iphigeneia and Mariam Have to Die." *Women's Writing* 6, no. 1 (1999): 27–45.

———, ed. Introduction to *Renaissance Women: The Plays of Elizabeth Cary, The Poems of Aemilia Lanyer*, vii–xxx. London: William Pickering, 1994.

———, ed. Introduction to *Three Tragedies by Renaissance Women: The Tragedie of Iphigeneia, The Tragedie of Antonie, The Tragedie of Mariam*. New York: Penguin, 1998.

Quilligan, Maureen. "Staging Gender: William Shakespeare and Elizabeth Cary." In *Sexuality and Gender in Early Modern Europe*, ed. James Grantham Turner, 208–232. Cambridge: Cambridge University Press, 1993.

Raber, Karen L. "Gender and Property: Elizabeth Cary and *The History of Edward II*." *Explorations in Renaissance Culture* 26, no. 2 (2000): 199–227.

———. "Gender and the Political Subject in *The Tragedy of Mariam*." *SEL: Studies in English Literature 1500–1900* 35, no. 2 (1995): 321–343.

———. "Gender, Genre, and the State: Elizabeth Cary's *Tragedy of Mariam*." Chap. 4 in *Dramatic Difference: Gender, Class, and Genre in the Early Modern Closet Drama*. Wilmington: University of Delaware Press, 2001.

Rankin, Deana. "'A More Worthy Patronesse': Elizabeth Cary and Ireland." In *The Literary Career and Legacy of Elizabeth Cary, 1613–1680*, ed. Heather Wolfe, 203–221. New York: Palgrave Macmillan, 2006.

Reeves, Margaret. "From Manuscript to Printed Text: Telling and Retelling the *History of Edward II*." In *The Literary Career and Legacy of Elizabeth Cary, 1613–1680*, ed. Heather Wolfe, 125–144. New York: Palgrave Macmillan, 2006.

———. "Writing 'for Profitable Use': Satiric Political Discourse in Women's Prose Fiction, 1628–1688." PhD diss., University of Toronto, 2004.

Roberts, Jeanne Addison. "Marriage and Divorce in 1613: Elizabeth Cary, Frances Howard, and Others." In *Textual Formations and Reformations,* ed. Laurie Maguire and Tom Berger, 161–178. Newark: University of Delaware Press, 1998.
———. "Revenge Tragedy and Elizabeth Cary's *Mariam.*" *Renaissance Papers 2003* (2003): 149–166.
Schleiner, Louise. "Lady Falkland's Reentry into Writing: Anglo-Catholic Consensual Discourse and Her *Edward II* as Historical Fiction." In *The Witness of Times: Manifestations of Ideology in Seventeenth-Century England,* ed. Katherine Z. Keller and Gerald J. Schiffhorst. Pittsburgh: Duquesne University Press, 1993.
———. "Popery and Politics: Lady Falkland's Return to Writing." Chap. 7 in *Tudor and Stuart Women Writers.* Indiana University Press: Bloomington and Indianapolis, 1994.
Serjeantson, R. W. "Elizabeth Cary and the Great Tew Circle." In *The Literary Career and Legacy of Elizabeth Cary, 1613–1680,* ed. Heather Wolfe, 165–182. New York: Palgrave Macmillan, 2006.
Shannon, Laurie J. "*The Tragedie of Mariam:* Cary's Critique of the Terms of Founding Social Discourses." *English Literary Renaissance* 24, no. 1 (1994): 135–153.
Shapiro, Arlene. "Elizabeth Cary: Her Life, Letters, and Art." PhD diss., State University of New York, Stony Brook, 1984.
Shell, Alison. "Elizabeth Cary's Historical Conscience: *The Tragedy of Mariam* and Thomas Lodge's Josephus. In *The Literary Career and Legacy of Elizabeth Cary, 1613–1680,* ed. Heather Wolfe, 53–67. New York: Palgrave Macmillan, 2006.
Simpson, Richard. Appendix to *The Lady Falkland, Her Life, from a Manuscript in the Imperial Archives at Lille. Also, A Memoir of Father Francis Slingsby from MSS in the Royal Library, Brussels,* 125–189. London: Catholic Publishing and Bookselling Company, 1861.
———, ed. "A Conversion from the Time of Charles I." *Rambler* 8 (1857): 173–189; 258–272.
Skura, Meredith. "Elizabeth Cary and Edward II: What Do Women Want to Write?" *Renaissance Drama* ns 27 (1996): 79–104.
———. "The Reproduction of Mothering in *Mariam, Queen of Jewry:* A Defense of 'Biographical' Criticism." *Tulsa Studies in Women's Literature* 16, no. 1 (1997): 27–56.
Starner-Wright, Janet. "Appropriations of Literacy: Exploring the Use of Prose Histories in Early Modern England." PhD diss., Lehigh University, 1997.
Starner-Wright, Janet, and Susan M. Fitzmaurice. "Shaping a Drama Out of History: Elizabeth Cary and the Story of Edward II." *Critical Survey* 14, no. 1 (2002): 79–92.
Stauffer, Donald A. "A Deep and Sad Passion." In *Essays in Dramatic Literature,* ed. Hardin Craig, 289–314. Princeton: Princeton University Press, 1935.
Straznicky, Marta. "Elizabeth Cary: Private Drama and Print." Chap. 3 in *Privacy, Playreading, and Women's Closet Drama, 1550–1700.* Cambridge: Cambridge University Press, 2004.
———. "'Profane Stoical Paradoxes': *The Tragedie of Mariam* and Sidnean Court Drama." *English Literary Renaissance* 24, no. 1 (1994): 104–134.

Straznicky, Marta, and Richard Rowland. Supplement to the introduction to *The Tragedy of Mariam, 1613*, ed. A. C. Dunstan with W. W. Greg, xxi–xxv. Reprint of 1914 edition. Oxford and New York: Malone Society, 1992.
Suzuki, Mihoko. "'Fortune is a Stepmother': Gender and Political Discourse in Elizabeth Cary's *History of Edward II*. In *The Literary Career and Legacy of Elizabeth Cary, 1613–1680*, ed. Heather Wolfe, 89–105. New York: Palgrave Macmillan, 2006.
Swan, Jesse. "A Bibliographical Palimpsest: The Post-publication History of the Octavo Pamphlet, *The History of the Most Unfortunate Prince King Edward II (1680)*." In *The Literary Career and Legacy of Elizabeth Cary, 1613–1680*, ed. Heather Wolfe, 107–124. New York: Palgrave Macmillan, 2006.
———. "Introduction: The 1680 Folio and Octavo Histories of Edward II by Elizabeth Tanfield Cary, Viscountess Falkland," in *Renaissance Women Online*, a subsidiary component of the *Brown University Women Writers Project*, 1999. By online subscription: http://textbase.wwp.brown.edu/WWO/rIntrosList.html [consulted October 4, 2006].
———. "Elizabeth Cary's '*The History of the Life, Reign, and Death of Edward II*': A Critical Edition." PhD diss., Arizona State University, 1993.
———, ed. Introduction to *Elizabeth Tanfield Cary's History of Edward II*. The Early Modern Englishwoman 1500–1750: Contemporary Editions, ed. Betty S. Travitsky and Anne Lake Prescott. Aldershot: Ashgate, forthcoming.
———. "Towards a Textual History of the 1680 Folio *The History of the Life, Reign, and Death of Edward II* (attributed to Elizabeth Cary, Lady Falkland): Understanding the Collateral 1680 Octavo *The History of the Most Unfortunate Prince*." In *New Ways of Looking at Old Texts, III: Papers of the Renaissance English Text Society, 1997–2001*, ed. W. Speed Hill, 177–190. Tempe, AZ: Arizona Center for Medieval and Renaissance Studies and Renaissance English Text Society, 2004.
Thoms-Cappello, Patrice. "Voice, Speculation and Authority in the Works of Elizabeth Cary." PhD diss., Drew University, 2002.
Travitsky, Betty. "The *feme covert* in Elizabeth Cary's *Mariam*." In *Ambiguous Realities: Women in the Middle Ages and Renaissance*, ed. Carole Levin and Jeanie Watson, 184–196. Detroit: Wayne State University Press, 1987.
———. "Husband-Murder and Petty Treason in English Renaissance Tragedy." *Renaissance Drama* 21 (1990): 171–198.
Valency, Maurice J. *The Tragedies of Herod and Mariamne*. New York: Columbia University Press, 1940.
Walker, Kim. "'By publike language grac't': Elizabeth Cary, Lady Falkland." In *Women Writers of the English Renaissance*, 124–145. New York: Twayne, 1996.
Weller, Barry. "Elizabeth Cary, Lady Falkland." In *Teaching Tudor and Stuart Women Writers*, ed. Susanne Woods and Margaret P. Hannay, 164–173. New York: MLA, 2000.
——— and Margaret W. Ferguson, ed. Introduction to *The Tragedy of Mariam: The Fair Queen of Jewry with The Lady Falkland Her Life: By One of her Daughters*, 1–59. Berkeley: University of California Press, 1994.
Wolfe, Heather. Lady Falkland's Letter to Lady Denbigh, ca. December 1626 [commentary and transcription]. In *Reading Early Modern Women: An Anthology*

of *Texts in Manuscript and Print, 1550–1770*, ed. Helen Ostovich and Elizabeth Sauer, 211–214. New York and London: Routledge, 2004.

———. "A Critical Edition of *Lady Falkland: Her Life* (1645) with Correspondence and Records of the Falkland Family (1625–1671)." 2 vols. PhD diss., University of Cambridge, 1998.

———, ed. *The Literary Career and Legacy of Elizabeth Cary, 1613–1680*. New York: Palgrave Macmillan, 2006.

———, ed. *Elizabeth Cary, Lady Falkland: Life and Letters*. Medieval and Renaissance Texts and Studies 230. Cambridge, England and Tempe, AZ: RTM Publications and Arizona Center for Medieval and Renaissance Studies, 2001.

———. "A Family Affair: The Life and Letters of Elizabeth Cary, Lady Falkland." In *New Ways of Looking at Old Texts, III: Papers of the Renaissance English Text Society, 1997–2001*, ed. W. Speed Hill, 97–108. Medieval and Renaissance Texts and Studies 270. Tempe, AZ: Arizona Center for Medieval and Renaissance Studies, 2004.

———. "The Scribal Hands and Dating of *Lady Falkland: Her Life*." *English Manuscript Studies 1100–1700* 9 (2000): 187–217.

Woolf, D. R. "The True Date and Authorship of Henry, Viscount Falkland's *History of the Life, Reign, and Death of King Edward II*." *The Bodleian Library Record* 12, no. 6 (1988): 440–452.

Wray, Ramona. "Case Study: Elizabeth Cary, Lady Falkland, *The Tragedy of Mariam*." In *Women Writers of the Seventeenth Century*. Tavistock, Devon: Northcote House, 2004.

Wynne-Davies, Marion. "'To Have Her Children With Her': Elizabeth Cary and Familial Influence." In *The Literary Career and Legacy of Elizabeth Cary, 1613–1680*, ed. Heather Wolfe, 223–241. New York: Palgrave Macmillan, 2006.

Zimmerman, Shari A. "Disaffection, Dissimulation and the Uncertain Ground of Silent Dismission: Juxtaposing John Milton and Elizabeth Cary." *English Literary History* 66, no. 3 (1999): 553–589.

NOTE

1. The essays in this volume are included in the bibliography for the sake of completeness. For a list of facsimile editions, contemporary editions, modern editions, and manuscript sources for Cary's writings up to 2001, see the bibliography in *Elizabeth Cary, Lady Falkland: Life and Letters*, ed. Heather Wolfe (Cambridge: RTM Publications, 2001), 493–496. For other useful bibliographies relating to Cary, see Purkiss (1994), xlix–liv, and Weller and Ferguson (1994), 317–328.

INDEX

Acontius, Jacobus, *Strategemata Satanae* 178
Alexander the Great 158
Allin, Rose 44
Anderton, Lawrence, *The Progenie of Catholicks and Protestants* 155
Andrewes, Lancelot 167
Arminianism 73
Askew, Anne 43–4, 45, 46
Aston, Walter, Baron 190

Bacon, Francis, Viscount Verulam 60, 61, 101
Baily, Richard 176
Baker, Richard 116
Bale, John 44, 45
Barberini, Francesco, Cardinal 171, 228
Barclay, William 98–9
Baronius, Caesar 167, 174, 176
Barrett, Edward, Baron Newburgh 190
Basse, William 214–15
Bellarmine, Robert, Cardinal 148, 152, 157, 158, 167, 174
Bellings, Richard 9, 208–13, 215, 216, 217
A sixth booke to the Countesse of Pembrokes Arcadia 208–13, 215
Benden, Alyce 43
Bentley, Thomas, *The Monument of Matrones* 67n45

Bible
books of the Bible: Exodus, 186; Leviticus, 186; Numbers, 59–60; 2 Kings, 186; Job, 230; Psalms, 226–8, 229; Wisdom, 47; Matthew, 172, 234
Douai Bible 226, 227, 228
and the genealogy of Christ 37
Latin Vulgate 226
Blundeville, Thomas, *The true order and methode of wryting and reading hystories* 54
Bodin, Jean, *Method for the easy comprehension of history* 89
Borgia, Cesare 92, 96
Bright, Timothy 45, 46
Buckingham, Duke of (*see* Villiers, George)
Butler, Walter, 11th Earl of Ormond 206

Cade, Anthony 152
Cadiz 72
Caesar, Julius 20, 54
Calvert, Cecil, Baron Baltimore 160
Calvin, John 172
Calvinism 73, 149, 157
Carew, Thomas 189, 235
Carleton, Dudley, Viscount Dorchester 10, 74, 150
Carlisle, Countess of (*see* Hay, Lucy)
Carr, Robert, 1st Earl of Somerset 81, 211

Cartwright, Thomas, *Confutation of the Rhemists translations* 148
Cary, Anne (Dame Clementia) 168, 223, 224, 225–8, 229, 230, 231, 234, 235, 236, 237, 238
Cary, Elizabeth (Dame Augustina) 223, 224, 235
Cary, Elizabeth, Viscountess Falkland (major works listed individually)
 and autobiographical criticism 57, 62
 epitaph and elegy on the duke of Buckingham 9, 183–200
 letters 10–11
 literary legacy 223–41
 lost writings 3, 8, 165–82, 207
 manuscript circulation and networks 2–3, 134
 prefaces and dedications to and by her 2, 9, 12n3, 13n9, 153–4, 194, 207, 208, 213, 214, 215
 translation of Ortelius's *Miroir du Monde* 12n2
 workshop for Irish children 205–7
Cary, Henry, 1st viscount Falkland 72, 111, 168, 190, 204, 210, 225
Cary, Henry, son of Henry 169, 170, 224
Cary, Lettice, Viscountess Falkland 233
Cary, Lorenzo 168, 184, 235, 237
Cary, Lucius, 2nd Viscount Falkland 165–74, 176–8, 184, 227, 232–8
 Discourse of Infallibility 173, 232–3, 234, 235
Cary, Lucy (Dame Magdalena) 168, 173, 205, 223, 224–5, 226, 228, 235, 236, 237, 238 (*see also The Lady Falkland: Her Life*)
Cary, Mary (Dame Maria) 170, 190, 223, 224, 235

Cary, Patrick 169, 170, 171, 206, 224, 228–31, 236, 237, 238
Cary, Rachel (Hungerford), dowager Viscountess Falkland 108, 139
Cary, Victoria 170, 190, 229, 231, 234, 238
Casaubon, Isaac 148, 174–5
Cassander, George 166, 174
Cavendish, Margaret 90
Cecil, William, Lord Burghley, *Execution of Justice in England* 43, 45
Chamberlain, John 74
Charles I 72, 100, 157, 169, 185, 186, 210, 212
Charles II 90, 98, 100, 129
Chillingworth, William 166–70, 173–8, 184, 224, 227, 232
 Religion of Protestants 175–7
Christine de Pisan 90, 94–6, 101
Churchill, Sir Winston 116
Clarendon, Earl of (*see* Hyde, Edward)
Clement, Cotton 46
Clitherow, Margaret 43, 44, 46
Con, George 171
Conway, Edward, Viscount Conway 190–1, 204
Cooke, William 114
Corbett, Richard 184
Cosin, John 171
Cotton, Robert 75
Cowley, Abraham 236

Daillé, Jean 167, 177, 178
Daniel, Samuel 97
Davenant, William, Sir 189, 235
Davies, John, of Hereford 194, 213
Denbigh, Countess of (*see* Feilding, Susan)
Devereux, Robert, 2nd Earl of Essex 211
Donne, John 22, 23, 24, 28
Drayton, Michael 73
Drury House, London 168

Du Perron, Jacques Davy,
    Cardinal   100, 101, 147–8,
    152–4, 156–9, 172, 174–8
    (*see also The Reply of the Most
    Illustrious Cardinal of Perron*)
Dublin, Ireland   9, 204
Durham House   172
Dutton, Robert   109

Earle, John   235
Edict of Nantes   167
Edward I   108
Edward II (*see History of
    Edward II*)
Eliot, John   184, 193, 194
Elizabeth I   19, 33n12, 97,
    151, 212
Elizabeth of Bohemia   150
English Benedictines
    Cambrai, Our Lady of
        Consolation   168, 224, 225,
        226, 235, 236
    Douai, St. Gregory's   229, 231
    Paris, Our Lady of Good
        Hope   225, 226, 234
    Paris, St. Edmund's   170
Erasmus, Desiderius   166, 174
Essex, Earl of (*see* Devereux, Robert)
Exclusion Crisis of 1680   89, 90,
    100

Featley, Daniel   152
Feilding, Susan (Villiers),
    Countess of Denbigh   72–3,
    190, 191, 193
Fell, Samuel   176
Feltham, Owen   189
Felton, John   185, 186
Fisher, Ambrose   152
Fisher, John   168
Floyd, John   152
Fortescue, John, *In praise of the laws of
    England*   90, 98
Foxe, John, *Acts and Monuments*
    43–5, 46

Gallican Church   167
Golding, Arthur   54
Goodwin, William   100
Gorboduc   84
"Graces," the   210
Great Tew   232
Great Tew Circle   165–6, 168–9,
    178, 184, 235, 236
Greneway, Francis   54
Grotius, Hugo   166, 174
Grynaeus, Simon, *De utilitate legnedae
    historiae*   54

Hackett, Nicholas   206
Hadsor, Richard   210
Harleian Miscellany (1744–46)   107,
    110, 114–115 (*see also* Oldys)
Harleian Miscellany (1808)   109, 110,
    117 (*see also* Park)
Harley, Edward, 2nd Earl of
    Oxford   113
Hay, Lucy (Percy), Countess of
    Carlisle   190
Hayes, James, Sir   108, 116, 139
Henrietta Maria   100–1, 148, 153,
    155, 157, 170, 171, 193, 207,
    210, 225, 228, 234
Herod and Antipater   42
History of Edward II   5–7, 71–144,
    195, 227
    and the duke of Buckingham
        71–88
    and revenge   203
    folio   77–9, 83, 89–101
    manuscript   118, 125–44
    octavo   77–8, 83, 107–24
    and political theory   89–105
    topicality   73–85
    characters: Edward II, 214, 215, 216;
        Gaveston, 75, 78, 80, 82, 84,
        90, 91, 92, 101, 138, 203, 214,
        215; Isabel, 84, 85–86, 91, 92,
        93, 94, 97, 98, 118, 119, 128,
        188, 217, 227 (comparison to
        Anna of Denmark and

History of Edward II—*Continued*
  Henrietta Maria, 80, 100–1;
  comparison to Elizabeth Cary,
  216); Mortimer, 85, 97, 118,
  119, 216; Spencer,
  91, 92, 93, 216 (comparison
  to Buckingham, 73–5, 78, 79,
  80, 84, 85, 188, 191)
Holland, Guy   168
Howard, Frances   211
Hubert, Francis   73
Huguenots   167
Hyde, Edward, Earl of
  Clarendon   165, 170, 228–9,
  230, 232, 234, 236, 237, 238

"Ignoto"   76, 82
irenicism   72, 157
Irish College, Rome   151
Irish language   206

James I   72, 74, 76, 80, 81, 148,
  157, 174–5, 185, 186, 212
  The trew law of free monarchies   100
  Vox regis   115
James II   100
Jewel, John   172
John, of Salisbury   90, 94, 95,
  97–8, 100
Johnson, Samuel   114, 116
Jonson, Ben   236, 237, 238
  Sejanus   84
  The Irish Masque at Court   211
Judaic law   24
Justinian the Second   158
Juxon, William   184

Knollys, Elizabeth, Countess of
  Banbury   11
Knott, Edward   176

The Lady Falkland: Her Life   3, 57,
  171, 205–8, 216, 223–4, 228,
  230, 232, 234, 238
Lambe, John   191, 192
Latimer, Hugh   172

Laud, William   176
Lee, Henry, Sir   190,
  211, 233
Lee, Thomas, Capt.   211
Leicester's Commonwealth   104n31
Lewes, Joyce   43
Lipsius, Justus   61
Livy   89
Locke, John   90
Lodge, Thomas, *The famous and
  memorable workes of
  Josephus*   39, 40, 47, 53–67
Luther, Martin   172, 233

Maccabees   36, 37, 40
Machiavelli, Niccolò   54, 89–94,
  96, 115, 216
Magaliano, Cosma   59
Malham, John   109–10
Malvezzi, Virgilio, *Discourses upon
  Cornelius Tacitus*   57
Manners, Frances (Cary), Countess
  of Rutland 190
Manners, George, 7th Earl of
  Rutland   190
Marlowe, Christopher
  Dido, Queen of Carthage   97
  Edward II   216
martyrdom   35–52
Mary Magdalene   46
Maryland   151, 160
Maunsell, Andrew, *First part of
  the catalogue of English printed
  bookes*   159
Maynwaring, Roger   100
Mompesson, Giles, Sir   74
Montagu, Elizabeth, Lady   60
Montagu, Henry, 1st Earl of
  Manchester   171
Montagu, Richard   171
Montagu, Walter   167, 171, 172,
  173, 225, 228, 233, 234, 237
  The Shepherd's Paradise   170, 234
More, Gertrude   225
Mornay, Philippe de, seigneur du
  Plessis-Marly   166

INDEX 257

Morwen, Peter, *Compendious and most marveilous history* 40–42
Mush, John 43

Neile, Richard, Bishop of Durham 171

O'Brien, Dermot, 5th Baron Inchiquin 206
Old English (in Ireland) 209, 210, 211, 212
Oldys, William 109, 111–4, 115, 116, 117, 118
Oratorian Fathers, Rome 171
Ortelius, Abraham 12n2, 211
Osborne, Thomas 113, 114, 115

Palatinate, the 72
Park, Thomas 109, 110, 111–3, 116–7, 118, 119
Parliament 72, 74–5, 79, 100, 185, 191, 210
Parliament of White Bands 78
Parsons, Robert, *A conference about the next succession* 90, 96, 99, 100
Patrizi, Francesco 54
Petition of Right 100
Phelips, Sir Robert 75
Philip II, King of Macedonia 11
Plutarch 11, 56, 61, 97
Poole, Elizabeth 98
Porter, Olivia 163n26
Potter, Christopher 178
Prideaux, Dr. John 176

Raleigh, Walter, Sir, *History of the World* 113
The Reply of the Most Illustrious Cardinal of Perron 7–8, 13n11–12, 128, 147–63, 165, 193, 195, 207
Roe, Thomas, Sir 150
Roman Catholicism
  in England 149–153
  schism and division 156–7
Russell, Lucy, Countess of Bedford 213

St. Winifred's Well, Holywell, Wales 150
Sallust 89
Sandys, George 237
Saville, Henry 54
Scott, Walter 229
Seneca, Lucius Annaeus 84, 207
Sforza, Caterina 92
Shakespeare, William 23, 29
Sheares, William 214
Shirley, James 189
Sidney, Henry 208, 209
Sidney, Mary
  as translator 159
  as dedicatee 213, 215
Sidney, Philip, Sir, 194
  Arcadia 208–9, 215, 217
  Astrophil and Stella 23, 24, 28
  Discourse on Irish Affairs 208
Smith, Thomas 177
Socinianism 166
sodomy 86
Somerset, Earl of (see Carr, Robert)
sonnets 17–34
Southey, Robert 110
Spanish match 72, 210
Spenser, Edmund
  Amoretti 23, 28
  The Faerie Queene 230
Stow, John, *Chronicles of England* 77
Suckling, John 170, 235, 236
Synod of Dort 157

Tacitus, Cornelius 84, 89
Tanfield, Elizabeth, Lady 190
Tanfield, Lawrence, Sir 204
Thucydides 89
Tomkins, Lucy 229, 230
The Tragedy of Mariam 4–5, 17–67, 128, 195, 227
  characters: Chorus, 30–31, 40, 45, 46, 47, 56, 61; Constabarus, 24–7, 29, 30, 31; Doris, 30; Graphina, 21–3, 40, 46; Herod, 27–9, 41; Mariam, 28, 29, 30, 38, 41, 42,

258   INDEX

The Tragedy of Mariam—*continued*,
   58–9, 62, 227; Nuntio, 36;
   Pheroras, 21–3; Salome,
   23–6, 29, 62;
   Sileus, 23–5; Sohemus, 29, 60
   and martyrdom   35–52
   and typology (Miriam, Mary,
      Mariam)   58–9
Triplet, Thomas   235
Trogus, Pompeius   54
Trumbull, William   63n2
Turner, Dr.   79

Urban VIII   228
Uvedale, Susan   231
Uvedale, William, Sir   229

Vaux, William, 3rd Baron Vaux   60
Villiers, George, Duke of
   Buckingham   71–85, 101,
   185–7, 189–93, 210
Villiers, John, Viscount
   Purbeck   191

Villiers, Katherine (Manners),
   Duchess of Buckingham   73,
   190, 191
Villiers, Mary Beaumont, Countess of
   Buckingham   73, 190, 191, 192
Vindiciae, contra Tyrannos   90, 99
Völkel, Johann, *De vera religione*   178

Weld, William   150
Wentworth, Thomas, Earl of
   Strafford   105n31
Weston, Richard, Earl of
   Portland   184
White, Thomas   177
Wickham, Hampshire   231
Windebank, Francis, Sir   10
Wood, Antony à   116–7
Woodman, Richard   43
Wright, Henry, *The first part of the
   disquisition of truth*   91

Yelverton, Henry, Sir   74–7, 83
Young, Elizabeth   44